Demanding
Accountability

Demanding Accountability

Civil-Society Claims and the World Bank Inspection Panel

Edited by
DANA CLARK, JONATHAN FOX,
AND KAY TREAKLE

ROWMAN & LITTLEFIELD PUBLISHERS, INC.
Lanham • Boulder • New York • Oxford

ROWMAN & LITTLEFIELD PUBLISHERS, INC.

Published in the United States of America
by Rowman & Littlefield Publishers, Inc.
A wholly owned subsidary of the Rowman & Littlefield Publishing Group, Inc.
4501 Forbes Boulevard, Suite 200, Lanham, Maryland 20706
www.rowmanlittlefield.com

PO Box 317
Oxford
OX2 9RU, UK

British Library Cataloguing in Publication Information Available

Library of Congress Cataloging-in-Publication Data

Demanding accountability : civil-society claims and the World Bank Inspection Panel /
  edited by Dana Clark, Jonathan Fox, and Kay Treakle.
    p. cm.
  Includes bibliographical references and index.
  ISBN 0-7425-3310-7 (alk. paper)—ISBN 0-7425-3311-5 (pbk. : alk. paper)
  1. World Bank Inspection Panel. 2. Economic development projects—Developing
countries—Evaluation. I. Fox, Jonathan, 1954– II. Treakle, Kay. III. Title.
  HG3881.5.W57C54 2003
  338.91'09172'4—dc21   2003008543

∞™ The paper used in this publication meets the minimum requirements of American
National Standard for Information Sciences—Permanence of Paper for Printed Library
Materials, ANSI/NISO Z39.48-1992.

Contents

Acknowledgments

First and foremost, we wish to thank our coauthors, whose contributions, in addition to their case study chapters, have included important experiences, perspectives, and insights that have informed considerably our analysis of the Inspection Panel: Victor Abramovich, Richard Bissell, Elías Díaz Peña, Majibul Huq Dulu, David Hunter, Cristián Opaso, Marcos Orellana, Maria Guadalupe Moog Rodrigues, and Aurélio Vianna Jr.

We would also like to thank the guest participants in our June 2001 authors' workshop in Washington, D.C., many of whom commented on early drafts of case study chapters and all of whom helped us to collectively analyze the broader patterns and trends across the claims. These include Soren Ambrose, Delphine Djiraibe, Oronto Douglas, Manuel Fernández de Villegas, Tom Griffiths, Steve Herz, Petr Hlobil, Madhu Kohli, Smitu Kothari, Satoru Matsumoto, Graham Saul, Steve Tullberg, Ka Hsaw Wa, and Nurina Widagdo.

Thanks are also due to Karen Decker, Abigail Parish, and Elizabeth Sweet, dedicated staff from the Bank Information Center who provided extensive support organizing the workshop and made helpful research contributions to the project. In addition, we thank Eric Brewer-Garcia for helping with the workshop, and Riccardo Rivera for checking citations.

The Inspection Panel members and secretariat staff who have shared so much of their time, perspectives, and lessons over the years deserve a special thanks. Eduardo Abbott, Edward Ayensu, Richard Bissell, Ernst-Günther Bröder, Antonia Macedo, Jim MacNeill, Alberto Niño, Maartje Van Putten, and Alvaro Umaña have all enriched our engagement with the claims process, and gave valuable help for our research on specific cases.

We also would like to thank our friends and colleagues who have generously commented on one or more chapter drafts, including Eduardo Abbott, John Ackerly, Robbie Barnett, Tom Barry, Peter Bosshard, Karen Decker, John Gershman, Robert Goodland, Lisa Jordan, Margaret Keck, Madhu Kohli, Smitu Kothari, Sydney Key, Juliette Majot, Wangchuk Meston, Josh Schrei, Hanna Schmuck, and Lori Udall. And many thanks are due to Lori Pottinger for editing an early version of the Jamuna chapter, and to Josh Karliner for editing both the Yacyretá and China/Tibet chapters.

For providing insider perspectives on the World Bank and the Inspection Panel in interviews and e-mail exchanges, we wish to thank Kristalina Georgieva, Maninder Gill, Robert Goodland, Ian Johnson, Steve Lintner, Robert Picciotto, Joanne Salop, Pieter Stek, and Shengman Zhang.

While many of the claimants are anonymous, and in some cases too numerous to list, we would like to acknowledge the many individuals and communities that have made the courageous and oftentimes daunting choice of filing their claims with the Inspection Panel. Their efforts on behalf of themselves, their families, their environment, and their future, have been profoundly inspirational. The organizations and individuals that have contributed to the efforts described in this volume are also to be acknowledged for their commitment to the principles of accountability, transparency, and sustainable development. They give us all hope that change is possible.

To our families and friends, we would like to note our deep appreciation for their support and encouragement during this project.

Finally, this project would not have been possible without the generous support from the C. S. Mott Foundation and the Ford Foundation. We would especially like to thank Ed Miller and Sandra Smithey, of Mott and Lisa Jordan, of Ford, for their strong commitment to the issues of accountability at international financial institutions.

Acronyms

ADB	Asian Development Bank
BIC	Bank Information Center
BP	Bank Practice
CAO	Compliance Advisor/Ombudsman (International Finance Corporation)
CIEL	Center for International Environmental Law
EA	Environmental Assessment
EBY	Entidad Binacional Yacyretá
EDF	Environmental Defense Fund (now known as Environmental Defense)
ED	Executive Director
EIA	Environmental Impact Assessment
FOE	Friends of the Earth
GABB	Grupo de Acción por el Biobío
GP	Good Practice
IBRD	International Bank for Reconstruction and Development
IDA	International Development Association
IDB	Inter-American Development Bank
IUCN	International Union for the Conservation of Nature and Natural Resources
IFC	International Finance Corporation
IRN	International Rivers Network
masl	meters above sea level
MIGA	Multilateral Investment Guarantee Agency

NGO	Nongovernmental Organization
NTPC	National Thermal Power Corporation
OD	Operational Directive
OP	Operational Policy
OED	Operations Evaluation Department
TGIE	Tibetan Government-in-Exile
UNDP	United Nations Development Program

Introduction: Framing the Inspection Panel

Jonathan Fox

The global political debate over the future of international economic institutions brings together both protest and proposals for change. Widespread civil-society action has put social and environmental justice issues on the international agenda, leading both official and alternative policymakers to respond with a growing array of institutional innovations. Some of these reforms may be dead ends, while others are potentially significant because they build leverage for further change. This book analyzes one such reform, a citizen-driven public accountability process called the World Bank Inspection Panel.

The World Bank has been a lightning rod for transnational protest for at least two decades, foreshadowing today's debate over economic globalization. The World Bank's global influence made it a strategic target for public interest campaigners seeking to link local and global struggles against socially and environmentally costly development strategies. In the process, advocacy coalitions have come together across borders and causes, linking mass mobilizations and direct action to media-savvy campaigners and to alternative policy analysts in often mutually reinforcing synergy. In the context of the great diversity of civil-society actors involved in questioning the dominant development model, the World Bank plays a key role by influencing the global "political opportunity structure" for joint action.[1]

For leaders of the dominant international institutions, the idea that they should be transparent and held publicly accountable was once unthinkable.[2] Sustained public pressure from human rights, environmental, and social justice campaigns is leading a wide range of international and national institutions to begin to accept these goals to some degree.

What difference does it make in practice when powerful global institutions become answerable—at least sometimes—for breaking their own rules? The Inspection Panel process allows local people who are affected by a World Bank–funded project to file a complaint and request an independent investigation into whether the bank complied with its own environmental and social policies. This book provides a comprehensive assessment of the process in practice, assessing the strengths and weaknesses of the panel process through case studies of key claims during its brief history. These original case studies offer insight into how local, national, and international civil-society actors mobilize to hold the World Bank accountable for noncompliance with its own commitment to fight poverty and pursue sustainable development. This case-based approach allows readers to come to their own conclusions about whether and how the Inspection Panel can serve as a political handhold in the hard climb toward increasing the voice and direct representation of people excluded from policy decisions.

This volume is the result of campaigners and analysts working together to learn from "*accountability politics,* or the effort to hold powerful actors to their previously stated policies or principles."[3] *Accountability* refers to the process of holding actors responsible for their actions. This involves *answerability*—usually formal processes in which actions are held up to standards of behavior or performance. For some, this definition is sufficient, while others prefer more rigorous criteria, which include sanctions for violations of standards. Accountability is inherently relational, and its meaning varies greatly depending on the actors involved (for example, contractual, corporate, and political accountability are all quite different). The standards themselves—what counts as compliance—as well as the scope and meaning of *public* accountability more generally, are all contested and shaped through political conflict.

The World Bank's accountability reforms combined promises to meet higher social and environmental standards with "more of the same" institutional behavior. The lessons from the World Bank's often contradictory responses to its critics can help to inform the broader, ongoing debate over the future of multilateral institutions.

The case studies of the Inspection Panel claims, primarily written by direct participants, are an especially rich source of lessons for understanding today's emerging transnational civil society. These studies provide original insights into the dynamics of civil-society efforts to challenge powerful global institutions and to shed light on the ways in which "globalization from below" can influence the institutions that guide "globalization from above."[4]

Because of the bridging nature of the Inspection Panel process, the questions examined here unfold at the crossroads of two distinct bodies of research, one dealing with transnational civil society and the other dealing with global governance and international institutions.[5] The lessons from this process are also critical for understanding new developments in international law.[6] Before the contested construction of the World Bank's minimum social and environmental standards and the creation of the Inspection Panel, the World Bank was a "lawless institution," insofar as it was insulated from any legal responsibilities to people directly affected by its actions.[7] The Inspection Panel's most important innovation is that it is designed to respond directly to grievances from citizens of developing countries about the environmental and social impacts of World Bank–funded projects.

WAVES OF PROTEST AND POLICY RESPONSES

Back in the 1980s, caught in the hot reflective glare of burning rain forests and dam-displaced villages, the World Bank first conceded that it needed mandatory minimum social and environmental standards. Since then, campaigners have repeatedly focused on vivid cases of "development disasters" that revealed the bank's persistent difficulty in meeting its own promises of reform.

Another wave of international protest shook the bank in the early 1990s. Local–global public interest networks were gaining increased leverage and credibility, bringing together broad-based protest movements and public interest groups in the South with environmental and human rights advocacy organizations in the North.[8] One wing of the campaign turned the tables on the bank's planned celebration of its fiftieth anniversary by organizing under the slogan "Fifty Years Is Enough." Meanwhile, the United Nation's 1992 widely hailed Earth Summit in Rio was encouraging international policymakers—including those at the World Bank—to at least pay lip service to the concept of "sustainable development."

To push for greater accountability and transparency at the World Bank, campaigners targeted a key pressure point, threatening to push for cutting U.S. congressional aid appropriations unless the World Bank agreed to reforms that directly addressed not just its "problem projects" but also the flawed decision-making processes that caused them. This strong message coming from the World Bank's external critics resonated with some donor-government policymakers as well as growing internal concerns about the need to improve the development effectiveness of its investments. In 1993, these pressures led North–South advocacy coalitions to win a pair of new procedural reforms: one greatly increased public access to information about bank projects and the other created the Inspection Panel.[9]

Like most formal accountability processes, the panel's scope is circumscribed by specific standards and procedures—an approach that empowers some strategies for change but not others. First and foremost, the panel's investigations can only examine those grievances that involve the bank's noncompliance with its own minimum policy standards.[10] The panel cannot challenge projects whose flaws fall outside those policies, nor can it examine actors other than the World Bank. For example, the panel cannot evaluate the roles of borrowing governments, except to the extent that their noncompliance with bank loan agreements and policies reflects a failure by the bank to adequately monitor a project. Since bank-funded projects are inherently bank–state partnerships, however, it is difficult to tell where the bank's role ends and the borrowing government's responsibility begins. When challenged on implementation failures, the bank and the borrowing government each tend to point the finger at the other. The boundaries of the panel's mandate are therefore regularly contested.

Both the Inspection Panel and the public information disclosure reforms were designed to use the power of "sunshine" to discourage the most egregious abuses and to empower pro-reform forces both inside and outside the institution. While many critics continue to question the bank's legitimacy, diverse public interest groups have followed up by testing the bank's reform commitments in an effort to consolidate policy reforms and prevent mere "greenwashing."

THE POLITICAL CONSTRUCTION OF INTERNATIONAL SOCIAL AND ENVIRONMENTAL STANDARDS

Like other multilateral organizations, the World Bank is formally accountable only to the 182 member nation–states that sit on its board of executive directors. The board is directly involved in bank decision making, approving every individual loan. The board makes decisions by a one-dollar, one-vote weighted system. Most decisions are reportedly by consensus and deliberations are highly confidential.[11] Borrowing governments have a dual role in terms of accountability relationships, both as members of the World Bank's board and as clients.

The board created the Inspection Panel in 1993 as a tool to encourage improved bank compliance with its own policies. Some members of the board implicitly accepted the crosscutting political principle that multilateral organizations should also be accountable to the people they directly affect. This change reflects the growing capacity of transnational civil-society advocacy campaigns to influence official discourse and policies in the international arena.

The panel's provisions for "third-party monitoring" may be a wave of the future in terms of policy innovations. So far, however, it is still too soon to tell how many other multilateral organizations will open up windows for accountability, or how far. The Inter-American Development Bank and the Asian Development Bank established accountability mechanisms in 1994 and 1995, but they have not been effective and they are now undergoing revision. The European Bank for Reconstruction and Development has a draft mechanism that it is expected to launch in 2003.[12]

Other multilateral agencies, in contrast, have not followed the World Bank's example of experimenting with public accountability mechanisms. The International Monetary Fund (IMF) and the World Trade Organization (WTO) still frame accountability narrowly in terms of how nation–states must respond to *their* authority.[13] In addition, the UN agencies still lack citizen-driven accountability mechanisms to deal with concerns from affected people about possible gaps between their policies and their own practices. Most donor-government bilateral foreign aid agencies, especially export credit agencies, also lack social and environmental accountability mechanisms, though this is beginning to change.[14]

The bank's social and environmental policies, backed by the panel's investigative capacity, sit in a middle ground among the broader array of global governance institutions. Some promote the unrestrained power of private capital, while others defend social and environmental justice. At one extreme are the international institutions that attempt to defend fundamentalist ideas about the sanctity of corporate property rights above all others. A new wave of international agreements give private investors enforceable powers to challenge the decisions of national governments when they interfere with their investments. The proposed Multilateral Agreement on Investment (MAI) would have institutionalized these "investor rights," but a wave of civil-society mobilization managed to defeat it in 1997–1998. In contrast, NAFTA's (North American Free Trade Agreement) little-known Chapter 11 protections for investors' rights, administered by secret tribunals, are well entrenched and are reproduced in many bilateral investment treaties and the draft proposal for the Free Trade Area of the Americas.[15] Meanwhile, the WTO continues to pursue a narrow property rights agenda at the expense of environmental and social concerns.[16]

At another pole, a very different set of universal principles defend human rights, environmental justice and sustainability, indigenous rights and women's rights, including such founding documents as the UN's Universal Declaration of Human Rights and subsequent agreements on civil, political, social, and economic rights. International agreements such as the International Labor Organization's Convention 169 on Indigenous Populations, Agenda 21, the global action plan that emerged from the 1992 Earth Summit in Rio de Janeiro, as well as many other environmental accords have also set promising precedents. However, most of these agreements have not led to the emergence of institutions with resources or enforcement powers. They therefore fall into the growing category of "soft law."[17] In contrast, the new International Criminal Court (ICC) is endowed with the authority to prosecute human rights violators from countries if their national judicial systems fail to act.[18]

These two competing sets of rights—one agenda for corporate investors versus another that puts people and the environment first—both assert universal mandates. For their respective advocates, each set of rights therefore trumps sovereignty (at least for countries that have agreed to cede some authority by treaty—or by contract, as in the case of World Bank loans). The World Bank's environmental and social policy reforms operate at an intersection between these two very different conceptions of universal rights. Most of the bank's money and power focuses on promoting policies and institutions that encourage conventional growth and economic globalization. At the same time, other parts of the bank, such as its social and environmental units, are charged with promoting sustainable development, poverty reduction, and more recently, "empowerment" of the poor.[19] The institution's various branches and factions pursue different goals and strategies, some with much more clout than others.

Public interest groups and policymakers continue to debate the significance of the bank's "sustainable development" reforms, and the degree to which they have led to changes in the institution's decision-making processes. In the process, the bank and advocacy groups have been involved in many other kinds of "stakeholder consultations" and "policy engagement" around the bank's social, economic, and environmental policies, with mixed results so far.[20] In practice, the bulk of the bank's lending, which involves macroeconomic and sectoral lending rather than antipoverty projects or infrastructure investments, has largely eluded the "sustainable development" policy reforms.[21]

The uneven degree to which the bank applies its own social and environmental policies in practice reflects the balance of power between pro-sustainable development forces between and within three different kinds of actors: civil societies, nation–states, and the bank itself.[22] This balance of power is not fixed or predetermined, however, and that is where potential levers for change such as the Inspection Panel can play a role.

ARENAS OF CHANGE: WHERE TO LOOK FOR LEVERAGE?

The Inspection Panel experience is a test case of the "reformability" of multilateral institutions. This raises a more general dilemma faced by the diverse actors that challenge the dominant globalization process: where do they look to gain leverage? Constituencies concerned about the environmental and social costs of corporate globalization differ over *where* the key alternative domain is located. In practice, advocacy strategies vary in terms of their relative emphasis on different *arenas* of change—the local, the national, or the international—depending on their own locations, resources, allies, and ideologies.[23] At the same time, these multilevel strategies are often mutually reinforcing. Specific campaigns often bring the actors together, most recently under the broad umbrella slogan "Another World Is Possible," associated with the World Social Forum—a Brazilian-led process of local–global convergence that has since inspired other "social forums" around the world.

Within the broad movement for global justice, some see local arenas as the principal sites for resistance and alternatives. For example, the International Forum on Globalization, an influential South–North coalition of critical intellectuals, NGO (nongovernmental organization) activists, and movement leaders, consistently stresses that the most promising alternative to top-down globalization is to strengthen *local* social, civic, and economic actors and institutions—based on grassroots democratic energy and innovation. This approach includes calls for public regulation to create space for grassroots initiatives, but it tends to be ambivalent about whether and how to empower nation–states and multilateral institutions.[24] Many panel claims emerge from grassroots causes that focus primarily on the local arena, get blocked, and then turn to an international instrument in an effort to shift the balance of power.[25] By using the panel, they are "thinking locally and acting globally."

Other campaigns focus primarily on the national arena and bolstering and democratizing nation–states. For example, the Hemispheric Social Alliance—a coalition of social organizations and NGOs that questions the proposed Free Trade Area of the Americas—consistently prioritizes the need to increase the leverage of nation–states. In this view, the key challenge is for nations to reshape the terms of integration with international markets by increasing their states' institutional and legal capacity to regulate trade and investment.[26]

A third campaign strategy focuses on the emerging alternative norms and institutions of global governance as a promising domain for defending social justice, the environment, and peace. Some advocates see new or reformed international institutions as a key pathway to offset the power of private capital and to challenge the impunity of human rights violators. For example, human rights defenders are pioneering a promising approach that seeks to enforce international human rights law in national courts.[27] The global governance approach includes within it diverse approaches, ranging from radical internationalists who want to contain or reverse corporate globalization, to moderates who promote global economic institutions that can redistribute from winners to compensate losers.[28] Both radical and moderate internationalists are skeptical that efforts limited to local or national arenas will be sufficient to offset the power of unregulated global capital.[29] Internationalists often differ, however, over how to weigh the conflicts between universal norms and national sovereignty. At the same time, many campaigners focused on local and national arenas wonder how and when changes at the international level will produce tangible progress on the ground.

The Inspection Panel is a test case for one current within the global governance approach: the focus on reforming the multilateral institutions. Reforming official discourse is easy for policymakers, but how do they react when they actually have to submit to official oversight bodies that investigate whether they are putting their enlightened-sounding promises into practice? Because of its focus on compliance, many different actors—bank management, both donor and borrowing governments on its board, other international agencies, public interest campaigners, and the panel itself—have staked it out as a major political battlefield.[30] Because the panel is a policy innovation designed to influence the actual behavior of the World Bank, this study will contribute to the broader debate over the "reformability" of dominant multilateral institutions.[31]

This analysis of the civil-society claims to the Inspection Panel examines cases where local, national, and international campaigns were mutually reinforcing. Local, national, and international arenas each offer advocacy campaigns distinct sets of allies, resources, and obstacles. Change initiatives in one arena are often interlinked with efforts in others.[32] The campaign case studies that follow will shed light on the different kinds of "vertical" linkages between arenas or "levels" of action, as well as the "horizontal" linkages between counterparts across sectors and borders. Both of these processes are key to strategies for empowering civil-society actors.

When analyzing patterns of unity and diversity among transnational social and civic actors, as well as when assessing their impact, where one stands depends on where one sits. The different case studies that follow assess the processes and outcomes in light of the interests and goals of the different actors involved. In some cases the goal was to prevent a project from happening, in other cases the goal was to get authorities to carry out a potentially positive project as promised, while in other cases the best that could be hoped for was some degree of mitigation or compensation for damages. In addition, several of the panel claims created opportunities for broader institutional reform that would affect future project decisions.

AN OVERVIEW OF THE BOOK

This book explores the Inspection Panel's case history in order to draw broader lessons about the dynamics of reform at the multilateral institutions. What difference did the panel make? Did panel claims produce tangible results for the communities involved? Did they lead to broader policy reforms? Who were the key actors behind the panel claims and how did they come together?

Although the civil-society actors, goals, and strategies involved in efforts to use the Inspection Panel process have been extremely diverse, they have all attempted to enter the same small but potentially significant international "policy space"—to put "a foot in the door" of a powerful global institution. The actors involved range from broad-based national advocacy coalitions to North–South partnerships that pursue a "boomerang" strategy by local campaigns to bring international pressure to bear against unresponsive nation–states.[33] Some panel claims led to significant direct impacts, such as policy reforms, or the withdrawal of bank funding for a potentially devastating project, while others led to minimal mitigation measures or had no impact at all. Several claimants had to face a political backlash from their governments, including human rights violations in some cases.

Each case study tells a different part of the story of the Inspection Panel's first eight years. The book is built around nine original case studies that together illustrate the strengths and limitations of civil-society efforts to use the panel process. The mix of cases is broadly representative of the many different kinds of campaigns and bank projects that have engaged the panel so far. The cases are all based on extensive, independent field research and reflect the views of direct participants in the claims.[34]

Chapter 1 provides overall context by explaining the Inspection Panel in terms of international law and the reform of international institutions. This chapter provides an overview of the Inspection Panel's history and dynamics, explaining its origins, procedures, and relationship to the World Bank's broader environmental and social policies. The chapter also offers analysis of the panel's changing relationship with the bank's management and board, as well as the uneven ripple effect on other international financial institutions.

Chapter 2 reviews the very first claim brought to the Inspection Panel, a claim that questioned the Arun III Dam project in Nepal. The Arun claim was a key test case, showing that a claim could provoke the cancellation of a project. The claim obliged then-incoming President James Wolfensohn to take sides in a preexisting internal debate over the project's viability, and revealed how transnational advocacy networks can sometimes tip the balance. The claim and the panel's report provoked the bank to withdraw its support of the project, which was considered a victory for the claimants and their international supporters. This tangible impact quickly established the panel as a viable institution.

Chapter 3 analyzes the claim dealing with the Rondônia Natural Resources Management project in Brazil, also known as the Planafloro project. The state of Rondônia was the site of one of the world's most visible and infamous "development disasters": the World Bank–financed Polonoroeste road and colonization project in the Amazon rain forest. With Planafloro, the World Bank and the Brazilian government tried to make amends by promoting sustainable development in the same province. This project was designed to promote participatory and sustainable natural resource management, but its problems in practice led a local/transnational coalition to submit an Inspection Panel claim. In contrast to many other campaigns, this one did not attempt to block a project; instead the goal was to promote compliance with its objectives. The claim led to a significant restructuring of the project, encouraging more power-sharing with local civil-society actors and the demarcation of protected areas.

Chapter 4 analyzes a claim involving the massive Yacyretá Dam, which is located on the Río Paraná on the Argentina–Paraguay border and was financed by both the World Bank and the Inter-American Development Bank. SOBREVIVENCIA/Friends of the Earth–Paraguay filed claims at both institutions on behalf of locally affected people. The chapter focuses on the World Bank process, including the responses of borrowing governments, bank management's attempt to distort the panel findings, the increased capacity of local communities to articulate and demand their rights, and the difficulty in translating the panel's findings into real change at the project level.

Chapter 5 documents a claim involving yet another large infrastructure project, the Jamuna Bridge in Bangladesh. The claim was brought by a local NGO, the Jamuna Char Integrated Development Project, on behalf of thousands of people who lived on seasonal islands—called *chars*—affected by changes in the Jamuna River due to the construction of the bridge. The claimants did not challenge the bridge project; rather, they objected to their exclusion from resettlement and compensation plans, given that their homes and livelihoods would be lost. Bank management and government responded quickly with an action plan that recognized the legitimacy of "*char* people" as affected people for the first time, but the resulting compensation plan was seriously undermined by the same systematic social discrimination that led to their exclusion in the first place.

Chapter 6 shows how a project campaign can lead to significant institutional reform yet offer little recourse for those displaced at the local level. The Pangue/Ralco hydroelectric dam complex on Chile's Biobío River raised questions about indigenous peoples' rights, the adequacy of environmental impact assessment, and how to extend accountability mechanisms to the growing private sector side of the World Bank's operations. Chile's Grupo de Acción por el Biobío filed a claim, which was rejected by the Inspection Panel on the grounds that it lacks jurisdiction over the International Finance

Corporation (IFC), the World Bank's private-sector lending arm. Nevertheless, the claim led President Wolfensohn to commission an environmental NGO leader to investigate the project. The chapter traces the history of the claim, the IFC scandal revealed by the independent review, and the resulting adoption of social/environmental policies and an accountability mechanism for both the IFC and MIGA (the Multilateral Investment Guarantee Agency, the World Bank's private-sector political risk insurance agency).

Chapter 7 provides a comparative analysis of the five Brazilian claims filed to the Inspection Panel. These claims involved three different projects: Planafloro, the failed Itaparica resettlement project, and the controversial Cédula da Terra "market-assisted" land reform program. All three projects were created in response to previous waves of social and environmental concern. In practice, however, all fell short, and the land reform project in particular provoked nationwide rejection. All three campaigns produced partial project changes, although in the Itaparica and land reform cases claimants saw the concessions as attempts to divide their social organizations. The analysis provides a national overview of the evolution of Brazilian public interest advocacy strategies, and their pioneering efforts to frame international campaigning in terms of their national campaigns to democratize the closed partnership between the World Bank and the Brazilian government.

Chapter 8 provides a vivid example of borrowing-government resistance to the Inspection Panel process. The industrialization of the Singrauli region in India, supported by the World Bank, has resulted in the involuntary displacement of hundreds of thousands of people and intense pollution. Local efforts to resist unjust resettlement and to utilize the Inspection Panel process were met with beatings and abuse. When the panel recommended an investigation, the government of India indicated it would not allow its entry into the country. As a result, the board confined the panel to a Washington-based "desk review." The Singrauli case underscores the devastating impacts of displacement, the board's inability to play an effective remedial role, the importance of national sovereignty concerns in the panel process, and management's failure to fully implement "action plans" developed in response to panel claims.

Chapter 9 tells the encouraging story of a case called Pro-Huerta (the Garden Program), where the panel process not only worked, but also set a precedent for applying social and environmental standards to macroeconomic adjustment loans. The social safety net conditions built into Argentina's structural adjustment program provided the leverage for the first Inspection Panel claim that focused on the impact of macroeconomic lending on antipoverty programs. The Inspection Panel claim led to an unusually rapid and positive policy response when the government of Argentina agreed to restore funding to the Garden Program, which helped the urban poor to grow their own food. This successful claim involving a macroeconomic structural adjustment project was quite different from most of the other cases, which focused on more "tangible" infrastructure projects.

Chapter 10 documents the China Western Poverty Reduction Project, one of the most important "turning point" cases in the history of the Inspection Panel—and in the World Bank's history. In 1999, the bank sought to support the Chinese government's plan to resettle approximately fifty-eight thousand poor farmers onto lands traditionally inhabited by nomadic Tibetan and Mongolian peoples. The project involved serious social and environmental risks, and local people sent letters seeking international support. Tibet solidarity groups worked with World Bank–watching organizations to generate widespread critical media coverage and skepticism in donor governments. The campaign against the project led to high-level diplomatic tensions between the bank, its largest borrower, and its largest donor; an unusually intense level of board engagement; a scathing report by the Inspection Panel; and, ultimately, the cancellation of the bank project. In addition to documenting the project's systematic violation of many of the bank's safeguard policies, the panel report went further to reveal dramatic weaknesses in the bank's entire system for avoiding and mitigating social and environmental risks. In response, bank policymakers developed a new strategy to bolster internal checks and balances to encourage more consistent staff compliance with social and environmental "safeguard" policies. Once more, a project campaign managed to leverage bankwide policy reform—although it is too soon to assess its impact in practice.

Chapter 11 assembles these detailed pictures into a larger portrait, taking stock of the panel experience by assessing its impacts on various actors, including the affected people and the bank itself. This chapter evaluates the trends that emerge across the full set of claims, including those not covered by case studies profiled in this book. For claimants on the ground, the results have varied widely, ranging from significant impacts to partial damage control, to no change at all. The full set of claims shows that the majority of panel claims over the first eight years have come directly from affected people and their NGO allies in the South, without even Northern coalition partners. The concluding chapter draws analytical lessons for understanding the dynamics of promoting public accountability.

On balance, the panel itself has been remarkably autonomous, permitting people negatively affected by World Bank projects the opportunity to gain some degree of international standing, access to transnational public interest allies, potential global media coverage, and even the possibility of some tangible changes in bank projects. In many of the cases, the process changed whose voices count, and who listens. Just how far the Inspection Panel's multiplier effects will travel within and across powerful institutions remains to be seen, but this innovative experiment is taking its place as one of many fronts in the larger political contest over how to redefine accountability from below.

NOTES

1. The *political opportunity structure* is a central idea in political sociology that refers to the contextual factors that encourage or discourage specific kinds of collective action and protest from below. For example, shared threats, the array of possible allies, the degrees and likelihood of repression, as well as splits or competition among elites, are all very relevant. For an overview, see Sidney Tarrow, *Power in Movement*, 2d ed. (Cambridge: Cambridge University Press, 1998).

2. *Transparency* refers here to public access to information about institutions and their actions, while *accountability* is widely understood as referring to those institutions' public *answerability* for their actions. Transparency is necessary but not sufficient for accountability.

3. Margaret Keck and Kathryn Sikkink, *Activists beyond Borders* (Ithaca: Cornell University Press, 1998), 16. The Inspection Panel is a subset of a growing category of checks-and-balances agencies, sometimes called institutions of *horizontal accountability* (Guillermo O'Donnell, "Horizontal Accountability in New Democracies," in *The Self-Restraining State: Power and Accountability in New Democracies*, ed. Andreas Schedler, Larry Diamond, and Marc F. Plattner [Boulder, Colo.: Lynne Reinner, 1999], 29–51). For conceptual discussions of different dimensions of accountability, see Mark Bovens, *The Quest for Responsibility: Accountability and Citizenship in Complex Organizations* (Cambridge: Cambridge University Press, 1998); Adam Przeworski, Susan Stokes, and Bernard Manin, eds., *Democracy, Accountability and Representation* (Cambridge: Cambridge University Press, 1999). For an effort to operationalize and measure different degrees of accountability of international institutions, see Hetty Kovach, Caroline Neligan, and Simon Burall, *Global Accountability Report 1: Power without Accountability?* (London: One World Trust, 2002–2003), available online at www.oneworldtrust.org [accessed May 26, 2003].

4. On transnational civil society, see, among others, Joe Bandy and Jackie Smith, eds., *Coalitions across Borders: Transnational Protest and the Neo-Liberal Order* (forthcoming); Jeremy Brecher, Tim Costello, and Brendan Smith, *Globalization from Below* (Boston: South End Press, 2000); Alison Brysk, ed., *Globalization and Human Rights* (Berkeley: University of California Press, 2002); and *From Tribal Village to Global Village: Indian Rights and International Relations in Latin America* (Palo Alto, Calif.: Stanford University Press, 2000); Robin Cohen and Shirin M. Rai, eds., *Global Social Movements* (London: Athlone, 2000); Alejandro Colas, *International Civil Society* (London: Polity, 2001); Donatella Della Porta, Haspeter Kriesi, and Dieter Rucht, eds., *Social Movements in a Globalizing World* (London: Macmillan, 1999); Michael Edwards and John Gaventa, eds., *Global Citizen Action* (Boulder, Colo.: Lynne Reinner, 2001); Ann Florini, ed., *The Third Force: The Rise of Transnational Civil Society* (Washington, D.C.: Carnegie Endowment for International Peace; Tokyo: Japan Center for International Exchange, 2000); John Guidry, Michael

Kennedy, and Mayer Zald, eds., *Globalizations and Social Movements: Culture, Power and the Transnational Public Sphere* (Ann Arbor: University of Michigan Press, 2000); Keck and Sikkink, *Activists;* Sanjeev Khagram, James V. Riker, and Kathryn Sikkink, eds., *Restructuring World Politics: Transnational Social Movements, Networks, and Norms* (Minneapolis: University of Minnesota Press, 2002); Gordon Laxer and Sandra Halperin, eds., *Global Civil Society and Its Limits* (London: Palgrave, 2003); David Lewis, ed., *International Perspectives on Voluntary Action: Reshaping the Third Sector* (London: Earthscan, 1999); Thomas Risse, Stephen C. Ropp, and Kathryn Sikkink, eds., *The Power of Human Rights: International Norms and Domestic Change* (Cambridge: Cambridge University Press, 1999); Jackie Smith, Charles Chatfield, and Ron Pagnucco, eds., *Transnational Social Movements and Global Politics* (Syracuse: Syracuse University Press, 1997); Jackie Smith and Hank Johnston, eds., *Globalization and Resistance: Transnational Dimensions of Social Movements* (Lanham, Md.: Rowman and Littlefield, 2002); Sidney Tarrow, *Power in Movement,* 2d ed. (Cambridge: Cambridge University Press, 1998); and idem, "Transnational Politics: Contention and Institutions in International Politics," *Annual Review of Political Science* 4 (2001): 1–20. For studies that specifically problematize North–South differences within civil society, see, for example, Clifford Bob, "Globalization and the Social Construction of Human Rights Campaigns," in Brysk, *Globalization and Human Rights,* 133–47; David Brooks and Jonathan Fox, eds., *Cross-Border Dialogues: US–Mexico Social Movement Networking* (La Jolla: University of California, San Diego, Center for U.S.–Mexican Studies, 2002); Michael Edwards and David Hulme, eds., *Beyond the Magic Bullet: NGO Performance and Accountability in the Post–Cold War World* (Bloomfield, Conn.: Kumarian, 1996); Jonathan Fox and L. David Brown, eds., *The Struggle for Accountability: The World Bank, NGOs and Grassroots Movements* (Cambridge: MIT Press, 1998); Lisa Jordan and Peter Van Tuijl, "Political Responsibility in Transnational NGO Advocacy," *World Development* 28, no. 12 (December 2000): 2051–66; and Paul Nelson, "Agendas, Accountability and Legitimacy among Transnational Networks Lobbying the World Bank," in Khagram, Riker, and Sikkink, *Restructuring World Politics,* 131–54.

    5. Most of the research and advocacy literatures focus *either* on the civil-society actors *or* the institutions. Previous studies that focused on their *interaction* include Patricia Feeney, *Accountable Aid: Local Participation in Major Projects* (Oxford: Oxfam GB, 1998), which compared project campaigns across international development agencies; Fox and Brown, *The Struggle for Accountability*; and Robert O'Brien, Anne Marie Goetz, Jan Aart Scholte, and Marc Williams, *Contesting Global Governance: Multilateral Economic Institutions and Global Social Movements* (Cambridge: Cambridge University Press, 1998), which compared the impact of civil-society campaigns on the World Bank, the IMF, and the WTO. For examples of studies that focus on the internal political dynamics within the World Bank as it grappled with how to respond to external pressures, see Natalie Bridgeman, "World Bank Reform in the 'Post-Policy' Era," *Georgetown International Environmental Law Review* 13, no. 2 (Summer 2001): 1013–46; Jonathan Fox "When Does Reform Policy Influence Practice? Lessons from the Bankwide Resettlement Review," in Fox and Brown, *The Struggle for Accountability,* 303–44; Eva Thorne, "The Politics of Policy Compli-

ance: The World Bank and the Social Dimensions of Development" (Ph.D. diss., Massachusetts Institute of Technology, 1998); and Robert Wade, "Greening the Bank: The Struggle over the Environment, 1970–1995," in *The World Bank: Its First Half-Century,* ed. Devesh Kapur, John P. Lewis, and Richard Webb (Washington, D.C.: Brookings, 1997), 2: 611–734.

6. For further discussion, see Dana Clark, chapter 1. Official World Bank publications on the Inspection Panel include Ibrahim F. I. Shihata, *The World Bank Inspection Panel* (New York: Oxford University Press/World Bank, 1994) and Ibrahim F. I. Shihata, *The World Bank Inspection Panel: In Practice* (New York: Oxford University Press/World Bank, 2000). Alvaro Umaña, a former member of the Inspection Panel, edited *The World Bank Inspection Panel: The First Four Years (1994–1998)* (Washington, D.C.: The World Bank, 1998). The Inspection Panel website has extensive information, including case findings and annual reports, available at www. inspectionpanel.org. Other studies of the Inspection Panel include Gudmunder Alfredsson and Rolf Ring, eds., *The Inspection Panel of the World Bank: A Different Complaints Procedure* (The Hague: Martinus Nijhoff, 2001); Flavia Barros, ed., *Banco Mundial, Participação, Transparência e Responsabilização* (Brasília: Rede Brasil sobre Instituições Financeiras Multilaterais, 2001); Richard Bissell, "Recent Practice of the Inspection Panel of the World Bank," *American Journal of International Law* 91 (October 1997): 741–44; Daniel Bradlow, "A Test Case for the World Bank," *American University Journal of International Law and Policy* 11, no. 2 (1994): 247–94; Daniel Bradlow and Sabine Schlemmer-Schulte, "The World Bank's New Inspection Panel: A Constructive Step in the Transformation of the International Legal Order," *Heidelberg Journal of International Law* 54 (1994): 392–415; Daniel Bradlow, "International Organizations and Private Complaints: The Case of the World Bank Inspection Panel," *Virginia Journal of International Law* 34 (1994): 553–613; idem, "The World Bank, the IMF and Human Rights," *Transnational Law and Contemporary Problems* 6, no. 1 (1996): 47–90; Sabine Schlemmer-Schulte, "The World Bank, Its Operations and Its Inspection Panel," *Recht der Internationalen Wirtschaft* 3 (1999): 175–81; Dana L. Clark, *A Citizen's Guide to the World Bank Inspection Panel,* 2d ed. (Washington, D.C.: Center for International Environmental Law, 1999), available online at www.ciel.org [accessed May 26, 2003]; Dana Clark, "The Rise and Fall of Accountability," *Watershed: People's Forum on Ecology* 6, no. 3 (March–June 2001): 52–55; idem, "The World Bank and Human Rights: The Need for Greater Accountability," *Harvard Human Rights Journal* 15 (Spring 2002): 205–26; Dana L. Clark and David Hunter, "The World Bank Inspection Panel: Amplifying Citizen Voices for Sustainable Development," in Alfredsson and Ring, *The Inspection Panel of the World Bank,* 167–89; Jonathan Fox, "The World Bank Inspection Panel: Lessons from the First Five Years," *Global Governance* 6, no. 3 (July–September 2000): 279–318; David Hunter and Lori Udall, "The World Bank's New Inspection Panel: Will It Increase the Bank's Accountability?" *CIEL Brief,* no. 1 (Washington, D.C.: Center for International Environmental Law, 1994); Lori Udall, *The World Bank Inspection Panel: A Three-Year Review* (Washington, D.C.: Bank Information Center, 1997); idem, "The World Bank and Public Accountability: Has Anything Changed?" in Fox and Brown, *The Struggle for Accountability,* 391–436.

7. David Hunter, former director of the Center for International Environmental Law, personal communication, January 29, 2003. This impunity resulted from the immunities afforded to multilateral institutions as well as the fact that international tribunals usually limit access: nation–states have access, but citizens are excluded. See also David Hunter, "Using the World Bank Inspection Panel to Defend the Interests of Project-Affected People," *Chicago International Law Review* 4, no. 1 (2003): 201–11.

8. For a more detailed analysis, see Fox and Brown, *The Struggle for Accountability,* which also includes a full bibliography of the vast critical literature on the World Bank. See also, among others, Catherine Caufield, *Masters of Illusion: The World Bank and the Poverty of Nations* (New York: Henry Holt, 1996); Susan George and Fabrizio Sabelli, *Faith and Credit: The World Bank's Secular Empire* (London: Penguin, 1994); Bruce Rich, *Mortgaging the Earth: The World Bank, Environmental Impoverishment and the Crisis of Development* (Boston: Beacon, 1994); and Bruce Rich, "The World Bank under James Wolfensohn," in *Reinventing the World Bank,* ed. Jonathon R. Pincus and Jeffrey A. Winters (Ithaca: Cornell University Press, 2002). On the "greening" of the bank, in addition to official publications, see Michael Goldman, "Constructing and Environmental State: Eco-Governmentality and Other Transnational Practices of a 'Green' World Bank," *Social Problems* 48, no. 4 (2001): 499–523, and Zoe Young, *A New Green Order? The World Bank and the Politics of the Global Environmental Facility* (London: Pluto, 2002). For links to key advocacy organizations that focus on the multilateral development banks around the world, see the Bank Information Center website, www.bicusa.org, and the Bretton Woods Project website, www.brettonwoodsproject.org [accessed May 26, 2003].

9. The panel is therefore one of the first international institutional reforms that was extracted by what has since come to be called a "fix it or nix it" bargaining strategy. The "fix it or nix it" slogan became prominent in the Seattle 1999 challenge to the WTO, but sums up a debate that goes back to the "Fifty Years Is Enough" campaign against the World Bank and the IMF in the early 1990s. This slogan can be read in two different ways: first, as a bargaining strategy, as in "either you fix it or we will try to nix it"; and second, as referring to the more reformist and radical wings of the movement against corporate globalization.

10. On the panel's procedures, see Dana Clark, chapter 1 and www.inspection-panel.org [accessed May 26, 2003]. The World Bank's social and environmental policies are now accessible at www.ifc.org/enviro/EnvSoc/Safeguard/safeguard.htm. The most recent internal bank policy assessment summarizes them as follows:

Safeguard policies provide a mechanism for integrating environmental and social concerns into decision-making. In general, they provide that (a) potentially adverse environmental impacts affecting the physical environment, ecosystem functions and human health, and physical cultural resources, as well as specific social impacts, should be identified and assessed early in the project cycle; (b) unavoidable adverse impacts should be minimized or mitigated to the extent feasible; and (c) timely information should be provided to stakeholders, who should have the opportunity to comment on both the nature and significance of impacts and the proposed mitigation measures. (World Bank, Environmentally and Socially Sustainable Development and Operations Policy and Country Services, "Safeguard Politics: Framework for Improving Development Effectiveness: A Discussion Note," June 5, 2002, 3)

11. On the broader debate about World Bank governance, see, among others, Stephanie Griffith-Jones, "Governance of the World Bank," report prepared for DFID (Department for International Development), 2001, available online at www.gapresearch.org/finance/ Griffith-Jones, 2000 [accessed May 26, 2003]; UNDP (United Nations Development Program), *Human Development Report 2002* (New York: United Nations Development Program, 2002); Devesh Kapur, "The Changing Anatomy of Governance of the World Bank," in Pincus and Winters, *Reinventing the World Bank;* and Ngaire Woods, "The Challenge of Good Governance for the IMF and the World Bank Themselves," *World Development* 28, no. 5 (May 2000): 823–41. For analysis of an unusual board vote about panel investigations, see Fox, "Lessons from the First Five Years."

12. The G-8 governments have called for all the MDBs (multilateral development banks) to create accountability mechanisms (see www.bankwatch.org). On the policy debate at the Asian Development Bank about how to bolster its accountability mechanism, see www.bicusa.org/mdbs/adb/index.htm.

13. For example, the IMF's approach to promoting transparency is to oblige nation–states to provide better financial data to private investors (Susanne Soederberg, "Grafting Stability onto Globalisation? Deconstructing the IMF's Recent Bid for Transparency," *Third World Quarterly* 22, no. 5 [October 2001]: 849–64). Because of a combination of its dependence on public funds, high visibility, the very tangible impacts of its projects, its own internal debates, and its self-proclaimed mission to fight poverty, the World Bank has been more vulnerable to challengers than, for example, the IMF or the WTO.

14. On bilateral aid agencies, see the International NGO Campaign on Export Credit Agencies, www.eca-watch.org. The Japan Bank for International Cooperation launched a public information policy in 2001 and has had significant public consultations to develop a complaints process. For Japanese public interest group assessments, see www.foejapan.org/en/aid/index.html and www.mekongwatch.org/english/index.html.

15. For a critique, see Hemispheric Social Alliance, *NAFTA Investor Rights Plus: An Analysis of the Draft Investment Chapter of the FTAA,* www.art-us.org/Docs/Invest-eng.pdf, June 19, 2001 [accessed May 26, 2003]. On the environmental policy issues in the FTAA (Free Trade Area of the Americas), see Carolyn Deere and Daniel C. Esty, eds., *Greening the Americas: NAFTA's Lessons for Hemispheric Trade* (Cambridge: MIT Press, 2002).

16. On WTO issues, see the respective websites of the International Center on Trade and Sustainable Development (www.ictsd.org) and the Center for International Environmental Law (www.ciel.org). In addition, in "Government without Democracy" (*The American Prospect* 12, no. 12 [July 2–16, 2001]: 19–22), Richard Longworth describes an opaque web of pro-business rule-writing involving banking, antitrust, accounting, and industrial standards as global governance without global democracy.

17. See, for example, Edith Brown Weiss, ed., *International Compliance with Nonbinding Accords,* Studies in Transnational Legal Policy, no. 29 (Washington, D.C.: American Society of International Law, 1997) and Kenneth W. Abbott and Duncan Snidal, "Hard and Soft Law in International Governance," *International Organization* 54, no. 3 (Summer 2000): 421–56.

18. See William Schabas, *An Introduction to the International Criminal Court* (Cambridge: Cambridge University Press, 2001); UNDP, *Human Development Report;* and updates from Human Rights Watch available online at www.hrw.org [accessed May 26, 2003].

19. These insiders have their own array of strategies and goals—some focus on damage control, while others invest their limited political capital to carve out enclaves of change. It is difficult to assess the latter approach because there are few comprehensive and independent field-based assessments of the results of the World Bank's investments that ostensibly promote social and environmental "best practices" (beyond its damage control–oriented "safeguard policies"). These loans are for basic health and education, pollution control, biodiversity conservation, participatory community development, indigenous land demarcation, gender-sensitive policy reform, and accountable governance. Some of the bank's own independent internal evaluations are now public and are often quite balanced and revealing (see www.worldbank. org/oed [accessed May 26, 2003]). See Andrés Liebenthal, *Promoting Environmental Sustainability in Development: An Evaluation of the World Bank's Performance* (Washington, D.C.: World Bank Operations Evaluation Department, 2002), on the very incomplete degree to which environmental priorities are incorporated across the institution, as well as Robert Picciotto, Warren Van Wicklin, and Edward Rice, *Involuntary Resettlement: Comparative Perspectives,* 2 vols. (New Brunswick: Transaction/World Bank Series on Evaluation and Development, 2001) and Gita Gopal, *The Gender Dimension of Bank Assistance: An Evaluation of Results* (Washington, D.C.: World Bank Operations Evaluation Department, 2002).

20. The most comprehensive multistakeholder experience so far is the World Commission on Dams (WCD), a joint civil society–business–government body that was convened by the World Bank and the International Union for the Conservation of Nature. The WCD addressed overlapping issues, including "involuntary resettlement," indigenous peoples' rights, and environmental assessment. See Sanjeev Khagram, "Toward Democratic Governance for Sustainable Development: Transnational Civil Society Organizing around Big Dams," in Florini, *The Third Force,* 83–114; Navroz Dubash, Mairi Dupar, Smitu Kothari, and Tundu Lissu, *A Watershed in Global Governance? An Independent Assessment of the World Commission on Dams* (Washington, D.C.: World Resources Institute/Lokayan/Lawyers Environmental Action Team, 2001); Patrick McCully, *Silenced Rivers: The Ecology and Politics of Large Dams,* 2d ed. (London: Zed, 2001); the regular reports in *World Rivers Review* (published by the International Rivers Network, available online at www.irn.org); and the extensive information resources of the WCD itself, available online at www.dams.org [accessed May 26, 2003]. The WCD reached an unprecedented degree of consensus on minimum social and environmental standards, although the World Bank and some governments later rejected them. In other issue areas that also directly affect powerful

vested interests, such as structural adjustment and extractive industries, various policy reviews and multistakeholder commissions have led some advocacy groups to question the benefits of "policy engagement." At the same time, the bank has also joined with more moderate NGOs to promote some less controversial international policy goals, such as basic education, biodiversity conservation, and the global partnership for the prevention of AIDS (acquired immunodeficiency syndrome), tuberculosis, and malaria.

21. The Inspection Panel has jurisdiction over sectoral and structural adjustment lending. See, for example, chapter 9 by Víctor Abramovich.

22. For an analytical framework that spells out patterns of interaction between these three sets of actors, see Fox and Brown, *The Struggle for Accountability,* and Fox, "Lessons from the First Five Years."

23. This approach, framing different challengers in terms of their approaches to *scale* and *space,* complements the "fix it or nix it" distinction between those challengers to globalization who want to reform the dominant institutions versus those who wish to abolish them. Similarly, Robin Broad's synthetic overview of the "global backlash" distinguishes crisply between those efforts to "roll back" the corporate-led globalization process, and campaigns that are trying to "reshape" it (see Robin Broad, ed., *Global Backlash: Citizen Initiatives for a Just World Economy* (Lanham, Md.: Rowman and Littlefield, 2002). As Broad points out, these two approaches often coexist or overlap in practice, depending on the issue, the campaign, and the political moment — as in the case of the distinction between local/national/international focus noted here.

24. See International Forum on Globalization, "Report Summary: A Better World Is Possible! Alternatives to Economic Globalization," www.ifg.org, 2002 [accessed May 26, 2003]. See also Edward Goldsmith and Jerry Mander, eds., *The Case against the Global Economy: And for a Turn toward the Local,* rev. ed. (London: Earthscan, 2001), among others.

25. Such campaigns constitute what Keck and Sikkink call the "boomerang pattern," which refers to a classic strategy of international human rights and environmental campaigns of the 1970s and 1980s. As Keck and Sikkink put it: "When channels between the state and its domestic actors are blocked, the boomerang pattern of influence characteristic of transnational networks may occur: domestic NGOs bypass their state and directly search out international allies to try to bring pressure on their states from outside" (*Activists beyond Borders,* 12–13). The subsequent shift in focus to "bringing the national arena back in" was made possible by the wave of transitions to elected civilian regimes. The Brazilian experience is one of the leading examples of this "nationalization" of transnational campaigning (see Aurélio Vianna Jr., chapter 7. Recent studies of cross-border public interest coalitions suggest that the tangible impacts of the boomerang strategy depend heavily on national actors and institutions (see Fox, "Lessons from the First Five Years"; idem, "Assessing Binational Civil Society Coalitions: Lessons from the Mexico–US Experience," in Brooks and Fox, *Cross-Border Dialogues,* 341–418; and Kathryn Hochstetler, "After the Boomerang," *Global Environmental Politics,* vol. 4 [November 2002]).

26. See Hemispheric Social Alliance, *Competing Visions for the Hemisphere: The Official FTAA Draft vs. Alternatives for the Americas,* www.ips-dc.org/projects/

global_econ/, January 2002 [accessed May 26]. For diverse advocates of empowering the nation–state, see Aurélio Vianna Jr., chapter 7; Samir Amin, "Convergencia en la diversidad," *La Jornada*, February 9, 2002; the cases in Laxer and Halperin, *Global Civil Society;* and Timothy Wise, Laura Carlsen, and Hilda Salazar, eds., *Confronting Globalization: Economic Integration and Popular Resistance in Mexico* (Bloomfield, Conn.: Kumarian, 2003).

27. Note, for example, the precedent-setting cases of Spanish and English court actions against Augusto Pinochet, Chile's former dictator. and the Belgian prosecution of Rwandans living in Belgium accused of genocide. Human rights advocates have also brought lawsuits against individual and corporate human rights violators in U.S. courts, including precedent-setting cases against the U.S. oil company Unocal for its operations in Burma and against retired Salvadoran generals living in the United States. These suits are based on U.S. laws, such as the Alien Tort Claims Act and the Torture Victim Protection Act, together with international human rights law. For details, see the respective websites of Human Rights Watch (www.hrw.org), EarthRights International (www.earthrights.org), and the Center for Justice and Accountability (www.cja.org), among others [accessed May 26, 2003].

28. For example, George Soros's global Keynesian proposals are explicitly designed to reform and empower existing international institutions to provide "global public goods" and save capitalism from its worst excesses (*On Globalization* [New York: Public Affairs, 2002]). See also Joseph Stiglitz, *Globalization and Its Discontents* (New York: Norton, 2002), who accuses the IMF of putting Wall Street's interests ahead of poverty reduction.

29. As Indian activist-scholar Smitu Kothari put it, "most groups now recognize that strengthening the local is a necessary but insufficient condition for resisting the global" ("Globalization, Global Alliances and the Narmada Movement," in Khagram, Riker, and Sikkink, *Restructuring World Politics,* 232–33).

30. While some World Bank policymakers saw the Inspection Panel and the prospect of improved compliance with its reform policies as being in the institution's long-term interest, many insiders resented and resisted the prospect of oversight and accountability.

31. As historical and comparative context for this debate, it is important to keep in mind that some apparent accountability reforms designed in response to protest are window dressing, which serves primarily to divide critics and to legitimate the status quo. For example, in the late 1970s, when major U.S. corporations and universities were pressured by mobilized students and local governments to divest from South Africa, U.S. investors used the Sullivan Principles, a set of limited voluntary employment standards, to try to divert attention from U.S. investors' structural support for apartheid. Similarly, when the then-proposed NAFTA agreement was hanging by a thread in the U.S. Congress, free trade advocates tipped the balance by creating weak side agreements in the name of environmental and labor standards.

32. In *Globalization from Below,* Brecher, Costello, and Smith make a strong argument for "multilevel strategies" (see p. 40). On the "vertical integration" strategy of simultaneously coordinated civil-society watchdog efforts at local, national, and international levels, see Jonathan Fox, "Vertically Integrated Policy Monitoring: A Tool

for Civil Society Policy Advocacy," *Nonprofit and Voluntary Sector Quarterly* 30, no. 3 (September 2001): 616–27.

33. On the key role of "national problem coalitions" in transnational advocacy campaigns, see L. David Brown and Jonathan Fox, "Accountability within Transnational Coalitions," in Fox and Brown, *The Struggle for Accountability,* 439–84.

34. The editors selected the cases based on two main criteria: (1) indications that the cases set broader precedents in some way, and (2) contacts with potential case analysts. At the time that this project's research agenda was being developed, only two African claims had been submitted by civil-society actors (two others had been submitted by private-sector actors). Since then, the distribution of panel claims across regions has become much more balanced, leading to an underrepresentation of African experiences in this study.

1

Understanding the World Bank Inspection Panel

Dana Clark

The World Bank Inspection Panel opened its doors for business in September 1994, and as of January 2003 it had received twenty-eight claims from around the world requesting an independent investigation into various World Bank–financed projects.[1] There are three Inspection Panel members, who serve for five-year, nonrenewable terms. The panel is tasked with investigating the World Bank's role in a project in response to complaints filed by local affected people and determining whether the bank has violated its own policy framework.[2]

The Inspection Panel provides local people with access to an international forum. It is a citizen-driven process through which people affected by World Bank–financed projects can seek to defend their rights and interests and hold accountable the world's largest development bank. It provides leverage and opportunity for civil society to insist that the bank honor the social contract expressed in the social and environmental policy framework: to finance projects that promote poverty alleviation and to avoid destructive projects.

The World Bank's environmental and social policies were adopted in the 1980s and early 1990s in response to external concern about the detrimental impacts of World Bank projects, internal concern about development effectiveness and increasing demands that the bank shift its lending practices toward more sustainable development.[3] As written, "the policies would require the World Bank to consult with local communities about decisions affecting their lives; carefully evaluate the risks (economic, social, environmental) associated with projects; avoid and minimise resettlement; [and] respect the rights of indigenous peoples and cultural property."[4]

Implementation of these environmental and social policies has been problematic, however, in part because of countervailing institutional pressures, including incentives that reward staff for lending large sums of money and pressure to meet annual lending targets. As civil society mobilized to resist the devastating impacts of high-profile "development disasters" on local communities and the environment, more and more voices called for significant reform of the institution or its abolition.

By the early 1990s, the bank was under increasing pressure to improve transparency and accountability. The creation of the Inspection Panel in 1993–1994 was essentially a publicly demanded response to a major credibility gap at the World Bank, whereby the words on paper and the fundamental objectives of the policies did not match the reality of implementation at the project level. It was hoped that this citizen-driven process would provide some means of holding the bank accountable to the people affected by its lending decisions, and that having such a mechanism in place would lead to the avoidance of further disastrous projects.

This chapter explores the origins of the Inspection Panel, including both internal and external pressures for reform that lead to the creation of this unique accountability mechanism. The chapter will also give an overview of the way the panel functions, examine its history, and document efforts to ensure its independence and define its powers.

ORIGINS: WHERE DID THE PANEL COME FROM?

External Pressure: The Narmada Campaign and the Morse Commission

Although the Inspection Panel's offices are housed within the ultramodern glass and cement World Bank headquarters in Washington, D.C., its origins can be traced back to a very different landscape, in the Narmada Valley of central India. The Narmada is India's most sacred river; its banks are lined with temples and shrines, and pilgrims regularly circumambulate the river. The economy of the valley is complex and robust, and the Nimad plains are blessed with "black cotton soil," which local farmers claim is the best in Asia.

The Narmada Valley is not, however, an idyllic or peaceful place. At present, there are plans to build more than three thousand dams on the Narmada River and its tributaries. The largest of these projects, the Sardar Sarovar dam and canal complex, is being constructed near the mouth of the Narmada, in the state of Gujarat. If the dam reaches its full design height of 455 feet, it will submerge "some of the most fertile land in India" and cause the forced eviction of hundreds of thousands of people, with the impacts falling most harshly on tribal people.[5]

For almost two decades, a village-level grassroots mobilization has resisted the Sardar Sarovar Projects (SSP), utilizing Gandhian principles of nonviolence and noncooperation, characterized most dramatically by the declaration that "we will drown but we will not move." The campaign against the SSP has insisted that development debates and decision making include a focus on issues of equity, including a genuine assessment of who benefits and who loses from large-scale projects such as Sardar Sarovar. Led by the Narmada Bachao Andolan (the NBA, or Movement to Save the Narmada), the grassroots movement and their supporters have also insisted that the World Bank be held accountable for its role in promoting the flawed project. Indian activists were particularly outraged that the World Bank gave its approval and financial support to the project in 1985, kick-starting the stalled construction, when the project had not yet had the benefit of environmental impact studies required by Indian law, and did not have the required clearance from the Ministry of Environment and Forestry.[6] The bank's approval of the project short-circuited domestic debate, violated World Bank policies, and led to flawed decision making. Medha Patkar, cofounder of the NBA, explained:

> the World Bank was really a crucial factor that was pushing a distorted decision-making process forward without considering the social impact, without considering the fulfillment of their own conditions and agreements. This is why they should be held responsible, making it necessary for donor country organizations to also question the World Bank through their respective executive directors so that the real issues would be raised, and the World Bank would be compelled to review the project completely.[7]

Campaign supporters in Europe, Japan, and North America raised concerns about the project with their governments and with the World Bank. A U.S. congressional oversight hearing in 1989 featuring testimony from Narmada activists "served as a catalyst for growing government concern in other major shareholder countries, particularly Japan."[8]

In late December 1990, thousands of people began a "long march" across the three states that would be affected by the project, with the goal of halting construction through peaceful occupation of the dam site.[9] When they reached the Gujarat border, the marchers found police blocking the road, and a standoff ensued. Medha Patkar and six others began a hunger strike, demanding that the Sardar Sarovar project be comprehensively reviewed.[10] Twenty-six days later, the fast was called off when it was announced that there would be a review of the project in India as well as a commitment from the World Bank to conduct its own independent review.[11]

The bank established an independent review team, which became known as the Morse Commission after its lead member, Bradford Morse, in the spring of 1991.[12] This was the first time that the bank had agreed to submit to a thorough independent review of one of its projects by outside experts. In June 1992, the Morse Commission issued its report. In a cover letter to the president of the World Bank, the commission concluded:

> We think the Sardar Sarovar Projects as they stand are flawed, that resettlement and rehabilitation of all those displaced by the Projects is not possible under prevailing circumstances, and that the environmental impacts of the project have not been properly considered or adequately addressed. Moreover, we believe that the Bank shares responsibility with the borrower for the situation that has developed.[13]

The report, which was independently published by the Morse Commission, described the bank's failure to comply with the involuntary resettlement, environmental assessment, and indigenous peoples' policies, and criticized the bank's knowing tolerance of India's violations of loan covenants.[14] The report further noted that "the problems besetting the Sardar Sarovar Projects are more the rule than the exception to resettlement operations supported by the Bank in India. . . . Projects are appraised and negotiated by the Bank despite the absence of resettlement plans, budgets, and timetables that meet the Bank's resettlement policy."[15]

The Morse Commission recommended that the bank "step back" from the SSP, noting that "the underlying difficulties—the failures that reach back to the origin of the Projects—cannot be overcome by a patchwork of studies."[16] On the same day that the Morse Commission released its report, NGOs issued a press release calling for a "Permanent Independent Appeals Commission," thereby launching the campaign for the creation of a new accountability mechanism.

The bank's response, however, was not to step back, but rather to propose a plan for moving forward with the project. Shripad Dharmadikary of the NBA characterized the bank's response as "callous, dishonest, and completely removed from reality,"[17] and the Morse Commission objected to what they considered a misrepresentation of their recommendations and findings.[18] International NGOs published a full-page advertisement in the *Financial Times* during the bank's annual meeting in September, calling on the bank to withdraw from Sardar Sarovar and threatening to cut off donor-country contributions to the bank if it did not.[19]

In October 1992, the board of executive directors convened to consider the Morse Commission report and management's plan. Patrick Coady, the U.S. executive director, stated that to continue with the project would send a "signal that no matter how egregious the situation, no matter how flawed the project, no matter how many policies have been violated, and no matter how clear the remedies prescribed, the Bank will go forward on its own terms."[20] Several executive directors called for a suspension of loans, but a majority voted to continue financing the project, and authorized management to proceed with a six-month action plan to address the environmental and resettlement problems.

Six months later, when the conditions of the action plan had not been met and it became clear that the bank would have to withdraw support, the government of India announced that it wished to cancel the remaining balance on the loan. The government pledged to continue the project without the bank's assistance, and the struggle against the dam shifted to a national debate in India. This decision, however, did not absolve the World Bank of its responsibility for ensuring that the project was in compliance with its policies and procedures.[21] Nor did it absolve the state and central governments in India from following the normative framework for resettlement and rehabilitation that had been developed for the Sardar Sarovar projects and subsequent dams on the Narmada.[22]

Internal Performance Crisis: The Culture of Approval

At the same time that the bank was beset by public controversy over Sardar Sarovar, it was also grappling with the findings of a scathing in-house review of its investment portfolio. The report of that review, known as the Wapenhans report, concluded that the World Bank was suffering from a performance crisis, with 37.5 percent of projects ranked as "unsatisfactory," and widespread violations of loan agreements.[23] The document made clear that the policy violations identified by the Morse Commission were not an aberration, but rather reflected a systemic part of the bank culture.

The Wapenhans report is best known for documenting the bank's internal "culture of approval,"[24] in which bank staff are rewarded for moving large amounts of money out the door. However, the report also provides crucial insights into how imbalances in the bank–borrower relationship have resulted in a failure to design projects that accurately reflect local capacity, commitment, or priorities. An annex to the Wapenhans report includes a summary of confidential interviews with borrowing-government officials, in which they reflect on some of the root causes of poor portfolio performance.

Demonstrating the effects of the bank's culture of approval, the interviews showed that borrowing-country counterparts felt that "The Bank seems more concerned with getting Board approval . . . than in arriving at a realistic agreement the borrower can live up to."[25] Other critiques focused on the lack of ownership of projects and policies, and the terms of the loan agreement, by the borrowing governments. The interviews revealed the unequal bargaining power and the differential technical capacity between borrowers and the bank. This is reflected, for example, in comments that the "Bank has far better lawyers and financiers;" and that "[d]uring negotiations, the Bank overpowers borrowers." Others complained about the bank's tendency to generate an overwhelming amount of paperwork, such that borrowers agree "to conditions and implementation plans that they don't understand fully, because there is no way . . . [they] can review all the documentation the Bank produces."[26] The summary of the borrowing government interviews further commented that the bank has "a built-in bias against project implementation and supervision."

Another function of the bank's culture of approval is the pressure for staff to meet year-end lending targets. Three of the projects profiled in this book involved loans that were rushed by management for board approval at the close of a fiscal year: Sardar Sarovar (discussed earlier), Singrauli (discussed in chapter 8), and China/Tibet (discussed in chapter 10). In each of those cases, policy requirements were violated in the context of pressure to have the project approved prior to the end of a fiscal year. Baseline surveys, consultations, and/or studies that are required by the safeguard policies were simply not done, or were not done well. The projects, therefore, failed to reflect the needs and aspirations of the local affected people.

Bringing It All Together: The Call for Institutional Reform

Thus, in 1992, the year of the Earth Summit in Rio de Janeiro, the year in which the world articulated a new commitment to sustainable development, the World Bank was faced with internal and external documentation that its lending practices were causing environmental disasters, exacerbating poverty, and failing to deliver effective or sustainable development.

Some of the NGOs involved in the Narmada struggle used the Morse Commission and Wapenhans reports to underscore the need for significant institutional reform. The Inspection Panel grew from the seeds of this experience. As explained by Lori Udall, who worked on both the Narmada campaign and the push for the creation of the Inspection Panel:

> The Morse Commission was viewed as independent and credible by the public. . . . For Bank critics, the extensive findings of the Commission, as well as attempts by Bank management to misrepresent the findings of its response to Executive Directors, confirmed the need for a permanent independent mechanism. The Morse Commission established a precedent for a body operating independently from Bank management and Executive Directors, and working on an independent budget.[27]

In the wake of the board's decision to continue funding Sardar Sarovar, NGOs carried through on their threat to cut public funding for the World Bank. Several U.S.-based organizations focused on blocking U.S. contributions for the tenth replenishment of funding for the bank's International Development Agency (IDA). The emphasis on IDA funds was timely, because IDA negotiations were being finalized in November 1992, just one month after the board had voted to continue supporting the Narmada project.[28]

In early 1993, the NGO reform effort gained support from Congressman Barney Frank, the new chairman of the Subcommittee on International Development, Finance, Trade and Monetary Policy, and Dr. Sydney Key, the staff director for the subcommittee.[29] Frank and Key were sympathetic to NGOs' proposals to improve transparency and accountability at the World Bank, and were particularly receptive to the model for an Inspection Panel that was being promoted by the Environmental Defense Fund (now known as Environmental Defense) and the Center for International Environmental Law (CIEL). The NGO proposal called for the creation of a permanent, three-member body that would respond to and investigate complaints from project-affected people, with an adequate budget for fieldwork and the ability to travel to the project area to investigate.[30] Both the NGOs and the subcommittee were also determined to improve the transparency of World Bank operations and simultaneously pushed for the creation of a new policy on information disclosure.

The *Financial Times* reported that the reform proposals "could radically alter the way the Washington-based development institution operates."[31] An article in the *Economist* described the reforms as follows:

> Mr. Frank is promoting two simple things. He wants more openness in the way the Bank processes and approves projects, including greater disclosure of financial, economic and technical information. Hitherto, poor countries, notably Brazil, have been indignant at the thought that their domestic dirty laundry could be hung up in the international breeze each time they negotiated with the Bank. Some rich-country members, including Britain, also dislike the idea, arguing that borrowers might be dissuaded from approaching the Bank. . . .
> . . . The second reform is to set up a permanent commission of outside worthies with power to review World Bank decisions if there is a legitimate case that the Bank's own guidelines have been breached.[32]

As the pressure was building from the outside, reformers inside the bank were also concerned about the systemic failures identified by the Morse Commission and the Wapenhans report. In February 1993, executive directors from The Netherlands, Germany, Malaysia, and Chile, with support from the Swiss executive director, circulated a proposal for a new accountability mechanism. They stated the following reasons for supporting an independent evaluation unit:

[I]n quite a few member countries the image of the Bank has been tarnished. The reaction of the public to the Wapenhans Report further accentuated this problem. Parts of the general public have the impression that there is a lack of accountability. . . . the creation of an independent evaluation unit that has the task to look into projects, could go a long way to dispel such concerns. . . . an independent "inhouse" evaluation unit could help avoid the repetition of painful recent experiences associated with the Narmada Project, the Pangue Project (Biobío), the Yacireta [*sic*] Hydroelectric Project and the Pak Mun Dam Project. An independent unit could provide the Board with a much needed objective assessment of the situation without relying on information from outside sources, whose objectivity is often difficult to assess.[33]

While the proposal constituted an important signal of willingness on the part of both donor and borrowing countries to confront issues of accountability and the need for reform, it did not include guarantees of independence and there were no provisions for the involvement of affected people.

Nonetheless, as reflected in the above quote, there was a desire on the part of both internal and external reform advocates to create a process that would help the bank avoid future development disasters with intractable implementation problems, such as those evidenced in Narmada, Yacyretá, and Pangue. The reformers hoped that by having a more rigorous screen for environmental and social risks, the bank could avoid getting involved in disastrous projects and prevent irreparable harm before it occurred.

In May 1993, Congressman Barney Frank opened a hearing on the tenth replenishment of IDA with the following words:

One thing should be very clear. There has been a great deal of dissatisfaction with the performance of the multilateral institutions. Much of it, in my judgment, is justified. The task we have is to see if a way can be found to improve substantially the way in which these institutions function so we do not find ourselves faced with a couple of unhappy choices, one of which would be to put money where we do not think it is doing much good, and the other would be to cut off money which would punish those who are already victimized by problems. That is the goal of this hearing.[34]

The hearing sent a clear message that the legislature of the bank's largest donor was serious about demanding institutional reform, and would be willing to withhold funds as an inducement to change. On June 10, 1993, the same day that the subcommittee met to approve a bill authorizing funds for IDA's replenishment,[35] the president of the World Bank circulated a paper entitled "Operations Inspection in the Bank: Issues and Options," which stated that "neither the President nor the Board want more surprises about problems with on-going projects."[36] The paper concluded that an inspection function was in the best interests of the bank, and "should be established immediately."[37]

On September 22, 1993, the same day that the House Banking Committee was meeting to mark up the subcommittee's bill, the board of executive directors issued a resolution authorizing the creation of the World Bank Inspection Panel.[38] Congressman Frank acknowledged that the bank had made progress, but said there was still "uncertainty about how some of these reforms will work out in practice." He therefore offered an amendment, which was adopted, authorizing funds for the first two years of the IDA replenishment, but withholding funds for the third year until there was evidence of significant progress by the bank.[39]

The Inspection Panel began operating in September 1994. The three original panel members were Richard Bissell of the United States (author of chapter 2 on the Arun Dam project, the first claim), Alvaro Umaña from Costa Rica, and Ernst-Günther Bröder from Germany. Ever since those first appointments, the board has followed the same geographic model for panel membership: one member from North America, one member from Europe, and one member from the global South.[40]

INTRODUCTION TO THE INSPECTION PANEL

International environmental lawyers who advocated for the creation of the Inspection Panel noted that by "adopting a compliance mechanism, the Executive Directors have made the Bank the only international institution explicitly accountable to citizens. As such, the panel is a remarkable advancement in international law."[41] The World Bank General Counsel also recognized that providing affected citizens with access to an international forum, "where they can submit their complaints and see them addressed," constituted "a progressive step in the development of both the law of international organizations and the international law of human rights."[42]

The Inspection Panel process is unique in that it gives local people access to an international accountability mechanism. This is quite significant because international law has traditionally been viewed as the realm of nation–states, with little space for the voices of non–state actors. Similarly, borrowing governments and bank staff have historically made decisions about projects affecting the lives of millions of people under the rationale that they are promoting the greater good of the country or of the global economic system, even if certain populations are targeted to bear the brunt of hardship caused by those development decisions. This approach is sometimes coarsely summarized as "you have to break a few eggs to get an omelet."

Box 1.1   Basic Questions and Answers about the Inspection Panel

- **How does the panel process work?** The Inspection Panel process is designed to be simple, and can be triggered by any two or more people[43] living in an area affected by a World Bank[44] project who believe that they have been, or are likely to be, harmed as a result of the bank's violation of its operational policies and procedures. Claimants must have already tried to raise their concerns with bank staff or management and not have received a satisfactory response. The executive directors, acting as a board, may also instruct the panel to conduct an investigation. To prevent retroactive claims on closed projects, a claim can only be filed up until the point when the loan has been 95 percent disbursed.[45]
- **Who is on the panel and how are they appointed?** Panel members are nominated by the president of the World Bank and approved by the board.[46] Though the nomination process has varied over the years, it has never overtly included the participation of civil society. Panel members can never work for the bank again after their service on the panel is over, and they cannot have been employed by the bank during the two years prior to their appointment. The panel also has a permanent secretariat with five staff and an annual operating budget of approximately $2 million.
- **What can it do?** The Inspection Panel can investigate whether the World Bank is in compliance with its policy framework. The panel does not investigate the actions or omissions of non-bank actors, such as borrowing governments, implementing agencies, or corporations, except to the extent that the bank has failed in its supervision of the borrower's relevant obligations under the loan agreement. During an investigation, the panel has access to the project area (with the permission of the borrowing government), can hold public hearings with affected communities, interview bank officials and government staff, accept submissions from third parties, and have access to all relevant documents and files. After its investigation, the panel issues a report, which it sends to bank management and the board of executive directors.
- **Then what happens?** After the panel submits its report, bank management has six weeks to prepare a report for the board indicating its recommendations for how to respond to the panel's findings. It is then up to the board to announce what remedial measures, if any, the bank will undertake.[47]

As a result, local people who are targeted to suffer displacement or other impacts by international development projects cannot necessarily rely on their own national governments to defend or respect their rights or interests because the government's priorities, as exemplified by the Singrauli case described in chapter 8 of this volume, are often to get people out of the way of the project. In such circumstances, the bank's policy framework constitutes an important set of rights for local affected people.

Local voices and local knowledge have long been marginalized in development decision making that is made in a top-down way, with decisions taken by political and economic elites. The Inspection Panel process helps to alter the balance of power at the World Bank, in that the process serves to elevate the voices and standing of local affected people, allowing them a platform from which to challenge flawed decision making by elites in the context of particular projects. This institutionalized channel for the expression of a distinct set of grievances can be quite valuable for both local people and the bank. However, as discussed in the concluding chapter of this volume, the institutionalized nature of this channel also helps explain why some groups will not use the panel to address their grievances: using the panel does, to a certain extent, mean buying into the system.

The Inspection Panel process is fundamentally a tool of the board of executive directors, those who give their approval to every project financed by the bank. The panel can help lead to better-informed decision making and provide the board with impartial opinions about policy violations. In contentious cases, the panel can serve as an "honest broker" between the often-conflicting accounts from local people and bank management. In addition, the panel process helps bring the reality of project impacts and policy violations into the boardroom, thereby making the reality harder to ignore. Finally, the process requires both bank staff and the bank's highest decision makers—the president and the board of executive directors—to be aware of and more responsive to the concerns of local people who bear the impacts of the bank's lending decisions. Some basic questions about the panel are addressed in box 1.1.

EVOLUTION OF THE PANEL PROCESS

The Early Years: Institutional Resistance to Accountability

The early years of the panel's operations, reflected in many of the case studies in this book, were somewhat contentious. There was a great deal of institutional resistance to this new mechanism that was suddenly looking through bank files, interviewing bank staff, traveling to project areas, and writing candid reports about problems in particular projects. The board and management both failed to abide by the terms of the resolution and the panel operating procedures, and the panel underwent a certain degree of adaptation as it sought to navigate hostile terrain.

Things got off to a momentous start with the first claim, filed on the Arun III Dam in Nepal just one month after the Inspection Panel started its operations. The board authorized the panel to conduct a thorough investigation into the project. The panel's investigation and subsequent report, in turn, helped convince incoming President James Wolfensohn to terminate World Bank support for the controversial project.[48]

At that time, nobody could have anticipated that it would take nearly five years before the board of executive directors would again authorize the panel to conduct a full investigation, or that that next full investigation would lead to the cancellation of another of the most controversial projects in the history of the World Bank: the infamous China Western Poverty Reduction Project.[49]

In between Arun (1994–1995) and the China Western Poverty Reduction Project (1999–2000), in every case where the panel recommended an investigation, the board either denied the panel authorization to investigate (in Planafloro, Itaparica, and EcoDevelopment) or limited the terms of reference of the investigation (in Yacyretá and Singrauli). Executive directors representing the countries where the projects were located banded together with other borrowing-country governments and some donors on the board to oppose the Inspection Panel's recommendations for an investigation. Some borrowing-country executive directors objected to the very concept and wording of "inspection," and sought to limit the panel's ability to operate in accordance with its mandate.[50]

The problem of borrowing countries blocking and objecting to panel investigations resulted from a structural weakness in the process, namely the requirement that the panel must have approval of the board to conduct an investigation. This weakness was identified early on by those who were monitoring the creation of the Inspection Panel. The NGO proposal had not allowed for board involvement in the panel's decision on whether an investigation was warranted. However, the board was not willing to accept a new process that would be beyond its control, and in order to give its approval to the panel concept, insisted on having the right to control whether the panel investigated a claim.

In testimony before Barney Frank's subcommittee before the board resolution was approved, Lori Udall specifically warned that the panel's independence could be undermined if executive directors from borrowing countries could block recommendations for an investigation:

> Since Board members from the Bank's borrowing countries often feel that scrutiny of projects is an infringement on their countries' sovereignty, many of

these Board members will possibly object to cases which originate in their country being brought to the panel. As a result, decisions about whether to take up a complaint may not be based on the merits of the case itself, but on the whims or biases of individual Board Members.[51]

This dynamic of board resistance to investigations played out dramatically during the early years of the Inspection Panel's operations, and it took a toll on the panel, civil society, and the board itself. The clear borrower/donor split that emerged at the board level over the panel process was embarrassing to the bank, especially since the board is accustomed to operating by consensus. The board often became paralyzed by the lack of consensus on how to proceed and would sometimes postpone discussion of the panel's reports and recommendations for months at a time. The panel resolution and procedures failed to define time frames within which the board must take action in panel cases, thus allowing unreasonable delays in decision making.

Meanwhile, bank management also resented the panel's scrutiny and strongly resisted being held accountable. Management responses to the Inspection Panel claims tended to deny policy violations and deny responsibility for problems identified in the claim (usually blaming the borrowing government for the problems instead). Management responses also tended to challenge the eligibility of claimants and propose "action plans" as alternatives to panel investigations.[52]

Management's action plan approach was frustrating to claimants and their advocates because rather than addressing the problems identified through an investigation, the action plans were designed to derail panel investigations and to instead convince the board to allow management to solve the problems. According to an attorney in the World Bank's legal department, "The effect of remedial action plans forwarded by Management shortly before the Board's consideration of the Panel's recommendation seemed thus to be that Management through them was successfully subverting the Panel process, as no inspections were authorized following the submission of such plans."[53]

Not surprisingly, management action plans failed to lead to effective remedial measures. One reason was that the plans were developed by the very actors who denied that there were policy violations and who were responsible for creating the problems that were articulated in the claim. In addition, the plans were developed without consulting the claimants or other local affected people. This reflects a structural imbalance in the panel process, which gives the people who caused the problems the task of designing and implementing the remedy to those problems, without allowing people affected by those decisions to have any comparable role. This is a frustration for the claimants and a key weakness in the process. Claimants in the Ecodevelopment case noted that: "As the petitioners, solely in whose favor the report has come out, we

feel that we have a right for participation and to contribute with effective recommendations in the process of the corrective measures to take place. The decision of the World Bank on the IP [Inspection Panel] Report has totally denied us this just and humane right."[54]

The action plan approach has also been problematic because of the role of
the Board, which has failed to fully embrace its responsibility to design and
oversee remedial measures in response to panel reports. There is a high degree of turnover among the executive directors, with a typical term lasting
only two years. Over time, most of the board members who were present
through the Narmada debate and the creation of the Inspection Panel were no
longer present, and many of the new board members did not necessarily recognize that the panel could be a helpful tool for the board to help ensure development effectiveness. As projects go through the claims process and time
passes, board members often lose sight of the fact that problems are still un-
resolved at the project level.

The Panel Adapts to a Hostile Environment

As it became less and less likely that the board would approve full investigations, the Inspection Panel adapted by packing a "mini-investigation" into the
preliminary stage of its analysis into whether a claim is eligible, which often
includes a field visit and a prima facie determination of policy violations. The
panel began including commentary on potential policy violations and harm in
its initial report to the board containing the panel's recommendation regarding an investigation.

This trend was accelerated by the Planafloro claim, which is discussed in
chapter 3 of this volume. In that case, the panel recommended an investigation based on its preliminary assessment of the claim and management's response. The board, not satisfied with the evidence of harm to the claimants,
responded to the panel's recommendation by asking the panel to do further research on harm and report back to the board. The panel responded with detailed evidence of harm and again recommended a full investigation. Ultimately, though, the board rejected the panel's recommendation for a full
investigation in favor of a management-generated action plan.

In claims following Planafloro, the panel was careful to emphasize the
harm suffered by the claimants as part of its preliminary assessment and
recommendation to the board, and this approach was validated by the board
during the first board review of the panel's operations.[55] In practice, however, this expanded preliminary assessment angered many board members
who felt that the panel's preliminary report and recommendation about how
to proceed contained information that was embarrassing for the govern-

ments in question, before the board had even authorized the panel to conduct an investigation.[56]

Meanwhile, claimants and NGOs were also dissatisfied with the way that the panel process was evolving. Their concerns included the marginalization of the panel, the dearth of investigations, the limited role of claimants in the process, the tendency of board decisions about investigations to be based more on the political resistance of powerful borrower governments than on the merits of a case, and the lack of remedies to problems. As a result, full-scale international civil-society campaigns were launched around many of the claims just to support the claimants' basic right to be heard, as NGOs put pressure on board members to vote in favor of the panel's recommendations. The Inspection Panel became a lightning rod for the debate over accountability and development effectiveness, as cases brought to the panel highlighted a pervasive lack of commitment to the requirements and objectives of the environmental and social policy framework on the part of both bank management and borrowing governments.

The 1998–1999 Review: A Watershed

In the aftermath of the tumultuous board meetings that resulted in the board rejecting the panel's recommendation for an inspection in the Itaparica case and confining the panel to a Washington-based desk review of Singrauli, the board finally recognized that it was not allowing the panel to operate in the manner that was intended under the resolution.[57] Board members were "frustrated that a mechanism that had been designed to help reduce their problems in dealing with difficult projects was instead generating more conflict at the Board."[58]

Accordingly, in March 1998, the board decided to initiate a second review of the panel process. A working group, consisting of three borrowing-country executive directors and three donor-country executive directors, was tasked with making recommendations to the full board on how to resolve the difficulties. As noted by Daniel Bradlow, a law professor who followed the review process and commented on the proposed changes, there were several problems with the reform proposal generated by the working group. First, the proposal

> seemed to be endorsing the management's "informal" practice of submitting an action plan to the Board before [the Board] had reviewed the Panel's recommendation. From the NGO perspective, this seemed to be formalizing precisely that management practice which the NGO's saw as a major cause of the problems with the panel process.[59]

The working group also proposed to change the standard for determining whether claimants have been harmed. The new benchmark for determining harm would compare the situation of the requesters at the time of filing the claim to what it would have been if there had been no project, as opposed to what it would have been if there had been full compliance with the bank's rules and procedures, thereby making it more difficult for claimants to demonstrate harm.

When the working group proposal was leaked, Washington-based NGOs responded by engaging the U.S. Treasury Department and the U.S. executive director to ask that the U.S. government demand public consultation on the proposal, and simultaneously launched an international campaign to "Save the Panel." Following the resulting public comment period, and substantial advocacy by NGOs from around the world, the board invited representatives of civil society, including several claimants, to attend a meeting to discuss the working group report. This extraordinary event marked the first time that representatives of people affected by bank projects had been invited into the boardroom to discuss a matter of policy. Following these consultations, the proposal was substantially modified. This outcome illustrates one of the most potentially powerful features of the panel, which is that it can help bridge the gap between top decision makers and those who actually feel the impacts of those decisions.

The board's "Conclusions of the Second Review of the Inspection Panel," released on April 20, 1999, reaffirmed "the importance of the Panel's function, its independence, and integrity." The board called on management to follow the resolution, to stop all communications with the board except as permitted under the resolution, and to "report to the Board any recommendations it may have, *after* the Panel completes its inspection and submits its findings."[60] In other words, management's action plans should be based on the panel's findings, not designed to preempt a panel investigation.

The board also resolved one of the key stumbling blocks that had developed in the panel process regarding how the board should respond when the panel recommended an investigation into a claim. Borrower- and donor-country executive directors reached a critically important compromise agreement whereby they clarified that "*If the Panel so recommends, the Board will authorize an investigation* without making a judgement on the merits of the claimants' request, and without discussion," except with respect to technical eligibility criteria, defined in the document.[61] In exchange, the panel's preliminary assessment period was reduced to a simplified evaluation of the eligibility of the claim. This compromise—a shortened preliminary assessment phase in exchange for a board commitment to respect the panel's recommendations for inspections—was one of the key outcomes of the second review.

In terms of the harm standard, the 1999 review "clarified" that

For assessing material adverse effect, the without-project situation should be used as the base case for comparison, taking into account what baseline information may be available. Non-accomplishments and unfulfilled expectations that do not generate a material deterioration compared to the without-project situation will not be considered as a material adverse effect for this purpose.[62]

In addition, the board deliberately decided to exclude the panel from supervision of remedial activities generated as a result of the claims process. The 1999 clarification stated that

"action plans" are outside the purview of the Resolution, its 1996 clarification, and these clarifications. In the event of agreement by the Bank and borrower on an action plan for the project, Management will communicate to the Panel the nature and outcomes of consultations with affected parties on the action plan. . . . The Panel may submit to Executive Directors for their consideration a report on their view of the adequacy of consultations with affected parties in the preparation of the action plans. The Board should not ask the Panel for its view on other aspects of the action plans nor would it ask the Panel to monitor the implementation of the action plans.[63]

While excluding an oversight role from the panel's mandate, the board also failed to create an alternative way to monitor any actions taken (or not) to bring projects into compliance with policies.[64] Claimants have found that remedial action plans often lack effective implementation because there is no systematic oversight by the board. This is particularly a problem in light of the high degree of board turnover noted above, because the board lacks institutional memory. Action plans, which can take a long time to implement, are forgotten and drop off the board's radar screen. As a result, local people are often denied meaningful remedies. This lack of oversight of remedial measures is a key weakness in the Inspection Panel process.

Recent History: The Tide Shifts

The first claim to test the board's agreement to allow the panel to investigate was the China Western Poverty Reduction Project, which is described in chapter 10 of this volume. In that case, sidestepping an objection by China, the board respected the panel's recommendation and authorized a full investigation—the first since the Arun claim. The board essentially adopted the claim as its own. The China Western Poverty Reduction Project marked a new stage in the relationship between the board and the Inspection Panel.

Following the China/Tibet case, the board has universally given authorization to the panel to investigate when it so recommends—getting back, finally, to the quasi-independent model of decision making that was originally envisioned. The approvals have all been granted on a "no objection" basis, which means that panel recommendations are circulated to the board and if no board member objects within three weeks, the recommendation is approved.

The board has also started to deal more aggressively with the problem of management undermining the panel's work. The cases profiled in this book reveal a pattern of bank management denying that anything is wrong in a project, denying that the policies have been violated, and seeking to undermine panel investigations. In its December 2000 report on an investigation into the Lake Victoria Environmental Management Project in Kenya, the panel found that management had violated the public consultation requirements of the bank's environmental assessment policy. Rather than making suggestions for what steps to take in light of the panel's findings, management disputed the panel's findings by issuing a rebuttal document that gave the impression that consultations had taken place. The panel, responding to management's overt challenge to its findings, issued a follow-up report that showed that management had manipulated information in such a way as to deliberately mislead the board. Ultimately, the board ordered management to withdraw its unauthorized report and rebuked staff and management for misrepresenting the facts and undermining the integrity of the panel process. According to the minutes of the board meeting, several board members "agreed with the Panel that Management's action in questioning its findings had damaged the Panel's credibility as an independent investigation mechanism for the Board."[65]

CONCLUSION

The Inspection Panel provides a forum where ordinary people can have their grievances heard and where local affected people have standing to challenge the development projects that so profoundly affect their lives. The claimants to the Inspection Panel have been in the forefront of some of the most pitched battles in the development debate, and as a result, the panel's case history profiles some of the most controversial projects in the World Bank's history. The following chapters demonstrate how fisherfolk, washerwomen, nomads, hydrologists, indigenous communities, subsistence farmers, the urban poor, and others have joined with national and international allies to challenge "expert" economists and elite decision makers. Through their efforts, the claimants have significantly altered the landscape of international financial institutions and have created a greater sense of public entitlement to accountability in development finance decision making.

The Inspection Panel is an innovative and extraordinary development in international law and the governance of international institutions, for it gives standing to non–state actors to hold an international institution accountable to a normative policy framework. As such, the panel is an important step forward in the struggle for accountability, building on past campaigns and making more enforceable the policy reforms established in the last two decades.

The panel concept has continued to evolve and to influence accountability discussions at international financial institutions around the world. The case studies in the Inspection Panel's brief history, including those portrayed in this book, have generated a new understanding of the flaws in the World Bank's lending paradigm and have identified areas for further improvement in the ongoing quest for accountability and sustainable and equitable development.

NOTES

1. The Inspection Panel's website is www.inspectionpanel.org. For a concise overview of the World Bank Inspection Panel, see Dana L. Clark, *A Citizen's Guide to the World Bank Inspection Panel,* 2d ed. (Washington, D.C.: CIEL, 1999), available online at www.ciel.org in English, Spanish, French, and Portuguese.

2. The relevant policies include the environmental and social policies, such as policies on environmental assessment, indigenous peoples, involuntary resettlement, and cultural property, as well as policies on project supervision and consideration of economic alternatives.

3. For a discussion of the evolution of environmental and social concerns at the World Bank, see Robert Wade, "Greening the Bank: The Struggle over the Environment, 1970–1995," in *The World Bank: Its First Half-Century,* ed. Devesh Kapur, John P. Lewis, and Richard Webb (Washington, D.C.: Brookings, 1997), 2: 654. For further information on the environmental critique of the World Bank's operations, see Bruce Rich, *Mortgaging the Earth* (Boston: Beacon, 1994) and Catherine Caufield, *Masters of Illusion: The World Bank and the Poverty of Nations* (New York: Henry Holt, 1996).

4. Dana Clark, "The Rise and Fall of Accountability," *Watershed: People's Forum on Ecology* 6, no. 3 (March–June 2001): 52.

5. The project authorities envision building 30 large dams, 135 medium-size dams, and 3,000 smaller dams on the Narmada River. Officials estimate that the Sardar Sarovar Dam will submerge approximately 37,000 hectares of land and 245 villages in three states — Gujarat, Maharashtra, and Madhya Pradesh. "Virtually all of the affected people in Gujarat are tribals. This is also the case in Maharashtra. In Madhya Pradesh approximately 40 percent of the people in the submergence area are tribals. . . . The canal network will require approximately 80,000 hectares for construction, more than twice as much land as the reservoir" (Independent Review, *Sardar Sarovar: Report of the Independent Review* [Resources Future International, Inc., 1992], 4–5 [hereinafter *Independent Review*]).

6. Chittaroopa Palit, "Gender Justice, People's Struggles and the State" (discussion during a workshop on "Engendering Resettlement Policies and Programmes in India," Institute for Development Studies and ActionAid India, New Delhi, September 12–13, 2002).

7. Medha Patkar, in conversation with Smitu Kothari, "The Struggle for Participation and Justice: A Historical Narrative," in *Toward Sustainable Development,* ed. William F. Fisher (Armonk, N.Y.: Sharpe, 1995), 175–76.

8. Smitu Kothari, "Globalization, Global Alliances and the Narmada Movement," in *Restructuring World Politics: Transnational Social Movements, Networks, and Norms,* ed. Sanjeev Khagram, James V. Riker, and Kathyrn Sikkink (Minneapolis: University of Minnesota Press, 2000), 232–33. A campaign organized by Japanese NGOs in coordination with the NBA convinced the Japanese government to withdraw its commitment to provide bilateral loans for the SSP. Kothari, "Globalization, Global Alliances." In addition, questions were raised in the Japanese Diet about SSP; the European Parliament scheduled a hearing; and questions were raised in the German, Finnish, and Dutch Parliaments. Lori Udall, e-mail communication with author, January 13, 2003.

9. Udall, e-mail communication with author.

10. Udall, "The International Narmada Campaign: A Case Study of Sustained Advocacy," in Fisher, *Toward Sustainable Development,* 213 (hereinafter "International Narmada Campaign).

11. Lori Udall, "The World Bank and Public Accountability," in *The Struggle for Accountability: The World Bank, NGO's and Grassroots Movements,* ed. Jonathan A. Fox and L. David Brown (Cambridge: MIT Press, 1998), 391–427, 398.

12. The review team's terms of reference were to assess the bank's performance regarding implementation of resettlement and rehabilitation as well as mitigation of environmental impacts. The review team was to use "the Bank's own polices, loan agreements and other governing documents as criteria" (Udall, "International Narmada Campaign," 215). In addition, the assessment was to "include, as appropriate, any recommendations for improvement of the project implementation in the above two areas" (World Bank, "Terms of Reference, INDIA—Implementation of Sardar Sarovar Projects: Assessment of Resettlement and Environmental Aspects," appendix A in *Independent Review,* 359–60).

13. Bradford Morse and Thomas Berger to Lewis Preston, president of the World Bank, June 18, 1992.

14. The report in particular criticized the bank's "incremental strategy" of policy compliance in which "[v]iolations of legal covenants are flagged and then forgotten; conditions are imposed and when the borrower fails to meet them, the conditions are relaxed or their deadlines postponed" (*Independent Review,* 56).

15. *Independent Review,* 53–54.

16. *Independent Review,* 355.

17. Shripad Dharmadikary to World Bank executive directors, October 9, 1992, as cited in Udall, "International Narmada Campaign."

18. "The Bank may decide that overriding political and economic considerations are so compelling that it's Operational Directives are irrelevant when decisions have

to be made about the Sardar Sarovar Projects. But it should not seek to reshape our report to support such decisions." Bradford Morse and Thomas Berger, to Lewis Preston, October 13, 1992, 1.

19. David Wirth, "Partnership Advocacy in World Bank Environmental Reform," in Fox and Brown, *Struggle for Accountability,* 63 (citing *Financial Times,* September 21, 1992, 6).

20. Statement of U.S. executive director Patrick Coady, executive directors' board meeting, October 23, 1992, as cited in Udall, "International Naramada Campaign," 219.

21. See World Bank, memorandum from Ibrahim F. I. Shihata to D. Joseph Wood, March 30, 1993: "In the brief Board discussion today of the cancellation of the Bank's loan for the Narmada Project, the impression was left that the Government of India is no longer legally obligated towards the Bank to carry out its obligations under the loan agreement. . . . this is not the case. Section 6.06 of the General Conditions applicable to all Bank loans . . . provides that '[n]otwithstanding any cancellation or suspension, all the provisions of the Loan Agreement and the Guarantee Agreement shall continue in full force and effect except as specifically provided in this Article.'"

22. For a current assessment of the situation in the Narmada Valley, see HLRN-HIC (Housing and Land Rights Network–Habitat International Coalition), "The Impact of the 2002 Submergence on Housing and Land Rights in the Narmada Valley: Report of a Fact-Finding Visit to Sardar Sarovar and Man Dam Projects," March 2003, available in PDF format at www.narmada.org.

23. World Bank, *Report of the Portfolio Management Task Force* (Washington, D.C.: World Bank, 1992) (hereinafter Wapenhans report).

24. Wapenhans report, ii; see also Ibrahim F. I. Shihata, *The World Bank Inspection Panel: In Practice* (Oxford: Oxford University Press, 2000), 3.

25. All quotes in this paragraph are from the Wapenhans report, annex B, 1–3.

26. Interestingly, bank management also has the capacity to "overwhelm" the board. Board members are besieged by paperwork most of the time, but particularly so at the end of the fiscal year, a time commonly referred to inside the bank as "bunching season."

27. Statement of Lori Udall, *Congressional Testimony before the Subcommittee on International Development, Finance, Trade and Monetary Policy,* serial no. 103-146, June 21, 1994, 13.

28. Udall, "The World Bank and Public Accountability," 402. This strategy of targeting IDA funds to leverage reform at the bank was not universally supported by NGOs; some international NGOs were concerned that threatening IDA funds, which go to the poorest countries, would have negative impacts on the poor (Udall, "The World Bank and Public Accountability").

29. As explained by Sydney Key, "the subcommittee made a policy decision to go well beyond the traditional approach of providing 'voice and vote' instructions for the U.S. executive directors and [decided] instead to use the leverage associated with its power to authorize funding to achieve fundamental institutional reforms" (Sydney Key, telephone interview by author, January 3, 2003).

30. David Hunter and Lori Udall, *Proposal for an Independent Appeals Commission* (Washington, D.C.: Environmental Defense Fund and CIEL, 1993). The Hunter and

Udall proposal was based on the recent experience with the Morse Commission. The idea of holding the bank accountable had been explored at a conceptual level for several years (see Chris Wold and Durwood Zaelke, "Establishing an Independent Review Board at the European Bank for Reconstruction and Development," *Duke Environmental Law and Policy Forum,* vol. 59, no. 2 [1992] and E. Christenson, *Green Appeal: A Proposal for an Independent Commission Inquiry at the World Bank* [New York: National Resources Defense Council, 1992]). In addition, Daniel Bradlow of American University's Washington College of Law put forward a proposal calling for the creation of an ombudsman. (Daniel D. Bradlow, "The Case for a World Bank Ombudsman," Hearings on Appropriations for International Financial Institutions, U.S. House of Representatives Subcommittee on International Development, Finance, Trade, and Monetary Policy, May 1993.)

31. George Graham, "Developing a More Worldly Bank," *Financial Times,* July 2, 1993.

32. "Got a Light?" *The Economist,* June 26, 1993.

33. World Bank, office memorandum from Fritz Fischer, Nicolas Flano, Eveline Herfkins, and Aris Othman, executive directors, to Lewis Preston, president, February 10, 1993. Ms. Herfkins, the Dutch executive director, played a key role in convincing other board members to support both the creation of the Morse Commission and the creation of the Inspection Panel (Lori Udall, e-mail communication with the author, January 13, 2003).

34. "Authorizing Contributions to IDA, GEF, and ADF," *Hearing before the Subcommittee on International Development, Finance, Trade and Monetary Policy,* serial no. 103-36, May 5, 1993, 2.

35. U.S. House of Representatives, Subcommittee on International Development, Finance, Trade, and Monetary Policy, Committee on Banking Finance and Urban Affairs, *Markup of Amendments to International Development and Debt Relief Act of 1993,* June 10, 1993.

36. World Bank, "Operations Inspection in the Bank: Issues and Options," June 10, 1993 (hereinafter "Issues and Options"). The paper evaluated two options: (1) the executive directors' February proposal, and (2) a management proposal for a more independent, permanent inspection panel. The paper recommended in favor of the latter.

37. "Issues and Options."

38. The World Bank, IBRD (International Bank for Reconstruction and Development) Resolution no. 93-10, IDA Resolution no. 93-6, *The World Bank Inspection Panel,* September 22, 1993 (hereinafter *Panel Resolution*).

39. House of Representatives, Committee on Banking, Finance, and Urban Affairs, markup of H.R. 3063, *The International Development and Debt Relief Act of 1993,* and H.R. 1257, *The Insurance Consumer Protection Act,* September 22, 1993. See also Andrew Taylor, "House Panel Cuts Contributions to Put Heat on World Bank," *Congressional Quarterly Weekly Report,* September 1993. Barney Frank was also putting pressure on the U.S. Treasury to take a more aggressive stand on the need for reform. "Frank said that the Treasury Department, which negotiated the U.S. contribution to the IDA, is not pleased with his move" (Taylor, "House Panel Cuts Contributions").

40. The current members of the Inspection Panel are Edward Ayensu from Ghana (whose term expires July 31, 2003), Maartje van Putten of The Netherlands (whose

term will expire in August 2004), and Edith Brown Weiss from the United States (whose term will expire in September 2007). For more information about panel members, see the Inspection Panel website, www.inspectionpanel.org.

41. David Hunter and Lori Udall, "The World Bank's New Inspection Panel: Will It Increase the Bank's Accountability?" *CIEL Brief,* no. 1 (Washington, D.C.: Center for International Environmental Law, 1994). Lawyers at the World Bank also shared this assessment. See Sabine Schlemmer-Schulte, "Introductory Note to the Conclusions of the Second Review of the World Bank," *International Legal Materials* 39 (2000): 243: "The creation of such a formal mechanism as the Bank's Inspection Panel by which non-state actors can hold the organization accountable for non-compliance with its own standards was unprecedented in the work of international organizations."

42. Ibrahim F. I. Shihata, "The World Bank Inspection Panel: A Background Paper on Its Historical, Legal and Operational Aspects," 25.

43. The two or more people must demonstrate a "common interest or concern." Claims can also be filed by authorized representatives of the affected parties, and by executive directors.

44. It is important to note that the Inspection Panel covers only IBRD and IDA operations of the World Bank Group; it does not cover the operations of the International Finance Corporation (IFC) or the Multilateral Investment Guarantee Agency (MIGA). A separate process, known as the Compliance Advisor/Ombudsman (CAO) was inaugurated in 1999 for IFC and MIGA projects. Chapter six, which profiles the struggle against the damming of the Biobío River in Chile, describes the origins of the CAO process.

45. After more than 95 percent of the funds have been disbursed, the project is deemed to be "substantially complete," and exempted from the panel process.

46. Members of the panel are to be "selected on the basis of their ability to deal thoroughly and fairly with the requests brought to them, their integrity and their independence from the Bank's Management, and their exposure to developmental issues and to living conditions in developing countries" (*Panel Resolution,* paragraph 4).

47. For a critique of the problems relating to remedial measures, see Dana L. Clark, "The World Bank and Human Rights: The Need for Greater Accountability," *Harvard Human Rights Journal,* vol. 216, no. 15 (2002).

48. See chapter 2 by Richard E. Bissell.

49. See chapter 10 by Dana Clark and Kay Treakle.

50. Thus, in Yacyretá, for example, the board authorized the panel to "review and assess" the project and proposed action plans in order to avoid the use of the term "inspection."

51. Udall, *Congressional Testimony,* 46, 56.

52. For additional information on panel claims and institutional responses, see chapter 11 of this volume, "Conclusions and Analysis: Lessons for Accountability."

53. Schlemmer-Schulte, "Introductory Note," 243, 245.

54. J. L. Subramani, J. P. Raju, Roy David, Shreekanth, and Narijundiah to the president, World Bank (undated), 3.

55. The board accepted this "harm assessment" as well as the preliminary assessment phase in its first review of the panel's operations (World Bank, "Review of the Resolution Establishing the Inspection Panel: Clarification of Certain Aspects of the Resolution," October 1996).

56. Some observers also felt that this trend detracted from the panel's accountability role, which is to identify violations of the bank's policies and procedures and then identify the harm that flows from those policy violations. See Schlemmer-Schulte, "Introductory Note," commenting that this resulted in an "exaggerated focus on the harm to requesters at the first stage of the Panel process that resulted in the Panel's practice in a reduced attention to the equally important question of the Bank's compliance with its policies and procedures" (243, 245).

57. For a discussion of Itaparica, see chapter 7 by Aurélio Vianna Jr., and for a discussion of Singrauli, see chapter 8 by Dana Clark.

58. Daniel D. Bradlow, Comments on the Report of the Inspection Panel Working Group Entitled "Second Review of the Inspection Panel 1998 Clarification of Certain Aspects of the Resolution," submitted to the World Bank Group, March 1999, 3 (hereinafter "Comments").

59. Bradlow, "Comments," 3.

60. World Bank, "Conclusions of the Board's Second Review of the Inspection Panel," April 20, 1999, paragraph 2 (emphasis added).

61. World Bank, "Conclusions of the Board's Second Review," paragraph 9 (emphasis added).

62. World Bank, "Conclusions of the Board's Second Review," paragraph 14.

63. World Bank, "Conclusions of the Board's Second Review," paragraphs 15, 16.

64. See Clark, "The World Bank and Human Rights," 219.

65. World Bank, minutes of board meeting of March 20, 2001, paragraph 11.

2

The Arun III Hydroelectric Project, Nepal

Richard E. Bissell

In any new international institution, the first year is pathbreaking: procedures are established, governance and staff capabilities are tested, and relationships with constituencies are established. The World Bank Inspection Panel in 1994–1995 was no exception. The Arun III Hydroelectric Project in eastern Nepal, which was the subject of the first request submitted to the panel, enhanced the sense of a new global initiative. Indeed, as a high-profile project involving the construction of a controversial dam, among many such controversies, Arun III was the focus of an extensive civil-society campaign and had an unprecedented degree of transparency for a World Bank project. People interested in the future of the World Bank may not be able to find the Arun Valley on a map, but they do know the kind of turning point it represented. The Arun III project was the "poster child" of the fiftieth-anniversary campaign against the World Bank. Without enumerating all the factors that came into play, an overview of essential factors is necessary to make some sense out of what transpired—ultimately, the cancellation of a billion-dollar project.

BACKGROUND

Citizen advocacy around the Arun project needs to be put in the context of a range of rapid changes and prior failures that deeply colored the experience of all stakeholders in this particular case. The Kingdom of Nepal was a fledgling democracy. While some of the trappings of democracy had been present for years, it was only in the early 1990s that the organic elements of democratic participation were put in place: freedom of the press, broadened legal protection of rights, generous access to education, viable opposition political parties, and competitive politics at the grassroots. Some sectors of society democratized faster than others, and, indeed, there was considerably more freedom in the capital, Kathmandu, than in the countryside. Thus, the establishment of the Inspection Panel at the time of rapidly escalating political debate brought together those opposing the government and those opposing this project. The government was unfamiliar with NGO activism—domestic or foreign—and was thus largely blindsided by the entire controversy.

The perception of large dams as a development instrument was also changing. In the richer countries, questioning of dams accelerated as environmental impact measurement became more sophisticated. The same methodologies would be used to question the much younger hydroelectric sectors in developing countries. The discrediting of the Sardar Sarovar project in the Narmada Valley of India in the early 1990s, punctuated by the termination of Indian government interest in World Bank financing, only added fuel to the fire—stoking public interest in the collateral effects of large dams.[1] The displacement of tens of thousands of families in the Narmada Valley became a graphic illustration of the costs offsetting the development benefits of large dam projects.

For governments on the rim of the Himalayas, like Nepal, this skepticism about the development effectiveness of large dams was both unexpected and, to some degree, embittering. Why, after all, should they be denied the benefits of clean, renewable power just because the more mature economies decided to cycle out of hydropower in their energy planning? As Nepal later learned, of course, they were not alone in this situation. Many of the early requests to the Inspection Panel focused on dam projects across all continents. These campaigns eventually culminated in the World Commission on Dams, which reported out in late 2000.[2]

Thus, the Arun request to the panel did not spring out of the blue; rather, it was just one step in a broader international campaign throughout the early 1990s to stop construction of large hydropower projects. The pressure that the Indian government and the World Bank received on Sardar Sarovar was developing on other projects, such as Arun III. Some governments, such as Nepal, did not realize the extent of the campaign until they became the targets.

The third contextual piece is the Nepalese government's prior experience with hydropower and associated social impacts. The Arun III project was a 402-MW design, while the largest hydro project prior to this was less than 70 MW. Even after Arun III was pared down to 201 MW for financing by the World Bank, the sheer scale of the project—for both the dam itself and the preparatory road-building work—was so substantial that it was beyond the capacity of Nepalese contractors. In fact, when the project bids were opened, there were no qualifying contractors from Nepal or India. An Italian firm won the bid, and Indian subcontractors were scheduled to do the work.

Earlier high dam hydro projects financed by the World Bank in Nepal had been badly implemented. The history of Marsyangdi was traced in appendix A of the Inspection Panel report on Arun as an object lesson of a failure of compliance with resettlement provisions.[3] Elsewhere in the same report, the panel expressed its concern about the lack of capability in the Nepal Electricity Authority (NEA) to supervise the contracts to foreign firms, especially regarding the social and environmental provisions.

One also has to keep in mind the imbalances in the entire energy sector of Nepal, an issue raised by those requesting an inspection, but excluded from the investigation by the board. The reduction of the size of the Arun III project to 201 MW implied a cost of $5 million per MW, causing an increased price of power to the Nepali consumer, estimated by some NGOs as rising 250 percent. The requesters also took issue with management's unsubstantiated estimates of the power market in the domestic Nepalese market and the absence of a power-purchasing agreement with India, the likely consumer of any large-scale power generation by Nepal. Furthermore, Nepal's inability to come to terms with India on a mutually acceptable tariff for power exported to the insatiable Indian market meant that the revenue from the Arun III project could not be securitized. In economic terms, the project was a speculative investment, with revenue estimates based on hoped-for levels of Nepalese consumption and/or exports to India at a "fair" price. Given India's history of predatory approaches to power agreements with its northern neighbors, there was good reason for the Nepalese to be skeptical of the "rate of return" estimates for this project as well as other hydro projects. India and Nepal, however, for separate reasons refused to come to an agreement that was predictable, enforceable, and able to overcome their traditional suspicions of each other.

Finally, it should be noted how unusual the Arun Valley is in Nepalese geography. Located at the eastern end of Nepal, it drains a region of southeastern Tibet with very substantial water volume throughout the year from melting snow and monsoon rains. This valley is in stark contrast to most of the rest of Nepal, where the rivers drain the south side of the Himalayas, and thus are limited in their hydro potential by being so seasonal. The Arun Valley is attractive to hydro engineers, for it has the ability to capture substantial power potential with run-of-the-river facilities rather than the large reservoirs required for all-year power generation in the rest of Nepal. Hydro planners in Nepal and the World Bank were reluctant to abandon such a desirable environment, even though it was recognized that the difficult terrain, inaccessibility, and absence of local development would raise collateral costs for the hydroelectric projects in the Arun Valley.

ORIGINS OF THE CLAIM PROCESS

The Inspection Panel was established in the summer of 1994. The panel was immediately approached informally by NGO representatives on behalf of several Nepalese requesters as to what issues could legitimately be raised in a formal request. Since the panel members had no prior experience on which to base a judgment, the Nepalese were urged to submit any issues they thought relevant, and in October 1994, a formal request was received in a joint petition from two NGOs in Kathmandu: the Arun Concerned Group and the International Institute for Human Rights, Environment, and Development (INHURED International). The central person in the claim to the panel appeared to be Gopal Siwakoti "Chintan," the executive director of INHURED and a person who had completed a law degree at the Washington College of Law at American University, and therefore had been exposed to the World Bank, to the establishment of the Inspection Panel, and to NGOs in Washington that could help with the mechanics of a request for inspection.

Siwakoti was later accused in the Nepal press of being a tool of NGOs based in Washington. His reply was telling:

> There are allegations that we might have been given money by other sources to file the case in the World Bank's Inspection Panel. Some even have said that the claim was prepared in Washington, D.C. by some American lawyers. It's all baseless. In my opinion, it is a perfect example of colonial attitude and inferiority complex. I am a lawyer. I have done my specialization in international human rights and environmental laws from the Washington College of Law. I have worked for an international organization, particularly on United Nations, international financial institutions and human rights matters, for more than two years as a staff attorney. I can challenge anyone in this country that I, and we as a group, has the strength and capacity of challenging the World Bank on the violations of its own policies and procedures. Of course, we request for documents and information about the World Bank from any groups since they are not available in Kathmandu.[4]

The degree of disorganization among the claimants became apparent when the members of the Inspection Panel visited Nepal on two occasions and became aware of the loose coalition that was behind the claim, which had been submitted on behalf of two "anonymous claimants" who lived in the Arun Valley. When the Inspectors met with the claimants on their second trip to Nepal, it was evident that they had highly specific complaints related to the project, but left to their own devices, they never would have been able to file a claim. The claimants themselves were not organized; indeed, the meeting with them had to occur covertly because the community at large had been entirely persuaded by government representatives that the project would be good for them. When the NGOs in Kathmandu took up their cause, they added a layer of macroeconomic issues on the claim of the local people. In terms of local representation, therefore, the request for inspection rested on the slimmest reed, and had to be considered as a filing by a national NGO on behalf of local claimants (as permitted under the resolution establishing the panel).

The very small number of local claimants—two being the minimum allowed under the panel resolution and procedures established by the panel— was established as legitimate in the initial screening of the request by the panel and the board. While most members of the board had a different expectation in mind, namely, that there would be recognizable, broadly representative NGOs filing the claims, the panel argued successfully that such NGOs would be unlikely to exist in a new democracy such as Nepal, and individual requesters would have to look outside their own community for organizational representation. In this way, the role of INHURED was legitimized, and a precedent was established for future claims to the panel.

At the same time, INHURED's involvement with the claim meant that issues important in the capital—macroeconomic planning and analysis of alternatives for the energy sector—were grafted on to a more standard test of safeguard policies (resettlement, environment, transparency, etc.) As far as the panel could tell, the awkwardness of these many strands in the request were never resolved in Nepal, and the panel and board worked them out by restricting the investigation to the issues that applied at the site of demonstrable material damage in the Arun Valley.

The greatest frustration for the claimant came from the shrinking scope of the panel's investigation. The claim included at least five major areas of alleged policy violations, divided on the one hand into those that derived from facts on the ground in the Arun Valley—issues germane to the safeguard policies—and on the other hand, into the macroeconomic decisions taken in Kathmandu with regard to the economy and the energy sector more broadly. In its response to the request, bank management singled out the alleged policy violations with regard to economic evaluation of investment operations (OP 10.04) as subjective in its standards and therefore inappropriate for panel review for potential violations. From management's point of view, if staff made a good faith effort to review alternatives and undertake related economic analysis, and the board was fully informed of the implications of various approaches, the policy had full compliance. The panel left it to the board to determine whether management had an appropriate interpretation of OP 10.04, but introduced several facts for the board to consider:

- Less than 1 percent of Nepal's hydropower resource had been developed and there was no complete inventory of hydropower sites that could be used reliably for long-term planning.
- Out of more than one hundred major potential hydroelectric sites that had been identified, there had been technical and economic screening of only eighteen projects where pre-feasibility or further engineering studies had been carried out. The latest least cost generation analysis had considered only eleven projects.
- The government had identified an alternative scenario of hydropower investments, consisting entirely of projects in the 10- to100-MW range that would actually cost 5 percent less than the Arun III proposal if demand growth were slower than anticipated.[5]

The claim also cited possible contradictions between the Arun project and the bank's poverty alleviation strategy. After reviewing management's response, the panel agreed that the fiscal demands of building Arun could have a "crowding-out effect" on poverty alleviation projects by causing rising electricity prices, rising costs of capital, and general constraint on public expenditure during peak construction years.[6]

When the board decided to authorize an investigation on February 2, 1995, it allowed the panel to inquire into only three areas: resettlement, environmental assessment, and indigenous people. The panel accepted that mandate as an adequate foot in the door, permitting a thorough review of the reality on the ground in the Arun Valley. The claimants in Kathmandu, on the other hand, were unhappy. Siwakoti argued that he would withdraw the request because the most important issues had been excluded from the investigation. The panel had to explain that once the board had authorized the investigation, it was not subject to being withdrawn. Just as the executive directors themselves could initiate an investigation, so their decision to act based on evidence submitted by a claimant meant that the decision to authorize an investigation had the effect of giving the panel an independent authority to pursue the issue, whatever the changing circumstances for the claimant. This independence for the panel, as designed in the resolution and procedures, prevented a group of claimants from pulling their request, thus subverting the investigation of policy violations. Because the claimants did not have direct access to the board, they had to rely on launching a process they could not control once it became an investigation.

The claimants' frustration became clear in their formal responses to the board's decision to authorize a limited investigation. Siwakoti wrote to the board of executive directors:

> We are highly disappointed with the way that the Board of Executive Directors (EDs) decided to allow the investigation of only some select areas relating to the project, such as environmental assessment, indigenous peoples rights and resettlement strategy. We have serious objections to the Board's arbitrary one-sided decision that has left out the investigation of some of the fundamental controversies which are of major concern to us. Economic analysis of the project, timely disclosure of basic project documents and information as well as meaningful public participation in this discussion, is of utmost importance. There is a lack of sufficient explanation as to why these issues of controversy were unilaterally removed from the investigation although specifically highlighted by the Panel and the Claimants. On the one hand, it seems that the Bank Management, the defendant of the Claim, has used all available means and tactics to directly influence the decision-making by the Board since it has the easy access to do so. On the other hand, the Claimants have neither the privilege of such access nor were they ever consulted by the Board before taking such a harsh decision against the claims for investigation. We strongly feel that this is a serious denial of justice to the Claimants by the Board, and the undermining of a fair adjudication process.[7]

The claimants had an important point. While they had no direct access to the board once the investigation was launched, their counterpart on the issue—bank management—found avenues to send new information and propose courses of action to the board throughout the process. The panel did not anticipate these repeated incursions into their independence by management, which had the unfortunate effect of creating asymmetrical access to the board between management and the claimants. The board refused to discipline senior management in this regard, and as a result, the practice of episodic "action plans" to the board by management evolved in an effort to short-circuit the panel investigations.

With this first case, the NGO community learned that its central role was to launch an inspection; after that point, its role was more supportive but not decisive, able to influence but not control in any significant way the process of investigation. The board's failure to achieve balance between the board and claimants on this issue clearly deterred some potential claimants from submitting claims to the panel.

SUPPORT FOR THE CLAIM PROCESS

Enormous interest in the Arun claim emerged at the national and global levels, owing in part to it being the first panel case, in part to the coincident fiftieth anniversary of the World Bank, and in part to the tumultuous nature of politics in Nepal. The least support came at the local level. The members of the panel witnessed this at a dozen public meetings in the Arun Valley, where the predominance of the opinion mobilized by the government and by the NEA suggested that the selective release of information had persuaded most residents that the arrival of construction crews would be a bonanza. If the claimants had substantial support in the valley, they were unable to demonstrate it. In the capital, however, the agitation against the project by NGOs, opposition political parties, and journalists was striking. At the same time, there was an active pro-Arun lobby in Kathmandu, many of whom wrote letters to the panel and insisted on meetings with panel members when in the country.[8] The fact that the political system was only partially democratic meant that some of the old habits for debating issues — with behind-the-scenes maneuvering and paranoia about the opposition — came through frequently in the Arun III controversy.

The instability of Nepalese politics also meant that members of coalitions sometimes changed roles as the government changed. The first free elections in Nepal's history had occurred in May 1991. In the fall of 1994, rioting broke out over the government's plans for development. When the Communist Party of Nepal (Unified Marxist-Leninist) took power in elections held on November 15, 1994, it became awkward for the requesters to discover that some of their allies, when ensconced in government, became as pro-Arun as the Congress Party had been. This change of government and the associated realignment of forces for and against Arun led to a delay of several months for the bank and the panel as they waited for the new Nepalese government to determine its willingness to support the project.

Globally, many NGOs followed the controversy closely and published articles about it. An extensive critique appeared in December 1994, including an interview with a World Bank staff member who resigned over losing the internal battle on Arun.[9] When the panel submitted a request to investigate in December and the board of executive directors went into a stall, many NGOs swung into action with press releases in support of the request.[10] Numerous letters were also sent to the president of the bank, Lewis Preston, urging his intervention in the procedural confusion of the board, which alternated between "informal consultations" and discussions with senior management.[11]

The diversity of interests represented among the claimants makes it difficult to generalize about the broader campaigns in Nepal, of which the Arun request was just one element. Some of the people involved in the request were particularly interested in alternative energy strategies and were actively pursuing other development contracts at the same time that they were arguing against the bank strategy on Arun. Others were interested in aligning with the forces fighting structural adjustment and found that the overall weakness of Nepalese economic institutions left the government quite dependent on the major donors. Insofar as Arun III was seen as enhancing the self-reliance of the Nepali power sector, thus diminishing dependence on India, there was a significant coalition in Nepal in favor of the project, where there is a long-standing anti-Indian sentiment.[12] Thus, those who opposed the project were frequently tarred as being Indian stooges. One of the leaders of the Nepali Alliance for Energy, Rajendra Dahal, responded by turning his opponents' arguments on their head:

> There is an intellectual and political class which sees Indian hands in everything. Kathmandu's elites always raise this Indian bogey. It is this class which is holding the key of Arun and other major water resources projects. It fears that if small projects are initiated, its interest and ego will be hurt. In fact, those creating the India-bogey are serving the interests of the Indians. The Alliance for Energy is for building our capability so that this sector is developed without depending on foreigners. Then we will not have to look for the Indian market to sell the surplus.

Dahal's final argument went to the question of how infrastructure projects are implemented:

> If Arun comes as it is . . . ultimately, it will benefit India more. The Indians will walk away with construction sub-contracts. They will also be selling their cement and other construction materials, besides laborers to Nepal. The Arun, in one way or another, will also help them to build their own capability which means that the next time Nepal plans another project, it would be the Indians who would be capable to do it for them.[13]

REACTIONS OF THE POWERFUL

The bank reacted in a variety of ways, as might be expected with the first request presented to the panel. Much of the initial response was led by the general counsel of the bank, Ibrahim Shihata, who argued behind the scenes that the claim was ineligible; nevertheless, management did not formally protest eligibility, aware that such a controversial first project for the panel could not be deemed ineligible on a technicality. The initial discussions among bank management included suggestions that the panel should accept the view of the general counsel and refuse to hear the complaint. The resolution establishing the panel had a provision inserted that required the panel to "consult" with the general counsel with regard to certain issues.[14] The panel accepted that view from the board and did consult with the general counsel, but the panel did not always accept the advice of the general counsel, particularly on eligibility. It was thus with some surprise that the board and management had to respond to a determination by the panel that the requesters were eligible and that, indeed, there was sufficient evidence to warrant an investigation.

The second phase of bank management's response, then, was to influence the board in an attempt to keep the investigation from going forward. For more than a month after submission of the initial findings of the panel in mid December, senior management met on several occasions with the board (with the panel excluded) to provide information that would preclude the need for an investigation. Management insisted that all the problems would be resolved if the board just had all the information available to staff, and in doing so, made it impossible for the panel to know what data was on the table at any given time. Ultimately, even the members of the board came to realize that there were certain essential pieces missing for them to be able to approve the loan (such as updated environmental assessments), and reluctantly agreed to authorize the panel to conduct an investigation in the field on three of the safeguard policies.

Even at that point, management did not desist from trying to move the benchmarks, in this case by announcing that they would, in any case, send a mission to the field to redesign the project to bring it up to the standards required by policy. The panel found it would be impossible to proceed with an investigation if there were also bank staff moving the goalposts, and therefore agreed to the board's request that the panel should wait until management had completed its remedial plan and then conduct its own investigation and field-based review of both the underlying project and the new complementary measures designed by management. In any case, the government of Nepal was vague as to whether it would agree to admit the Inspection Panel into the country, a step required by the resolution since this was to be an investigatory visit. Clearance for a field visit by the panel came only on March 15, in a letter from the minister of finance to the bank.[15] In the meantime, a bank staff mission was dispatched in April 1995 to review the environmental impact assessment and the environmental mitigation plan, improve environmental monitoring, review the resettlement action plan, and launch a living standards monitoring survey. All of these measures should have been taken much earlier in the design and appraisal processes. Nevertheless, when the mission had returned, the panel received a complete report from management on May 18, 1995, about remedial measures.[16] With that in hand, the panel moved quickly to send its team to the field, with a return date of June 5 and a rapid completion of their report.[17]

In general, bank staff were forthcoming with information as called for under the resolution establishing the panel. The original internal project review had caused a major split among staff over the wisdom of approving financing. The energy department, in particular, had taken their dissent on the project to the level of the senior vice president before being finally overruled, and technical experts in various departments, such as the South Asian department, expressed unhappiness within and outside the bank. Many of the staff in the social development and environment departments made available their articulate, well-researched memoranda on the Arun III project, which had been generated over a decade of internal debate. The analysis was sound, but the data was frequently out of date, which was a fundamental weakness of the project. The bank management did not insist on current data, and the borrower was largely unequipped to provide it even if the bank had insisted.

As a result of such a dramatic split in views among the staff, the executive directors of the bank were caught in a dilemma. In the best of all worlds, from their point of view, they would not have had to react at all. They realized, however, that they had created a mechanism that required them to make a decision about whether to go forward with an investigation. When the executive directors hesitated, management seized the opportunity to throw even more information at the board. In accepting this information, the board put the panel and the requesters in an untenable position. The resolution clearly did not allow for multiple submissions by management of their view. Once word about this development got out to the NGO community, protests began rolling in about the subversion of the panel process.[18] The board remained uncomfortable with the situation. When it became clear that many of the directors from developing countries were opposed on grounds of sovereignty, the question became even more difficult. The compromise eventually negotiated informally by the board was only a temporary solution: It allowed management to go ahead and redesign the project, but also allowed the panel to complete its investigation afterwards. The solution clearly fell outside the terms of the resolution, and left no one satisfied. The executive directors were only relieved of their unwanted role in decision making when the incoming president, James Wolfensohn, decided to terminate bank involvement in the project later that summer.

Within Nepal, the submission to the Inspection Panel caused a firestorm, made even more intense by the instability of the government in power. The announcement of the field visit by the panel members was an occasion for the claimants to brag publicly about their role in putting Nepal and the Arun III project on the world stage.[19] The government in power during the first phase defended the project, despite the pressure it would place on the national budget and the crowding-out effect it would have on alternative power investments. Because most of the analysis for the project had come from bank staff, much of the reaction from the government and its allies was focused less on substance than on the perceived lack of deference to traditional authority shown by the claimants. Owing to the chronic impoverishment of the Arun Valley, the region had been a hotbed of opposition to the government prior to the controversy over the claim, and it was tipping politically in the direction of the opposition party. Nevertheless, that discontent did not swing in the direction of opposing the dam, but rather toward complaining that the valley was not getting its fair share of the national budget. The NEA and the government were thus able to rapidly swing public opinion in their direction among valley residents by arguing that the claimants and NGOs were jeopardizing this potential flow of money and jobs into the valley. The pro-project forces, dealing with a largely illiterate population, did not bother with sophisticated arguments, and instead simply ensured that the prevailing political and community authorities in the valley were on their side.

This approach broke down over the alignment of the access road to the dam site. Two different routes for constructing the road up the valley had been designed over the years. The first went along the ridges, where most of the people lived and most towns were located. That was good for the local authorities, who saw a potential road as an economic boon for moving goods and people in and out of the valley (to date, everything was carried by local porters; some ten thousand were estimated to be employed in the valley).

When the project was redesigned in the early 1990s, however, the bank persuaded the government to shorten the access road to the dam from 175 kilometers to about 120 kilometers by going straight up the valley floor, avoiding all the towns, and minimizing elevation change. That shattered the political support of the local leaders, since a good road going up the valley would attract the people and commerce away from the existing towns on the hilltops and drive down the price of land on the hills, even while putting thousands of laborers out of business. It also divided the government ministries: the Ministry of Roads and Transport wanted to remain with the high ridge alignment, whereas the Ministry of Water Resources wanted the valley route in order to get the dam built more quickly and to avoid the construction difficulties on steep slopes.[20] At the local level, these tensions over the road route (an entirely secondary issue from the bank's point of view) became dominant, and when the inspectors held their town meetings on the ground, the roads were clearly of much greater importance than any dam built up in the mountains.

The strong views of the people in the valley on the road issue and their mixed reaction to the petition to the panel (depending on where they lived in terms of the potential road alignment), illustrated the extent to which both the claimants in Kathmandu and the bank staff missed the main point for the residents of the area. The project was designed to meet a power need in Nepal, and the principal concern of the NGOs in Kathmandu was over the strategy behind that decision. This perspective can be seen in the letter from the Arun Concerned Group protesting the February 2 decision of the board to permit only a limited investigation. It was even clearer in a letter from the Alliance for Energy protesting the exclusion of the "examination of alternatives" issue from the proposed investigation.[21] For the people in the valley, who had never had much access to electrical power, the dam and the transmission lines were largely irrelevant. Indeed, as a run-of-the-river facility with little impact on their water resources, it would have a very small footprint locally. As a result, the power side of the equation was not a local issue. On the other hand, the livelihoods of the people of the valley would be massively affected by the construction of the road, where it was routed, who used it, and how it was managed. Since the government had already bought some of the land for the ridge alignment, there was a major legacy of liabilities that no one in the government was inclined to resolve. The panel insisted that the bank had responsibility, along with the government, to unravel those title and remuneration issues on the ridge alignment whether or not it went forward with the valley route and dam project. The local leaders were appreciative of having someone interested in their problems, and the government was actively resistant to doing anything. Unfortunately, it was unlikely that anything would be done about the damage from construction that had already begun along the ridge alignment if the overall project did not go forward.

IMPACTS OF THE CLAIM PROCESS

The greatest impact of the claim was the cancellation of World Bank participation in the Arun III project. The politicization of the project that occurred following submission of the request was immediate, unavoidable, and brought to a head all of the doubts about the World Bank's handling of large infrastructure projects.

The report of the Inspection Panel was issued on June 22, 1995. It included two major themes for the executive directors to consider: (1) through strenuous effort for the first half of 1995, the bank staff, working with the government of Nepal, had apparently brought the *design* of the project into compliance with the policies of the bank, yet (2) the panel believed the government of Nepal and the bank supervisory mechanisms were incapable of *carrying out* the project as designed, and adverse impacts on the people of the Arun Valley were almost certain. The history of bank infrastructure loans in Nepal made the track record quite clear—and there were few successes to point to, even with projects significantly smaller than the Arun project. The panel, however, was not asked whether the project should go forward; its mandate was to report its finding on compliance with policies and procedures and to provide whatever information was needed to assist the board in its decision. The board was not happy to be faced with yet another decision and looked to President James Wolfensohn, who had just assumed office on June 2, to find a solution for them.

Wolfensohn consulted with the panel, with outside advisors such as Maurice Strong, and with senior bank managers—all of whom conveyed the lukewarm support or opposition that the project engendered outside the South Asia department. Wolfensohn resolved to find a formula for withdrawing the bank from the project. The escalating tone of rhetoric surrounding the panel report was the only persuasion that he needed to move quickly.[22] His solution was to negotiate a new power-sector package for Nepal, which would consist of smaller, alternative approaches to meeting Nepal's electricity needs. On August 3 Wolfensohn announced that

Large complex projects require institutions like the World Bank to weigh the benefits against the risks and then decide on their feasibility. The judgment made over a year ago in the case of Arun came out in favor of the project after substantial internal debate. Irrespective of whether that was the right or wrong decision at the time, I concluded that under today's circumstances and with the information at my disposal, the risks to Nepal were too great to justify proceeding with the project. The public debate on this controversial project was valuable in that it served to heighten the concerns of Bank staff about the risks faced by the project. It also led to a review by the World Bank's Inspection Panel of environmental and social aspects of the project with the result that measures to address these concerns were strengthened. Although this project will not go ahead, the Panel's work remains relevant to the Bank's operations in general and to future investments in Nepal's power sector in particular.[23]

The report from the panel was thus considered moot and the board never took a decision on it. Since the formal process was interrupted at several times during the first and second stages and the closure of the case was inconclusive, the impacts of the claim have to be considered in an indirect manner.

Without attempting to attribute individual outcomes entirely to the work of the Inspection Panel and the claim presented, some or all of the following immediately followed the president's decision:

- The bank drastically reduced its involvement in the development of the Nepali energy sector. In fact, the entire South Asian region saw a drastic cutback in energy investments on the basis of the Arun case, and there were several subsequent complaints filed with the panel about Indian projects. While the bank talked about developing energy alternatives in Nepal, little was done.

- The Arun Valley received no further attention from the bank. The Nepali government did, on the basis of its own resources, steadily build the ridge alignment of the road, and has almost reached Chainpur with its construction. The Nepali government did not, of course, abandon the Arun III project entirely. On several occasions after 1995, there were negotiations with other financiers who said they were interested in developing the project abandoned by the World Bank. As of this writing, none had come to fruition. The needs identified for the Arun Valley in terms of small-scale development were not met, other than continuing technical assistance from bilateral German and British programs. A small Nepali company has also developed a small 3-MW hydropower project on one of the Arun's tributaries, with the intention of selling the power to the national grid.
- The government of Nepal expressed great bitterness about the bank's abandonment of the Arun project. Despite Wolfensohn's attempt to sugarcoat the outcome, the decision was a fait accompli when he talked with Nepali Prime Minister Man Mohan Adhikary. The Water Resources Ministry in Kathmandu put out a statement saying that "His Majesty's Government expresses surprise and dismay at the cancellation of the project at a time when a lot of investment and exercise had been put and the project was at the implementation stage."[24] The bank exacerbated this bitterness by implying in its press release that the Nepali government was at fault for the collapse of the project.[25]
- Many of the NGOs proclaimed this a victory akin to the bank withdrawal from the Sardar Sarovar project in India several years before. They expressed gratitude to Wolfensohn, and a hope that this would allow them to develop a strong working relationship with the bank for the first time. While it did not stop the "Fifty Years Is Enough" campaign, it certainly slowed down some of the elements of that coalition, with the thought that confrontation might be changed to dialogue.
- The claimants were energized by the development and described it as a great victory. As Siwakoti was quoted, "It is a historic victory for Nepal and a crushing defeat for the management of the World Bank. The statement made today by the Bank President vindicates all the main points we have been making in our campaign against Arun III. Until today our claims were totally refuted by the Bank's management. Now their new President has in effect accepted that we were right all along."[26]
- Because the process could be counted a victory for the claimants, it encouraged others to file claims, which did then happen on a growing scale.

At the same time, the serious departures from the published Inspection Panel procedures by the bank management and board confused potential claimants by putting less predictability into the process.

- The outcome of the case encouraged anti-dam activists to attack other dam projects, both individually and as a function of policy. As Patrick McCully of the International Rivers Network put it, "Hopefully this is a sign of reality on the part of the Bank that large dams make no economic, environmental or social sense."[27] At the time of the Arun withdrawal, World Bank managing director Gautam Kaji was quoted as saying, "Clearly there is a need for some introspection on this one."[28] The cumulative efforts led eventually to the establishment of the World Commission on Dams (WCD) in 1998, with the bank as a co-initiator.

INSTITUTIONAL CHANGES

As the first case to come before the Inspection Panel, the Arun III claim necessarily had a major impact on the institutional perspectives of the bank and the panel itself. Much less clear, however, is its impact on the institutions in Nepal. The flux and political change in Nepal was so great during the 1995–2000 period that it is hard to attribute any impact from the request for inspection. The chronic weakness of the Nepali government was magnified by the shaky control of the political parties in power as the country emerged into an increasingly open political system. Ministries contended openly with each other for control of the social and economic agendas. The power structures built around the road system, the power sector, and the management of water resources were largely uncoordinated during this period. The power sector is said to have become healthily diverse, with a mix of larger and smaller projects, bringing an end to power brownouts in 2000.

In Washington, on the other hand, World Bank management, its board of executive directors, and the Inspection Panel were sailing in uncharted waters. The role of management in an inspection remained unclear. The appropriate scale and scope of the panel's "preliminary review" was hotly debated. Some essential elements of the procedures promulgated by the panel itself had been preserved during the Arun case, but at the cost of generating significant opposition to the panel process from some members of the board. The debate over the case revealed the extent to which a majority of the board thought they had voted for the establishment of the panel as a "fig leaf" to placate the environmental community, rather than out of any genuine interest in ensuring compliance with the bank's policies and procedures.

The panel insisted that management and staff were accountable for ensuring that the policies were implemented. Historically, the culture of the bank had been to focus on the technical design of the projects to be funded and then to leave implementation issues to the borrower. The policies, on the other hand, called for staff to be responsible for the effective implementation of projects, not only during the active phase of loan disbursement, but even during the life of the project as the loan was repaid—an interpretation that shocked most staff, until it was confirmed by the bank's own general counsel. This definition of management responsibility should not have been unexpected, coming as it did on the heels of the Wapenhans report, which assessed the failure of so many bank-financed projects being attributable to so little attention being paid to implementation.[29]

The two-pronged attack on the bank record, from outside and inside, was sobering indeed, especially when management began summing up the cost of doing effective supervision missions and implementation oversight of all bank projects. The ultimate impact of the panel's work on Arun III, with subsequent hammering on the theme of accountability for implementation, was that within five years the bank's leadership attempted to shift responsibility to borrowers for implementation. This line of thought arose in the second review of the panel's functions in late 1998, with an intensive debate over "unbundling" of responsibilities and accountability between the bank and borrowers.

The institution also focused on the fact that the Arun case dealt in large part with a project in preparation. While the panel used the evidence of direct damage from the prior loan, the real focus was on the anticipated harm to be done by the road alignment leading to the dam site. Some board members argued that damage had not yet been proven and therefore the claim should not be eligible, but management took a much more dynamic approach, arguing that they could fix any prospective problems with the design, in collaboration with the borrower. This attitude foreshadowed the later insertion of "action plans" in virtually all inspections. Thus, they dispatched an outstanding team to the field in early 1995 to fix any evident problems and bring the design up to standards set in bank policies. Management learned two lessons from that episode: (1) it was entirely feasible to upgrade the design of any project still in the appraisal process to meet bank policies—a process called "panel-proofing" among bank staff, and (2) projects upgraded to that extent were very unlikely to be implemented according to design, given the limited capacity of the borrower and the limited budget available for the project. The projects were thus likely to be judged harshly in terms of compliance with the safeguard policies in particular, for which the bank's only answer was to pin responsibility for implementation on the borrower, or to withdraw from the project entirely.

The bank also learned from the Arun case that it would have to be more open and transparent with project information. The insistence by civil society, both within Nepal and aboard, for greater release of information was eventually agreed to in practice. Some board members and parts of management even believed that they could prevent release of the final report of the panel to the public. It was not until August 18, two weeks after the final meeting of the board on this subject, that the secretary agreed to send the report to an NGO that had requested it. The decisive point was that "excerpts of the Panel's Report are being leaked to the local press which is causing distortion of the facts and embarrassment to the Bank."[30] The bank has been much more open about panel affairs ever since that object lesson in the Arun case.

NOTES

1. See the valuable discussion of the Narmada precedent as a precursor to the Arun III campaign in Lori Udall, "The World Bank and Public Accountability," in *The Struggle for Accountability: The World Bank, NGOs, and Grassroots Movements,* ed. Jonathan A. Fox and L. David Brown (Cambridge: MIT Press, 1998), 394.

2. World Commission on Dams, *Dams and Development: A New Framework for Decision-Making* (London: Earthscan, 2000), available at www.dams.org.

3. Inspection Panel, "The Inspection Panel Investigation Report: Nepal: Arun III Proposed Hydroelectric Project and Restructuring of IDA Credit-2029-NEP," June 22, 1995, appendix A.

4. Gopal Siwakoti "Chintan," "No Foreign Hand in ARUN Campaign," *Spotlight,* February 24, 1995, 17. This statement by Siwakoti was a reaction to public statements from a pro-Arun activist, Ram Sharan Mahat, and others, denigrating the standing of INHURED and its staff: "Eyebrows have also been raised over the sophisticated language used in the petition filed by Gopal Siwakoti 'Chintan' and Ganesh Ghimire on behalf of 'two anonymous persons' to the Bank requesting for inspection to review the project. 'The language can only be the work of a professional American lawyer of considerable standing who knows all details of the Bank's rules and regulations and which rules have been violated in Arun,' said Mahat in an apparent reference to [Lori] Udall who is a lawyer by profession. 'No Nepali may have written it'" (Ram Sharan Mahat, "Not to See a Foreign Hand is Non Sense," *Spotlight,* February 24, 1995, 24).

5. Inspection Panel, "The Inspection Panel Report on Request for Inspection: Nepal: Proposed Arun III Hydroelectric Project," request no. RQ94/1, December 16, 1994, 7.

6. World Bank, "Arun III," request no. RQ94/1.

7. Gopal Siwakoti and Ganesh Kumar Ghimire, claimants, to members of the board of executive directors, February 22, 1995.

8. See, for instance, Pushba Raj Pradhan, "An Intriguing Claims Petition to WB against Arun III Project," *Review,* November 18, 1994, and "Expedite Arun III, Acharya Urges," *The Rising Nepal,* February 21, 1993.

9. Lori Udall, "Trampling on Nepal," *Multinational Monitor* (December 1994): 22–25, and idem, "Panel Calls for Arun III Probe; Bank Management Tries for Delay," *BankCheck Quarterly* (December 1994): 1, 14.

10. International Rivers Network, "World Bank Attempts to Derail Independent Inspection Panel Probe of Arun III Dam," press release, January 6, 1995, and Sierra Club, "Sierra Club Charges World Bank with Violating Environmental Policies," press release, January 9, 1995.

11. Lori Udall, International Rivers Network, Chad Dobson, Bank Information Center, Peter Bosshard, Berne Declaration, David Hunter, Center for International Environmental Law, Larry Williams, Sierra Club, Korinna Horta, Environmental Defense Fund, Elizabeth May, Sierra Club–Canada, Brent Blackwelder, Friends of the Earth, Randall Hayes, Rainforest Action Network, Barbara Bramble, National Wildlife Federation, Lief Packalen, Swallows of Finland, Lutz Ribbe, Euronature, and Maike Rademaker, Urgewald, to Lewis Preston, president, World Bank, January 5, 1995; Gopal Siwakoti, also on behalf of other claimants, to Lewis T. Preston, January 5, 1995; Frank Almond, Intermediate Technology Development Group, to Lewis Preston, January 6, 1995; and others.

12. The reasons for India to sabotage the Arun project are laid out in an article by Sushil Sharma, "Arun III: The Power Politics," *Spotlight,* February 24, 1995, 15–21.

13 Rajendra Dahal, "To See a Foreign Hand Is Nonsense," *Spotlight,* February 24, 1995, 16.

14. The World Bank, Resolution no. IBRD 93-10, Resolution no. IDA 93-6, *The World Bank Inspection Panel,* September 22, 1993, paragraph 15.

15. Bharat Mohan Adhikari, minister of finance, to D. Joseph Wood, vice president, World Bank, March 15, 1995.

16. Jean-Francois Bauer, World Bank, memorandum to Eduardo G. Abbott, Inspection Panel, "NEPAL: Proposed Arun III Project," May 18, 1995.

17. Inspection Panel, "The Inspection Panel Investigation Report: Nepal: Arun III Proposed Hydroelectric Project and Restructuring of IDA Credit-2029-NEP," June 22, 1995.

18. Management also used the delay to attempt to force the new (Marxist-Leninist) government of Nepal to commit formally to the project as written to shore up management's position with the board. See protests by NGOs in Ken Ritchie, Intermediate Technology–U.K., to Huw Evans, U.K. executive director, February 28, 1995; see also Alex Wilks and Nicholas Hildyard, *The Ecologist,* to Huw Evans, February 24, 1995. Some of the details of this issue were covered in "World Bank Ignores Green Concerns over 500m Dam Project," *Guardian* (U.K.), January 9, 1995, 12.

19. INHURED International, "World Bank Inspection Panel Arriving in Nepal to Investigate Arun III Project," press release, Kathmandu, May 26, 1995.

20. The reputation of the Ministry of Roads had always been weak and the panel was the recipient of a scathing and sarcastic letter from a pro-Arun NGO about the abject inability of the ministry to meet any of the targets on a ridge alignment (Kedar Karki, Rural Awareness Centre, Nepal, to the Inspection Panel, January 24, 1995).

21. Bikash Pandey, Alliance for Energy, to Lewis T. Preston, February 27, 1995.

22. In a letter to Wolfensohn, June 2, 1995, for instance, INHURED International, one of the Arun requesters, accused the bank of "crimes against humanity": "Without compassion, the heinous crimes against humanity that your organization, and others in league with it, have committed in the last fifty years will continue, and even intensify, as the power corrupts the very essence of life itself. We entreat you sir, to end the economic genocide of peoples and nations Third World-wide. 50 years was enough! 51 years is too much!"

23. World Bank, "World Bank and Nepal to Develop Energy Alternatives to Arun Project," press release, August 3, 1995.

24. Reuters, "Nepal Shocked over Bank's Refusal to Back Dam," August 4, 1995.

25. See note 23.

26. International Rivers Network, "World Bank Scraps Nepal Loan," press release, August 4, 1995.

27. International Rivers Network, "World Bank Scraps Nepal Loan," press release, August 4, 1995.

28. Alver Carlson, "Arun Dam Reversal Poses Questions on W. Bank's Role," *North American Business Report,* August 13, 1995.

29. World Bank, "Effective Implementation: Key to Development Impact," R92-125, November 3, 1992.

30. Daoud L. Khairallah, memorandum to the files, "Arun III: Release of the Inspection Panel Report," August 18, 1995.

3

The Planafloro Inspection Panel Claim: Opportunities and Challenges for Civil Society in Rondônia, Brazil

Maria Guadalupe Moog Rodrigues

In July 1995, civil-society organizations from the Brazilian state of Rondônia in the Amazon presented a request for the investigation of the Planafloro project to the World Bank Inspection Panel. The Planafloro Inspection Panel claim was not simply a technical device to bring the bank to compliance with its supervision and monitoring policies. It was, primarily, a critical strategy in a long-standing and increasingly fierce, contentious relationship between the Rondonian state government and local civil-society groups.

The Planafloro project's goal was to promote sustainable development, but well into its third year of implementation, the project was failing to meet its environmental and social objectives. While civil-society groups criticized the government for its neglect of Planafloro's environmental provisions, the latter charged civil-society groups with placing obstacles in the state's path toward sustainable development. The strategy of demanding an investigation of the Planafloro project by the Inspection Panel had immediate and long-term impacts on both the project's implementation and the balance of political forces in the state. Due to space constraints, this chapter addresses Planafloro's implementation problems only indirectly. The focus is on the political mobilization that such problems triggered within Rondônia and abroad, and in particular, on the role of the Inspection Panel claim in this mobilization process.

The history of the Planafloro Inspection Panel claim illustrates a gradual process of political empowerment experienced by local Rondonian civil-society organizations. This process occurred in a political context characterized by the weakness of local democratic institutions and the control of state resources by local political elites. While the Inspection Panel claim represented a watershed in the relations between the state and civil-society groups in Rondônia, it cannot be evaluated in isolation. In fact, the claim was a part of a larger set of initiatives deployed by a transnational advocacy network of organizations concerned about Rondônia's environment. The coalition originated in the mid 1980s as a reaction to the social and environmental devastation caused by road construction and settlement schemes, which were the core elements of the World Bank–funded Polonoroeste (the Northwest Brazil Integrated Development Program, 1983–1987).[1] Ironically, the Planafloro project was devised to "correct" the negative social and environmental consequences of Polonoroeste.

Despite the strengths of transnational advocacy networks,[2] and of the Rondônia network in particular, one must also account for their limitations. Unfortunately, this issue has been underexplored. For instance, there is an established assumption that participation in transnational advocacy networks contributes to the political empowerment of local civil-society organizations.[3] Closer analysis of the Rondônia network, and of the processes related to the Planafloro Inspection Panel claim, suggests that such an assumption requires theoretical refinement. In fact, the political gains that local Rondonian groups obtained through their participation in the Rondônia network were accompanied by increased technical and political burdens. Neither the transnational advocacy network nor the Rondonian groups themselves had the capability of shouldering these new burdens or responsibilities. As a result, the political empowerment obtained by the Rondonian groups in the wake of their request for the investigation of the Planafloro project was compromised in the long run.

Both analysts of and activists in the processes of transnational cooperation on environmental issues must use caution. Local actors' participation in transnational advocacy networks tends to increase their political capacity and visibility. What is not self-evident, however, is whether increased political capacity is a structural process or a temporary condition. Distinguishing between these two outcomes is one of the goals of this chapter. In addition, analysis of the Planafloro Inspection Panel claim should enhance understanding of the conditions under which the political empowerment of local groups, as a result of their participation in transnational advocacy networks, may be sustained.

This chapter will proceed with a brief background on the origins of the Planafloro claim. Particular attention is given to the role played by the claim strategy in "renewing the energies" of the Rondônia network and realigning its internal balance of political forces. A discussion of the reactions of the World Bank and the Brazilian and Rondonian governments to the claim follows, together with an analysis of the claim's impacts on Rondônia's politics and on the state's environment. Finally, the concluding section assesses the institutional consequences of the Planafloro claim for the consolidation of advocacy efforts to increase the transparency of Brazilian public policies and for the long-term political empowerment of Rondonian civil-society organizations.

Data for this research derived from thirty open-ended interviews with environmental and human rights activists, government officials, and World Bank staff and consultants, conducted in Brazil and Washington, D.C., in 1994 and 2000. The identity of interviewees is protected by pseudonyms, as most of them remain engaged in political, social, and environmental struggles in Rondônia. Data were also obtained from the analysis of reports, letters, and e-mail correspondence; aide-mémoires, and summaries of meetings from the archives of advocacy organizations concerned about Planafloro and the project's funding and implementing agencies; publications on the Brazilian experiences with the Inspection Panel; and newsletters and newspaper articles in the Brazilian and international media.

INNOVATION IN A LONG-STANDING STRUGGLE: THE DILEMMA OF DEVELOPMENT VERSUS ENVIRONMENTAL PROTECTION

Negotiations on the Planafloro project started in 1987. The five-year lapse between the start of negotiations and approval of the project loan by the World Bank Board of Executive Directors in March 1992 derived, in part, from the need to respond to the scrutiny of the international environmental movement.[4] Eventually, a coalition of international environmental NGOs led by the Washington, D.C.–based Environmental Defense Fund (or EDF, now known as Environmental Defense, or ED) and Brazilian activists and civil-society organizations (including research institutes, professional associations, and grassroots groups) succeeded in altering the design of the Planafloro project. The loan agreement listed a series of environmentally related measures to be implemented before disbursements were initiated.[5] The loan agreement also required the establishment of participatory mechanisms, such as a decision-making body (*Conselho Deliberativo*, or CD) composed of an equal number of representatives from governmental agencies and civil-society organizations.

Implementation of the Planafloro project began officially in 1993. Despite the promises of its design, it immediately generated frustration among sectors of Rondonian civil society. This became evident in conversations with activists during a visit to the region in November 1994. One interviewee said that she "never imagined getting to December 1994 without the creation of a single extractive reserve."[6] Another explained that "from a legal point of view, the state has breached its contract with the bank since none of the (environmental) preconditions have been implemented."[7]

Local Cleavages

Analysts have explained the early lack of interest among Rondonian groups in challenging Planafloro's implementation in two different ways. One explanation is that local groups (and foreign NGOs) may not have understood the nature of Rondônia's political climate and may have erroneously believed that their participation in Planafloro's decision-making institutions would allow them to play an actual role in Planafloro's implementation.[8] On the other hand, local groups may not have had the technical capacity for the enterprise.[9] This chapter puts forward a different explanation: lack of interest derived more from the political pragmatism of Rondonian groups than from their political and technical immaturity.

In the early 1990s, local groups viewed the Planafloro project as a concrete opportunity to establish a political space and an arena of leverage vis-à-vis the state of Rondônia. Just one year prior to the approval of the project, Rondonian NGOs and grassroots groups had formed an umbrella organization, the Forum of NGOs and Social Movements of Rondônia, or the Rondônia Forum. They were supported by national advocacy and grassroots organizations, such as the now-extinct Instituto de Estudos da Amazônia (Institute for Amazon Studies, or IEA); the Conselho Nacional dos Seringueiros (National Rubber-Tappers Council, or CNS); and by international NGOs, such as Oxfam, the World Wildlife Fund (WWF), and the EDF.

The mandate of the Rondônia Forum was to monitor public policy in Rondônia, and specifically, the Planafloro project. The forum and many of its affiliated organizations, such as the Organização dos Seringueiros de Rondônia (Rondônia Rubber-Tappers' Organization, or OSR), the Karitiana Indigenous Peoples' Organization, and the Federação de Agricultores de Rondônia (Federation of Agricultural Workers of Rondônia, or FETAGRO), held seats in Planafloro's decision-making and budget allocation institutions. While Rondonian civil-society organizations were aware of the political and bureaucratic hurdles to their effective participation, being a part of Planafloro's formal institutions still represented the conquest of a political space.[10] It would have been inconsistent for Rondonian organizations that were, at least formally, partially responsible for Planafloro's implementation, to challenge the project in its early stages.

It is beyond the scope of this chapter to narrate the context and details of the various efforts that the Rondônia Forum and its national and international allies deployed between 1992 and 1994 to keep Planafloro in line with its stated environmental objectives.[11] These efforts unfolded in both the international and domestic arenas. Internationally, members of the Rondônia transnational network, led by the Rondônia Forum, pressured the World Bank to intensify its monitoring of the project. NGOs gathered information on Planafloro's lack of or irregular implementation and drafted independent evaluation reports.[12] They denounced the project's mismanagement in letters to the bank's management team and to the institution's high-ranking officials.[13] On the domestic front, representatives of the forum and of its member organizations spent uncountable hours in strategic meetings among themselves and with World Bank monitoring staff and government officials, devising ways of improving Planafloro's environmental performance. The Rondonian government, however, would ignore its commitments as soon as bank staff left the area. The most effective strategy deployed during this period by Rondonian activists was a lawsuit (civil action) against the Brazilian land agency INCRA (Instituto Nacional de Colonização e Reforma Agrária, or the National Institute for Colonization and Agrarian Reform). In 1993, the forum charged the agency with violating the state's zoning law. The courts favored the forum and INCRA was ordered to halt colonization plans in areas designated exclusively for the creation of extractive reserves and conservation units.

From the outside, this might have appeared to be a coherent set of initiatives implemented by a coalition of like-minded activist organizations, but from the inside they rather resembled a mosaic or an impressionist painting. Despite the Rondônia Forum's coordinating efforts, the individual—and sometimes disparate—agendas of its allies and member organizations account for this "mosaic" of strategies. Such strategies unfolded in parallel, and sometimes in contradiction, to one another. For instance, the rubber-tappers organization and CIMI (Conselho Indígena Missionário, or Missionary Council for Indigenous Peoples, an indigenous peoples' advocacy group linked to the Catholic Church) favored negotiation with the government over confrontation. For these groups, the World Bank was, first, a strategic ally, even if structurally it was also a part of the problem. They perceived Planafloro as their only chance at guaranteeing resources for the demarcation of extractive reserves and indigenous lands. Planafloro's emphasis on conservation units made the landless peoples' organization MST (Movimento dos Sem Terra) and the organization of rural workers, FETAGRO, ambivalent supporters of the project. The movements' leadership was sensitive to the link between environmental protection and sustainable development, but strategies to support restrictions on settlement projects and farming land were hard to "sell" to their rank and file.

There were also cleavages among grassroots groups, on the one hand, and the more "internationalized" members of the coalition (such as the forum's leadership, certain advocacy and support NGOs, and international environmental groups). The latter approached Planafloro from the perspective of the broader multilateral development bank campaign (MDB Campaign) and aimed at challenging federal and regional development policies in Amazônia.[14] As such, their strategies privileged pressure on—and even confrontation with—the Brazilian and Rondonian governments and the World Bank over dialogue and negotiation (tactics that were often preferred by local grassroots groups).

The diversity of agendas and expectations within the Rondônia advocacy network is best illustrated by the tensions triggered by the forum's lawsuit against INCRA and the network's legitimacy crisis that this unleashed. Such a crisis, discussed below, was characterized by a period of intense tensions among network members at all levels, which greatly weakened their mobilization efforts.

The Legitimacy Crisis of the Rondônia Network

The carefully researched and documented lawsuit against INCRA convinced the courts that the agency had neglected to conduct mandatory environmental impact assessments for its planned colonization projects in Rondônia and disrespected the Rondonian zoning law. The forum's lawyer at the time, who drafted the lawsuit, explained: "INCRA has expropriated a huge area, around 400 square kilometers, for the settlement of landless people. But this is happening in an area designated (by the Zoning Law) for extractive reserves."[15] The courts responded to the lawsuit by issuing a provisional order mandating INCRA to stop all settlement in Rondônia.

In June 1994, backed by this favorable result in the case against INCRA, the forum wrote a letter to the World Bank requesting the interruption of disbursements for Planafloro.[16] The request was grounded on evidence that neither the Brazilian nor the Rondonian governments were seriously committed to the environmental aspects of project implementation. Letters from international environmental and human rights NGOs to the bank, the lobby of Brazilian NGOs in the national Congress, and the coverage of committed sectors of the national and international media supported the forum's request for suspension of disbursements.

In August 1994, in response to the forum's letter, the World Bank sent a monitoring mission to Brazil prepared to accept the forum's request for interruption of the Planafloro project. According to a Washington, D.C., environmentalist, the bank "was going out of its mind with worry that it would be forced to suspend (Planafloro) and was facing still another massive scandal in Rondônia."[17] Yet when the bank mission arrived in Rondônia it encountered a different scenario from what it had expected. Rondonian civil-society organizations had replaced the confrontational tone of their June letter with a pragmatic willingness to negotiate.

What had changed between June and August 1994? The answer lies in the diversity of agendas and expectations among the members of the Rondônia network. The request for suspension of Planafloro's disbursements was a bold yet precipitated strategy that addressed the concerns of the forum's leadership and was supported by its national and international allies. If followed through, this strategy could have turned into an important symbolic victory for those concerned about the environmental sustainability of development policies in Brazil. Grassroots organizations representing rubber-tappers and agricultural workers in Rondônia, however, had to be sensitive to the expectations of their rank and file. Planafloro may have been tainted with problems, but it represented these populations' best chance at obtaining concrete benefits, such as access to rural credit and the demarcation of extractive reserves. Staff at the OSR, for instance, stated emphatically: "never, speaking for the OSR, have we been in favor of suspending Planafloro. We were in favor of adjustments in the program but we could not throw it all away. For us it would have been a major loss."[18]

The forum leadership thus did not have the necessary political support and internal consensus to pursue the interruption of the Planafloro project. It opted instead to be responsive to the interest of its bases and negotiate with the government and the World Bank in August 1994. With hindsight, this proved to be a "strategic error"[19] that led the forum to a legitimacy crisis, from which it only recovered through the process of preparing the 1995 Inspection Panel claim.

In the post-negotiations phase, the forum and its member organizations faced a series of challenges. First, they needed to strike a balance between their continued roles as participants in—and independent monitors of—Planafloro. Second, they had to be responsive to project implementation commitments that they assumed during negotiations with the bank, which they soon found to be beyond the limits of their technical capacity.[20] Third, they needed to regain the trust of national and international allies, who had supported the request for the interruption of Planafloro, only to see that request being withdrawn a few months later. During the course of 1994, it became evident that the forum and its affiliate organizations could not meet these multiple challenges.

These difficulties, combined with increasing levels of frustration among Rondonian activists with the lack of Planafloro's positive results, launched both the forum and the Rondônia network as a whole into an unprecedented legitimacy crisis (see box 3.1). In December 1994, Rondonian civil-society organizations finally reassessed their position vis-à-vis the Planafloro project,

---

Box 3.1.   The Rondônia Forum's Legitimacy Crisis

- "The Rondonian NGOs, today, are undergoing an identity crisis, a huge operational crisis. The forum is in a bad shape. It is essentially an internal crisis. It may be able to maintain an external image, but internally, it is disastrous!"[22]
- "Planafloro's delay in establishing the extractive reserves is causing the rubber-tappers' movement to be discredited."[23]
- "Planafloro has promised the Indians a lot, but it hasn't delivered anything! Up until now, Planafloro has served only as a marketing tool. It promised to place forty doctors in indigenous areas and a high number of nurses, but it all remains as it was, and health problems have [been] aggravated in indigenous areas."[24]

---

a process that was defined by the forum's executive secretary as the "end of its romantic phase."[21]

The Planafloro Inspection Panel Claim

In early 1995, when international NGOs such as Friends of the Earth (FoE) and Oxfam suggested the Inspection Panel claim strategy to the Rondonian organizations, their suggestion fell on fertile ground. Although the research for the Inspection Panel claim was financed, initiated, and essentially completed by staff and consultants with international environmental NGOs (FoE, CIEL [Center for International Environmental Law], and Novib [Netherlands Organisation for International Development Co-operation]), the decision to request the Inspection Panel's investigation was made by local and international groups working together.[25]

The Planafloro Inspection Panel claim essentially denounced the World Bank's failure to adequately monitor project implementation. For instance, the bank remained oblivious to the fact that the Brazilian and Rondonian governments had failed to harmonize development policies with Planafloro's objectives. As a result, the project had been compromised in four main areas: land tenure, the creation of conservation units, the implementation of environmental protection measures, and support to indigenous communities. A fundamental aspect of the Planafloro claim, and the key to understanding why it became such a catalyst in resolving the Rondônia Forum's legitimacy crisis, was its main goal. Rather than expecting that the panel's investigation would lead to the interruption of Planafloro, the claimants wanted the investigation to "contribute to the solution of the ongoing problems of execution of Planafloro."[26]

During the year that elapsed between the request for interruption of disbursements for Planafloro in June 1994 and the claim to the Inspection Panel filed in June 1995, the forum and its member organizations reached a new level of political maturity. This process was the result of the Rondonian groups deepening their experience in negotiating with both the government and the World Bank, building or rebuilding bridges among groups that had not previously shared a common vision on development and environmental issues, experiencing the frustrations of Planafloro, and confronting their own institutional weaknesses in the context of the project. These experiences unfolded in parallel with a growing awareness—this time among all groups—that Planafloro's environmental promises would remain unfulfilled.

The Inspection Panel strategy was a novelty well suited to inaugurate a "new phase" in the relations between the forum's members and its national and international allies, and between the forum and Planafloro's implementing and funding agencies. For the forum's leadership, in particular, the Inspection Panel claim and its emphasis on resolving Planafloro's implementation problems—rather than terminating the project—was an opportunity to assert its accountability to local grassroots organizations.[27]

Several sources acknowledged the political cohesion of Rondonian civil-society organizations during the Inspection Panel process. An outside observer explains: "the forum was experiencing a crisis. The Inspection Panel claim reunified groups inside and outside Rondônia."[28] Inside Rondônia, representatives of organizations that had once questioned some of the forum's previous strategies also lent support to the claim, regardless of its consequences. The rubber-tappers' representative affirmed, "I was favorable to the Inspection Panel claim from the beginning . . . even if it meant interrupting the project,"[29] and staff at FETAGRO recalled, "during the Inspection Panel claim, we had a common position with these groups (environmentalists, indigenous peoples, and rubber-tappers)."[30] As the following section will demonstrate, the political cohesion among Rondonian civil-society organizations triggered by the Inspection Panel claim had consequences that went beyond the scope of that specific strategy.

IMPACTS OF THE CLAIM: CHALLENGES AND OPPORTUNITIES IN RONDÔNIA AND BEYOND

Institutional Responses to the Planafloro Claim

The Planafloro claim, filed on June 17, 1995, provoked reactions from four sets of actors: the Brazilian federal administration, the Rondonian government, the World Bank Board of Executive Directors, and the bank's

Planafloro management team. In the reactions of each of these actors one can identify, in different degrees, the tension between forces that were supportive of the claim—or at least, sensitive to it—and those who adamantly rejected its charges. This political battle had consequences at several levels. Outside the World Bank, international civil-society groups questioned the effectiveness of the panel as an international accountability mechanism. After all, the board of directors ultimately rejected the investigation recommended by the panel. Within the World Bank, the Planafloro claim triggered processes of redefinition of eligibility criteria and reevaluation of the panel's role, which aimed at narrowing the scope of its responsibility.[31] Finally, in Brazil, the debate generated by the claim created important leverage opportunities for local civil-society groups vis-à-vis the Rondonian government.

The first set of responses to the claim came from the World Bank's Planafloro management team, in tandem with Brazilian authorities. Management presented a document arguing for the dismissal of the Planafloro claim to the board of directors. The document stressed technical irregularities of the claim, but did not challenge the essence and merit of the charges made by the Rondonian organizations. The response of bank management consisted, first, of counterfactual assumptions: management claimed that Planafloro's beneficiary populations would have been worse off without the project. Second, bank management argued that the panel resolution required claimants to prove that "material adverse harm" had derived from the bank's actions. Using a narrow definition of this directive, the bank management argued that the panel should dismiss the claim. Their argument was that Planafloro's failure to produce *potential or planned* benefits to target populations did not characterize *actual* "material adverse harm."[32]

While denying the charges made in the Planafloro claim, the bank's management team also responded by intensifying its oversight of the project, including pressuring the Brazilian and Rondonian governments to implement key environmental measures. At least one analyst has described these actions and others that unfolded on the same path, such as the management team's action plan of 1996, as "schizophrenic." He asked, "why is management deploying efforts to fix problems whose existence it denies?"[33]

The Planafloro claim generated a long and convoluted process of political negotiations as well as serious divisions among members of the bank's board of directors. Eventually, the board decided to accept an action plan proposed by the Planafloro management team as a legitimate substitute for a panel investigation. The plan simply proposed to increase oversight of Planafloro. The acceptance of an action plan as a substitute for an investigation established a precedent that has affected the panel's effectiveness in other claims. Action plans have become a routine alternative to a panel investigation. As a consequence, rather than receiving an independent assessment of the problems, claimants are left with a remedy created by the very actors who allegedly caused the problems.

The Brazilian government was primarily concerned with asserting its national sovereignty. The country would not subject itself to an investigation by international experts, regardless of the nature of their mandate. Representatives of the Rondônia Forum, of the rubber-tappers' organization, and of indigenous peoples met with the Brazilian executive director during their trip to Washington, D.C., in October 1995 to lobby bank officials on behalf of the Planafloro claim. In the meeting, they were told that the ED would seek to block a panel investigation.[34]

The Rondonian government's reaction to the Inspection Panel claim was also immersed in contradictions. Such contradictions can be best understood as consequences of the pressures exerted on the then-newly elected administration of Governor Walter Raupp. The first set of pressures that Raupp had to face came from the World Bank, by means of increased levels of monitoring, including visits to the area by high-ranking bank officials and by executive directors.[35] The second set of pressures came from the Brazilian federal government, which wanted to avoid, at all costs, further international scrutiny of development policies in Rondônia. The pressures from the federal government carried significant leverage with the Raupp administration, since the cancellation of Planafloro would lead to the paralysis of all new loan negotiations for the state.[36] The third set of pressures endured by the Raupp administration came from grassroots groups who had signed the Planafloro claim, such as the landless movement and Rondônia's federation of rural workers, FETAGRO. These groups had political links with the Partido dos Trabalhadores (the Worker's Party), a party that had joined the ruling coalition by endorsing Raupp's candidacy in the state's runoff elections. Finally, the Rondonian government remained under pressure from the state's economic and political elites, who resisted Planafloro's social and environmental measures.

Given the political context described above, the measures adopted by the Rondonian and federal administrations immediately after the filing of the claim were not surprising. On July 28, 1995, federal and state land agencies signed an agreement transferring federal lands to the state of Rondônia. The agreement had been an unfulfilled precondition to the Planafloro loan and was a necessary step in the process of creating several conservation units and extractive reserves. In the month following the land agreement, the Rondonian government created fifteen extractive reserves. Before the end of the year, the geographic limits of most indigenous areas in Rondônia had been established. In the course of 1996, "notable progress" was observed in the management of conservation units and in the establishment of social and economic infrastructure in extractive reserves.[37]

The speed with which some of these actions were implemented raises questions about the role of the Inspection Panel claim in this process. The prevailing explanation is that the Inspection Panel claim, and the World Bank's consequent lobbying of the Brazilian and Rondonian governments, were instrumental for the adoption of such important measures (land agreement, demarcation of extractive reserves, and indigenous lands).[38] Yet individuals directly linked to the processes preferred to highlight the contribution of strategies that historically preceded the Planafloro claim. The importance of ongoing mobilization and incremental pressure strategies is evidenced in the fact that many of the most important environmental measures proposed by Planafloro became effective immediately after the presentation of the Inspection Panel claim. Such timing suggests that the actual decision to implement such measures may have predated the claim. In other words, while the Planafloro claim created the momentum for the adoption of environmental protection measures, the decision to make them effective seems to have been forced upon the Rondonian government by years of advocacy by the transnational network, together with pressures from the World Bank, which had grown increasingly dissatisfied with project implementation.[39]

Despite the fact that the implementation of environmental protection measures had become inevitable in the context of the Planafloro project, the Rondonian state was determined to create loopholes to "pacify" its "developmentalist" clients, that is, the state's economic elites, particularly logging interests. Indeed, the Raupp administration issued a series of regulations that directly undermined Planafloro's environmental accomplishments. Rondonian civil-society organizations, however, were able to block all but one of these attempts—further evidence of their political strength in the wake of the Inspection Panel claim.[40]

The Inspection Panel Claim and the Political Empowerment of Rondonian Civil-Society Groups

The escalation of tensions between Rondonian civil-society organizations and the state reinforced the decision of the Planafloro World Bank management team to facilitate or mediate a dialogue between them.[41] This goal was pursued through several initiatives, such as the World Bank–sponsored workshop on Planafloro's participatory management in March 1996 and the bank's commissioning of an overdue evaluation of the project, conducted by independent consultants in April 1996. In fact, staff in the World Bank's mission in Brazil acknowledged that these initiatives were a direct result of the Inspection Panel claim and "a function of the competence that the (Rondonian) civil society demonstrated in questioning the way Planafloro was being implemented. Through the Inspection Panel claim, the World Bank changed its perception of Planafloro [and] realized it had to change strategies. [In] order to reach a 'win-win' situation, there had to be collaboration among government and civil society."[42] This "new vision" culminated in the bank's sponsorship of the June 1996 Planafloro Evaluation Seminar.

Civil-society groups had the upper hand in the evaluation seminar for two reasons. First, the working document for the seminar was the final report of the April 1996 evaluation. The evaluation had reiterated most of the charges contained in the Inspection Panel claim and thus further legitimated the position of Rondonian civil-society organizations. Second, the Rondonian government's lack of capacity became apparent at the onset of the June seminar. Bank staff reported:

> the forum was well prepared. NGOs had better proposals—better formulated and with more details than those from the government. There were speeches from representatives of several sectors of the population, and when it was the government's turn, the Secretary of Planning did not say anything. The government lacked the capacity to make a competent defense against the NGOs. So it decided to negotiate.[43]

The political pragmatism of Rondonian civil-society organizations again became evident in the negotiations that occurred in the evaluation seminar. It is important to note that as early as October 1995, in the aftermath of the meeting between Rondonian civil-society activists and the Brazilian ED, the Rondonian groups had realized that an Inspection Panel investigation would not occur and were preparing alternative strategies. The focus of their efforts was on guaranteeing that a portion of project resources actually reached its beneficiaries.[44] For that to happen, civil-society groups also recognized that they would have to negotiate with the government.

Negotiations with the Rondonian government focused on two related demands from civil society. The first was that Planafloro funds be streamlined and that several governmental bureaucracies be excluded from the project. The second was that a portion of the reallocated money be directed to expand a project subcomponent that provided funds for community initiatives. The independent evaluation had identified this subcomponent as relatively successful. At the conclusion of negotiations, the Rondonian civil-society organizations had achieved their goals. One third of Planafloro's remaining budget (approximately $20 million) was directed to a community initiative fund, denominated *Projeto de Apoio a Iniciativas Comunitárias* (Project for the Support of Community Initiatives, or PAIC), and many state bureaucracies had been excluded from Planafloro. The Rondonian government, however, maintained control over the project in terms of its overall administration and responsibility for its remaining components, that is, environmental conservation and transportation infrastructure.

The PAIC: Conquests and Challenges

In hindsight, the conquest of the PAIC was a mixed blessing for Rondonian civil-society organizations. Among the PAIC's main blessings was the increased legitimacy that Rondonian civil-society organizations and leadership obtained vis-à-vis their rank and file, since their struggle had finally translated itself into concrete potential benefits to local communities.[45] A second benefit was the intensification of the dialogue between local organizations and governmental agencies and the growing perception within the latter that local leadership is both knowledgeable about environmental and social problems in Rondônia and able to propose alternative development models. Finally, according to some cautious evaluations, the PAIC may contribute to Rondônia's environmentally sustainable development.[46]

The PAIC also had its "curses," however. The first such curse was the high level of demands and expectations that it generated—expectations that local organizations were unprepared to meet. The second relates to the fact that local groups' focus on the PAIC alienated their national and international allies. The latter have come to perceive the PAIC as addressing narrow local interests, with little to contribute to larger issues, such as public policies for the Amazon region or the effectiveness of the Inspection Panel.

Frustrations with the PAIC started at the onset of its implementation. Formal and informal evaluations of the PAIC to date highlight the enormous challenge that it has presented to the limited technical capacity of Rondonian organizations. For instance, the bureaucratic requirements for the approval of funds were difficult to meet. Communities depended upon accredited consultants (*tecnicos*) to draft the projects according to PAIC's technical requirements. The processes of selecting and training *tecnicos* were cumbersome and often manipulated by the government.

A problem that derived from this *indústria de tecnicos* (industry of *tecnicos*) was that some encouraged the speedy formation of community associations. Most of these associations were formed in response to the opportunities generated by the PAIC, rather than being based on the level of organization and consensus of specific communities. Finally, the PAIC's regional selection committees, composed of both governmental and NGO representatives, were overburdened by both the number of proposals that they had to evaluate and the number of screening processes that had to be conducted. These problems are best illustrated through the words of individuals who were directly involved in these processes (see box 3.2). Rondonian leaders' assessment of the problems with the PAIC implementation has been confirmed by a 1998 evaluation

Box 3.2.   Evaluating the Community Initiatives Program

- "The Rondonian civil society had to stretch itself to come up with capable people to draft manuals, define the PAIC priorities, its beneficiaries. . . . The effort was to formulate the PAIC manual in the least complicated format possible. But there must be limits. For instance, the association applying for PAIC funds had to be in existence for at least one year. But this condition was waived for indigenous populations. On the one hand, such an exception was positive, on the other, it created serious problems. From one minute to the other we went from twelve indigenous associations in the state of Rondônia in 1994 to thirty-six in 1996–1997. Many of these associations did not even know what their mission was. The FUNAI *tecnico* (staff of the Brazilian Indian Agency, FUNAI [Fundação Nacional do Indio]) kept pushing the Indians by saying 'you must create the association in order to obtain the (PAIC) money.' This generated an enormous expectation. Also in 1996, the CUNPIR (Coordination of the Union of Indigenous Peoples and Nations of Rondônia) assumed responsibility for the Planafloro's indigenous health component. Yet the organization did not have the technical capacity that the project required. For instance, estimates for the payment of personnel were so badly done that in the end CUNPIR could only pay its field staff. There was no money for project management, monitoring, etc. . . . In 1997 the CUNPIR drowned in debt and imploded."[48]
- "(With the PAIC) there was significant progress in defining and conquering an important political space, yet civil-society organization did not have 'legs' to conduct the required political monitoring of such a large program. This is a problem. Some people back then said that the civil society had been co-opted. I do not think so. Co-optation requires an intention and this was not the case. The government itself was the first to resist the PAIC. What happened was that many organizations became involved with the execution of PAIC, and in the end there were not enough human resources to continue to monitor the initiative. . . . Not only there was a lack of human resources with political capacity, but also people with technical knowledge, mostly in the areas of finances and budget."[49]
- "Maybe co-optation occurred to a certain extent, but in large part the problem was related to the lack of capacity of these organizations in implementing the (PAIC) projects. They were not fully aware of what they were committing to. With all the heavy bureaucratic demands of the initiative, there was no way they could do anything else. Many organizations were unprepared and had troubles with the accounting part of the projects."[50]

commissioned by the World Bank, which warns about the lack of sustainability of many PAICs, an outcome resulting from both the nature of the projects approved and the degree of legitimacy of recipient organizations.[47]

Despite the technical difficulties involved in implementing the PAIC, the hardest blow suffered by the initiative came two years after its formulation. Governor Raupp campaigned for reelection in 1998, and in a desperate move to gain the support of civil servants whose salaries had been withheld due to lack of public funds, Raupp arbitrarily (and illegally) diverted the PAIC's money to the state's payroll.[51] The consequences were dire for community associations and NGOs that had already committed the diverted PAIC resources. Projects were paralyzed, crops were lost, and frustrated suppliers initiated lawsuits against associations that failed to pay for products they had ordered. In spite of all these problems, representatives of local organizations and some of their national allies still perceived the PAIC as an important conquest for the civil society, politically as well as environmentally (see box 3.3).[52]

The issue of the PAIC's contribution to environmental protection is particularly relevant for an assessment of the degree of success of the Planafloro Inspection Panel claim. Critics such as Brent Millikan point out that Planafloro's restructuring has diverted material and administrative resources

---

Box 3.3.   The PAIC's Contribution

- "In my evaluation, the PAIC was a complete and very positive experience, despite its flaws. Sure, there were many badly implemented projects, projects that lacked a participatory approach, there was a lot of internal confusion within the communities, but there are also many projects in the field that would not have been there were it not for the PAIC. . . . Unfortunately, in the long term. I think that the continuity of the program is a remote possibility given the state's political and economic situation."[53]

- "The PAIC is thus a way of transferring resources from the state to civil-society organizations that are most permeable to environmental issues. The project is important because it promotes a more decentralized style of management and a more sustainable agriculture."[54]

- "What the rubber-tappers and the indigenous communities discuss today is the desire to increase production, but this is within the scope of the PAICs. Yet the communities also want to guarantee the area's environmental preservation. For them it is important to recover areas that have been degraded by logging or colonization."[55]

away from the project's environmental component. In addition, since Rondonian civil-society organizations have focused all their energies on the PAIC, the state has become freer to neglect its environmental commitments.[56] So far, Millikan's predictions have been accurate. In fact, the relative success of the claim may have triggered an unprecedented move from Rondonian political and economic elites against initiatives to preserve the environment. In 1998, a conservative coalition led by the Partido da Frente Liberal (Liberal Front Party, or PFL) replaced the Raupp administration in the state's government. This coalition immediately initiated a series of measures aiming at curtailing some of Planafloro's post-claim environmental achievements.

The Rondonian state's successive backlashes against the environment have contributed to the reappearance of old cleavages among the Rondonian civil-society groups. Since Raupp diverted the PAIC funds, both MST (the landless movement) and FETAGRO have advocated ending any involvement of civil-society groups with the Planafloro project. Representatives of rubber-tappers, indigenous peoples, and small producers' associations, however, have opted for continuing their involvement in project implementation and dialogue with governmental agencies. These divisions have deepened in the context of the challenges brought about by Rondônia's conservative forces.

The cleavages among Rondonian civil-society groups have generated new challenges for monitoring the Planafloro project and for initiatives aiming at resisting the state's backlash against the project's environmental component. Despite cleavages, however, local groups have come together on occasion, particularly to pressure the state to return to the beneficiary communities the PAIC resources diverted in 1998. The second approximation of the zoning process was another instance in which local civil-society groups have continued to join forces on behalf of the environment in Rondônia.

In part due to the differences that have divided Rondonian civil-society groups in recent years, their effort to monitor Planafloro, the zoning process, and other public policies in Rondônia have followed a different path than in previous initiatives. Rondonian groups have remained focused mainly inward—and on their constituency-specific agendas—and as a result have weakened their links to activists groups at national and international levels. On a brighter note, it is important to stress that this "inward process" (some would label it a "process of isolation") may be the result of some positive developments. Since the rejection of the Planafloro claim, but because of the impact it had on Rondonian politics, local groups have felt empowered to confront the state's political elites directly, without necessarily resorting to national/international arenas or allies. Such an increased degree of autonomy also becomes evident through the fact that most mobilization strategies that have been implemented to guarantee the social and environmental rights of Rondonian populations has unfolded under the leadership of grassroots organizations such as OSR or FETAGRO. As explained by one of FETAGRO's leaders, "the federation's space to influence the state machine—its ability to be perceived as a political reference—have occurred as a result of (activism around) Planafloro."[57]

Before closing this section it is important to ask the following questions: first, Have local Rondonian groups been empowered as a result of their participation in the Rondônia Forum and in the Planafloro transnational network? In many aspects, they have. In the last ten years, and particularly since the Planafloro Inspection Panel claim, Rondonian groups have become more visible in the political scene; increased their membership base; gained significant knowledge about the state bureaucracy's mode of operation; gained direct access to and initiated dialogue with selected state agencies; increased their technical skills through participation in challenging procedures such as the formulation of the PAIC and the Rondonian Zoning Plan; and found common ground among themselves on issues that were once the sources of cleavages, such as land use and conservation units. The second question is, Has participation in transnational advocacy networks empowered Rondonian groups to the point that they are now capable of checking the power of economic elites and their tradition of appropriating state resources to their private benefit? The answer to this question is, generally not. While leading to valuable conquests on behalf of the Rondonian environment, the political empowerment obtained by local groups through their participation in the Planafloro transnational network was not sufficient to structurally alter the balance of political forces in the state. In the next section I discuss some of the reasons for the remaining weaknesses of Rondonian local groups and suggest strategies to overcome such weaknesses.

CONCLUSIONS

This chapter evaluated the strategy of demanding the investigation of the Planafloro project by the Inspection Panel. It emphasized the impact of that process on the political empowerment of local civil-society organizations in Rondônia. In doing so, this study questioned the "empowerment" assumption dominant in the literature on transnational advocacy networks. It demonstrated that participation in a transnational advocacy network may lead to a relative political empowerment of local civil-society groups. Yet this very process also imposes significant demands on these groups' capacity. These unaddressed demands, in the long run, may compromise the political space that was obtained by local groups at the height of the transnational mobilization.

The strategy of demanding the investigation of the Planafloro project produced concrete improvements in project implementation, despite the fact that the World Bank Board of Directors rejected the investigation itself. The strategy produced impacts not only on the Rondonian environment, but also on the state's politics. In its immediate aftermath, the Planafloro claim altered the balance of political forces in Rondônia, creating conditions for the reallocation of project funds, which directly benefited the project's primary beneficiaries.

The claim strategy, however, is also to blame, at least in part, for the Rondonian government's backlash against Planafloro's environmental provisions. The leverage and political visibility that civil-society organizations obtained as a result of their role in the Inspection Panel claim threatened the interests of local political and economic elites. The latter have since stepped up their efforts to reverse Planafloro's environmental gains. The conservative backlash has taken place in part as a result of the political vacuum that has been left unchecked by the Rondonian groups and their national and international allies. This political vacuum is the result of two interrelated factors. On the one hand, local groups, overwhelmed by the technical demands of implementing the PAIC, lacked the capacity to continue to adequately monitor Planafloro's other components. On the other hand, the increased demands on the political and technical capacity of local groups contributed to the emergence (or reemergence) of cleavages among them, cleavages that related to their goals and participatory strategies in both the Planafloro project and other policies aiming at the sustainable development of the state.

It is here that this study of the Planafloro Inspection Panel claim can contribute the most useful insight: it highlights the importance of perceiving—and planning for—such a powerful strategy in the long term. Neither the Rondonian organizations nor their international allies were prepared to seize the opportunities and confront the challenges that the Inspection Panel claim created. Local groups tried bravely to occupy the spaces for participation in Planafloro that were opened to them as a result of the claim. In many instances, however, they were overwhelmed by their own lack of technical and human resources. This very shortage of resources explains the decreased political activism of the Rondonian groups.

One of the activities that was most compromised as a result of the intensification of demands on local activists was the maintenance of institutional and personal links between Rondonian advocacy groups and their national and international allies. Local activists have neglected key activities such as feeding common information channels and participating in conferences and workshops to share common experiences and articulate complementary strategies. As a result, Rondonian groups have missed important opportunities to strengthen their struggles through a higher degree of engagement in national initiatives for the democratization of policy making at regional and national levels.

This situation reflects a perverse irony. The success of strategies such as the Planafloro claim increases the demands on the political, technical, and financial resources of local civil-society organizations. Since these groups' capacity is usually limited, growing demands on their resources have constrained their ability to maintain or intensify their networking initiatives. This is unfortunate since the preservation and intensification of their interorganizational links would likely increase Rondonian organizations' own institutional resources. Instead, their isolation (under the burden of their new responsibilities) contributed to widening preexistent cleavages between local groups and their once national and international allies.

As previously indicated, testing the autonomy and effectiveness of the Inspection Panel was among the main goals of international NGOs that supported the Planafloro claim. Many of these organizations interpreted the rejection of Planafloro's recommended investigation as the end of a promising process. In doing so, they overlooked the fact that such a rejection did not prevent the beginning of a new phase in the struggle for an adequate implementation of Planafloro in Rondônia.

One consequence of this incomplete evaluation of the impact of the Planafloro claim was the distancing of international groups from the processes that unfolded in Rondônia in the wake of the claim. Thus, when Rondonian groups were in dire need of technical assistance to keep up with the demands of the PAIC and of the zoning process, international NGOs were distancing themselves from Rondônia. In this light, the case of the Planafloro Inspection Panel claim provides yet another illustration of the continuing challenges of institutionalizing transnational partnerships among local and global actors. They further corroborate Jonathan Fox's claims on the fragility of Northern–Southern advocacy coalitions.[58]

Quite possibly, the key element in processes of institutionalizing Northern–Southern advocacy coalitions is the mediation of organizations or networks of organizations with a national reach. This "link" has been chronically missing in the case of the Rondônia network. Historically, Rondonian groups have had direct access to international NGOs (and vice versa) due, in large part, to the personal connections established among leadership in Rondônia and abroad from the time of the Polonoroeste mobilization. Since then, however, Brazil has democratized and its civil society has been actively devising mechanisms to increase popular participation in policy making. Successful examples of this effort are the Brazil Network on Multilateral Development Banks (Rede Brasil sobre Instituições Financeiras Multilaterais) and collective bodies such as the Brazilian National Forum of NGOs (Fórum

Brasileiro de ONGs) and Social Movements on the Environment and Development (Fórum Brasileiro de ONGs e Movimentos Sociais para o Meio Ambiente e Desenvolvimento). Rondonian organizations, however, have been noticeably absent from these mechanisms. The challenges of Rondonian politics and the overstretching of local organizations due to their commitments within Planafloro may explain their incapacity to establish stronger links with national advocacy entities. Yet this very incapacity has further compromised their chances of advancing technically and politically.

Finally, a different aspect of the same problem is the tendency of international NGOs to bypass, often inadvertently, national clearinghouses and collective mechanisms. They often do that in response to pressures to assert their legitimacy through direct alliances with local grassroots groups. Yet one consequence of such a tendency is that international NGOs often miss opportunities to contribute to structural change in national arenas. Unless international groups, which are often the most resourceful elements of transnational advocacy networks, commit their resources to long-term struggles that are incremental and national in scope, transnational advocacy efforts will remain limited to the sporadic successes of specific local strategies and campaigns.

NOTES

1. The Polonoroeste, a road and settlement project, aimed at furthering Rondônia's integration into the national economy.

2. See Margaret Keck and Kathryn Sikkink, *Activists beyond Borders: Advocacy Networks in International Politics* (Ithaca: Cornell University Press, 1998).

3. Thomas Princen, "NGOs: Creating a Niche in Environmental Diplomacy," in *Environmental NGOs in World Politics: Linking the Local and the Global,* ed. Thomas Princen and Matthias Finger (London: Routledge, 1994); Lisa Jordan and Peter Van Tuijl, "Political Responsibility in Transnational NGO Advocacy," *World Development,* vol. 28, no. 12 (2000); Tamara Jezic, "Ecuador: The Campaign against Texaco Oil," in *Advocacy for Social Justice: A Global Action and Reflection Guide,* ed. D. Cohen, R. Vega, and G. Watson (Bloomfield, Conn.: Kumarian, 2001).

4. See Keck and Sikkink, *Activists beyond Borders,* and Maria Rodrigues, "Environmental Protection Issue Networks in Brazil's Amazônia," *Latin American Research Review,* vol. 35, no. 3 (2000).

5. Such measures were to conform to a social-environmental zoning plan, which was among the cornerstones of the Planafloro project.

6. Sônia [pseud.], staff member from the Rondonian NGO INDIA, interview by author, tape recording, Rondônia, November 24, 1994.

7. Paulo, staff member from the Rondônia Forum, interview by author, tape recording, Rondônia, November 22, 1994.

8. Margaret Keck, "Planafloro in Rondônia: The Limits of Leverage," in *The Struggle for Accountability: The World Bank, NGOs, and Grassroots Movements,* ed. Jonathan Fox and David L. Brown (Cambridge: MIT Press, 1998), 181–218.

9. Brent Millikan, "Planafloro, Modelo de Projeto Participativo," in *Bancos Multilaterais e Desenvolvimento Participativo no Brasil,* ed. Jean Pierre Leroy and Maria C. Soares (Rio de Janeiro: Federação das Associações para a Assistência Social e Educação [FASE, or the Federation of Associations for Education and Social Assistance]/ Instituto Brasileiro de Análises Sociais e Econômicas [IBASE, or Brazilian Institute for Social and Economic Analyses], 1998); Breno [pseud.], former consultant for the Rondônia Forum, interviews by author, Rondônia, November 22, 1994, and Brasília, May 19, 2000; Pedro [pseud.], Working Group staff member, telephone interview by author, tape recording, February 9, 2001.

10. The inclusion of Rondonian civil-society organizations in the decision-making body of the Planafloro project (the *Conselho Deliberativo*) was a response from both the World Bank and the Rondonian government to pressures for grassroots participation in the project. This response was formalized in an agreement signed on June 20, 1991, by the Rondonian governor and twelve local civil-society organizations.

11. See Keck, "Planafloro in Rondônia"; Keck and Sikkink, "Activists beyond Borders"; Millikan, "Modelo de Projeto Participativo"; idem, "O Painel de Inspeção do Banco Mundial e o Pedido de Investigação sobre o Planafloro," in *Banco Mundial: Participação, Transparência e Responsabilidade: A Experiência Brasileira com o Painel de Inspeção,* ed. Aurélio Vianna Jr., et al. (Brasília: Rede Brasil, 2001), 79–122; Rodrigues, "Environmental Protection."

12. Comite de Avaliação Independente (COMAI), "Plano Agropecuario e Florestal de Rondonia—Planafloro—Relatorio de Avaliacao" (n.d., mimeographed).

13. Forum of NGOs and Social Movements of Rondônia to Mark Wilson, the World Bank, June 15, 1994.

14. The Multilateral Development Bank Campaign, organized in the mid 1980s by international environmental NGOs, pressured the World Bank to become accountable to the environmental and social costs of its development initiatives.

15. Paulo [pseud.], interview, November 22, 1994.

16. Forum of NGOs and Social Movements of Rondônia to Mark Wilson, June 15, 1994.

17. Estevão [pseud.], staff member in a Washington, D.C.–based international environmental NGO, telephone interview by author, Washington, D.C., March 1, 2001. Sectors of the Rondônia media also interpreted the August 1994 World Bank mission as a step toward the suspension of disbursements (see, e.g., Rolim de Moura, "Missão do Banco Mundial chega para discutir suspensão do Planafloro" [Mission from the World Bank arrives to discuss Planafloro's interruption], *O Progresso,* August 5, 1994).

18. Silvio [pseud.], staff member at OSR, interview by author, tape recording, Rondônia, May 23, 2000.

19. Fernando [pseud.], Rondônia Forum's executive secretary between 1994–1996, interview by author, Brasília, March 21, 1995.

20. Fernando [pseud.], interview, March 21, 1995.

21. Fernando [pseud.], interview, March 21, 1995.

22. Miguel [pseud.], PNUD (Programa de las Naciones Unidas para el Desarrollo) consultant, interview by author, tape recording, Rondônia, November 23, 1994.

23. Silvio [pseud.], interview by author, tape recording, Rondônia, November 22, 1994.

24. Afonso [pseud.], leader of the Karitiana indigenous people, interview by author, tape recording, Rondônia, November 22, 1994.

25. Eduardo [pseud.], staff member, Friends of the Earth–Amazônia Program (Brazil), interview by author, tape recording, São Paulo, June 5, 2000; Fernando [pseud.], interview, by author, tape recording, Rondônia, May 29, 2000; João Batista [pseud.], staff member of FASE, interview by author, tape recording, Rio de Janeiro, December 11, 2000.

26. Forum das ONGs e Movimentos Sociais que Atuam em Rondônia and Friends of the Earth/Amigos da Terra–Programa Amazônia, "Request for Inspection Submitted to the World Bank Inspection Panel on the Planafloro–Rondônia Natural Resources Management Project," Porto Velho, July, 25, 1995, 5.

27. This was a political necessity given that membership of grassroots organizations in the forum had increased from two in 1991 to thirteen in 1995, while the number of support/advocacy groups had remained almost the same (between nine and twelve).

28. Olavo [pseud.], former staff member at the Rede Brasil sobre Instituições Financeiras Multilaterais, interview by author, tape recording, Brasília, May 19, 2000.

29. Silvio [pseud.], interview, May 23, 2000.

30. Marcelo [pseud.], leader of FETAGRO, interview by author, tape recording, Rondônia, May 23, 2000.

31. For details, see discussions on attempts to limit the powers and mandate of the Inspection Panel available online at www.ciel.org.

32. Millikan, "O Painel de Inspeção," and Fernando [pseud.], interview, May 29, 2000.

33. Millikan, "O Painel de Inspeção," and Breno [pseud.], interview, May 19, 2000.

34. Fernando [pseud.], interview, May 29, 2000.

35. "Cronograma dos Fatos—Governo toma medidas pressionado pela repercussão das denúncias" [Chronogram of facts: Government takes action under permission from the impact of charges], *Noticias do Forum*, vol. 4, no. 3 (December 1995).

36. "Banco Mundial tenta evitar a denúncia," *Noticias do Forum*, vol. 4, no. 3 (December 1995).

37. Roberto Smeraldi and Brent Millikan, "Planafloro—Um Ano Depois—Análise Crítica da Implementação do Plano Agropecuário e Florestal de Rondônia um Ano Após o Acordo Para a sua Reformulação" (Amigos da Terra Internacional–Programa Amazônia e Oxfam, São Paulo and Porto Velho, August 1997, mimeographed).

38. Keck, "Planafloro in Rondônia," and Millikan, "O Painel de Inspeção."

39. Estevão [pseud.], interview, March 1, 2001, and Sérgio [pseud.], member of the World Bank Planafloro management team, telephone interview with author, tape recording, Cuiabá, June 9, 2000.

40. For a discussion of these legislative disputes, see Maria Rodrigues, "Redes Transnacionais de Advocacia Pública: Estratégias e Impactos—O Projeto

Planafloro e o Painel de Inspeção do Banco Mundial," *Contexto Internacional,* vol. 24, no. 1 (2002).

41. Sérgio [pseud.], interview, June 9, 2000, and Davi [pseud.], World Bank staff member at the Brazilian mission, interview by author, tape recording, Brasília, May 19, 2000.

42. Davi [pseud.], interview, May 19, 2000.

43. Davi [pseud.], interview, May 19, 2000.

44. Fernando [pseud.], interview, May 29, 2000.

45. Other analysts may question such an assessment based on the fact that the PAIC resources have taken a long time to reach—when they have, in fact, reached— their intended beneficiaries. While this criticism is valid, it is also important to high-light that given the volume of resources available through the program, the percent-age that has reached Rondonian communities is significant. This is particularly true when one considers the "new PAICs," whose disbursements began in 2000.

46. For instance, John Bowder, "Report: World Bank Mid-Term Supervision Mis-sion for the Program of Support to Community Initiatives (PAIC), Planafloro (loan 3444-BR)," consultant report, November 20–December 3, 1998.

47. Browder, "Report."

48. Júlio [pseud.], consultant for the CUNPIR, interview by author, tape recording, Rondônia, May 23, 2000.

49. Paco [pseud.], executive secretary of COOTRARON (Cooperativa de Trabalho Múltiplo de Rondônia, or the Rondonian Cooperative of Multiple Works) and former executive secretary of the Rondônia Forum, interview by author, tape recording, Rondônia, May 23, 2000.

50. Breno [pseud.], interview, May 19, 2000.

51. Júlio [pseud.], interview, May 23, 2000.

52. For a technical evaluation of PAIC's contributions to Rondônia's environmen-tally sustainable development, see Browder, "Report."

53. Paco [pseud.], interview, May 23, 2000.

54. Manuel [pseud.], staff member at the World Wildlife Fund–Brazil, telephone interview by author, tape recording, Brasília, May 26, 2000.

55. Júlio [pseud.], interview, May 23, 2000.

56. Millikan, "Modelo de Projeto Participativo" and "O Painel de Inspeção."

57. Interview with Marcelo [pseud.], interview, May 23, 2000.

58. Jonathan Fox, "Assessing Binational Civil Society Coalitions: Lessons from the Mexico–US Experience" (paper presented at the 2000 International Congress of the Association for Latin American Studies, Miami, March 16–18, 2000).

4

Accountability at the World Bank: What Does It Take? Lessons from the Yacyretá Hydroelectric Project, Argentina/Paraguay

Kay Treakle and Elías Díaz Peña

On December 26, 1996, the Inspection Panel recommended that the bank's board of executive directors authorize a full investigation of one if its most notorious development projects—the Yacyretá Hydroelectric Dam, located on the border between Argentina and Paraguay. The recommendation was in support of a claim submitted to the panel by SOBREVIVENCIA/Friends of the Earth–Paraguay, an NGO in Paraguay. The claim, which had been filed in September 1996, asserted that the project had "serious impacts on [local people's] standards of living, their economic well-being, and their health," and that the harm was caused by violations of World Bank environmental and resettlement policies, among others.[1] Yacyretá was the sixth claim filed with the World Bank's Inspection Panel since its inception, and the third that the panel had recommended for an investigation.

This chapter describes why the claim was filed and what happened during the several phases of the process, which took more than two years. While the Yacyretá project is a colossal failure when examined from just about any angle—financial, economic, political, social, and environmental—this chapter will highlight the bank's failures to protect the environment and compensate displaced people in violation of its own policies. The chapter also illustrates how local citizens, with support from local and international NGOs, have used the bank's Inspection Panel to pressure for justice, accountability, and solutions to their problems.

While the process has been daunting for the claimants, it has had some positive results, particularly because it galvanized local citizens to press for greater political space in Paraguay to assert their rights. From the standpoint

of accountability at the World Bank, however, the conclusions are less opti-
mistic. Thousands of local people affected by the project are still waiting for
proper compensation for the loss of their livelihoods and the deteriorated
quality of their environment.

BACKGROUND ON YACYRETÁ

One of the largest and most complex construction projects ever undertaken in
Latin America, the Yacyretá Hydroelectric Dam straddles the Parana River
between Paraguay and Argentina. The dam is a joint project between the two
countries and has been built and managed by the Entidad Binacional Yacyretá
(EBY), a supranational entity. Located downstream from the cities of Encarnación, Paraguay, and Posadas, Argentina, the Yacyretá Dam is about 35 meters high at the main channel closure and 67 kilometers long. The dam crosses
Yacyretá Island, submerging the Apipe rapids and most of the island in a lake
formed when the dam's two spillway gates were closed in 1994 and the reservoir was filled to its first (and present) stage of 76 meters above sea level
(masl). If the reservoir is raised to its originally designed elevation of 83
masl, the powerhouse would generate 3,100 megawatts of electricity for Argentina and a 250-km-long reservoir would cover 1,650 square km, flooding
some 93,000 hectares in Paraguay and 29,000 hectares in Argentina.

An important feature of the Yacyretá project is that while the energy produced will be used exclusively by Argentina, most of the adverse impacts of
the project are in Paraguay. Most of the dam, both spillways, and the powerhouse are all in Paraguayan territory, as are most of the losses of housing,
means of livelihood, and land.

While the long history of Yacyretá started with studies undertaken in the
early part of the century, and the two countries signed the treaty establishing
Yacyretá in 1973, construction did not get underway until 1983, when the
original estimated cost of the project was $1.35 billion.[2] Since its inception,
Yacyretá has been fraught with corruption scandals, gross mismanagement,
construction delays, and cost overruns amounting to billions of dollars.[3]

The World Bank and the Inter-American Development Bank (IDB) have
together loaned over $1.7 billion to the government of Argentina for Ya-
cyretá.[4] Initial loans covered construction of the main civil works, including
the powerhouse, earth dam, navigation, locks, irrigation intake, migratory
fish elevators, and purchase of turbines.

When the banks began negotiating new loans in 1991, however, construction was 85 percent complete, nine years behind schedule, and the estimated cost of the dam had risen to about $8 billion. To complete con-

struction, the Argentine government requested new loans from the World Bank and IDB in 1992 to pay for "complementary works." These projects included housing for displaced people, parks, schools, sewage treatment facilities, and environmental mitigation measures, which at that point were only 15 percent completed.

By that time, both banks had adopted strong environmental and resettlement policies, largely as a result of international NGO campaigns that exposed the enormous ecological and social disruption caused by large-scale infrastructure projects.[5] As the World Bank and IDB prepared new loans for Yacyretá, they required the borrower to prepare an Environmental Impact Assessment (EA) and a resettlement plan. Moreover, the policies also required that affected citizens be consulted in the development of the project, and in order to have informed participation, new bank policies gave citizens the right to have access to relevant information about the project prior to the loans' approval.

Both the EA and resettlement studies identified a number of critical environmental and social impacts that would need to be mitigated in order for Argentina to receive the loans. Some of the impacts included the following:

- Flooding of over 93,000 hectares of land in Paraguay and 29,000 hectares in Argentina, including more than 50,000 hectares of forest, large and small islands, marshes and grasslands. Ninety-eight percent of the land to be flooded was classified as being composed of biologically unique natural ecosystems.
- Irreversible disruption of fish biodiversity and fishery resources upon which a sizeable population depend.
- Involuntary resettlement of over 50,000 mostly urban poor people in the two countries, as well as indigenous Mbya peoples and peasant fisherpeople (who had already been relocated far from islands in the river to marginal lands in Paraguay).
- Increased health risks from schistosomiasis, malaria, and other diseases.
- Pollution of the urban waterfront areas and the reservoir from untreated sewage, industrial, and agricultural wastes.[6]

The bank loans were predicated on a three-stage plan to install turbines and begin electricity generation while conducting, in phases, environmental mitigation and resettlement activities. The reservoir would be filled to seventy-six, seventy-eight, and then eighty-three masl over a period of several years. The project also included a plan to ensure implementation and financing of the remainder of the resettlement activities as well as recurring costs of environmental monitoring and mitigation.

NGOs in the region and internationally[7] opposed the two loans on the grounds that the environmental assessment was inadequate and that both the environmental mitigation and resettlement plans were dependent on an improbable financing arrangement. Chief among the complaints were a lack of baseline data to determine the extent of the biodiversity losses and impacts; inadequate identification of "compensatory reserves" (areas that were supposed to compensate for flooded wildlands); absence of a plan to maintain minimum water flow in a principal branch of the river, the Aña Cua; and an underestimation of the number of people who had the right to compensation and resettlement. The resettlement plan, they said, was based on a faulty census conducted by EBY in 1989–1990, and did not benefit from effective consultation with affected people.[8]

An international NGO campaign to oppose the loan, aimed at lobbying executive directors at both banks, did not succeed. But it did compel the World Bank (largely at the urging of the then-U.S. director, Patrick Coady) to include in the loan agreement stronger conditionality, more money for environment and resettlement activities, and promises for rigorous bank supervision of the project. The IDB also increased the amount of its loan to $130 million and designated it for environmental mitigation and resettlement activities that would result from filling the reservoir above seventy-six masl.

A specific condition that would be crucial to future advocacy efforts, including the Inspection Panel claim, was that before EBY could raise the level of the reservoir to seventy-six masl, the required environmental mitigation and resettlement measures had to be completed to the satisfaction of the World Bank.

Over the next few years, construction of the dam continued, though chronically behind schedule. Particularly lagging were resettlement and environmental mitigation activities. However, with two turbines installed, EBY decided to close the spillways in 1994 and begin generating electricity. Neither the World Bank nor the IDB objected to this decision, even though the required environmental and resettlement actions had not been taken. The decision to close the spillways and create the reservoir at its first stage of seventy-six masl blatantly violated the loan agreement. The banks' failure to object in 1994 was apparently based on an agreement that EBY would complete all requirements by 1995.[9]

This promise was eclipsed by the 1995 peso devaluation in Mexico, which was followed by a macroeconomic crisis in Argentina. Referred to as the "tequila effect," the financial crisis caused reductions in public spending, including a complete cutoff of the government's counterpart funding commitment to Yacyretá. The Argentine government refused to spend another dime on Yacyretá until the project was privatized.[10] Meanwhile, the creation of the reservoir led to significant deterioration in the lives of thousands of affected people in both countries.

THE WORLD BANK AND IDB INSPECTION PANEL CLAIMS

In September 1996, SOBREVIVENCIA submitted a claim to the World Bank's Inspection Panel and the first claim to the IDB's Independent Investigation Mechanism.[11] The claim was filed by SOBREVIVENCIA in its own right and as an authorized representative of anonymous affected people from Paraguay. It was a last-resort action by local people to assert their rights after years of frustrated attempts to obtain adequate and timely compensation from EBY and to bring concerns to the attention of bank management.

SOBREVIVENCIA found that bringing the claim to the World Bank and the IDB with locally affected people was quite difficult. The democratic process, which started in Paraguay in 1989, had not changed EBY, which remained an agency characterized by authoritarianism and corruption. EBY routinely abused peoples' rights, threatened affected communities, generated intrigue directed at dividing organizations, and discredited those leaders whom they could not co-opt. The bank officials in charge of the project largely supported EBY's positions and actions.

Because of their negative experiences with EBY, local people were afraid that a claim would only bring retaliation to those who signed. Several workshops were conducted with different groups of affected communities to explain the nature and terms of reference of the inspection mechanisms. The workshops carefully avoided the possibility of raising false expectations about the power of these mechanisms to solve the communities' problems. The claim process was supported by the Center for International Environmental Law (CIEL), the Bank Information Center (BIC), and International Rivers Network.

In September 1996, when given guarantees that the Inspection Panel procedures allowed them to keep their names confidential, a number of affected people agreed to sign as claimants. They decided to file jointly to both banks since both were responsible for financing the project and implementing protections. SOBREVIVENCIA filed the claim on its own behalf and as authorized representatives of local people.[12]

The claim alleged that "Socio-economic impacts include loss of jobs and livelihood and forced resettlement to smaller homes of poorer quality. Workers in occupations including ceramic-making—mainly bricks and tiles—and fishing have lost their resource base. Others, including washerwomen, bakers and pastry makers . . . have lost customers concerned over the effects of lower water quality on the goods they produce and the services they provide."[13]

The claim also cited numerous health problems caused by poor water quality, including increased respiratory infections, diarrhea, rashes, skin and intestinal parasites, nutritional disorders, and stress-related conditions. It asserted that the rising water table "has also incapacitated sanitation systems and destroyed crops" and that "untreated sewage is discharged into the lake and instead of being carried downstream—as before the reservoir was filled—it stagnates in the proximity of homes now near that water level."[14] Irreversible impacts on fish resources, inadequate removal of biomass from the reservoir area, and the failure to establish adequate compensatory reserves were also cited in the claim. The claim alleged violations of bank policies on environment, resettlement, wildlands, information disclosure, indigenous peoples, and project supervision, among others, and asserted that these violations of policy caused material harm to local people.

The claimants requested several remedies, including adequate compensation and retraining for people who had lost their homes and livelihoods, legal establishment and effective protection of compensatory wildlife reserves, a halt to privatization of the project unless an evaluation were first conducted of the economics of privatization and its environmental and social impacts, and maintenance of the reservoir at seventy-six masl until all necessary environmental and social mitigation measures had been completed.

Phase 1: The Panel Recommends an Inspection

In early December 1996, panel member Alvaro Umaña and the panel's executive secretary, Eduardo Abbott traveled to Argentina and Paraguay. Accompanying them was Dr. Angus Wright, chair of the IDB's investigation team for Yacyretá. Together, the World Bank and IDB panel representatives met with SOBREVIVENCIA, affected people, project sponsors, government officials from both countries, and bank staff.

Based on their preliminary assessments, both panels recognized that the claimants were eligible and that there was evidence to confirm allegations of harm related to loss of livelihood, health risks, water pollution, and resettlement, and accordingly recommended full investigations. The World Bank panel's recommendation to the board found that the decision to raise the level of the reservoir to seventy-six masl may have violated bank policy and that the bank had tolerated violations of the loan agreement.[15]

Bank management responded by challenging the eligibility of the Yacyretá claim on several grounds. They denied that the problems raised in the claim resulted from "any alleged Management violation of the Bank's policies and procedures." They claimed that "all resettlement and environmental mitigation activities required prior to reaching the current reservoir level of 76 masl have been met . . . except some pending matters which are being addressed through appropriate financing and supervision." Management challenged the eligibility of the claimants since they were from Paraguay and the borrower was Argentina, and their response contained a rebuttal disputing most of the allegations in the claim.[16]

Phase 2: The Ball Moves to the Board's Court

It took a full two months for the board to decide what to do with the panel's recommendation on Yacyretá. At its first informal meeting to discuss the recommendation in early February 1997, the board split over whether to approve an inspection, with the donor countries in favor and the borrower countries opposed. The Argentine executive director, Julio Nogues, launched the strongest attack, mobilizing borrowing countries to oppose the panel, the claim, and the claimants. At the board meeting, Mr. Nogues objected to an investigation and accused the panel of operating outside its own resolution and placing the country in a precarious financial situation owing to the recent financial crisis.[17] He also took issue with the claimants' eligibility because they were Paraguayan and the loan was to Argentina. This was early in the panel's history and there was a strong reaction from some borrowing countries to the very term "investigation," which to some implied wrongdoing. They were worried that the panel process would focus on the role of the government rather than on the role of the bank.

For the first time in a panel deliberation, the donor-country directors unanimously supported the panel's recommendation. The strongest advocates included the United States, The Netherlands, and Switzerland. The board split between North and South, and because donor countries hold a majority of votes, had a vote been taken, the panel recommendation would have been approved. President Wolfensohn was uncomfortable with the split, however, and hoped to build consensus for an investigation.[18] A decision about the panel's recommendation was postponed.

NGOs from North and South conducted a vigorous international campaign to convince the executive directors to support the claim and allow the panel to investigate. Their goal was to ensure that the board understood that the NGO community was paying close attention to the panel process, and that a failure to accept the panel's recommendation for an investigation would damage the bank's credibility. Letters supporting the claim were also sent from members of Congress in both Argentina and Paraguay. A letter to President

Wolfensohn, signed by twenty-six NGOs from around the world, summed up their view of the stakes riding on the board's decision:

> To deny an inspection of this claim would deny the claimants the fair hearing they seek and would undermine the credibility and utility of the Inspection Panel as a forum to which directly affected local people can turn for impartial review. If a claim as strong and compelling as that presented in Yacyretá is turned away by the Board, it may be difficult for NGOs to continue to support the Panel process. We consider the Yacyretá claim to be an important test of both the Inspection Panel process and the Board's commitment to reform.[19]

The board met again three weeks later. In addition to deliberating over the panel's recommendation, the board heard a presentation from bank management about a new action plan generated by the implementing agency, EBY. The plan had two parts. Plan A addressed those environment and resettlement actions that should have been completed *prior to* filling the reservoir to seventy-six masl and Plan B proposed actions that the borrower considered necessary to continue operating the reservoir at 76 masl.

While effective actions and remedies are a desired outcome of the claims process, the board's acceptance of the action plan undermined the panel process; it gave management direct access to the board to present its point of view, without making a similar allowance for claimants, who had not been consulted, and indeed, had not even seen the action plan, and hence were unable to develop a meaningful response.

Distracted by the borrower's action plans and unable to reach consensus on the term "investigation," the board authorized the panel to undertake a *review* of the existing problems of the Yacyretá project in the areas of environment and resettlement and provide an *assessment* of the adequacy of the action plan.[20] The board gave the panel four months to complete its work.[21]

Phase 3: The Panel Opens Space for People Affected by Yacyretá

The Inspection Panel, working together with the IDB's investigation team, returned to Yacyretá in May and July of 1997. They met with municipal authorities, government, and EBY officials in both countries. The field visit also included meetings with affected people and their organizations and visits to relocation sites, where the inspectors examined crumbling houses and poorly constructed facilities. The panel had conversations with relocated families, who had lost their means of subsistence, and observed areas affected by the reservoir. The field visit gave the inspectors a vivid picture of the reality of the situation at the project site.

News that the claim had been accepted by the boards of both the World Bank and IDB, along with the presence of the two panels in the field, was a turning point for the long-neglected affected people. Years of intimidation and the lack of response from government institutions had practically destroyed the organizations of affected communities. The panel's obvious independence from EBY provided important space to citizens to voice their complaints in an atmosphere free of intimidation and disregard, and generated hope among the community organizations that their joint efforts could make a difference.

One immediate consequence of the panel's visit was that EBY began meeting with community leaders. For some, this was the first time that their complaints had elicited such a response from EBY. Practically all dam-affected groups began organizing within sectors and then formed networks across sectors. The buildup of public pressure had an effect on the government, both locally and nationally, with some officials joining in efforts to form a new organization, the "Association of Municipalities Affected by Yacyretá," to pursue compensation for communities previously denied by EBY.

The panel's field visit was not the only catalytic feature of the emerging social movement at Yacyretá, but it gave strong impetus to community organizing. Ultimately, the panel's final report and findings would provide the communities with official confirmation of their claims; they hoped to use the report to pressure EBY and the banks to accept community participation in designing solutions to their problems.

Phase 4: Shoot the Messenger

The panel delivered its report, a "review and assessment" of the Yacyretá project, to the board on September 16, 1997, almost one year after the claim was filed. The findings were unequivocal:

> Despite extensive but inconsistent supervision efforts, the Bank has failed to bring the project into compliance with relevant Bank policies and procedures due to a poorly conceived Project design in the first place, compounded by changing standards and regulations over time, EBY bureaucratic procedures and lack of financial resources.[22]

In addition to the explicit policy violations cited, the panel found fundamental inadequacies in the action plan proposed by management. It criticized bank management for failing to consult with locally affected people, and called into question the financing arrangements for completion of the action plans and for completion of the dam to eighty-three masl:

> The investment required to reach elevation 83 masl has been estimated by Management to be at least $700 million beyond [that required for execution of] Plans A and B. This however does not take into account the actual costs of remaining

expropriations (including thousands of hectares of land), resettlement of urban populations on both sides of the reservoir, and replacement of infrastructure (railroads, ports, airport) which would render the Management's estimate wholly inaccurate.[23]

The panel's report also confirmed the problems with resettlement and implementation of environmental actions that SOBREVIVENCIA and local organizations had raised in the claim and called on the World Bank and IDB to provide "financial and technical assistance to correct the harms that have been identified."[24]

Despite these findings, the board's consideration of the panel's report on Yacyretá suffered another delay. At the time the report was submitted, the board was also considering two other controversial Inspection Panel claims: Itaparica Resettlement and Irrigation Project in Brazil and the National Thermal Power Corporation (NTPC) Power Generation Project in Singrauli, India. The panel recommended inspections for both claims; the board effectively rejected both recommendations due to the continued North–South tensions and the Southern countries' organized efforts to block the panel.[25] Instead, President Wolfensohn proposed a board review of the Inspection Panel. The outcome of the collision of claims was in effect a decision to "shoot the messenger."

Thus, between September and early December 1997, the board put discussion of the panel's findings on the Yacyretá project on hold while they began a review of the panel. After months of waiting, during which the Inspection Panel's report had not officially been made public, the board finally scheduled a discussion of Yacyretá for December 9, largely because then-U.S. executive director, Jan Piercy, insisted that the claim be de-linked from the board panel review.

Donor-country executive directors had expressed great concern about the panel's findings, and were anxious for the bank to push for immediate resolution of the problems by revising the action plans with the participation of the claimants and local communities. They were concerned that the bank's economic analysis was flawed and wanted a credible analysis of the costs of raising the level of the dam to the full design height of eighty-three masl. There was also support for a follow-up role for the panel.

Any hope that the board would move in the direction of resolving the problems and prescribing remedies were dashed, however, when it finally met on December 9, 1997. The meeting was again contentious and inconclusive, with another split between North and South that resulted in yet another postponement of final decisions. The board thanked the panel for its report and asked management to report back about the progress of implementation of the action plan in six months. The board then agreed to revisit the panel's report in early 1998.

The board then went forward with its review of the panel, described in chapter 1. As part of the review, the panel convinced board members to hear directly from claimants who had practical experience with the process. On February 3, 1998, representatives from Yacyretá, Itaparica, and Arun traveled to Washington, D.C., to present their experiences to the full board and President Wolfensohn. Madhu Kohli also prepared a written statement about the Singrauli claim for the board.

LIES, DAM LIES, AND PUBLIC RELATIONS

While in Washington for the meeting with the board, Yacyretá claimant Pedro Arzamendia sent a letter to request that President Wolfensohn come to Yacyretá to see for himself the desperate living conditions of the people. A similar letter was sent to President Iglesias of the IDB. The letter also requested that the panel report be translated into Spanish and that the action plans be made available to the public, so that the affected communities could understand the panel's findings and the work that was supposed to be done to solve problems cited in the claim. The letter complained that the action plans were created without the participation of the people, and concluded, "the communities affected by the Yacyretá Project are waiting anxiously for the decision of the Directors of the World Bank, concerning the actions that the Bank will take in this case."[26]

Arzamendia returned to Encarnación with the hope that his visit to Washington would result in positive action in Paraguay. Instead, on March 20 an advertisement paid for by EBY appeared in the Paraguayan newspaper *Ultima Hora,* which reprinted a February 27 letter signed by Isabel Guerrero, the World Bank's acting vice president for Latin America and the Caribbean. Her letter was addressed to Arzamendia on behalf of President Wolfensohn, and said:

> the Bank is satisfied with the conclusions of the report which affirm that its policies on resettlements, environment, community participation, and others were fully respected and applied in the case of Yacyretá. . . . We have complete confidence in the institutions and people that work with us to implement the Action Plan agreed to.[27]

The bank's letter was published in several newspapers before having been received by either Arzamendia or SOBREVIVENCIA. The claimants were shocked that the Guerrero letter blatantly lied about the findings of the Inspection Panel report with regard to violations of bank policy. The Guerrero letter gave the impression to the Paraguayan public that the bank's official response to the Inspection Panel claim was that the bank believed that everything was fine with the project and with EBY.

On April 8, 1998, SOBREVIVENCIA wrote a letter to President Wolfensohn in response to the Guerrero letter:

> It is incomprehensible to us . . . that your name would be attached to affirmations so far from reality—deliberate affirmations by the Entidad Binacional Yacyretá to discredit sincere and honest claims regarding the deprivation of authority to community leaders and municipal authorities who request only the right to just compensation for their communities.[28]

SOBREVIVENCIA further asserted that because the panel report had not been translated into Spanish to be accessible to the local people, bank policies related to participation and information disclosure continued to be violated. SOBREVIVENCIA demanded that a new action plan be developed with the peoples' genuine participation and that the bank publish a retraction in Paraguayan newspapers to counteract the misinformation from the Guerrero letter.

Outraged by the lack of response from the bank, and especially because the Guerrero letter effectively gave EBY a license to continue to lie about the Inspection Panel findings,[29] NGOs turned to the press to get President Wolfensohn's attention. On May 4, an article in the *Financial Times,* "Row Brews over Bank Role in Dam Project," was the lead story in the bank's internal daily press file.[30] The article contrasted the Guerrero letter with the Inspection Panel's report, and referred to the bank's "apparent attempt to play down a critical report from its international inspection panel." Finally alerted to the situation, Wolfensohn was apparently angered by the actions of his staff, and for being kept in the dark.

Four days later, SOBREVIVENCIA received the first of several letters from Shahid Javed Burki, vice president for the Latin America and Caribbean region (whom Ms. Guerrero had earlier been acting on behalf of). Burki said, "Ms. Guerrero's letter . . . conveyed an *incomplete* description of the Bank Inspection Panel's Report."[31] NGOs were outraged that bank management still couldn't seem to tell the truth about the panel's findings. The Guerrero letter was inaccurate, not incomplete. Phone calls to bank external relations staff resulted in a second letter from Burki, sent on May 12, making a correction. This time, the line read "Ms. Guerrero's letter . . . conveyed an *erroneous* description of the findings of the Bank Inspection Panel's Report."[32] Burki's letter said that the bank took the Inspection Panel findings seriously and that the panel had recommended that the bank "redouble its efforts to strengthen participation, supervision and institutional capacity under two action plans." He promised to make the panel report available in Spanish, as well as the EBY action plans, and said, "In the meantime, we are confident that meetings with the affected populations and organizations representing them, will continue to take place—as they have taken place over the last year in accordance with the EBY Action Plans."[33]

Burki's comment implies that such meetings with local people were common, but again, bank management's interpretation of EBY's behavior was far from what was really taking place. Earlier in the year, hundreds of local citizens had blocked the road to Encarnación to protest the squalid conditions in the affected zone, exacerbated by abnormal flooding, and to demand a meeting with Joaquín Rodriquez, the Paraguayan head of EBY. Riot police, paid for and transported by EBY, attacked protestors with lead pipes, sending about twenty people to the hospital. Six of the protestors camped outside EBY offices and held a hunger strike for four days before Rodriguez would agree to meet with them.[34]

Quickly following the Burki letters, World Bank staff met with affected people in Encarnación. During one of these meetings, World Bank Task Manager William Partridge said, "Your petitions and requests contain factual errors and a series of false information but apart from this, it is not our role to discuss or agree with solutions in the cities of the different countries." Partridge also blamed delays in the mitigation programs on the "lack of participation and support on the part of the population."[35]

Two weeks after Burki's letter to SOBREVIVENCIA, there was still no translated Inspection Panel report, no publicly available action plan, and no retraction to the Guerrero letter in Paraguayan newspapers. Thus, despite bureaucratic pronouncements in Washington, nothing in the field was being done to counteract the original misleading letter. SOBREVIVENCIA decided to send a representative to visit the bank in Washington to find out whether anyone there had any intentions of making the truth known in Paraguay. On May 26, coauthor of this chapter, Elías Díaz Peña met with Mr. Burki and Ms. Guerrero. Mr. Burki promised that he would immediately publish a retraction, ensure the panel report was translated by the end of the week, and make the action plans publicly available. He also agreed that SOBREVIVENCIA should help to organize meetings with the affected people in Paraguay during the next mission of the bank, the week of June 16, which Burki would head.

The next day, President Wolfensohn met with Díaz Peña, along with David Hunter (CIEL), Alvaro Umaña (chair, Inspection Panel), and Shahid Javed Burki. President Wolfensohn was extremely concerned about Yacyretá and the irresponsible actions of his staff. He apologized for the way the bank had handled the Inspection Panel report and said that he was personally committed to fixing the problems at Yacyretá. He promised a translation of the report and public participation in the action plan, and directed Burki to go to the region and solve the problems. He indicated that he supported the panel and its findings "one hundred percent," and told SOBREVIVENCIA to contact him directly if things did not go well.

Not surprisingly, things did not go well. EBY took note of SOBREVIVENCIA's visit to Washington. On June 3, newspaper, radio, and television reports in Paraguay, using the head of EBY, Joaquín Rodriguez, as a source, falsely claimed that SOBREVIVENCIA was "boycotting" an emergency World Bank loan to Paraguay for repairing damages from El Niño. Rodriguez called SOBREVIVENCIA unpatriotic and politically motivated, and said they were causing harm to their own people.[36]

Misinformation escalated tensions in Paraguay. Worried about further political retaliation and possible human rights abuses in the project area, SOBREVIVENCIA, CIEL, and BIC sent another letter to Burki on June 4 asserting that the misleading allegations by EBY appeared to have had the bank's support since no retraction had yet been printed in the newspaper. The letter expressed concern that such allegations seemed to follow a "pattern of members of the Bank or EBY publicly stating that progress under the project is satisfactory to the Bank, and that the problems are being caused by the affected people or their representatives." The letter demanded that the bank immediately publish a retraction to appear in all major Paraguayan newspapers, a retraction that

> (a) acknowledges that the letter written by Ms. Guerrero was erroneous and should not have been published; (b) acknowledges that the World Bank Inspection Panel has found serious problems with the project and the Bank respects the findings of the Panel and is committed to solving the numerous social and environmental problems; and (c) states that SOBREVIVENCIA had nothing to do with the cancellation of funds to Paraguay, and that Mr. Rodriquez' published statements to the contrary are incorrect.[37]

On June 6 the bank finally took out paid advertisements in several Paraguayan newspapers that included a press statement and Burki's May 12 letter to SOBREVIVENCIA.

A "SHOCKING" SITE VISIT

In response to President Wolfensohn's instructions to fix the problems at Yacyretá, Burki led a high-level mission to Paraguay and Argentina June 18–20, 1998. The mission went to Asunción, Encarnación, and Posadas (Argentina) and, as previously agreed, the visit was partly arranged by SOBREVIVEN-

CIA. Prior to the mission, EBY had deliberately lowered the level of the reservoir, placing many previously flooded houses well above the water line. Local people showed the bank's representatives signs that the water level had been obviously lowered rapidly, and was now lower than at any time since the reservoir was first created in 1994.

For the first time, SOBREVIVENCIA and local leaders were given the opportunity to explain the reality of their situation to bank management. The mission was taken to neighborhoods where Burki talked to affected people. A public meeting in Encarnación attracted over one thousand people; many testified about the way their lives had been impoverished by Yacyretá. At the end of the meeting, Burki, a native of Pakistan, summed up by saying, "I come from one of the poorest countries on earth and I have never seen such misery as I have seen here today."[38]

Vice President Burki's report back to the board of directors described the misery, poverty, hunger, and complete lack of social services in the dam's area of influence in Paraguay. The mission observed that the situation was probably worse than when the panel went to the field in 1997, and acknowledged that the reservoir was not being maintained at seventy-six masl. Indeed, the mission admitted that thousands of people had been displaced by the reservoir *above* seventy-six masl:

> Some of the most serious social problems stem from the fact that hundreds, if not thousands of people have been displaced by the seasonal rise of the reservoir waters beyond level 76m, while they may not be considered as eligible project beneficiaries, having not been covered in the census taken in 1990.[39]

Bank management acknowledged that families not covered by the original resettlement census were nevertheless living in extreme poverty and needed to be included in some type of development plan.

> To sum up our impression from the Paraguay field visit: we were shocked to see the situation on the ground. More people than the original census of 1990 would suggest, have been touched by the project, and many live in utmost poverty right next to one of the World's grand engineering achievements. So far, because of a legalistic rather than a social welfare approach, their plight is addressed neither by EBY nor by the local Paraguayan Government in a satisfactory way.[40]

NO ACCOUNTABILITY, LITTLE PROGRESS

Nearly five years after Burki's visit, and almost six years after the two Inspection Panels issued their reports on Yacyretá, there had been no World

Bank or IDB board mandates to directly solve the problems at Yacyretá and bank management had done little to follow up to ensure that the action plans were being implemented

Despite the lack of effective action on Yacyretá, both the World Bank and IDB to some extent improved their attitude with respect to the affected populations' claims. During 1998, the IDB carried out a series of meetings and workshops with local affected peoples' organizations, NGOs, and local governments to discuss possible solutions. A Multi-Sectoral Forum was created, which included representatives of EBY, members of the national Parliament, the IDB, the World Bank, the Coordination of Affected Peoples Organizations, NGOs, local governments, and national government institutions. The World Bank changed staff and named new project managers for Yacyretá, both in Buenos Aires and Asunción

Dramatic social and political events in Paraguay during March 1999, led by organized civil society, resulted in a total change of the government. These events also marked a milestone in the process of participation of the communities affected by Yacyretá. The Paraguayan director of EBY was changed and a new round of dialogue was initiated within the framework of the Multi-Sectoral Forum. The coordinator of the forum was appointed to the board of directors of EBY and new hopes were raised among affected populations that their participation in the design and implementation of the mitigation and compensation plans would finally be effective and significant.

Unfortunately, concrete solutions to the problems caused by Yacyretá are not in sight. To date, there has been no credible evaluation to assess the real social, environmental, and economic impacts that the present level of the reservoir has caused. Both governments are still committed to raising the elevation of the reservoir level to eighty-three masl and are trying to minimize the costs to EBY for resettlement, compensation, and environmental mitigation measures.

Despite these ongoing problems, civil-society organizations in the region have expanded their activities and built better and larger alliances to resist and propose solutions to the damage caused by Yacyretá, as well as other proposed or existing large dams in the region. The NGO pressure on the banks and EBY has grown more organized and coordinated, with Argentine organizations, which are part of the transnational Rios Vivos Coalition, joining the Paraguayan organizations to monitor the project. This alliance is making concrete recommendations for the finalization of the Yacyretá project and has launched a campaign based on these recommendations called "Yacyretá, No More DAMage."[41]

Meanwhile, the organization of communities affected by Yacyretá, called FEDAYIM (Federación de Afectados por Yacyretá de Itapua y Misiones), presented a new claim to the World Bank Inspection Panel and the Independent Inspection Mechanism of the IDB in May 2002—nearly six years after the original claim was filed. This new claim includes the cases of families affected by the increase of flooding in urban areas; environmental degradation and pollution caused by the reservoir, and the subsequent impacts on public health, lack of proper compensation, and relocation to affected families, and more. In August 2002, the World Bank Board of Directors accepted the claim, and as we go to press, the Inspection Panel is investigating. Organizations from Argentina are considering the presentation of another claim to both banks' Inspection Panels, concerning the leakage of reservoir water to the Ibera wetlands in Argentina. The IDB has yet to respond to the claimants.[42]

CONCLUSION

The Yacyretá claims process has been an enormous challenge for those who initiated the claim, as well as for all of the actors who have tried to move it through the bank. What are the outcomes of this process? Has the claim resulted in accountability? Have social and environmental problems been resolved to the satisfaction of the claimants?

Institutional Accountability Remains Illusory

Despite all of the efforts during the Yacyretá claim process, the bank's management and executive directors have not been held accountable for the persistent social, environmental, and economic consequences of the Yacyretá project. The Paraguayan and Argentine people are still paying the price for the institutions' failures. Indeed, even with an inspections panel, individual and institutional accountability remains elusive.[43]

The bank's culture also fosters an environment in which bank staff tend to deflect the blame for failures from themselves onto the borrowing governments (which are often acting on advice and instructions from the bank). Given the historic problems with EBY, it has been easy for bank staff to accuse it of failing to implement bank policies. Indeed, bank staff often tried to portray themselves as champions of the people in the face of EBY's obstreperous bureaucracy, claiming that they put pressure on EBY to consult with affected citizens. The long time span of projects such as Yacyretá also leads to high staff turnover, which results in staff avoiding responsibility. Consequences that are felt today can often be ascribed to decisions taken by someone else years ago. The 1992 World Bank loan had four task managers in eight years.

The board's final role in the Inspection Panel process, as outlined in the resolution, is to consider the findings of the panel and to determine what action, if any, should be taken. Granted, the language in the resolution is weak and does not actually compel the board to assign remedies. The board exists to make decisions for the institution and the *expectation* is that it should not simply hear findings but also address them. On each occasion when the board had the responsibility to discuss Yacyretá, it met informally, came to no conclusions, and delayed any action into the future. The only actors who consistently followed the panel procedures were the claimants and the panel (see box 4.1). As we have seen, the other actors in the process—management and the board—undermined and subverted the process to avoid accountability.

Active Involvement of International Civil Society Is Essential

The bank is almost impenetrable to most citizens: it is a large and complex institution removed from the communities affected by bank-financed projects. In the case of Yacyretá, in order for the claims process to be used, Paraguayan citizens needed contact with international NGOs to learn that the Inspection Panel was an option. In preparing their claim, citizens also relied on NGOs that understood bank policies to determine which applied in the Yacyretá project and how their experiences may have been a result of violations of those policies.

As in other cases cited in this book, as soon as the panel accepted the Yacyretá claim, the claimants were officially left out of the process. While the panel met with claimants both in Washington, D.C., and in country, the claimants did not have formal access to the process. Their only recourse was to engage with international NGOs that could in effect be their advocates in front of executive directors and management, and to the international press. With Yacyretá, NGOs in Washington had to monitor the progress of the claim relentlessly to keep SOBREVIVENCIA and the local claimants informed.

The politicization of Yacyretá also forced the international NGO community to generate pressure on the board of directors and President Wolfensohn to approve an investigation. Without that pressure, the board would have swept Yacyretá under the rug. Without an organized international civil society, and especially without advocates in Washington, the claimants would have been completely at the mercy of bank management's attempts to whitewash the panel's report in the Paraguayan press. The necessity for such an organized civil society is disappointing but not surprising. The Yacyretá claimants went to great lengths to establish the legitimacy of their claim, following all of the rules and procedures, including many years of field work documenting the dam's problems. When the panel accepted their claims as valid and worthy of an inspection, the claimants should have been able to rely on the bank to implement its part of the bargain. Unfortunately, bank policies and procedures are not necessarily complied with unless there are aggressive public interest watchdogs ensuring that those in power implement them.

But even with policies and watchdogs, both externally and internally, one cannot conclude that the claims process has led to accountability. Ongoing attempts by a coalition of local citizens' organizations, municipal and provincial governments, and NGOs to insert themselves in a process of problem solving with the banks and EBY have been thwarted by continued lack of access to meaningful participation. Due process does not exist at the World Bank, and without a more democratic governance structure at the institution, the bank will continue to act with impunity.

The Panel Process Fosters Citizen Empowerment

Despite these serious shortcomings, citizens affected by Yacyretá have been able to use the Inspection Panel as a way to legitimately challenge the banks, EBY, and governments. The policy and accountability mechanisms that the banks themselves have made available gave the claimants tools to prove that they have been harmed by the failure of the World Bank and the IDB to enforce the policies and loan agreements that were designed to protect them. The panel reports of both the World Bank and IDB confirmed that the problems are real and that the responsibility for correcting them lies with the official actors. Moreover, the reports underscore the absolute necessity of effective public participation in overcoming years of distrust and suspicion, which has become the main obstacle to problem solving at Yacyretá.

The people affected by Yacyretá still have a long struggle in front of them. They continue to demand that the negative social, economic, and environmental impacts be satisfactorily solved and compensated. Citizens empowered by the findings of the Inspection Panel have called on the banks, EBY, and both governments to establish a permanent independent monitoring mechanism with the power to assess the impacts of the dam at the present level of the reservoir and the potential impacts at the final stage of the reservoir at eighty-three masl. They are demanding that the mechanism incorporate their full participation in the design and implementation of solutions. Even though the banks' boards have not responded formally to the claim, the citizens have. They are demanding that their voices be heard and that their rights are upheld; and they are engaged in a process of creating the solutions to their own problems.

Box 4.1. The Panel Process Reviewed
by Local Community Leaders

SOBREVIVENCIA interviewed five key local community leaders to gauge their feelings and thoughts about the Inspection Panel process. A brief summary of their responses follows:[44]

- Panelists were honest people, genuinely concerned about the problems caused by the project. They contacted the affected people directly and saw the situation in the field themselves.
- Panelists induced hope among affected people; motivated their organization; and fostered strength, optimism, and self-confidence in local organizations.
- Local community leaders learned about the banks and their policies, particularly those related to the rights of populations affected by projects financed by the banks. Community leaders also learned about EBY's structure and functioning. A lot of information that had been withheld by EBY was made available to the people through the panel process.
- The affected population shed their fear of EBY, learned to take matters into their own hands with regard to claims for their rights, and became confident in their ability to solve problems by themselves.
- Thanks to the strengthening of local community organizations and the respect shown to them by both panels, local and national authorities listened to and respected these organizations. Participation of affected communities in discussions with EBY's officials only started with the Inspection Panel process.
- EBY and the banks were forced to recognize the problems caused by the project. As a result, some mitigation projects have been designed, albeit without the participation of affected communities, civil-society organizations, or local governments; these projects were then ineffectively implemented.
- Local community leaders and many people from all sectors of society have realized that the elevation of the reservoir to its designed final level is not viable when its social, economic, and environmental consequences are taken into consideration.
- The Inspection Panel's recommendations should have been binding for the banks and for EBY, and their implementation should have been monitored by the panel itself. This would be the only way to assure that the panel's findings and recommendations are effectively implemented. The way it is now, the panel is an institution that cannot actually make significant changes within the bank or in the projects.

NOTES

1. Inspection Panel, "Request for Inspection, Argentina/Paraguay: Yacyretá Hydroelectric Project Panel Report and Recommendation," December 24, 1996 (hereinafter "Panel Recommendation").

2. For a critical history, see Gustavo Lins Ribeiro, *Transnational Capitalism and Hydropolitics in Argentina: The Yacyretá High Dams* (Gainesville: University of Florida Press, 1994). For impact on the region's people and the local social movements, see Carmen A. Ferradas, *Power in the Southern Cone Borderlands: An Anthropology of Development Practice* (Westport, Conn.: Bergin and Garvey, 1998).

3. Current estimates of the costs to complete the project run at $8 to $10 billion and it is more than eleven years behind schedule (Inspection Panel, "Review of Problems and Assessment of Action Plans, Argentina/Paraguay: Yacyretá Hydroelectric Project," September 16, 1997 [hereinafter "Panel Review and Assessment"]).

4. World Bank loans totaled $895 million; IDB loans totaled $840 million. Amounts compiled from official World Bank and IDB project documents, on file with the authors.

5. See Robert Wade, "Greening the World Bank: The Struggle over the Environment, 1970–1995," *The World Bank: Its First Half-Century*, ed. Devesh Kapur, John P. Lewis, and Richard Webb (Washington, D.C.: Brookings, 1997), 2: 611.

6. Ing. Juan David Quintero Sagre et al., "Informe de Evaluación Ambiental Proyecto Hidroeléctrico Yacyretá," report prepared for EBY, May 30, 1992, and Maria Clara Mejia, "Plan de Acción para el Reasentamiento y Rehabilitación: Informe Final," report prepared for EBY, April 1992.

7. The NGOs included SOBREVIVENCIA, Centro de Estudios Ambientales, FUNAM (Fundación para la Defensa del Ambiente, or Environment Defense Foundation), International Rivers Network, and BIC.

8. Comments made by SOBREVIVENCIA at the IDB consultation on the Yacyretá Environmental Assessment and Resettlement Plan. The consultation was held in Ayolas, Paraguay, in July 1993.

9. Inspection Panel, "Request for Inspection, Yacyretá Hyrdroelectric Project," September 1996, 1 (hereinafter "Request for Inspection").

10. Privatization of the operation of Yacyretá would require the approval of both the Argentine and Paraguayan Congresses; the necessary legislation failed in both.

11. For an analysis of the IDB's mechanism, see Angus Wright, "Reflections of a Member of the Inter-American Development Bank Inspection Panel" (paper presented at the 1998 International Congress of the Latin American Studies Association, Chicago, September 24–26, 1998).

12. Because of the potential for retaliation, the claim states, "the names of those persons who have authorized SOBREVIVENCIA to represent their interests have been made available only to the World Bank Inspection Panel and are otherwise to remain confidential" ("Request for Inspection," paragraph 1).

13. "Request for Inspection," paragraph 3.

14. "Request for Inspection," paragraph 4.

15. "Panel Recommendation," paragraphs 26 and 29 to 31.

16. World Bank, "Argentina, Second Yacyretá Hydroelectric Project Management Response to the Request for Inspection," September 30, 1996 (hereinafter "Management Response").

17. Julio Nogues, statement to the board of directors of the World Bank, "Yacyretá Hydroelectric Project, Panel Report and Recommendation," February 5, 1997. An important precedent was set by the panel in response to challenges to the eligibility of the claimants. In their recommendation for an investigation, the panel found that despite the panel resolution, which established that claimants needed to come from the "territory of the borrower," claimants from Paraguay had standing in this case because they were directly affected by the project. Thus, they were able to overcome the eligibility objections of both the bank management and Julio Nogues.

18. This assessment is based on discussions between Kay Treakle and staff from board members' offices who attended the meeting.

19. Dana Clark and David Hunter, CIEL, on behalf of twenty-five undersigned organizations, to Wolfensohn, January 31, 1997 (on file with the authors).

20. Emphasis added.

21. The IDB's board of directors waited until after the World Bank Board had taken action, and then followed suit with the appointment of its own panel of three investigators, headed by Angus Wright. For an analysis of the IDB's process, see Wright, "Reflections," 4.

22. "Panel Review and Assessment," 4.

23. "Panel Review and Assessment," 5.

24. "Panel Review and Assessment," 5.

25. See chapters 7 and 8 on Itaparica and Singrauli.

26. Pedro Arzamendia to Wolfensohn, February 1, 1998 (on file with the authors).

27. Isabel Guerrero, acting World Bank vice president for Latin America, to Pedro Arzemendia, February 27, 1998, as printed in *Ultima Hora* (Paraguay), March 20, 1998.

28. SOBREVIVENCIA to Wolfensohn, April 8, 1998 (on file with the authors).

29. EBY's official comments on the Inspection Panel denounced the panel members as communists, and at one point they asserted that the panel had been eliminated from the bank ("Técnicos del Banco Mundial; Unos agitadores comunistas?" *ABC Color* [Asunción, Paraguay], January 14, 1998, and "Acusan de revoltosos y comunistas a funcionarios del Banco Mundial," *Noticias* [Asunción, Paraguay], January 14, 1998).

30. "Row Brews over Bank Role in Dam Project," *Financial Times,* May 4, 1998.

31. Shahid Javed Burki to SOBREVIVENCIA, May 8, 1998 (on file with the authors; emphasis added).

32. Burki to SOBREVIVENCIA, May 12, 1998 (on file with the authors; emphasis added).

33. Burki to SOBREVIVENCIA, May 12, 1998.

34. "Violenta represión contra afectados," *Nacionales,* February 26, 1998, 28, and "Yacyretá y la ley de garrote," *ABC Color,* February 16, 1998, 55 (on file with the authors).

35. "El Banco Mundial Apoya Política de la EBY," *Noticias* (Asunción, Paraguay), May 18, 1998 (on file with the authors).

36. "Sobrevivencia Quiere Biocotear un Préstamo para el Paraguay," *Noticias* (Asunción, Paraguay), June 3, 1998 (on file with the authors).

37. SOBREVIVENCIA, CIEL, and BIC to Shahid Javed Burki, June 4, 1998 (on file with the authors).

38. Abid Aslam, "Development–Paraguay: World Bank to Bill Its Victims," Inter Press Service, June 25, 1998 (on file with the authors).

39. From the staff presentation reporting back to the World Bank Board of Directors on June 23, 1998 (report on file with the authors).

40. Staff presentation to the World Bank Board of Directors, June 23, 1998.

41. SOBREVIVENCIA–Paraguay, "Yacyretá, No More DAMage," June 2002.

42. See February 18, 2003, letter to IDB President Enrique Iglesias from BIC on behalf of NGOs and claimants from Latin America, concerning the IDB's lack of responsiveness to the Yacyretá claim and two others that were filed with their Independent Investigation Mechanism, available online at www.bicusa.org [accessed May 24, 2003].

43. The task manager responsible for Yacyretá during the claim process, William Partridge, was reportedly fired for having written the Guerrero letter that lied to the Paraguayan people about the outcome of the claim.

44. Interviews for this section were conducted in Encarnación, Paraguay, by Elías Díaz Peña. Interviews with Jorge Urusoff were conducted in September and December 2001, and July and October 2002. Interviews with Angela Miranda were conducted in December 2001 and October 2002. Both Urusoff and Miranda are leaders of an affected peoples' organization, FEDAYIM, which presented the second Yacyretá claim to the Inspection Panel in May 2002.

5

The Experience of Jamuna Bridge: Issues and Perspectives

Majibul Huq Dulu[1]

REALIZING A DREAM: THE JAMUNA BRIDGE

The Jamuna is one of the world's largest rivers. It originates in western Tibet and flows through northeastern India, where it is known as the Brahmaputra, and then flows south through Bangladesh before joining the Ganges and discharging into the Bay of Bengal. The Jamuna is also known as the "dancing river," because it constantly shifts its boundaries and over the years has been known to completely change channel and location. The river forms a geographic barrier that divides the western half of Bangladesh from the east. During monsoon season, the braided Jamuna swells to twenty kilometers wide in places.

The decision to build a bridge across the Jamuna enjoyed widespread political support in Bangladesh and the bridge became a symbol of national unity, linking the two halves of the country and providing reliable transportation across the river. In addition to automobiles, the bridge also supports a railway line, an electric power line, telecommunications facilities, and a gas pipeline. The objective of the project was to stimulate "economic growth by facilitating cross-river transport of passengers, freight and transmission of power."[2]

The Jamuna Bridge project was financed by the World Bank, the Asian Development Bank, the Japanese Oversees Economic Cooperation Fund, and the government of Bangladesh. The government began raising money for the project in the early 1980s, when it introduced the "Jamuna surcharge," a tax levied on a wide array of goods and services, through which virtually everyone in Bangladesh contributed to the Jamuna Bridge.[3] The World Bank loan for approximately $200 million was approved by the board of executive directors on

February 25, 1994.[4] The bridge was inaugurated on June 23, 1998. The Jamuna Multipurpose Bridge Authority (JMBA), the government agency in charge of all undertakings related to the bridge, posted a sign at the bridge proclaiming: "Welcome to the miracle over the Jamuna. Once a dream, today reality."[5]

As the project got underway, the planners decided to channelize the Jamuna, reinforcing the banks with rocks and concrete to narrow the river underneath the bridge. The theory was that this would minimize the length of the bridge and thereby save construction costs, although it was recognized that there was a significant risk that the bridge would be suspended over a dry riverbed if the Jamuna continued to shift her boundaries. The decision to narrow the broad and shifting Jamuna had serious impacts on the flow of the river. The river currents were altered and intensified by the construction, making erosion less predictable and more rapid.

These impacts on the flow of the river meant that life was less secure for the people living on sandy islands called *chars* that exist in the midst of, and are frequently flooded and eroded by, the ever-shifting Jamuna River. As this case study will show, the country's long-awaited dream caused nightmares for the people who live on the islands in the Jamuna.

The Jamuna Char Integrated Development Project (JCDP), an NGO working with local people living on the chars in the Jamuna River, tried repeatedly to call on project authorities to respect the rights of the *char* people. JCDP pointed out that the char people were bearing significant impacts from the construction yet had been excluded from project planning and design, as well as from the compensation packages being developed for resettlement. The original resettlement plan focused only on the people living on the mainland.

As this chapter will explain, JCDP's advocacy efforts on behalf of the char people, including a claim to the World Bank Inspection Panel, resulted in significant changes in project design and the development of an Erosion and Flood Policy to compensate for losses caused within a particular impact area of the bridge. There have been problems in implementation, however, which have undermined the effectiveness of the remedy to the policy violations.

Life on the Chars

Approximately five hundred thousand people live on chars in the Jamuna River in Bangladesh.[6] They are among the poorest and most vulnerable people in the country.[7] Public facilities such as schools and health centers are rare, and most char people have no formal education. The char people's primary economic activity is agriculture, which they supplement with fishing, small trade, wage labor, and animal husbandry. Older chars have dense vegetation cover, and are planted with rice, jute, wheat, pulses, and vegetables.

Despite the challenges, families have lived on chars for generations, and they hold legal land ownership documents. They have developed methods for identifying shifting lands and establishing ownership. If a homestead is flooded during the monsoon, people will temporarily live on the rooftops of their submerged houses until the waters recede. They shift their livestock to the nearest flood shelter, embankment, or road. When a char is eroded, the inhabitants will shift to a neighboring char, rebuild their village, and keep the same village name. Kinship groups move together, helping each other in times of crises. Occasionally, char families will take shelter on the road or embankments of the mainland, but they return to the chars as quickly as possible. In this environment, land is clearly the most important asset.

Although char people face a great deal of prejudice and discrimination from mainland people, they are proud of their identity and their way of life. "On the chars we are free as birds. We move from one place to another," stated Iqbal Akanda.[8] Char society is characterized by mutual help and solidarity, often reflected in common laws and obligations. "We always help each other. If a family's homestead is eroded, they can move to any other place, without asking the owner, because tomorrow the owner could be in the same situation," Shamsul Hoque Khandoker explained.[9]

Impact of the Jamuna Bridge on the Char People

Although the char people have adapted to the river's normal floods and erosion, they have suffered badly from human interference with the flow of the river. The living conditions in the impact area of the Jamuna Bridge have deteriorated severely since river-training construction relating to the bridge began in 1994, especially for char-dwellers who used to live in the vicinity of the bridge and the main channel northwest of the bridge.[10] Some chars that had been stable for more than thirty years were washed away within a few days, leaving the inhabitants with little opportunity to salvage their belongings or harvest crops. Due to increased intensity of erosion and instability of the chars, many families have had to move three or more times since the bridge construction began.

In addition to the increased erosion and flooding resulting in loss of homesteads, agriculture, livestock, and income, the char people have also suffered from a severe disruption of social and cultural traditions. Some of the people whose land has been eroded are now living in slum-like conditions on the mainland, where they have shifted to nontraditional work as day laborers and rickshaw-pullers. Traditional occupations such as gardening and animal husbandry are impossible on the mainland due to lack of space. Charwomen in particular have suffered severe deterioration of their living conditions, social status, and personal security. Having been relatively free on the chars to visit neighbors and other villages, they are now bound to the home; otherwise, they are harassed by the mainland men. The women also reported tensions within the family as their husbands became unemployed.[11]

Ignoring the Char People

The World Bank and the JMBA prepared a resettlement action plan for about one hundred thousand mainland people displaced from about three thousand hectares of land that was acquired for the approach roads, guide bunds, bridge, and additional infrastructure.[12] The project plans, however, largely ignored the impact of the bridge on the people living on the chars. It is not clear whether the char-dwellers were intentionally ignored to save money or whether the failure to take their plight into consideration was simply the result of an oversight by project planners. In any case, the fact remains that no compensation measures were planned for the char people until the JCDP, the only local NGO working in that area, filed a request for inspection to the Inspection Panel on August 18, 1996.

The project authorities should have been aware of the potential impacts on the char people and should have taken steps to explicitly include them in the resettlement plan and compensation packages. World Bank staff in Washington, D.C., wrote letters to the JMBA and the bank's Dhaka mission, asking about provisions taken for the inhabitants of the islands.[13] The standard response from the Dhaka mission was that erosion is a natural phenomenon, and that it would be impossible to assess the degree to which future erosion was caused by the impacts of the bridge. The JMBA and World Bank Dhaka argued that a compensation package for char people was impractical because the impact of the bridge on the chars would only be measurable after the embankments were completed.

The Role of the Jamuna Char Integrated Development Project

The JCDP was created in 1990 with the mission of improving the lives and livelihood of char-dwellers. JCDP works on capacity-building among char-dwellers to address issues of education, livelihood, and disaster preparedness. JCDP also helps provide basic services like health, education, and infrastructure for coping with floods.

Besides working on development projects to improve the living conditions of the char people, the author became active on World Bank policy issues in the late 1980s, in opposition to the World Bank–supported Flood Action Plan (FAP), which originally aimed to embank all the major rivers in Bangladesh, including the Jamuna, a plan that would have had serious environmental impacts and would have endangered the chars through increased erosion.[14] An international campaign against the FAP resulted in significant changes to the plan. Although JCDP had established contacts with organizations in the United States, The Netherlands, and Germany during the FAP campaign, these contacts had not continued beyond FAP, and thus JCDP did not have a broad base of international support when filing the Jamuna Bridge claim.[15]

THE ORIGIN OF THE CLAIM PROCESS

Frustrating Attempts to Raise Concerns with World Bank and Project Authorities

From the time construction of the bridge project started in 1994, JCDP repeatedly wrote letters to and requested meetings with World Bank staff in Dhaka, the Ministry of Finance, the Ministry of Communication, and the JMBA. JCDP was hoping to raise project authorities' awareness about the disastrous impact of the bridge project on the char-dwellers and the urgent need for mitigation measures and compensation.[16]

JCDP spent a considerable amount of time and money trying to make the government of Bangladesh and the World Bank staff aware of the need to consider the impacts on the char people. The NGO asked the responsible authorities if studies had been conducted on the impact of the bridge on the livelihoods of the inhabitants of the islands, and which compensation measures were planned for these people. Few of the letters received a reply, and when the World Bank Dhaka officials eventually took the time to meet with JCDP, they said "On the chars? Only ducks are living out there in those sandy lands."[17]

The char-dwellers themselves revealed the problems with the project and requested JCDP to act on their behalf. Based on past experience with the FAP, JCDP took a multipronged approach to the bridge campaign—social mobilization, lobbying, and advocacy. Social mobilization originated at the grassroots, through committees and groups formed by local people, with elected public representatives. This grassroots mobilization framed the issues within the ambit of constitutional rights and the World Bank's policy framework. It reflected the perspectives of the local people who, from the beginning, had been demanding that the project authorities pay attention to causes of displacement and destruction of livelihood and threats to survival emanating from the project-induced factors. JCDP drew on international lobbying with organizations—NGOs, foundations, European lobby groups, World Bank executive directors, parliamentarians, journalists, and environmental activists—to exert pressure on donors involved in the project to address the plight of the char people.

Challenges to Filing a Claim: Lack of Access to Information

As mentioned before, most of JCDP's letters to the JMBA and the World Bank office in Dhaka received no reply, and meetings were often cancelled at the last moment.[18] The process of writing letters and seeking project documents took several months, until eventually JCDP gave up or managed to get documents from another source. The organizations—JMBA, the World Bank, and later BRAC (the Bangladesh Rural Advancement Committee)—either did not react to the letters or would reply that requested documents were with another party.

By refusing or delaying access to documents and project information, the project authorities frustrated JCDP's ability to take action, as written documents are necessary to make an argument viable. Starting in late 1994, JCDP sent approximately sixty-five letters and two hundred e-mails to the World Bank office in Dhaka, World Bank management in Washington, D.C., the JMBA, the government of Bangladesh, BRAC, and the Inspection Panel, in addition to telephone calls and meetings. For example, in January 1995, JCDP wrote to the World Bank's Dhaka office to summarize the concerns and frustrations of the char people:

> Again, I would like to draw your attention to the fact that the construction of Jamuna Multi-purpose Bridge would likely to have severe adverse affect on the lives and livelihood of the char dwellers. . . . It is evident from the document of the JMBA authority that the resettlement and rehabilitation issues of char people haven't been taken into account. In order to reveal all these above mentioned aspects and to devise a strategy to deal with them, we intended to launch a process of dialogue with World Bank which unfortunately seem to be unsuccessful because of WB's apparent silence. We indeed, would like to draw Bank's attention to the problems and hope that a fruitful process could be launched as immediate as possible.[19]

The next hurdle to filing a claim was to learn that the Inspection Panel existed. JCDP came to know about the panel process from a World Bank consultant working in the region in 1995, but the next challenge was to get information about how the panel operated. Finally, JCDP requested and received a copy of the Inspection Panel policy and procedures. However, once JCDP got access to documents relevant for filing the request for inspection, it was very difficult to understand them. None of the documents—the project documents, bank policies, or panel procedures—were available in Bengali, and the English version contained technical terminology that was challenging for the requesters. Since JCDP did not have access to the Internet at that time, it also lacked information or guidance from other requests that had been filed with the Inspection Panel.

Preparing the Claim

The decision to approach the Inspection Panel was taken after more than one year of attempts to get attention from institutions and organizations within Bangladesh, most importantly the World Bank and the JMBA. To file a request for inspection was the last step, which JCDP tried to avoid with every possible means. Once it decided to file a claim, JCDP did a substantial amount of work with limited resources to investigate the Inspection Panel process and prepare extensive documentation to support the claim. It was a daunting task for JCDP to fulfill the criteria set by the Inspection Panel. Initial efforts were directed toward collecting information to corroborate that the Jamuna Bridge would have an immediate and long-term effect on the lives, livelihood, and socioeconomic structure of char people.

To meet this challenge, JCDP carried out an in-depth investigation that reached out to thousands of people.[20] JCDP undertook a baseline survey of seventy-five char villages in 1996 to collect information about the number of villages, households, schools, mosques, crops, and other information.[21] JCDP attached an annex to the claim, which summarizes the results of the baseline survey and "identifies 75 chars by name and indicates for each its settlement pattern, main agricultural products, nature of vegetation, type of housing, economic activities of char people other than agriculture, and provides a brief socio-economic assessment."[22] JCDP also had to establish that the char people had land title and were paying taxes. The lack of communication facilities between chars made the effort to collect signatures and land ownership documents very time-consuming and difficult.

As it worked to prepare the claim, JCDP was also continuing to try to get information from World Bank officials and the JMBA. JCDP analyzed project documents and bank policies. In preparing the analysis for the claim, JCDP found that the environmental impact assessment admitted, although in a limited and conservative way, the effect of the bridge on char people.[23]

REQUEST TO THE INSPECTION PANEL

JCDP wanted to solve this problem within Bangladesh and tried all possible ways to convince the authorities to comply with operational directives of the World Bank, to no avail. Therefore, on August 18, 1996, JCDP filed a request to the World Bank Inspection Panel on behalf of the char people.[24] More than three thousand char people provided signatures or thumb prints for the claim, authorizing JCDP to act on their behalf. The letters of authorization stated, "we protest against the pervasive destruction and damages caused by Jamuna

Multi-purpose Bridge and press home the demand to incorporate us in compensation and mitigation plans."[25]

JCDP claimed that the project omitted compensation provisions for the char-dwellers, that the affected communities had not been consulted about either impacts or mitigation related to the project, and that these failures would adversely offset JCDP's development efforts in the chars and result in aggravated poverty. The claim illustrated in detail the specific damages already affecting some chars, for which the people had not been appropriately compensated. JCDP argued that the policy violations would lead to additional direct and material adverse effects on the chars, the char people and their livelihood:

> Chars, unique in land type and settlement history, distinct in mode of life and existence, are at stake, specially in the Jamuna region, owing to the changes to the river channel as well as river morphology caused by the Jamuna Multipurpose Bridge Project. . . .
>
> We appeal to the inspection panel, to stand beside us in support of our right to survive, sustain our long-standing knowledge, and protect the social coherence achieved through our perennial struggle for lives and livelihood.
>
> Damage to ecological balance to such a degree because of this kind of human actions amounts to a deliberate denial of our right to live or exist. Our existence is rooted in the process of erosion and accretion, appearance and disappearance of chars. We derive our subsistence from the land and water, the char and the river. Our agriculture, fishery, transportation, rituals, social harmony have an inseparable link with the river. The Jamuna Bridge, as predicted and already proved (to our dismay) is severely dismantling all these.
>
> Mitigatory plans, apparently well-fashioned and envisaged in order to comply with official order, have neither taken notice of these issues, nor are aware of the fact that the chars are not a barren land but are full of cacophony of life, both human and non-human. We urge all to be aware of this fact. This is of vital importance that we the people of char have experienced several embankments, existent or planned to protect the mainland people, and at the cost of our lives and livelihood. . . . We, the char people, who have acquired the knowledge from experience through ages and apply those in every step of our life, clearly understand that we and our nature around us have become undue victims of the bridge project.[26]

The claim alleged violations of the bank's policies on Environmental Assessment (OD 4.01 and annexes), Involuntary Resettlement (OD 4.30), and Involvement of NGOs in Bank-Supported Activities (OD 14.70). The char people did not participate in the development of the resettlement plan. The claim noted that 74 percent of the people interviewed by JCDP had "said there had been no official attempt to inform them about the plans undertaken by the authority having direct impact on their lives and livelihood."[27] Disclosure of information was deliberately obstructed.

Backlash against JCDP

The request for inspection took the project authorities by surprise. It was a shock for the institutions in Bangladesh, and their reaction was in turn a shock for JCDP. Just a few days after the request had been sent to the Inspection Panel, representatives of JMBA and officials from the World Bank office in Dhaka started to threaten JCDP, asking them to immediately stop their activities regarding the impact of the bridge.[28]

The government of Bangladesh, primarily the Ministry of Communication, threatened directly and indirectly to stop JCDP's work.[29] The director of JCDP, Majibul Huq Dulu, was warned to stop speaking out about the bridge. The staff of JCDP received numerous telephone calls and encountered threats. Most of the national newspapers published articles that attacked the integrity of the director and JCDP, stating that JCDP is against the Jamuna Bridge and thus against the uplift of the country, which was not, in fact, JCDP's position.[30]

In response, JCDP sent an appeal to approximately two hundred NGOs and donor agencies working on development issues in Bangladesh, explaining the decision to file a claim and seeking their support:

> After receiving complaints from the char people, our long-time partners in improving the conditions of perhaps the most vulnerable segment of Bangladesh population, we sought to find remedies. We approached the authorities concerned, especially the Jamuna Multipurpose Bridge Authority . . . but to no avail. The authorities not only ignored our plea but also sought to ignore the fact that the chars and char people did at all exist, let alone admit that these people would also be directly affected and need to be compensated. . . . As many as 17 chars have already been washed away as a result of the increased water discharge due to the narrowing of the river channel through training. These chars will never be accreted again and the inhabitants have already been forced into the state of environmental refugees. . . . The denial of compensation to these char people runs contrary to the World Bank rules on involuntary resettlement. And as part of our effort to establish people's right[s], we have been forced to lodge a complaint with the Bank's Inspection Panel, an independent body that probes into complaints from people in the Bank-financed project areas or their representatives. And we went to the Panel after being duly authorised by the representative *char* people. . . . Under the circumstances, we urge all friends and fellow fighters of people's rights to extend support and co-operation.[31]

Because of the political profile of the Jamuna Bridge, however, no other national groups would collaborate with or offer support to JCDP. Only one international donor organization, the Swiss Development Agency, replied to JCDP's appeal for support and showed its concern. The reason for others' reluctance was clear: to question the feasibility and sustainability of the Jamuna Bridge project, or to raise questions about compensation for affected people, would mean risking being labeled "antigovernment" and "antidevelopment." Most NGOs in Bangladesh avoid confrontation with international donors and the government out of fear that if they raise critical questions, the NGO Affairs Bureau of the government of Bangladesh will terminate their ability to exist and put a stop to their activities.[32] Thus, JCDP was fairly marginalized in the NGO community in Bangladesh.

Bank Management's Response: An Action Plan

On September 7, 1996, even before its response to the claim was due, bank management announced that the JMBA had approved a new policy that it described as "generous and simple," covering compensation for all erosion as well as increased flooding that adversely affects crops in the bridge impact area.[33] In its response to the claim on September 20, management stated that the char people would receive compensation through the new Erosion and Flood Policy (EFP), which would supplement the project's Revised Resettlement Action Plan (RRAP) and the Environmental Action Plan (EAP).[34] The project resettlement plan had addressed those on the mainland affected by the construction approach road and structural changes to the riverbanks. The EFP applies to char people as well as those living on the riverbanks and provides that those "who experience erosion for any reason will be compensated, and those affected by increased flooding due to the bridge will also be compensated."[35] The plan demarcated an area that would be eligible for compensation for losses due to erosion and floods.

Management's response also stated that "for some time" the bank had shared "the concerns expressed to the Inspection Panel by the char dwellers."[36] Management insisted that it had been planning to implement the RRAP in stages and that the bank simply hadn't been able to identify the affected char people prior to the claim. The bank further noted that it had been requesting an erosion and flood policy from the government since 1994, but that the "completely new concept of compensating project-induced erosion and flooding raised complex political and technical issues and led to substantial debate and controversy."[37] The government was concerned about the precedent that would be created by such a compensation plan.[38] Bank management noted, correctly, that the EFP "represents a new era in environmental legislation and practice in Bangladesh. The EFP includes compensation for all erosion in the bridge impact area, whether due to bridge impact or any other factor. Increased flooding that adversely affects crops would also be compensated."[39]

In this case, management essentially alleged that it intended to bring the project into compliance with bank policies and that the EFP would satisfactorily address the claimants' concerns. This type of response from bank management has been rare in the Inspection Panel process, though it is consistent with the Inspection Panel procedures governing management's response: "Management shall provide the Panel with evidence that it has complied, or intends to comply with the Bank's relevant policies and procedures."[40] The panel's job was to evaluate the eligibility of the claim, the degree to which management's response seemed likely to bring the project into compliance with bank policies, and the extent to which it remedied past problems.

The Panel's Preliminary Assessment of the Claim and Management's Response

In light of management's response and action plan, the panel requested and received an extension of time within which to conduct its preliminary assessment of the claim and management's response. The Inspection Panel interviewed bank staff in Washington, reviewed bank files, evaluated the EFP, and conducted a five-day field visit to the project area and Dhaka in October 1996. The panel met with some of the requesters, visited the chars, and met with representatives of the World Bank, the government of Bangladesh and the JMBA.

During its visit to the project area, the panel flew to the bridge site by helicopter, which minimized its interaction with local people. There were communication failures and scheduling difficulties, which disappointed some char people who had expected to meet with the panel. In one case, char people had readied local boats for the panel to use, but somehow the panel's change of plans was not communicated and these people waited in vain for the Inspection Panel to show up.[41] The panel interviewed very few people around bridge area.

Although the EFP adopted by the bank and JMBA in September 1996 called for consultation and participation of the people, there had been no increase in their participation, except leaflets circulated on the mainland. Local people hoped to raise these and other grievances with the Inspection Panel during its visit in October 1996, but their ability to communicate freely with the Inspection Panel was hindered by the fact that the panel did not travel with an independent translator.

Despite these shortcomings of the field visit, the Inspection Panel's report did capture the concerns of the char people. The panel submitted its report to the board on December 2, 1996.[42] The panel found that the claimants "have been left uninformed and out of the design and appraisal stages of the project, including the environmental and resettlement plans aimed at mitigating adverse effects on people and nature."[43] The panel rejected management's explanation for the exclusion of char people, noting that the policy framework mandates their participation:

> Once a project area has been identified, the environmental assessment and resettlement guidelines (ODs 4.00, Annexes and 4.30) call for identification of irreversible impacts and consultation with potentially affected parties. The policy guidance is clear and unambiguous. . . . Although in this particular project the impacts of erosion could not be quantified with certainty in advance, erosion of *chars* was almost certain to happen and the *char* people should have been consulted in this process. The Panel has not received evidence that this kind of consultation ever took place.[44]

The panel concluded that the char people "have not been appropriately informed about the project and invited or allowed to participate in the design and implementation of mitigation and compensation activities—the policies on participation appear to have been and continue to be violated."[45]

However, in light of the commitments made by bank management and the government to bring the project into compliance, and the fact that the claimants expressed satisfaction with the action plan, the panel did not recommend an investigation of the claim. "The Panel concluded that although some policies and procedures on resettlement and environmental assessment had not been followed, the EFP seemed to address the Requesters' concerns, obviating the need for a full investigation."[46] Thus, the panel provisionally accepted the action plan, saying that it could "constitute an adequate and enforceable framework that would allow—and show the intentions of— Management to comply with the policies and procedures relevant to the Requesters' concerns. *This framework would have to be revised and expanded to meet policy requirements and a full and informed participation of affected people would be needed to ensure its success.*"[47]

In April 1997, the board met to consider the panel's report and recommendation. During that meeting, the panel stated that although it was not recommending an investigation, there were important issues that needed additional review. The panel's decision not to recommend an investigation was based on the assumption that "management would follow through on its commitments under the EFP."[48] The executive director representing Bangladesh "assured the Board that the Government of Bangladesh (GOB) was fully committed to the compensation plan."[49] In addition, the "legal opinion of the Senior Vice President and General Counsel, which had been provided to the Panel, was that the EFP could be regarded as a fully enforceable covenant of the loan agreement."[50] Ultimately, the board approved the panel's recommendation that there not be an investigation, asked management to submit a periodic progress report on the status of implementation of the EFP, and also requested that the panel participate in a review of management's progress report.[51]

The Char Peoples' Response to the Claim Process

The report prepared by the Inspection Panel included the broad concerns of JCDP and the char claimants. The panel found that management did not comply with policies and procedures, although it was possible for them to do so. Even now, it is not possible to say that the bank's policies on resettlement, the environment, and participation have been complied with.

The char people accepted management's action plan, which was supposed to mitigate and compensate the people who suffered the direct and indirect effect of the bridge on the chars. On paper, this plan was responsive to the concerns raised in the claim except that it was not developed in consultation with local people. Unaware of the pitfalls that lay ahead, the claimants thought that management's action plan would satisfy their concerns, so they agreed that a full investigation was not necessary. The claimants would soon discover, however, that implementation of the plan was neither simple nor generous.

Compensation for Erosion and Flood-Affected Persons: Benefits Don't Trickle Down

The Bangladesh Rural Advancement Committee (BRAC), the largest NGO in Bangladesh, was contracted by JMBA to implement the Guidelines for Compensation of Erosion and Flood Affected Persons (GCEFAP).[52] Unfortunately, the participation of local people was further compromised by the methodologies employed by BRAC in administering the compensation program. The BRAC offices were set up on either side of the river, in Bhuapur on the eastern side and Sirajgonj on the western mainland. BRAC staff did not visit the chars regularly, and it posted notices only on the mainland, rather than on the chars. Given the fact that many of the char people are illiterate, BRAC's method of posting notices on the mainland meant that many char people did not have effective notification of their rights to compensation. BRAC distributed some posters and handbills in Bengali, but the char people had to travel to the BRAC offices on the mainland to get detailed information about the EFP.

JCDP encouraged the char people to file for compensation and assisted them in filing their claims. By doing so, JCDP was actually doing the work BRAC was supposed to do. Hundreds of char-dwellers could not even process applications for getting compensation. BRAC and JMBA are bureaucratic and do not support the people to establish claims. In this sense, there has not been any change at JMBA as a result of the claim—the bureaucratic tangles and the attitude of the institutions involved continue to work to the detriment of the local affected people. There is no independent institution that oversees the implementation of the EFP.

Thus, the process of applying for compensation was not easy for char people, and they encountered a number of complexities that forced many of them to abandon their claims. The process was lengthy, difficult to access, complicated, time-consuming, and imposed a high documentation burden on local people. For example, char people had to provide original land records; in situations where those records were lost or destroyed by floods, BRAC did not accept government-certified copies or testimonials. In addition, people had to provide registration cards (issued by BRAC), an application form with two passport-size photos, the purchase deed and original land mutation records. a record of ownership changes, a land tax receipt, and the exact size of the affected land.

The design flaws can be traced to many interlocking factors, including the number and formality of documents required; the disconnect between the operations of BRAC and the daily life of the char people; and an unsympathetic approach from BRAC and its employer, the JMBA. The end result is that many claimants were effectively denied compensation, and many others spent more time and money navigating the compensation process than they actually received in compensation. This was especially true for claimants with the smallest land holdings. On average, a claimant spent a total of seven working days and incurred processing and travel expenses of 782 Taka, in addition to the loss of daily income (with a minimum wage of 50 Taka per day).[53]

There were many other problems associated with the compensation program, including the following:

- Char people were never compensated for losses due to flooding.
- Very few people were compensated for the erosion that took place in 1998, 1999, and 2000 because JMBA and BRAC failed to provide clear instructions about how and when to file claims. The deadlines for filing compensation have closed, and many people were left out. The confusion was compounded by the fact that char-dwellers who received compensation were not told the year for which compensation was being given.
- No compensation was paid for eroded community facilities (such as schools, mosques, etc).
- Widows were not paid.
- Partial payments made by BRAC make it difficult for the char people to receive full compensation for their losses.

The Situation Deteriorates, with No Effective Supervision

The compensation deadline for the project-affected persons was changed numerous times, making the situation more confusing. When the compensation program ended in February 2001, hundreds of eligible people were not registered as project-affected persons and are now denied the right to get compensation within the framework of the EFP. Some people have received only partial compensation. The appeals of the affected peoples remain unheeded. The affected people are entrapped in a bureaucratic tangle. A budget of fifty million Taka was initially allocated to fund the EFP.[54] However, BRAC has not kept precise data on the number of households affected by erosion and/or land losses, nor is it clear how many claims for compensation have been submitted or paid.[55]

In summary, the EFP was flawed for two main reasons. First, instead of BRAC traveling to the chars to provide information and document claims, the char people had to travel to BRAC's offices on the mainland. Thus, char people were required to come forward at their own initiative to take advantage of the compensation program. This presupposes that they were informed about when and how to apply for compensation, when in fact they were not involved in planning or implementing the project and were not provided with adequate information or support to file for compensation. Second, although the EFP was supposed to deal with erosion and flooding, the Entitlement Matrix states that "[t]he matrix covers the impact of erosion only" and that losses due to flooding are "[t]o be mitigated through a Flood Preparedness and Relief Programme sponsored by JMBA."[56] This promise to provide another program in the future never materialized.

Insufficient Monitoring

Although the char people welcomed the Inspection Panel's role in monitoring and supervision of the action plan, in the opinion of the claimants, the panel did not follow up properly. The panel returned to Bangladesh in June 1998 to investigate a claim filed against a World Bank sectoral adjustment loan for the jute industry. During that visit it did some brief follow-up on the char peoples' claim. The second visit and consequent report had considerable shortcomings. The Inspection Panel's ability to get a comprehensive and objective view on the compensation project was hampered by the short duration of both visits to the chars and its failure to travel with an impartial interpreter. The panel mission members also met with JCDP in Dhaka in June 1998 after visiting the chars.

Although the panel's 1998 report found problems in implementation of the compensation program, the panel didn't undertake any follow-up activities because it did not have board authorization to do so. The NGOs and project-affected people never learned what happened at the bank after the panel submitted its report. When JCDP wrote to the Inspection Panel seeking clarification, the response was that "the Panel is no longer involved in the process."[57] After receiving this information, JCDP and some char people questioned the overall use of the Inspection Panel. They were frustrated by the panel's failure to follow up on the outcome of the action plan and to see it through to completion. Claimants' descriptions of the process were often full of frustration:

> What is the use of this investigation at all? Who has the benefit? We certainly do not. We just waste our time with trying to get compensated. The Government simply does not want to give any money to us, and only BRAC earns out of it. The whole project is a cheat. They are making fun of us![58]

Local Impacts of the Claim Process

This general frustration with the panel process is prevalent in the whole impact area. The char people have reacted by focusing on daily activities and trying to survive. Many have given up trying for compensation and some refuse the payment as they feel humiliated, but some still keep on fighting for their rights.

The devastating impacts of the bridge are now a fact of life for the char people. Nobody has yet received compensation for wage loss. Unnecessary complications are barring people from registering their names as eligible persons for compensation. As mentioned earlier, management's response to the Inspection Panel alluded to a process of assessing possible damage after the construction of the bridge, which is yet to be taken up. Even the delineation of the affected area and fixing boundaries was not done properly.

With the commencement of the EFP, interest in the issue waned, and by 2000 very few people in Bangladesh were aware that there was an ongoing problem. Nonetheless, through the request to the Inspection Panel, the char people got a voice at the international level. The visits by the World Bank and the Inspection Panel to the chars showed them that at least somebody outside Bangladesh is aware of the impact of the bridge on their livelihoods. Thus, the request worked as a tool for empowerment of the char people. Never before have they attracted so much attention within the country than from the date the request was sent and the compensation project launched.

The bank has described the compensation program as a precedent-setting plan for the government of Bangladesh. The bank should recognize that any such plan would require strong institutional capacity on the part of JMBA and the government. However, the policy guidelines have not been translated into an institutional and legal framework that would facilitate effective implementation.

The claim process redefined the relationship between the state and NGOs, and unveiled the contradictions and inherent dynamics of bank management. It seems there is a lack of understanding of how borrowing governments should comply with bank policies while implementing World Bank–financed projects. The changes seen from this claim in Bangladesh could be summarized as follows: first, the introduction of EFP sets out the principles of determining the level of impact on char-dwellers and provides a set of rules to govern future actions. Second, the request for inspection successfully established that the char people have the right to get compensation. One of the most important achievements was that char people now have a legal right to resort to court if they are not properly compensated. Several cases have been filed to realize compensation.[59]

CONCLUSION

The request for inspection filed on the Jamuna Bridge project is unique in several ways. First, it was filed completely from the grassroots: three thousand char-dwellers signed it, most with thumbprints. JCDP, the organization representing the char people, filed the request without any international support. International organizations and advocacy groups did not know that a request was going to be submitted on the bridge. Thus, the request took the World Bank as well as advocacy groups by surprise. There were pros and cons to this approach. On the one hand, it was recognized as a truly grassroots complaint. On the other hand, international groups were hampered in their ability to support the request because they had to become familiar with the issue first and get in contact with JCDP, which was not easy since e-mail access was still limited at that time. As international support was weak, it was easier for Bangladeshi institutions involved to prejudice the media against JCDP.

The request differed from others in another way: the claimants said they were satisfied with management's response in developing the Erosion and Flood Policy and thus agreed that the Inspection Panel did not need to undertake an investigation. The atmosphere on the chars was very positive after the EFP was decided upon as an action plan, because the char people trusted that there would be proper implementation. They were quite convinced that the EFP, and in a broader sense the JMBA and government, would take care of all the damages they have suffered.

If the char people had known how this policy was to be applied, however, they surely would have asked for better support from the Inspection Panel. One could claim that JCDP and the claimants were not careful enough regarding the content of the policy. Indeed, to laymen the policy sounds generous and simple, but it actually has many weaknesses and pitfalls. One should not forget that the EFP was adopted only a few days after the request for inspection reached the World Bank in Washington.

The issues and problems raised by char people and later corroborated by the Inspection Panel team were accentuated further because the implementation lacked monitoring and a framework for ensuring accountability and transparency. Several issues that the EFP focused on have gone unheeded or simply dropped away from the bank's agenda. Many people have not yet received proper compensation. The time period for establishing eligibility for compensation should be reviewed and extended because the process has not yet compensated all affected persons.

The EFP was significant because it was the first time that people in Bangladesh were to be compensated for losses from river erosion irrespective of the cause. In this sense, the panel claim helped to set a precedent in Bangladesh, at least for World Bank–funded projects. It will likely have an impact for future projects of a similar nature, such as a planned bridge over the Ganges.[60]

Although the EFP remains largely rhetoric in the absence of an effective monitoring process, the claim did bring changes in the lives of char people. They have received some financial compensation, and it was the first time that an EFP policy was developed in the history of the country and the World Bank. This is a victory and the claim sets a precedent for all the fringe areas around the globe for how the bank's policies could be enforced within the panel framework. JCDP's experience with the Inspection Panel was exciting, although it also demonstrated the limitations of the panel.

NOTES

1. I was assisted by Sultan Bakhsh and Fazlul Huq Ripon. As a consultant on behalf of JCDP, Hanna Schmuck Widmann carried out a research study on Jamuna Bridge funded by the Interchurch Organisation for Development Co-operation (ICCO); JCDP thankfully acknowledges her effort for the study.

2. Inspection Panel, "Report and Recommendations, Bangladesh: Jamuna Bridge Project," December 2, 1996, 7 (hereinafter "Report and Recommendations").

3. The tax covered commodities such as food, paper, books, and clothing, as well as services such as water supply, gas, electricity, telephone service, and bank deposits. By 1991, when the tax was abolished, 5.08 billion Taka (equivalent to U.S.$102 million) had been collected from Bangladeshi citizens.

4. Alvaro Umaña, ed., *The World Bank Inspection Panel: The First Four Years* (Washington, D.C.: World Bank, 1998), 128.

5. The Jamuna Multipurpose Bridge Authority (JMBA) was established in 1986 as part of the Ministry of Communications. It became the Jamuna Bridge Division.

6. Irrigation Support Project for Asia and the Near East, *National Charland Study Coordinated by the World Bank* (sponsored by U.S. AID [Agency for International Development], 1993), 4–2.

7. The char people have a mean household income of between 800 to 1,200 Taka per month (the equivalent of U.S.$16 to 24 per month). See JCDP, "Baseline Survey Report," May 1998.

8. Iqbal Akanda, interview by Hanna Schmuck, Jungipur, Bangladesh, October 17, 1994.

9. Shamsul Hoque Khandoker of Jungipur, interview by Agence Presse Télévision, Paris, 1990.

10. Results of research by Hanna Schmuck conducted from 1994–2000.

11. Kamla Begum of Megharpotal, interview by author, August 10, 2000.

12. World Bank, "Implementation Completion Report," June 2000, annex 10, 37.

13. Kazushi Hashimoto, World Bank, to Ismail Mobarek, task manager, World Bank, September 20, 1996. This letter was sent after construction had already begun.

14. This original plan proposed by a French engineering consortium was later given up and changed to the "Flood Action Plan" with several polder and embankment projects all over the country (Flood Plan Coordination Organization, 1995).

15. International NGOs that JCDP had worked with included Information, Alternatives and Opposition (IAO) Network International, a German NGO founded as an opposition network to the FAP, and the U.S.-based International Rivers Network (IRN) and Center for International Environmental Law (CIEL).

16. Most of the letters are enclosed in the request for inspection (JCDP, "Submission to Inspection Panel: A Request for Inspection on the Effect of the Jamuna Multi-Purpose Bridge on the Jamuna Char Inhabitants," August 18, 1996; hereinafter "Request for Inspection") and the Inspection Panel's "Report and Recommendations" (see, e.g., Majibul Huq Dulu, JCDP, to Mohammad Ali, executive director of JMBA, February 12, 1996; Majibul Huq Dulu, JCDP, to Arun Benerjee, World Bank office in Dhaka, February 12, 1996; Majibul Huq Dulu, JCDP, to Arun Benerjee, World Bank, January 23, 1995).

17. Arun Benerjee, World Bank statement made to Majibul Huq Dulu, JCDP, during a meeting at the World Bank office in Dhaka, February 1995.

18. Ironically, the World Bank claimed that it could not contact JCDP, as explained in letters from the World Bank office in Dhaka attached to the "Request for Inspection."

19. Majibul Huq Dulu, JCDP, to Arun Benerjee, the World Bank, January 23, 1995; attached to claim to Inspection Panel, annex 2.

20. JCDP, "The People's View" (1996); JCDP, "The Other View" (1996).

21. JCDP, "Baseline Survey Report," May 1998. JCDP's baseline survey contains important data about the situation of the chars before compensation measures were decided upon after the request for inspection. However, this survey has not been used as a reference by the World Bank or BRAC, the NGO carrying out the compensation program.

22. Inspection Panel, "Report and Recommendations," 7.

23. Inspection Panel, "Report and Recommendations," 3.

24. JCDP, "Request for Inspection."

25. "Request for Inspection," annex 1.

26. "Request for Inspection," 14–15.

27. "Request for Inspection," 9.

28. Threat and intimidation by telephone to author. Secretary, JMBA, personally visited the NGO Bureau and took away all the JCDP files.

29. The NGO Affairs Bureau audited JCDP in February 1997 (the NGO Affairs Bureau wanted to find loopholes within JCDP's institutional structure).

30. The front page of the Bangladesh daily newspaper *Shangbad,* October 23, 1996, reported that the author, the representative of the claimants, had mismanaged money. Another article claimed that "without any registration JCDP became an NGO and put a petition to the Inspection Panel, without knowing the char and saying that the chars will be affected" (*Janakantha,* October 28, 1996). *Shangbad,* October 30, 1996, wrote that JCDP had filed the request for inspection without having a discussion with the World Bank and the JMBA.

31. Fazul Huq Ripon, JCDP, letter to multiple recipients, September 17, 1996.

32. In Bangladesh, every NGO has to seek approval from the NGO Affairs Bureau, an office under the Ministry of the Prime Minister, to be authorized to work. The NGO Affairs Bureau can refuse approval of an NGO and a project without having to state a reason for the refusal (*NGO Affairs Bureau Guidelines,* clause 12, articles A and B).

33. Inspection Panel, "Report and Recommendations," 8.

34. Inspection Panel, "Report and Recommendations," 5.

35. Inspection Panel, "Report and Recommendations," annex 2, iii.

36. Inspection Panel, "Report and Recommendations," annex 2, i.

37. Inspection Panel, "Report and Recommendations," annex 2, 3.

38. The "Implementation Completion Report" notes that the bank had identified the exclusion of the char people as early as 1994, but the "GOB was initially reluctant to establish entitlements for victims of floods or erosion, pointing out that this would set a difficult precedent in a country like Bangladesh with winding rivers where erosion occurs naturally due to shifts in channels and flooding occurs naturally every year. However, following a complaint to the Bank's IP and a preliminary investigation by the Panel, GOB agreed to adopt a compensation policy that would be time-bound and limited within the bridge project's impact area" (paragraph 4.2.7).

39. Inspection Panel, "Report and Recommendations," annex 2, 4.

40. Inspection Panel, "Operating Procedures" (1994), paragraph 27.

41. Kader, chairman of Kawakhola Union, interview by the author, Serajganj, December 1997.

42. Inspection Panel, "Report and Recommendations."

43. Inspection Panel, "Report and Recommendations," 17.

44. Inspection Panel, "Report and Recommendations," 14–15.

45. Inspection Panel, "Report and Recommendations," 17–18.

46. Inspection Panel, "Report on Progress of Implementation of the Erosion and Flood Action Plan," August 17, 1998, paragraph 2.

47. Inspection Panel, "Report and Recommendations," 18 (emphasis added).

48. World Bank, "Summary of Discussion of Board of Executive Directors of the Bank and IDA, April 3, 1997" (summary dated April 17, 1997), paragraph 2 (hereinafter "Summary of Board Meeting").

49. "Summary of Board Meeting, paragraph 3.

50. "Summary of Board Meeting," paragraph 2.

51. "Summary of Board Meeting." See also Ibrahim F. I. Shihata, *The World Bank Inspection Panel: In Practice* (New York: Oxford University Press, 2000), 117.

52. BRAC, which employs fifty thousand people, was "hesitant to participate in the resettlement compensation program" (World Bank, "Summary of Board Meeting," paragraph 14).

53. The rate of the minimum daily wage amounts to 3 kg of rice.

54. Inspection Panel, "Report and Recommendations," paragraph 37.

55. BRAC gives conflicting figures in its year-end report (BRAC, "Compensating the Erosion Affected Persons. EFAP Project of JMBA: Phase-End Report, Period: May 1997–April 2000" [August 2000]).

56. Inspection Panel, "Report and Recommendations," annex 5, attachment 1.

57. Eduardo Abbott, secretary of the Inspection Panel, e-mail correspondence to Sultan Bakhsh, JCDP, February 22, 2000.

58. Zainul Bhuya, interview by Hanna Schmuck, Rehai Chunduni, February 15, 1999.

59. According to the existing land law, a person or his or her heir can go to court for compensation within one hundred years (Land Reformation Law, government of Bangladesh).

60. The World Bank also sees the EFP as being very important: "The adoption of this principle is a highly significant milestone. For the first time in Bangladesh, and possibly anywhere in the world, the Government has accepted responsibility for compensating and assisting people suffering from flooding and erosion caused by a development project" (World Bank, "Implementation Completion Report," annex 10, 39).

6

The Biobío's Legacy:
Institutional Reforms and Unfulfilled Promises
at the International Finance Corporation

David Hunter, Cristián Opaso, and Marcos Orellana

This chapter chronicles the tragedy of the *Mapuche/Pehuenche* people and
the defense of their homeland along the pristine Biobío River.[1] The Biobío is
the most important river in Chile—historically, culturally, and economically.
In the late 1980s, proposals emerged from Chile's government-owned utility
to build a series of dams that would flood the heart of the ancestral home of
the Pehuenche, a culturally distinct group of the Mapuche people. The dams
would also destroy one of the world's foremost white-water recreational
rivers, inundate close to twenty-two thousand hectares of one of Chile's most
biodiverse riparian habitats, and threaten the survival of several endemic fish
species.

ENDESA, a government-owned utility, began exploring the Upper Biobío
basin for possible hydroelectric sites as early as the 1950s. By the late 1980s,
ENDESA had studied a series of six potential sites in the Biobío basin, and
concluded that at least three (Pangue, Ralco, and Huequecura) were economically feasible.[2] By March 1990, when Chile's democracy was restored after
the seventeen-year Pinochet dictatorship, the Pangue project had already received the necessary water rights and several administrative permits. The
Pangue project was the first of the Biobío dams planned for construction, but
it made little economic sense by itself. The more destructive Ralco Dam was
the key project in the series, being the only one capable of storing enough water to compensate for interannual hydrological differences.

ENDESA's plans to dam the Biobío sparked opposition as soon as they were
made public. A budding Chilean environmental movement and a resuscitating
Mapuche movement waged a ten-year campaign opposing the project. Despite

115

the opposition, the International Finance Corporation (IFC) approved the Pangue project in December 1992, and the dam was completed in 1996. The second dam in the proposed series, Ralco, is expected to become operational by late 2003.

WHAT'S AT STAKE IN THE BIOBÍO

The Last Frontier of the Mapuche

The history of the Mapuche people, of which the Biobío region's Pehuenche people are a part, is a long story of racism and systematic violence conducted by various conquerors that have returned repeatedly to destroy Mapuche culture, life, and property. The conflict is no longer cloaked in the canons of "civilization" and "Christianity," but in the more secular notions of "rates of return" and "low costs of production." Rhetoric aside, little has changed for the Pehuenche; the dam builders, like the Spanish before them, seek to deprive the Pehuenche of their ancestral rights to land and force them from their homes.

For centuries, the Biobío River was the last line of defense for the Mapuche. The Spaniards, who conquered the Aztec and Inca empires, never prevailed over the Mapuche territories south of the Biobío River. After Chile gained independence in 1810, the government regarded the Mapuche as citizens of the republic, and annexed their territories to the new state without their approval. In 1881, the Chilean army, jointly with Argentina, conducted an ethnic cleansing campaign against the Mapuche.[3] The military destroyed the resistance and finally wrested control over the Mapuche territory for the Chilean state. The Mapuche have steadily lost their land ever since, and the population is now fragmented and cornered into a fraction of their original territory.[4] Some scholars estimate that by 1929 the Mapuche held only 6.4 percent of their traditional territories.[5] Under Pinochet's dictatorship, thousands more hectares of Mapuche land were taken.[6]

Currently, the Upper Biobío basin is home to some nine thousand Pehuenche,[7] who live in several distinct communities. The Pehuenches are seminomadic; in summer, they move toward the high Andes to collect the fruits (called *pehuén*) of the ancient Araucaria trees and to celebrate their religious ceremonies. The pehuén is central to the group's culture and affirmation of group identity; people self-identify themselves as Pehuenche (*che* = people, thus People of the *Pehuén*). In winter, the Pehuenche return back to their lowland winter homes. The Pangue/Ralco dams would flood important parts of these winter homes, permanently and irreversibly disrupting their complex cultural relationship with the land and seasons.

These disruptions also attack the cultural foundation of the Pehuenches, and thus threaten the existence of the group as such. The Pehuenche are integrated with their environment in a material and spiritual way that defines their cultural identity. Their customs reflect the symbolic meaning attributed to the natural components of their lands, rivers, and forests. For example, the community elders believed that the damming of the river would force *Punalka,* the spirit of the river, to leave the community, bringing misery to the land and people. These religious and spiritual beliefs are central to the group's self-identity. Thus, The Pangue/Ralco dams threatened the very existence of the Pehuenche as a distinct, cultural group. Rodrigo Valenzuela, a leading anthropologist initially hired by the project sponsors to study the consequences of the dams, concluded that the dams would extinguish the Pehuenche culture from the area.[8]

Threatening a Unique Ecosystem

Not only is the Biobío important to the Pehuenche and Chilean history, but it also represents a unique and valuable environmental resource. The Biobío basin is rich in biological diversity, housing a large number of endemic and endangered species. The river cascades 380 kilometers down from the Andes to the Pacific Ocean, providing world-class whitewater rafting and habitat for at least three endemic fish species.

The Pangue/Ralco dams posed several serious environmental threats to the Biobío region. Damming the river would deprive downstream ecosystems of critical organic nutrients, exacerbate downstream pollution problems, increase the erosion from released waters, and reduce nutrient deposits in the Arauco Gulf, one of Chile's richest fishing areas. The construction of the service road would also open the door to increased logging of several important and rare trees, including the Araucaria. The reservoir and increased logging along the access road would destroy habitat for several rare species of mammals, reptiles, birds, and plants.

Much of the opposition to the Pangue/Ralco dams was fueled by the lack of studies for many of the environmental and social impacts. Pangue's long-term downstream ecological impacts, including impacts on fish populations, were never satisfactorily studied and remained controversial throughout the ten-year campaign. Despite repeated promises from ENDESA, for example, cumulative impacts of the six proposed dams on the Biobío (or even of Pangue and Ralco together) were never assessed while IFC was reviewing the project or prior to the government's approval of both dams. IFC staff ignored the obvious linkage between Pangue and Ralco, accepting ENDESA's promise to study cumulative impacts only after additional dams (other than Pangue) were proposed.

THE INTERNATIONAL CAMPAIGN TO DEFEND THE BIOBÍO AND THE PEHUENCHE

The National Context

Following the seventeen-year dictatorship of General Pinochet, a democratically elected government took office in Chile in 1990. With democracy came heightened expectations, not only regarding civil and political liberties, but also the democratic participation of civil society in the development process. Yet Chile's transition back to democracy had its obstacles, and many of the ruling power structures did not change significantly. The 1980 constitution enacted by the military dictatorship limited the judicial system's independence, established an electoral system that overrepresented the right-wing political spectrum, and empowered a National Security Council that could convene itself to veto executive branch decisions.

The political power was reinforced by the enormous economic power that was consolidated during the privatization process that took place during the military dictatorship. The Pinochet dictatorship built a strong economy through top-down exploitation of four primary resources—minerals, agriculture, fisheries, and forests—while largely ignoring environmental and community concerns. ENDESA was among the corporations that benefited from the military's privatization of public assets, services, and public enterprises, and, at least until its sale in the late 1990s to the Spanish company ENDESA–España, it was controlled by some of the same people who were in charge of the privatization process during the dictatorship.[9]

Ultimately, the economic paradigm that the new democratic government implemented differed little from the preceding authoritarian rule. Behind a discourse of "growth with equality," the new democracy also followed a model that did not include the meaningful participation of civil society in the design of long-term development projects, least of all the involvement of affected people. In this context, the Pangue/Ralco controversy crystallized a broader clash between opposing models of development, and the Biobío River became a symbol of the debate between a development paradigm that valued the participation of affected people and one that saw development as a top-down process responsive to the interests of financial elites and central governments.

The Opposition Organizes against the Dams

The first public denunciation of ENDESA's plans for the Upper Biobío came in 1985 at a national scientific congress organized by the Chilean NGO Centro de Investigación y Planificación del Medio Ambiente (CIPMA). Katherine Bragg, a North-American ethnobotanist who had lived and conducted research among the Pehuenche, exposed the plans for the dams and raised concerns about the tremendous potential impact on the fragile ecosystem and vulnerable Pehuenche communities.

By the end of 1991, the Pehuenche communities had held open meetings to determine their position regarding the proposed series of dams. Most traditional leaders, with the support of affected families, agreed to resist the dams. The traditional leaders of the Pehuenche communities subsequently released public statements denouncing the construction of the Pangue/Ralco dams (see box 6.1). They also rejected the government's division of their lands, condemned overexploitation of the forests, and demanded the immediate suspension of all construction in their territories.

**Box 6.1. The Women's Movement:
Leaders of the Pehuenche Opposition**

Statement by Nicolasa Quintreman Calpan

They talk to us about wealth, about giving us money. But we have pure air to breathe, we have pure water, the trees that provide us with shade, we have the *pehuén* (Araucaria tree) that feeds us, the sun that gives us the light of day, and we are close to the stars and the moon, that give us light at night. We live in harmony with animals, we have Mother Earth. What wealth are they talking about?

If you don't want to barter, if you don't want to get out in good terms, then the Good Men [government-appointed commission that is supposed to set a price for expropriated land] are going to come and they are going to take you out the wrong way. So they say. But I believe nothing of what they say. I always have to believe He who gives light, He who left the world. This is why I am afraid of no one. . . .

"What do those old women know?" they said. Older women are the ones that know the most, because we know of the mountains, of the volcanoes. We know what is going to happen, that is why we warn way in advance. . . . If Ralco goes ahead we will perish. If the *Pehuenche* perish, so will everything, because without *Pehuenche* the world is not going to be strong.

Also in 1991, Chilean citizens and colleagues from other countries created the Grupo de Acción por el Biobío (GABB), which publicized the impacts of the proposed dams and began an intense advocacy campaign that would last over ten years (see box 6.2). The campaign to save the Biobío would be among the most important tests of Chile's new democracy, as well as a test

---

Box 6.2.   Interview with Juan Pablo Orrego, Grupo de Acción por el Biobío (GABB), July 2000[10]

When was the GABB created?

In 1991 I was in charge of communications at the newly created Special Commission for Indigenous Peoples when a producer from ESPN called. They were preparing a story on a descent down the Biobío, and they wanted to invite Chileans who could talk about the issue of the Biobío dams and their potential impacts on the watershed and on the Pehuenche people. . . . We ended up going on ESPN's white-water adventure with a lawyer, José Aylwin. While descending through Pangue's flooding area, Gary Lemmer, our ecologist and oarsman, was insistently telling us "all this is going to disappear under the water." We were absolutely shocked. Back in Santiago we met with Katherine Bragg. We decided to take action, and so . . . GABB was created. We rented a small office-room in Bellavista, with support of the kayaker/environmentalist *gringos*. We had serious problems finding information about the project, but then one day Rodrigo Valenzuela, an anthropologist originally hired by ENDESA to evaluate the impact of the Biobío dams on the Pehuenche, appeared on the doorsteps of our office with a social impact study and many documents and maps that accurately described the monstrous project.

We elaborated a strategy in which the Pehuenche Lonkos (leaders) played a crucial role as the representatives of the communities. We made the mistake of idealizing things, believing that the indigenous community and their traditional authorities were still functioning. We did not see clearly the many divisions within and among the Pehuenche communities, as well as among the Mapuche in general, nor the extent to which the institution of the Lonkos had eroded. This was the source of many of the problems we had in the years to come.

When did you first meet with bank officials in Washington, D.C.?

Due to the mounting public opposition to the construction of the Pangue Dam, in 1992 ENDESA created the Pehuén Foundation to a great extent just to offer the Pehuenche subsidies of up to 80 percent for food and tools. To obtain these benefits, though, families had to sign as members of the foundation. While the IFC was evaluating the loan, ENDESA presented those who had signed . . . as supporters of the project. In 1992 we traveled with Lonko Antolín Curriao to Washington, D.C., where we met with the board and the president of the bank. There, management said they were supporting the dam because of its minor environmental impacts and because it did not involve the resettlement of any Pehuenche. Then, Antolín clarified that Pangue would flood the lands of nine of his children. There was havoc. The president's dagger look to his technicians for providing false information was evident and cut across everyone in the room. At the end, the IFC helped broker loans from private banks, ignoring both the substantive issues of the series of dams and the fact that management misled the board.

Your leadership in this campaign has been recognized worldwide. You received the Goldman Prize in 1997 and the 1998 Right Livelihood Award in Stockholm. Did these recognitions help your cause?

The prizes helped to draw international attention to our struggle. The ñañas (women) also obtained the Petra Kelly award of the Heinrich Böll Foundation in Berlin. However, the prizes further alienated the more radical Mapuche organizations, which could not tolerate the fact that *huincas* (foreigners) were leading the defense of the Biobío. . . . GABB always preached nonviolent active resistance, and we supported and worked with the ñañas, who inspired the whole resistance movement. All this did not fit into these groups' political agendas. . . . GABB was accused of manipulating the conflict for its own advantage. A delegation of the Consejo de Todas las Tierras (a radical Mapuche organization) even showed up in Stockholm to disparage GABB and me as its most visible speaker. I was accused of stealing millions of dollars and of becoming famous at the expense of the Pehuenche. I was also declared persona non grata in the Upper Biobío by the many Pehuenche who very poorly negotiated with ENDESA, and who threatened to beat me up and worse if I kept coming to the Biobío.

The *Nguillatour* incident can exemplify the problems of working there. On October 11–12, 1996, we . . . organized a *Nguillatún* (a traditional religious ceremony) with the ñañas in the context of the opposition to the dams. It got out of hand. We hired buses and invited everybody from all over the country. Thousands came, indigenous and nonindigenous. A delegation of indigenous leaders from the U.S. and other countries were also invited. . . . The Sunday when the ceremony concluded, at 3 A.M., under heavy rain, the camp was assaulted by the radical Mapuche, who tried to drive everyone away with stones and sticks, lead by a Mapuche woman in trance who screamed that the *huinca*'s throats had to be cut because they were killing the river. The situation finally became so violent, difficult, and polarized that we decided we could not help the defense of the Biobío and of the Pehuenche through GABB, so the organization virtually ceased to exist in May 2001.

for the international environmental rhetoric that emerged in the hopeful days after the 1992 Earth Summit. The controversy also engaged international NGOs actively pushing reforms at the World Bank Group, including the IFC.

Although this chapter focuses primarily on the international parts of the campaign, the majority of the efforts to save the Biobío and the Pehuenche were waged at the national and local levels, as the project became the first major test of Chile's new environmental and indigenous rights laws and institutions. Jaime Toha, Chile's minister of energy, labeled the Biobío controversy "the main eco-economic conflict" facing the transitional government. Given ENDESA's substantial economic and political power, the government's treatment of Pangue/Ralco was arbitrary and outside the law, undermining the credibility of the democratic government itself. Both the environmental impact assessment law and the laws meant to protect indigenous land rights were violated. Two heads of CONADI (the indigenous peoples' agency Corporación Nacional de Desarrollo Indígena) and the head of CONAMA (the environmental agency Comisión Nacional del Medio Ambiente) were removed by the government or resigned because of their opposition to the Ralco Dam. The government also largely ignored two resolutions taken by the Lower House of Parliament that demanded a halt to the Biobío projects until energy alternatives and negative impacts were explored fully.[11]

From the beginning, the campaign to save the Biobío was also international. Katherine Bragg, who first publicized the proposals for damming the Biobío, helped to spark interest in North America. Environmentalists, whitewater rafters, and human rights activists all join together at different times in the campaign. Articles aimed at mobilizing these different constituencies appeared in journals as early as 1987.[12] The campaign was one of the earliest international campaigns to take advantage of the Internet and the globalization of the environmental movement.

The presence of IFC financing provided the key international hook for the campaign on the Biobío. The IFC, which is the World Bank Group's private sector arm, is the world's largest multilateral source of financing for corporate investment in developing countries. Before the 1980s, IFC mainly supported commercial and manufacturing activities. Privatization trends throughout the world in the 1980s provided new opportunities for the IFC to finance large infrastructure projects. One of these projects was the Pangue Dam.

When the IFC became involved with the Pangue Dam project, however, the institution was ill-prepared to handle such an environmentally and socially sensitive project. During the review of Pangue (i.e., beginning around 1990), the IFC relied on just one environmental professional, responsible for reviewing potential environmental impacts of more than one hundred projects annually. This "environmental advisor" was tasked with "advising management on environmental matters and review[ing] potential projects."[13] IFC finally established an "environmental unit," which was expanded in 1992 to three full-time professional staff and four environmental consultants. In addition to being understaffed, the policy framework for the IFC was ambiguous during this period. IFC had developed its first written procedure for environmental review of projects in 1989, and in many ways the Biobío would become the first test of that procedure.

THE CAMPAIGN TO PREVENT IFC APPROVAL OF THE PANGUE DAM

Beginning in 1990, GABB worked closely with several U.S. groups, including Friends of the Earth (FoE), the Natural Resources Defense Council (NRDC) and International Rivers Network (IRN), to keep the Biobío high on the international agenda. Reform of the IFC was a major priority of these and other organizations in both the United States and Europe. Fueled by regular information from GABB, as well as occasional field visits, these groups began raising questions to the IFC, its board of directors, and donor governments regarding the project's environmental and social impacts.[14] Letter campaigns by rafters and conservationists targeted both the IFC and Chile's leaders. Articles appeared in leading newspapers in Chile, the United States, and Europe. Several organizations even prepared a comprehensive, alternative study of Chile's national energy needs and the feasibility of meeting those needs through energy conservation.[15]

Much of the debate around IFC financing focused on potential violations of applicable World Bank Group policies. With no policies of its own, the IFC told environmental groups that it followed World Bank policies. By putting arguments in terms of policy violations, opponents of the dam gained support from donor governments who were interested in ensuring a consistent, transparent, and predictable policy framework at the World Bank Group. The donor countries were unlikely to question the development decisions made by the newly democratic Chile, but could legitimately question how the IFC conducted its business.

With the focus on policy violations, some issues gained in importance—for example, the IFC's failure to assess the cumulative impacts of the proposed dams. The IFC always backed ENDESA's self-serving and patently false position that Pangue was a stand-alone dam and therefore it was not necessary to evaluate the economic, environmental, and social impacts of the other proposed dams on the Biobío River. In spite of clear indications that Pangue was only the first in a series of functionally interconnected dams, the IFC always looked at Pangue as an isolated project.

Restricting the scope of the environmental impact assessment (EIA) enabled ENDESA and IFC to distort the debate, suppress criticism, and move on with the proposed dams, one by one. Pangue may have been promoted first precisely because, among the proposed dams, it raised the fewest issues. Pangue's reservoir would flood relatively small amounts of native forest and dislocate relatively fewer families. Pangue would thus be the foot in the door for Ralco and the other dams. The access road would be built, the community divided, and criticism muted by the creation of jobs, the collection of taxes, and the supply of electric energy. By presenting Pangue first, attention was distracted from the more serious environmental and social impacts of the Ralco Dam, which would flood an area seven times larger than Pangue and would require the resettlement of close to one hundred families.

The IFC was fully aware of these issues at the time of approving the Pangue loan in late 1992. As early as 1991, a World Bank consultant informed the bank that "both ENDESA and its critics see Pangue as the first of several (up to six) large hydroelectric projects on the upper Biobío river."[16] One year later, the IFC-financed consultant who was supposed to look at energy supply alternatives and their impacts concluded that a cumulative impact study was probably not necessary because "no other project was currently under review," yet the same report listed the Ralco Dam as one of the expected sources of future energy by the year 2000.[17] This hypocrisy was apparent throughout the IFC's handling of the Pangue project, including the information it gave to the board.[18]

Independent observers also recognized that ENDESA had not adequately assessed Pangue's long-term impact on certain native fish or, more generally, the downstream impacts of the dam. The United States argued to the IFC Board that fish life cycles, migration habits, and the establishment of fish conservation areas should be studied before the IFC Board reviewed the project.[19] Instead, IFC staff assured the board of directors that these studies were underway and that adequate mitigation, particularly through minimum flow requirements, would be implemented.[20] Yet, as the independent review would later find, four years after the approval of the loan and with most of the loan disbursed to ENDESA, downstream impacts had not been studied, nor had minimum flow requirements been addressed.[21]

Although the IFC did ultimately approve financing for Pangue, the campaign successfully raised indigenous and environmental concerns to the highest levels of the IFC and its donors. The project was delayed several times as ENDESA and IFC staff were forced to respond to these concerns (see box 6.3).

Box 6.3.   Statement by Berta Quintreman Calpan

And what do they expect to do? Do they expect to simply destroy the earth? Do they study to destroy the earth? One has to study so that people remain in good standing, not to destroy the earth. The earth is sacred, it is where all of us are living, the whole world. Why have they harmed it, contaminating the water, interrupting the waters? I have my water over there where I live. Night and day it flows, clean, without any contamination, flowing as Nuke Mapu Chao (Mother Earth Father) left it, with no one interrupting it.

. . . These people worked without permission. They did everything under the table. Nothing with the people. Blind and deaf. One has to have a clear vision, one has to listen with one's ears. . . .

. . . That is what the *Mapuche-Pehuenche* word says. We are not going to use foul ways to take land away from the people. We are gentle people. We knock at the door, we are not going to arrive and come in without knocking at the door. When they came, the people from ENDESA, they did not knock at the door. As if they were the owners of the land. Why do they lie so much? Lies have never been a good thing. They have never won either. Truth has always won everywhere. And they waste so much paper with their lies. I also know how to write and I also know how to read. But I don't use paper, I only use my mind and my heart.

The Pangue campaign also set several important precedents in how IFC reviews projects:

- The Pangue project was the first time the IFC publicly released an environmental assessment before the board's review, thus providing an opportunity to evaluate the report and inform the IFC Board about the assessment's deficiencies.
- The Pehuén Foundation was the first foundation created in Latin America to benefit indigenous communities with a guaranteed lifelong revenue stream from a bank-financed project.
- The Pangue project was the first IFC project ever to gain less than unanimous support by the board of directors because of environmental and social concerns. Even with added conditions, the United States abstained

from supporting the project because of the failure to assess its environmental aspects adequately.

• The Pangue loan agreement contained an unprecedented number of comprehensive environmental and social conditions.

THE INSPECTION PANEL CLAIM

After the IFC's approval of the Pangue loan, the international campaign became less active. The project went forward, and after receiving a report on downstream impacts in 1993, the IFC released its initial disbursement in 1994. When it became clear that many of the conditions that the IFC staff had promised the board were not being met, however, GABB once again reached out to international networks. In this second phase of the international campaign, the leading international partners were the BIC (Bank Information Center), CIEL (Center for International Environmental Law), FoE, and IRN

GABB and its international partners again brought clear evidence of failures in project preparation and monitoring to the attention of the highest levels of the bank and donor governments. The U.S. Environmental Protection Agency (EPA) reviewed the documentation and concluded that the 1993 downstream impact study did not "constitute the study that IFC promised" at the time of board approval.[22] More generally, EPA concluded that IFC "assurances . . . made to the Board and elsewhere about environmental mitigation do not appear to have been implemented. As in other dam projects of the Bank, the tendency of 'build now, study later' with respect to fish impacts is evident here." [23]

Perhaps more disturbing, by 1995 it was clear that the Pehuén Foundation, established to support the Pehuenche people, was instead being abused by ENDESA as a tool of acculturation. After visiting the region, a U.S. State Department official wrote the World Bank's regional environmental chief with the following concerns:

[T]he Pehuen Foundation (FP) seems to have become a divisive element in the community it was supposed to benefit. During my January 1995 visit to the upper BíoBío valley, I heard several reports that FP representatives continue to use access to the Foundation's benefits as a means of pressuring local residents into supporting dam construction on the BíoBío. Many members of the local community told me they thought the real purpose of the FP was to dislodge them from their homeland. These and other difficulties with the Foundation's operations appear to be related to the Foundation's managerial structure, to the level of community involvement in the project, and perhaps to the issue of adequate supervision on the ground.[24]

Such continuous oversight by a donor government was relatively unprecedented among IFC-financed projects, and ensured that the Pangue project continued to get the attention of top management, if for no other reason than to placate the IFC's largest donor. Significantly, the U.S. government's letters always received substantive replies from the IFC staff, while letters raising similar concerns sent from GABB and the affected communities were often ignored.

Eventually, based on advice provided by CIEL and FoE, GABB decided to submit a claim to the Inspection Panel together with the local Pehuenche and hundreds of Chileans living in the basin and elsewhere. In November 1995, after six months of preparation, GABB simultaneously filed both a petition to World Bank President James Wolfensohn and a formal claim to the Inspection Panel. The complaints were submitted on GABB's own behalf and that of 385 other concerned people—including 47 Pehuenche, 194 citizens from Concepción (located at the mouth of the Biobío), 145 Chileans from other cities, and three members of Parliament.[25] The petition to President Wolfensohn was distributed simultaneously to the IFC Board of Directors in an explicit effort to persuade them either to extend the Inspection Panel's jurisdiction to the IFC or authorize an independent inspection of some sort, assuming that the Inspection Panel would not have jurisdiction. In an open letter to Wolfensohn, forty-six NGOs from seventeen countries supported the claim.[26]

The Inspection Panel claim and identical petition detailed alleged violations of eight different IFC or World Bank policies,[27] specific violations of Chile's 1993 Indigenous Law, and abrogation of rights under the Chilean Constitution to a contamination-free environment, to be heard and to participate in matters that affect the country. The claim also identified specific unmet promises that had been made by both the IFC and the borrower at the time the IFC Board approved the Pangue loan, including the following:

- in violation of a promise made by IFC staff in the project summary presented to the IFC Board,[28] work had begun on the Ralco Dam without any cumulative impact assessment;
- adequate assessments of downstream impacts and long-term impacts on fish had yet to be completed (although those studies were allegedly part of the loan conditions);
- no flow management regime had been developed as required by an agreement with the regional government in Chile and presumably by the loan agreement; and
- a variety of promises were broken regarding the structure, independence, and scope of the Pehuén Foundation.

These arguments raised the stakes at the IFC. If true, then either IFC staff had deliberately misled the board of directors, ENDESA was deliberately and strategically misleading IFC staff, IFC staff was incompetent with respect to supervision, or a combination of the three. The debate was no longer whether the project was good for Chile—which in the IFC's view was a question better left to Chile's democratic government—but rather why the IFC tolerated the failure to comply with relatively straightforward mandates emanating from top management. These questions were clearly within the critical institutional interest of IFC.

As anticipated, the Inspection Panel rejected the claim because it has no jurisdiction over IFC projects. IFC staff argued that the claim was exaggerated and no investigation was necessary. However, the claim itself was well documented, broadly supported by international civil society, and legitimized by the U.S. government's own findings.[29] Still relatively early in his tenure, Wolfensohn had shown a willingness to use controversial projects (particularly those developed before he was in charge) as a way to push reforms within the institution, while at the same time scoring public relations points with outside constituencies.[30] GABB and the northern NGOs supporting the complaint hoped that Wolfensohn would see the petition for an independent review as a valuable opportunity to gain both public relations points and to obtain information valuable for IFC reform.

THE INDEPENDENT REVIEW

In March 1996, Wolfensohn finally authorized an "impartial internal review of the environmental and social implications of the project. The review would determine whether the Pangue project is in compliance with applicable World Bank policies, and whether there have been any violations of environmental and social covenants contained in IFC's Investment Agreement with [ENDESA]."[31] President Wolfensohn appointed Dr. Jay Hair, the former head of the U.S.-based National Wildlife Federation and then-president of the International Union for the Conservation of Nature (IUCN), as an independent investigator to review the project. The selection of Dr. Hair was made without the input or approval of any of the claimants or environmental groups active in the Biobío campaign. At the time of an initial meeting between Dr. Hair and the Washington-based NGOs monitoring the project, he had already been briefed on the project by IFC staff but had not yet reviewed any underlying documents other than the claim. Dr. Hair was openly skeptical that the allegations made in the claim could be true, given assurances he had received from IFC staff. The NGOs, in turn, questioned Dr. Hair's terms of reference, which did not guarantee the final report's public release.[32]

Despite the initial tension, over time the environmental groups became convinced that Dr. Hair and his team had conducted a fair investigation. Their concerns over disclosure of the report were warranted, however, as IFC and ENDESA moved to censor and suppress the report's release. The review team argued that they had been careful not to quote any confidential documents or otherwise violate IFC's information disclosure policy.[33] On the other hand, ENDESA put substantial pressure on IFC and Wolfensohn, essentially threatening legal action if the report was released.[34]

On July 15, 1997, one year after Wolfensohn authorized the independent review—at least three months after a draft of the report was completed and a month *after* the Chilean government finally approved the Ralco EIA— Wolfensohn released a heavily redacted version of the report of the independent review. Close to a third of the report was censored and never made public.

Dr. Hair and his team were furious, as suggested by the following letter to Wolfensohn:

> [T]he IFC-redacted version of the Pangue Report eliminated about one third of the original text. In the IFC redacted version it is not possible for the reader to tell whether a word, a sentence, a paragraph, a page, or several pages were deleted. While we understand that the primary purpose of the review/redaction process was to address potential legal and/or proprietary business issues it is clear in reviewing the original text that the redaction process went well beyond a reasonable interpretation of that intent.
>
> There are numerous deletions that appear to have been made for no other reason than to avoid embarrassing the individuals who made certain decisions regarding the Pangue project or how it was supervised by IFC.[35]

The Independent Review's Findings

Even the redacted version of the independent review provided a remarkable indictment of IFC's handling of the Pangue/Ralco projects. The review validated virtually every allegation in GABB's original claim. The report not only documented specific violations of World Bank policies, but also specified several instances when IFC staff withheld information from IFC's board of directors—information that may have changed their support of the project.[36] Among other things, the review concluded the following:

> From an environmental and social perspective IFC added little, if any, value to the Pangue Project. Its failure to adequately supervise this project—from beginning to

end—significantly increased the business risks and diminished the public credibility for both the World Bank Group (particularly IFC) and its private sector partner. There is no indication at this time (April 1997) that IFC has in place the necessary institutional operating systems, or clarity in its policy and procedural mandate, to manage complicated projects such as Pangue in a manner that complies consistently with World Bank Group environmental and social requirements and recognized best practices.[37]

Throughout Pangue's loan preparation, IFC staff repeatedly told concerned NGOs that IFC followed World Bank policies, but the review team found no evidence that the IFC had ever informed ENDESA of what, if any, World Bank policies applied. This disconnect between what IFC staff told outside advocates and what it conveyed to the borrower resulted in significant confusion and, ultimately, a wide range of policy violations.[38] The review team found significant violations and shortcomings regarding the IFC's treatment of environmental impacts, information disclosure, wildlands, cultural property, indigenous peoples, involuntary resettlement, and project supervision, as well as violations of commitments contained in the loan agreement.

Perhaps most damning was the IFC staff's general disregard for the environmental and social issues raised by the Pangue project. The review team concluded that IFC's staff never seriously considered the environmental and social aspects of the dam in determining whether to finance the project. Indeed, the review found that the IFC had no systematic mechanism for even identifying environmental and social standards.

> It was particularly troubling . . . to discover in the very *first* Pangue Project document—the Project Data Sheet (March 8, 1990)—the statement that although "it appears that . . . the project has significant environmental and socio-economic impacts, proper design, planning and implementation should reduce such impacts to levels acceptable to the World Bank and others."
>
> How, at that early stage in the development of the Pangue Project, could a conclusion of such magnitude [have] been reached without any identified performance standards, compliance criteria or supporting data? The only logical conclusion is that the environmental and social aspects of the IFC project were secondary to financial, construction design and technology considerations.[39]

Apparently, the IFC's environmental and social review of the Pangue project was designed to come to one of two preordained outcomes: either the project was in compliance or any problems would be mitigated. The disregard for environmental and social factors was essentially built into IFC's review system, resulting from the lack of capacity to review environmental and social impacts, the lack of relevant policies, and the ultimate authority of the investment officers to accept or reject the environmental findings.

The Pehuén Foundation and the Downing Report

The independent review team also confirmed most of the findings previously reached by an independent anthropologist whom the IFC employed to investigate the operation of the Pehuén Foundation.[40] Marketed as a first-of-its-kind arrangement in South America, the Pehuén Foundation was supposed to share benefits from the dam projects with the local indigenous communities. It was an integral part of the IFC's response to early outside pressure and was part of the pitch made to gain the IFC Board's approval for the project. The foundation was supposed to promote sustainable development in Pehuenche communities, facilitate benefit-sharing from the project, mitigate adverse impacts from the project, and preserve and reinforce the cultural identity of the Pehuenche.[41]

In response to the growing concerns over the foundation's misuse as a tool for acculturating the Pehuenche, the IFC hired Theodore Downing to evaluate the foundation. Downing's report concluded that the net loss in natural resources for the Pehuenche economy was appreciably greater than the benefits that the foundation provided to the community.[42] Downing also highlighted the lack of meaningful community participation in the foundation's implementation, a lack of staff expertise in working with indigenous peoples, and a conflict of interest between other corporate goals and its official mandate. For example, a majority of the foundation's board, including the president, was appointed by a subsidiary of ENDESA. The people in charge of the foundation's operations thus had vested economic interests in the construction of the Ralco Dam.

Downing's contract included a clause allowing him to provide the results of his research to the Pehuenche in a culturally appropriate fashion. Downing intended to present a summary of his findings to the three Pehuenche communities, to ENDESA and the IFC, and to civil society in a seminar. Two weeks after Downing delivered his report in May 1996, the IFC presented a summary of it to ENDESA. The company promptly threatened to sue the IFC and Downing if they disclosed the anthropologist's report to either the Pehuenche or the public. As a result, the IFC sought to prevent public disclosure of the report, sparking substantial controversy within and outside the IFC.

Finally, in December 1997, eighteen months after originally receiving the report, the IFC informed Downing that it would not proceed legally if he disclosed the report, as long as he stated that the report was not an official

IFC document. During these months of delay, the Ralco EIA process required by the new Chilean Environmental Framework Law was under way. Thus, ENDESA's litigation threats and IFC's refusal to disclose the report effectively prevented the community from having access to critical information that revealed extensive environmental harm as well as threats to Pehuenche culture and forceful resettlement from their ancestral lands. These findings, if revealed in a timely manner, could have had a decisive impact over the EIA process.[43]

The independent review concluded that "From the Project's inception, the *Pehuenche* have not been informed participants of ^actions which have a substantial bearing on their future. *Pehuenche* Board members had little knowledge of Foundation statutory objectives, finances, their juridical and fiduciary rights and obligations as Board members, or staff salaries or benefits."[44] The review team also chastised the IFC for failing to translate the Downing report into Spanish and release it publicly. The report concluded that the "entire matter on how the IFC has dealt with indigenous peoples associated with the *Pangue* project has been and continues to be very unfortunate."[45]

IFC's Response: Too Little, Too Late

When it came, IFC's response to the independent review and the Downing report would be too late to have any meaningful benefit for local people or any effective oversight over their borrower. In a February 1997 letter to the Chilean minister of finance, President Wolfensohn announced the IFC's intent to hold ENDESA in default of the loan and to disclose both the independent review and the Downing report. He said:

> I regret to inform you that ENDESA appears to have taken a less than constructive approach to its environmental and social obligations in particular with regard to the preparation of a satisfactory cumulative impact assessment for the Ralco project and is in a situation of imminent default under the IFC financing agreements.
>
> You should also be aware that two independent reviews of the project— drafts of which have been made available to Pangue—are highly critical of IFC's handling of the environmental appraisal and supervision of the Pangue project and of the compliance of Pangue S.A. and ENDESA with their obligations under the IFC agreements. It is our intention to disclose these two reports, despite the strong objections of Pangue S.A. We will of course remove any confidential business information but we owe it to our shareholders and to the other stakeholders of our organization to be as transparent and open as possible.[46]

By this time, however, ENDESA's need for IFC was over. On March 6, 1997, Chile's President Eduardo Frei inaugurated the Pangue Dam. Five days later, ENDESA prepaid its $150 million loan to the IFC in a deliberate effort to avoid complying with the many promises it made to gain IFC's financing years before. As a result of the prepayment, IFC's only remaining leverage in the project was its 2.5 percent equity interest in PANGUE S.A.

On April 25, 1997, the IFC and ENDESA reached a final agreement on how to address outstanding environmental and social issues arising from IFC's investment in the Pangue Dam project. According to the agreement, PANGUE S.A. once again reaffirmed its commitment to ensure compliance with the environmental requirements previously introduced in the loan agreement. After years of violating the original environmental covenants of the loan agreement, the IFC attained nothing more from its client than *another* promise of future compliance.

Having used IFC financing to ensure the viability of the project, ENDESA subsequently walked away from most of the environmental and social conditions. IFC, for its part, was complicit in this process, failing to place clear enforceable terms in the loan agreement and stalling enforcement of the loan conditions. By the time IFC belatedly started to take significant steps to demand compliance, the Pangue/Ralco projects were on firm financial footing, had received all necessary project approvals, and were nearing completion. At that point, ENDESA simply reneged on its promises with impunity. Moreover, the IFC negotiations that left ENDESA off the hook were done in secret and occurred *before* either the independent review or the Downing report were released to the public, thus insulating IFC from any public pressure until it was too late.[47]

THE GREENING OF THE IFC

More than any other project in IFC's history, the Biobío controversy drove reforms at the IFC. Persistent pressure from GABB and its international allies, especially the Swedish Society for Nature Conservation (SSCN) in Sweden, Urgewald in Germany, and U.S.-based CIEL, FoE, and BIC, eventually convinced IFC management that they had neither sufficient policies in place nor the commitment and capacity to implement them. The clear findings of the independent review left no doubt of the need for fundamental reform at the IFC. The following discussions highlight some of the institutional changes arising from the Biobío campaign, lingering issues at the IFC and, most important, the failure of this process to respond to the plight of the affected Pehuenche communities.

Internal Environmental and Social Review

The Independent Review's findings that IFC had never identified clearly which World Bank policies applied to the Pangue/Ralco projects led the IFC, beginning in 1998, to review systematically its environmental and social policy framework. The IFC decided to adopt each of the World Bank's environmental and social safeguards after evaluating and modifying them in light of the IFC's private-sector focus.[48]

In addition, the IFC strengthened its professional capacity to review environmental and social issues. At the time the IFC was first reviewing the loan application for the Biobío dams, the IFC had one environmental professional with limited Spanish language skills. It now has eighty environmental and social issues staff, many with significant experience. The IFC now requires that all projects receive specific approval from the environmental and social unit. In contrast, at the time of the Pangue project, approval of the project was entirely at the discretion of the investment officer, and the environmental staff served merely as advisers.

Despite these improvements, the IFC is still struggling with its environmental and social role. Environmentally and socially harmful projects are still a common part of the IFC's portfolio. There is still no effective environmental and social screen for projects, and the investment officers still operate under a culture of approval that has yet to reflect a complete institutional shift toward environmental and social sustainability. Moreover, many observers believe that the momentum for reform that emerged from the acknowledged mismanagement of the Biobío project has stalled in recent years.

Information Disclosure and Business Confidentiality

In 1994, the IFC established an information disclosure policy, which attempted to balance the private sector's need for confidentiality with the public's right to know about projects. In part because of criticism raised in the independent review, in September 1998 the IFC issued a revised policy on disclosure of information, which was accompanied by a *Good Practice* manual aimed at orienting project sponsors toward enhanced public consultation and disclosure.

Under the 1998 information disclosure policy, the IFC is making more information available than in the pre-Biobío days. But the institution continues to operate under an unacceptable standard that allows the business client unilateral prerogative in labeling information as "business confidential." The

IFC has never implemented the independent review's recommendation to make environmental and social loan conditions public.

In sum, the institution has not formally changed any of the practices that led to the conflict over release of the independent review's report, and continued conflicts over information disclosure can be expected in the future. The continued failure to release the specific language of environmental and social conditions in loan agreements could lead to a repeat of the Biobío case. If local communities do not know the rights and protections they have received in the loan agreements, they will have no way to effectively monitor IFC's supervision or a project's implementation.

IFC'S COMPLIANCE ADVISOR/OMBUDSMAN

Part of the motivation behind filing the Biobío claim to the World Bank's Inspection Panel was to highlight the need for an accountability mechanism that covered the private-sector arms of the World Bank Group, the IFC, and the Multilateral Investment Guarantee Agency (MIGA). As a result of the Biobío claim and continued NGO pressure,[49] in early 1996 the board directed the IFC and MIGA to study how an inspection mechanism could be applied to their operations.[50] The IFC and MIGA announced their intention to create an inspection mechanism and initially outlined their proposals for the mechanism in a number of meetings with NGOs and industry and two internal documents.[51]

Opened in 1999, the new Compliance Advisor and Ombudsman (CAO) office uses both an ombudsman and a compliance advisory role to attempt to resolve complaints from project-affected persons and address issues of policy noncompliance within the institution. The CAO is appointed by and reports directly to the World Bank president and is thus independent of IFC staff and management. The CAO operates by using a problem-solving mixture of fact-finding, consultation, mediation, and conflict resolution.[52]

The office controls its own hiring of staff and consultants, and has thus far been allowed to operate free from undue influence by IFC management. Although the ombudsman process does not provide the same clear procedural process of the World Bank's Inspection Panel, it is designed to offer a more flexible and solution-oriented structure. The general effectiveness of the CAO's office in responding to the complaints of project-affected people is still difficult to evaluate, given that relatively little information is available on specific claims. There is thus a trade-off between flexibility and predictability, as claimants and other interested parties wait in vain for the CAO to provide information about its various reviews.

CONCLUSION: INSTITUTIONAL REFORMS
AND UNFULFILLED PROMISES

The Biobío campaign met with appreciably different levels of success when viewed from the international, national, or community perspectives.

International Impacts

At the international level, the Biobío campaign has to be considered the single most successful campaign in catalyzing positive reforms at the IFC, and along with the campaign around the Narmada Dam in India, it is one of the most influential campaigns leading to reform of international financial institutions. The Biobío campaign forced the IFC to come to grips with the emerging paradigm of sustainable development. In addition to the policy and institutional reforms discussed above, the Biobío campaign also crystallized fundamental identity issues faced by the IFC: what makes the institution operationally different than any private commercial bank, what public interest does it serve, and why should it continue to exist?

As the independent review found, the IFC added no value to the environmental and social aspects of the project. Given that ENDESA so easily prepaid its loan to the IFC as a means of avoiding accountability, one must question what, if any, positive development impact derived from IFC's participation in the Pangue project. Indeed, if the IFC fails to provide any added value on environmental or social aspects, and if its capital can be so easily replaced through commercial markets, then why does the IFC even exist? Or at least why does it warrant public financial support? These questions continue to plague the IFC, which still struggles to articulate how it implements a poverty alleviation mandate that is worthy of public support (particularly in light of the growing reach of private capital markets).

The IFC has failed to implement many of the independent review's specific recommendations that relate to these mandate issues. For example, the IFC has never adopted the independent review's recommendation that the IFC prescreen their private-sector clients "to ascertain objectively, in advance, their capacity and their top management's willingness (both culturally and from a human/financial resources perspective) to comply with specific World Bank Group requirements."[53]

The IFC should also consider the past performance of companies and blacklist those companies that demonstrate, as did ENDESA in the Biobío case, a blatant disregard for environmental and social concerns. Such a screen could increase the long-term leverage IFC has over companies like ENDESA. This issue could have important implications beyond the Biobío project. In

August 2001, for example, IFC's ombudsman faulted the IFC for not recognizing the poor record of the Shell Corporation before allowing it to control a recent IFC project in the Niger Delta.[54]

National Impacts

The Biobío campaign also had significant implications for the development of democratic institutions at the national level in Chile. The institutions and laws of Chile's fledgling democracy proved to be little match for the underlying economic powers promoting the Pangue/Ralco dams. The Chilean legal framework at the beginning of the 1990s was clearly inadequate to address the environmental and human rights issues involved in major development projects like the Pangue/Ralco dams. The domestic standards were a patchwork array of sectoral norms, which did not require basic environmental management tools such as environmental impact assessments. Moreover, during the time of Pangue's planning and construction no governmental institution had the authority or expertise to address the environmental or indigenous rights issues at stake. The indigenous peoples' law and the environmental framework law were not put in place until 1993 and 1994, respectively.[55]

The demonstrably weak governance structures in Chile highlight a recurring failure of the World Bank Group, including the IFC. These institutions regularly ignore or make unrealistic assumptions about governance structures in borrowing countries to justify supporting and promoting large, high-risk development projects (at least risky to the local communities). Chile was under dictatorial rule when the Pangue/Ralco projects were conceived, and they were pushed through while Chile's nascent democratic institutions were still being formed. The lack of domestic standards and institutions should have alerted the IFC to the need for particular vigilance in ensuring that minimum rights of the communities are fulfilled. The bank's operational directives may be the only viable source of "law" ensuring the participation of affected people, assessment of environmental impacts, mitigation of adverse environmental and social effects, or screening of environmentally unsound projects. Controversies like the Biobío project illustrate the need for the IFC to consider governance capacity and commitment to its environmental and social standards when preparing project loans.

Local Impacts

At the community level, the Biobío campaign must be viewed, at least until now, as mostly a failure—this, regardless of the long-term political empowerment that the struggle against the dams will probably mean for the Pehuenche and the political and economic benefits that might still be negotiated. The Pangue Dam was built and Ralco has been largely unaffected by the campaign and is now moving ahead at full speed. Despite the efforts of the claimants, the IFC successfully avoided considering the linkages between Pangue and Ralco, and avoided dealing with cumulative impacts. In addition, the Pehuenches have received little, if any, meaningful compensation for their losses. The independent review and the Downing report chronicled the harm done to the Pehuenche, but in the end, the IFC did little to ensure that they were compensated.

While the campaign was going on both internationally and nationally, ENDESA successfully employed a "divide-and-conquer" strategy to undermine Pehuenche opposition in the Biobío communities. Employing propaganda, threats, and alcohol, the company was able to co-opt a growing number of Pehuenche. The communities were ill-equipped to face such external pressure, particularly given the limited availability of credible, independent information regarding their rights, even under the Indigenous Law. Moreover, the communities lacked the recognized authority to exclude ENDESA representatives from their territories. Fear and mistrust began to appear within the communities, and the communities were gradually divided. Some families decided to barter their land, while others resisted. Some families moved to the resettlement area, while others remained on their lands, vowing to stay even if their lands were flooded.

Despite the pressure, six Pehuenche families, most of them headed by women, remain staunchly opposed to the project. These relatively few people that have withstood the tremendous pressure to sell their lands in an effort to preserve their culture are the true heroes of the campaign, but ultimately they have received little to show for their effort.

The failure of the Biobío campaign to return real benefits to the local Pehuenche communities reflects in part the different goals of the international and national players in the campaign. The international groups wanted to stop the project, but they also saw the project as a vehicle for reforming the IFC. For the Pehuenche and GABB, however, stopping the project was the highest priority goal. It is not that these goals conflicted, but rather that the international campaign could not actively engage over the long-term at the national or subnational level. Facing choices about how to spend resources among literally dozens of similar development controversies around the world, these groups often prioritize according to the likelihood that the project can catalyze broader policy reforms. For example, the international part of the campaign was largely dormant for several years after the project was approved by the IFC, until failures to implement the IFC-imposed conditions became clear. During this time, Chile's national institutions and civil society were addressing the environmental assessment and the Pehuenche's rights.

The international networks are necessarily less effective when engaging at the national level. The major driving force for reform—the independent review of the project—was (like the Inspection Panel after which it was patterned) ultimately limited to reviewing the activity and conduct of the IFC. Any of the report's conclusions that may have implicated the company or Chile were never disclosed. Thus, the independent review proved to be relatively ineffective for changing the behavior of the company in the country. Had the report's conclusions about ENDESA's conduct been made public at the outset, the campaign's overall impact on the Pehuenche's plight could have been greater.

EPILOGUE

The IFC has yet to accept its share of responsibility for the plight of the Pehuenche. In July 1998, GABB submitted to top bank management a proposal that would compensate the Pehuenche for enduring the negative social and environmental impacts of the Pangue/Ralco project. GABB suggested, among other things, that the "IFC transfer the ownership of their equity (2.5%) to the local Pehuenche communities, through an organization that they recognize as representative of their leadership and interests and in order to finance their plans for sustainable development."[56] The World Bank president never responded to this suggestion.

Interestingly enough, one avenue of recourse may be through the IFC's ombudsman, created in response to the original Pangue Inspection Panel claim. Among the first complaints sent to the IFC ombudsman was one on behalf of a Pehuenche family living near the Biobío that was never considered for relocation and that has been living in miserable conditions for the past three years. The CAO investigated this complaint—the Sotomayor claim—and then convinced the company to provide additional support in the form of new land, some livestock, and a small trust fund to be managed for the education of the children.

Encouraged by the result of the Sotomayor claim, on July 1, 2002, local residents negatively affected by the Pangue/Ralco dams filed a petition with the IFC ombudsman to address outstanding issues resulting from the hydroelectric projects. As of January 2003, the ombudsman's work was still underway, representing perhaps the IFC's last chance for providing meaningful redress to the Pehuenche for the damages caused by a dam that should never have been built, and certainly would never have been financed by the IFC had it lived up to its environmental and social responsibilities.

Almost eight months after the filing of the petition, the CAO office had yet to come up with its initial results of the investigation. Time will soon tell if the IFC's accountability mechanism will make a difference on the ground for those it is supposed to serve. As with the previous Hair investigation, the CAO inquiry of early 2003 was occurring at a crucial time for the dam projects. Tired after years of a very difficult struggle and with the Ralco Dam construction going ahead around them, some of the Pehuenche families decided to swap their lands. In December 2002, several Pehuenche families filed a petition with the OAS (Organization of American States) Human Rights Commission alleging that the government was violating their rights. Two days later, in view of the urgency of the situation, the Inter-American Commission on Human Rights requested precautionary measures to prevent irreparable harm to the petitioners, which induced the Chilean government for the first time to try to negotiate a settlement with the families. Proposals for the creation of a new indigenous county in the Upper Biobío, the purchase of disputed land in all the vicinity, a percentage of Ralco Dam profits, and proper environmental monitoring of the dams were on the table.

Still unclear is whether the IFC's accountability mechanism (the CAO) will complement the negotiation and help to at least partly reverse the tragedy that has befallen the Pehuenche or whether, as in the past, the accountability mechanism will serve more as a mea culpa that is interesting for historians and useful for the public image of the bank than as a mechanism for correcting and compensating the damage caused by the IFC's mistakes.

NOTES

1. The story of the struggle to save the Biobío River is explored in a more detailed version of this chapter, at www.bicusa.org.

2. Rodolfo Von Bennewitz, "Hydrological Resources of the BíoBío Basin" (paper presented at the University of Santiago, Chile, 1990), 83–130.

3. José Bengoa, *Historia de un Conflicto* [History of a conflict] (1999), 21.

4. Jorge Calbucurá, *Legal Process of Abolition of Collective Property: The Mapuche Case* (Uppsala: Uppsala University).

5. José Bengoa, *Historia del Pueblo Mapuche, Siglo XIX y XX* (Santiago, Chile: Sur, 1985).

6. See, e.g., Maggie Bowden, "UN Sub-Commission on the Promotion and Protection of Human Rights," E/CN.4/Sub.2/1999/SR.19, paragraphs 29, 48, and Domingo Namuncura, "UN Commission of Human Rights," E/CN.4/1998/SR.19, paragraphs 25–28 (discussing marginalization of the Mapuche).

7. See Raúl Molina and Martín Correa, *Territorio y Comunidades Pehuenches de Alto BíoBío,* Comisión Especial de Pueblos Indígenas (Santiago: CONADI, 1996).

8. ENDESA presented a report to the IFC that distorted Valenzuela's conclusions; the anthropologist sued (unsuccessfully) and subsequently joined GABB (see Jorge

Moraga, *Aguas Turbias, La Central Ralco en el Alto BíoBío,* Observatorio Latinoamericano de Conflictos Ambientales [Latin American Observatory of Environmental Conflicts], 2001, 29–30).

9. See María Olivia Monckeberg, *El Saqueo de los Grupos Ecónomicos al Estado Chileno* (Santiago: Ediciones B, 2001), 108–26.

10. Juan Pablo Orrego, interviewed by Marcos Orellana, Santiago de Chile, July 14, 2000.

11. Lower House of Parliament, *Proyectos de Acuerdos,* March 18, 1993, and April 11, 1993.

12. See, e.g., John Sears and Katherine Bragg, "Bio-Bio: A River Under Threat," *The Ecologist,* vol. 17, no. 1 (1987); Michael Powers, "Last Stand of the BíoBío: What's Happening to Chile's Grand Canyon?" *Canoe* (July 1990); "Four Hundred Pehuenche Families Refuse to Be Driven Off Lands," *South and Meso American Indian Information Center Newsletter* 5, no. 3–4 (December 1990).

13. IFC, *IFC and the Environment: 1992 Annual Review* (1992), 5.

14. See, e.g., IRN to Alan Hooper, senior investment officer, IFC, November 26, 1990, and IRN to Martin Riddle, environmental officer, IFC, December 27, 1990.

15. University of Chile, Prien *Uso Eficiente de la Electricidad en Chile,* June 1996.

16. Scott Guggenheim, consultant to the World Bank, to Kent Lupberger, the World Bank, November 7, 1991.

17. Monenco, Inc., "Assessment of Electric Power Generation Alternatives," draft, October 1992, S-6, S-13 to S-14.

18. See, e.g., Lewis Preston, president of the IFC, report to the IFC Board of Directors entitled "Report to the Board of Directors on a Proposed Investment in Empresa Electrica Pangue S.A. Chile" (restricted document), IFC/P-1169, November 23, 1992 (acknowledging plans for six dams on the Biobío, but claiming that the IFC would look at cumulative impacts only when asked to review future projects).

19. Mark M. Collins Jr., U.S. alternate executive director, statement to the IFC Board of Directors, December 17, 1992, 2–3.

20. IFC, "Summary of Discussions at the Meeting of the Board of Directors of IFC," December 17, 1992, paragraphs 39–40.

21. Pangue Audit Team, *Pangue Hydroelectric Project (Chile): An Independent Review of the International Finance Corporation's Compliance with Applicable World Bank Group Environmental and Social Requirements,* April 1997, executive summary, 3–4 (hereinafter *Independent Review*).

22. Christopher Herman, U.S. EPA, memorandum to Nancy Katz, June 26, 1995, 2 (reviewing the IFC's "Response to Questions on Pangue," June 16, 1995).

23. Herman, memorandum to Katz, June 16, 1995, 1.

24. Charlotte Roe, Department of State, to William Partridge, environmental chief, Latin American Division, World Bank, November 13, 1995, 1.

25. See Cristián Opaso and Juan Pablo Oreggo, GABB, to James Wolfensohn, president, the World Bank Group, November 17, 1995.

26. "Open Letter to World Bank President and Board of Executive Directors on the Need to Extend the Inspection Panel's Mandate to Cover the IFC and MIGA" (undated).

27. "The BíoBío Dams in Chile: Violations of World Bank Policies and Lack of Accountability at the IFC, Claim before the Inspection Panel of the World Bank and Petition before the IFC Board of Executive Directors," filed by GABB on behalf of Pehuenches and other Chileans, November 1995 (hereinafter cited as "Biobío Inspection Panel Claim").

28. See IFC, "Project Summary," 14.

29. See, e.g., Charlotte Roe, Department of State, "IFC and the Pangue/Ralco Projects in Chile: Issues Raised by the BíoBío Complaint" (undated memorandum).

30. See, e.g., Richard Bissell, chapter 2 of this volume.

31. IFC, "Terms of Reference: Independent Advisor for Internal Review of Pangue Project," June 7, 1996, paragraph 4.

32. David Hunter and Dana Clark (CIEL) and Andrea Durbin (FoE–U.S.) to Jay D. Hair, independent advisor, IFC, July 22, 1996, and Jay D. Hair, independent advisor, IFC, memorandum to Dana Clark, David Hunter, and Andrea Durbin, July 23, 1996.

33. *Independent Review,* 23.

34. Gaston Aigaren, chief executive officer, Pangue S.A., to Assad J. Jabre, vice president, IFC, March 1997: "Because the report clearly contains confidential and proprietary information and because Pangue explicitly declines to consent to its dissemination, any dissemination would be a breach of this [nondisclosure] requirement. Dissemination of the Hair report could also jeopardize the ability of the IFC and Pangue to continue their effective work on ongoing aspects of the Pangue Project." See also James Wolfensohn to Jay Hair, June 2, 1997 (citing risks of litigation and liability as reasons for redacting some of the report).

35. Jay Hair to James Wolfensohn, July 25, 1997.

36. *Independent Review,* 3, paragraphs 7–10.

37. *Independent Review,,* executive summary, 4, paragraph 18.

38. *Independent Review,* 26–27.

39. *Independent Review,* 35–36.

40. *Independent Review,* 87.

41. Theodore Downing, "Independent Review of the Pehuén Foundation," May 7, 1996, paragraph 3.

42. Barbara Johnston, "The Pehuenche, the World Bank Group and ENDESA S.A.," report of the Committee for Human Rights of the American Anthropological Association, April 20, 1998, 15, and Theodore Downing, "Independent Review of the Pehuén Foundation," paragraph 28.

43. See, e.g., Mauricio Huenchulaf, national director, CONADI, to James Wolfensohn, president, IFC, April 15, 1997 (noting the "urgent" need to release the Downing report while the Ralco EIA was being reviewed). Downing ultimately filed a claim before the American Anthropological Association (AAA) advancing the Pehuenche's human rights and his own rights as an anthropologist. Downing argued that the IFC's threatened legal action effectively precluded him from acting according to his professional ethical codes by delivering the findings of his research to the Pehuenche. The AAA confirmed Downing's allegations and challenged the IFC to compensate the Pehuenche for damages done and to adopt a permanent policy of protecting the human rights of project-affected people (see Barbara Johnston, "The Pehuenche, the World Bank Group").

44. *Independent Review,* 85. The ^ mark in the *Independent Review* denotes where text has been censored by the IFC.

45. *Independent Review,* 87.

46. James Wolfensohn, president of the World Bank Group, to Eduardo Aninat, minister of finance, February 7, 1997. Pressure from ENDESA and disagreements over what should be considered confidential kept the *Independent Review* from being disclosed for six more months.

47. IFC failed to learn its lesson from ENDESA's effort to avoid IFC oversight by prepaying its loan; several years later Basic Oil Company prepaid its loan for construction of a pipeline through a Guatemalan wildlife reserve rather than meet the promises it had made to the IFC (in an agreement IFC had brokered with Conservation International) (see Ian Bowles et al., "The Environmental Impacts of International Finance Corporation Lending and Proposals for Reform: A Case Study of Conservation and Oil Development in the Guatemalan Peten," *Environmental Law* 29 [1999]: 103). To avoid recurrence of this problem, the IFC should require performance bonds or insurance to ensure that environmental and social promises made to gain IFC approval are kept once the project is underway.

48. Among the policies adopted in this way were IFC equivalents of the World Bank policies on environmental assessment, natural habitats, pest management, forestry, and international waterways.

49. See, e.g., David Hunter, CIEL, and Andrea Durbin, FoE–U.S., "Proposal for Independent Review Panel for IFC and MIGA," July 31, 1997.

50. World Bank Group, report to Committee on Development and Effectiveness, "Integrated Accountability Mechanism for IFC and MIGA" (undated), 7 (in which the board instructed the IFC and MIGA to "develop a proposal on an inspection mechanism designed to meet the needs of the private sector").

51. IFC and MIGA report to the Committee on Development Effectiveness, "Proposed Inspection Mechanism for Private Sector Projects: IFC and MIGA Inspection Panel," June 27, 1996.

52. IFC, "Compliance Advisor and Ombudsman, Operational Guidelines," April 2000, 7.

53. *Independent Review,* 158.

54. Office of the Compliance Advisor/Ombudsman, "Assessment Report: Complaint Filed to the CAO Regarding the Nigeria Delta Contractor Revolving Credit Facility," August 2001, 4.

55. Chile's weak environmental and social governance system was considered by the bank as early as 1991, but was never viewed as a significant reason to postpone the project (see Scott Guggenheim, consultant to the World Bank, to Kent Lupberger, November 7, 1991).

56. Cristián Opaso, "The BíoBío Hydroelectric Project: A Lesson Not Fully Learned," World Commission on Dams Regional Consultations for Latin America, São Paulo, Brazil, August 1999.

7

The Inspection Panel Claims in Brazil

Aurélio Vianna Jr.

USING THE INSPECTION PANEL REFLECTS
SOCIAL AND POLITICAL LEARNING

The World Bank Inspection Panel is an important transnational instrument that makes it possible for civil-society actors to register complaints about bank-funded projects in their countries without having to go through their national governments. This study will analyze the main trends in Brazil's extensive experience with the Inspection Panel, which so far has involved five separate claims involving three different projects. In each case, the analysis focuses on how these citizen campaigns, which tried to use the panel process, unfolded in the local, national, and transnational arenas.

The panel was created as a response to pressures from the transnational movement of civil-society organizations to reform and increase transparency and participation in the World Bank, but so far it has been used by civil-society actors in relatively few countries of the global South. Moreover, these claims have addressed just a few projects, and have involved a limited number of organizations. The explanations may vary—from mere lack of knowledge about the panel's existence on the part of civil-society actors in some countries, to an assessment by some civil-society organizations (CSOs) that the panel process is not likely to be able to advance their struggles and demands.[1] In addition, while the decision to create the Inspection Panel was a response to transnational protests, including strong Southern mobilizations, its specific procedures and institutional process responded more to the demands of the Northern NGOs.

Translated by Charles Roberts

The Brazilian experience helps to shed light on this dilemma. More claims to the panel have come from Brazil than from any other country, but not just because of the large number of projects the bank financed there, nor because Brazil's projects are necessarily the most disastrous in the world. The Brazilian experience suggests that civil-society decisions to make panel claims in a given country are the result of a process of social and political learning.[2] This process includes, first, the accumulation of CSO expertise about both public policy advocacy in general and the World Bank in particular, and second, their analytical assessment that submitting a claim might bolster a specific campaign.

The broader national political context is extremely relevant. In Brazil, the process of re-democratization is crucial for understanding both the civil-society actors and their advocacy strategies. This transition to democracy included the 1988 Constitutional Assembly, when civil society became politically networked through grassroots organizations associated with the Catholic Church (Christian base communities and pastoral committees), mass social movements (such as MST—the Movimento dos Sem Terra, or Landless Movement), trade unions that organized into national federations (such as the Central Única dos Trabalhadores, or CUT), and, finally, organizations that supported grassroots movements. This highly diverse group of organizations demanded the right to participate in the formulation of Brazil's public policies. Their campaigns produced results, including laws that created important new policy instruments, such as the National Public Policy Councils, balanced government–civil society power-sharing bodies that debate and carry out social policies; the possibility of having recourse to the Public Ministry, a judicial body that receives complaints from society; and the increased use of congressional committees and public hearings.

It was in this context, in the second half of the 1980s, that the demands for the right to participation, and for *effective* participation, came to the fore in the institutional culture of Brazilian civil-society organizations. This process gathered steam in the 1990s, when a considerable number of groups identified themselves as NGOs in the context of the 1992 United Nations Conference on Environment and Development and the parallel Global NGO Forum, held in Rio de Janeiro.

Brazil's democratic transition and the launching of participatory institutions in the national government happened at the same time that the international debate was heating up about the World Bank and the need for public information access, participation, and accountability. The debate about the Inspection Panel and other bank policy reforms came at a time when Brazilian CSOs were engaged with similar issues in the domestic arena.

There are at least two different ways to assess the effectiveness of panel claims—one is direct, and involves the project-specific issues driving the claims themselves. On the other hand, the possible indirect impacts of panel claims are quite different. For example, the process of making a panel claim can empower a local organization, which then seeks to bring about change in a local project or policy. The greater the number of different "actors" involved (local and national governments and civil-society organizations), the more difficult it is to assess the direct impact of a claim, thus making it almost impossible to determine what would have happened had the claim not been submitted.[3] Specifically, this hypothetical question is what would have happened without the *claim,* since none from Brazil led to a full panel inspection. Because each claim represented a specific moment in a broader process of struggles around specific projects involving demands to the government and to the World Bank, it is difficult to separate the distinct impact of using that specific tool.

Looking at panel claims through a national lens contrasts with a "World Bank–centered" analysis, which focuses on whether the bank's policies were violated and what project changes could be attributed to the panel process. The direct stakeholders who bring claims always have an eye on their own interests, which will differ from those of the World Bank as an institution, and even from the goals of the bank staff charged with carrying out its social and environmental policies. For example, from the standpoint of Brazilian CSOs, or even in terms of the impact on the communities affected by these projects, the most important result of engaging with the panel process may be to create or strengthen civil-society coalitions and their advocacy capacity. It is also important to keep in mind that the use of the panel in Brazil, more than elsewhere, provoked a political backlash from the Brazilian government's representative on the bank's board of executive directors. Paradoxically, one of the main impacts of the Brazilian panel claims was that the Brazilian government sought to limit the panel's autonomy and operational capacity at the global level of the bank's board of directors.[4] In the context of these dilemmas, this study focuses on the ways in which Brazilian CSOs used the panel process and on the limitations and advantages they encountered.

Brazilian CSOs became involved in the debate on the World Bank through two different pathways: the broad public campaigns against foreign debt and the more focused responses to socioenvironmental disasters.[5] Yet while the different campaigns around foreign debt linked the World Bank, the Inter-American Development Bank, and the International Monetary Fund with macroeconomic disasters in the eyes of the broader public, the environmental issue, or the socioenvironmental issue, created a different image. Through this lens, the public associated World Bank–financed infrastructure projects with socioenvironmental disasters, while later the bank's (or banks') "new face," became one that finances environmental and social projects.

In other words, it was *not* the broader campaigns on the World Bank in Brazil—such as the campaign around the debt—that led several civil-society organizations to study how they might take advantage of the World Bank's social and environmental policies. It was the World Bank's increased involvement in projects with very tangible, local social and environmental impacts—in the 1980s destructive impacts and in the 1990s ostensibly positive impacts—that appears to have drawn CSO attention to the bank's reform policies. CSOs sought to respond to those projects in Brazil in which they felt they had—and were considered by others to have—a very direct stake.

PLANAFLORO: PRESSURING THE BANK AND LEVERAGING CHANGES IN NATIONAL POLICY[6]

The Program for the Integrated Development of Northwestern Brazil (Polonoroeste), financed by the World Bank in the 1980s, was a typical developmentalist project that caused environmental and social destruction in the Brazilian Amazon. This classic "development disaster" became the target of an international campaign seeking environmental and social policy reform in the mid 1980s.[7] The Polonoroeste campaign became a paradigm case of the "boomerang effect," as Margaret Keck and Kathryn Sikkink call it,[8] in which a coalition of local organizations, together with national and international counterparts, brought pressure to bear on the bank, which in turn pressured the Brazilian government and the state government, leading to a major change in the project. The project was restructured, in a context of political transition toward democratic consolidation and still-weak civil-society organizations.

This campaign led to the design of a new project, Planafloro, with a loan targeted to the same Amazonian state of Rondônia, which was supposed to prevent the negative impacts of disorderly small-farmer settlement fostered by Polonoroeste. In other words, even before the Inspection Panel was created, a campaign with both international and national dimensions was able to halt a project and provoke the design of another project at least ostensibly intended to ameliorate some of the effects of the first one.[9] At the same time, this new project also reflected the interests of the bank task manager and his clients in the state and federal governments. They appropriated the environmental/sustainable development rhetoric that was so much in vogue in the run-up to the Earth Summit, using CSO rhetoric to package a project they wanted anyway. The specific NGO critiques at the time (including that of the Environmental Defense Fund) were based on the perception that their rhetoric was being hijacked for the purposes of the bank–government agenda, which in general proved to be true.

The Planafloro project provoked the formation of a new statewide civil-society advocacy coalition, the Rondônia NGO Forum. In 1994, the forum's (then) principally NGO leadership used the federal courts to challenge the state and federal government for allowing violations of environmental zoning. The forum was internally divided, however. The major small-farmers' organizations hadn't been involved in the strategy, and the grassroots groups (Indians, rubber-tappers, local environmentalists) were not adequately prepared for the possibility that their policy advocacy strategy might work. When the forum publicly called on the bank to suspend the Planafloro loan, with support from international NGOs, it collapsed under the weight of its own success. The bank staff (realizing that they were legally and politically very vulnerable) and the state government went all out to get the forum to agree to anything that would get them to drop the demand for suspension. In the absence of a strategy that would allow grassroots leaders to build a constituency for reforming the project or broader alliances with other civil-society actors, the forum was reduced to two isolated NGO activists (one foreign) negotiating with an army of bank staff, the entire state government, and a host of federal agencies. The two agreed to a hypercomplex action plan, with dozens of points and stipulations about CSO participation that were overly ambitious on logistical grounds alone.[10]

The Inspection Panel case was presented the next year by the forum (involving local NGOs, the small-farmers association, the rubber-tappers' union, and indigenous groups), together with an international NGO that lacked networks in Rondônia, based on an a priori assumption that bringing a panel case was a good thing. For the NGO activists who prepared the claim, it was a means to recover from the debacle of the suspension request. The forum never regained the leverage it had with the national legal strategy (which was dropped in favor of the panel case, more out of preference—or fear—than because it had run its course). They had, in effect, traded a more direct strategy—the courts—for an indirect one—the Inspection Panel.

In August 1995, the panel recommended to the World Bank's board that it carry out a complete investigation of Planafloro. The then-executive director for Brazil (Marcos Caramuru) asserted that this would constitute meddling in national sovereignty, leading to an impasse, whereupon the panel engaged in further preliminary investigations that resulted in another recommendation for an inspection. As an alternative to the panel investigation, the project manager submitted an action plan to improve project implementation, which allowed the board to reject the panel's recommendation for an investigation in favor of the action plan's more ad hoc approach.

The project's difficulties on the ground persisted, and it was only after the bank's 1996 mid-term evaluation that changes really happened. The very fact that these different actors signed a document in 1996 itself merits a more in-depth analysis.[11] The changes proposed for the project (independent of their effectiveness) emerged from the momentum of the legacy of the international and national network of alliances organized around Polonoroeste. International NGOs played a key role in the negotiations—a reflection of their bargaining power and the Amazon's international salience. The government authorities even showed an unusually high degree of deference to the NGOs' direct involvement (despite the government's opposition to such involvement). The state and federal governments' agreement to include a power-sharing arrangement with local CSOs in the project may have reflected their lack of a sense of ownership of the project, considering it to be a narrowly "World Bank project" in which the NGOs were very influential. In effect, the state government's role suggests that it considered the Planafloro project itself as a federal/World Bank intervention in the state of Rondônia, which it sought to use for its own purposes.

The result of the whole project restructuring process was greater control by the Rondônia-based CSOs, and the earmarking of a significant fraction of project resources for CSO projects in the state. There were, however, major problems in terms of their participation in the project's consultative and deliberative councils and in the effective disbursement of the resources earmarked to the CSOs. In December 1999, these issues led the Forum of NGOs and the Federation of Agricultural Workers of the State of Rondônia (the main small-farmers association, which had separated from the forum) to step down from all of the project's joint decision-making bodies.

The CSOs of Rondônia created the Forum of NGOs and Social Movements of Rondônia as a coalition for civil-society participation in Planafloro. In other words, one immediate effect of the claim was to "facilitate" the broader organization of civil society. This does not mean that the existence of the project "created" or strengthened civil society in the state of Rondônia. Polonoroeste and Planafloro no doubt encouraged transnational and statewide alliances of CSOs. Their advocacy campaigns strengthened the Rondônia CSOs at some points, and at other times weakened them, but in the process, they became political actors.

The Accumulation of the Brazilian CSOs' Understanding of the World Bank and the Panel: Rede Brasil and the Bank's Liaison Officer

In 1995, more than thirty CSOs launched the Brazilian Network on Multilateral Financial Institutions (Rede Brasil sobre Instituições Financeiras Multilaterais). The Rondônia Forum, as well as several organizations that had participated in the process that resulted from the Planafloro panel claim, were among the founders of the Rede Brasil. Large national "flagship" NGOs were also key founders, such as INESC (Instituto de Estudos Socio-Econômicos, or Institute of Socioeconomic Research), IBASE (Instituto Brasileiro de Análises Socio-Econômicas, or Brazilian Institute of Social and Economic Analysis), and FASE (Federação de Órgãos para Assistência Social e Educaçional, or the Federation of Social and Educational Agencies), which brought strong technical capacities and political reputations to the new network. Key founding trade unions brought a broad social base to Rede Brasil, including the National Federation of Agricultural Workers (Confederação Nacional dos Trabalhadores na Agricultura, or CONTAG), which includes more than three thousand peasant unions nationwide, the Pólo Sindical de Itaparica (Itaparica Union Coalition), a coalition of peasant unions from the northeast and politically aligned with CONTAG, and the National Federation of Bank Employees, one of the most powerful white-collar trade unions.

With the creation of Rede Brasil, a wide range of organizations forged a common agenda, ranging from the "Bank bashers" to those seeking to reform projects already receiving multilateral funding. Rede Brasil, based on a partnership between domestic CSOs with the Environmental Defense Fund (EDF; now Environmental Defense) and Oxfam–U.K., sought to serve as an issue-based coalition pulling together organizations affected by, or interested in, the multilateral financial institutions, without, however, seeking to represent them. This facilitated the membership of different types of organizations. Both a national trade union federation with hundreds of thousands of members and a local NGO with twenty members could participate on an equal footing and without political problems, because Rede Brasil could support its member organizations' demands without claiming to represent them.

Rede Brasil clearly emerged from international campaigns promoted by Northern NGOs. Brazilian CSOs that had participated in international campaigns, together with Northern NGOs with a long track record of Brazilian partnerships, developed a strategy that encouraged Brazilian CSOs to deal with the IFIs (International Financial Institutions) in the national arena, and not just as grassroots organizations that are part of "international" alliances that lobby in Washington to have the multilateral banks pressure the Brazilian government. For Brazilian CSOs, Rede Brasil came to operate as a clearinghouse on this issue, even for unaffiliated CSOs.

Just when Rede Brasil was launched, the World Bank hired a liaison officer to relate to Brazilian civil society, which helped various CSOs learn more about the bank's role and responsibility in relation to different projects in Brazil.[12] Through seminars, meetings, and publications, the World Bank and its policies came to have a place in the debates of many Brazilian CSOs. Rede Brasil responded to CSO demands in this process and has helped to create claims by holding training courses in which the panel was noted as one possible avenue for advocacy.

The debate on the use of the Inspection Panel and other World Bank policies was discussed with organizations that had always questioned the legitimacy of seeking to have a U.S.-dominated multilateral institution pressure the Brazilian government. The Planafloro experience was seen as an exception, because of both the nature of the project and the NGOs involved, but the panel claim put the possibility of using bank policies on the agenda of a broader group of Brazilian CSOs. Rede Brasil's most significant contribution as a coalition of constituency-based social organizations and NGO allies was to increase Brazilian CSO awareness of the IFIs and the possible range of strategies for action.

Rede Brasil's Post–"Boomerang Effect" Strategy

In 1997, Rede Brasil was actively engaged in what it considered a new political advocacy strategy toward the multilateral institutions and international alliances. In this approach, the political rationale for bringing a claim before a multilateral institution was determined not by Brazil's status as client or victim, but by its status as shareholder. And CSO demands (including claims to the Inspection Panel) were based on the belief that the Brazilian government was represented on the boards of these institutions, as a minor shareholder in the case of the World Bank, and as a major shareholder in the case of the Inter-American Development Bank (IDB). In addition, Rede Brasil included on its agenda the struggle to change the multilateral balance of power within these institutions, promoting the "one country-one vote" position instead of the ruling "one dollar-one vote" principle.

Interestingly, this position opened some important official doors for Rede Brasil, both in the Brazilian federal government, including in the Ministry of Planning, and among members of the Brazilian Congress, who came to better understand development policy issues. In this view, requesting a panel investigation into the World Bank's operations in Brazil could no longer be considered a call for external intervention, since the Brazilian government was a member of the board that created the rules that made possible the very existence of the panel. And if the government, in the context of structural adjustment, sought to convey to the Brazilian public that the IMF was not the monster it appeared to be, in part because the government was a member of the fund, why not use the same logic for the World Bank and the IDB? That is, because Brazil is a shareholder of these banks, they are not strictly "foreign" institutions and therefore outside of the national public sphere.

This direct advocacy approach was bolstered when Rede Brasil asked a member of the Brazilian Congress, Ivan Valente, to request a copy of the

World Bank's Country Assistance Strategy (CAS), a key document whose public release had been the target of relatively ineffective international campaigns. He filed an information request with the executive branch, and the Ministry of Planning responded by sending the document to the Chamber of Deputies. When the Congress turned the CAS over to Rede Brasil, which translated and published it, this breakthrough encouraged Brazilian CSOs to take greater political initiative in their approach to the multilateral financial institutions.[13] This was an example of how Brazil's broader political context—the new constitution plus greater room for maneuver for Congress—and civil society's new engagement with the issues of the multilateral institutions, paved the way for Brazil's second panel claim, whose approach differed markedly from the first.

ITAPARICA: USING THE PANEL AS PART
OF A NATIONAL CAMPAIGN STRATEGY

The Itaparica project was a milestone in the World Bank's policy on involuntary resettlement. For the first time, the bank was financing a project that, it claimed, was limited to resettling those displaced, rather than supporting the construction of the dam itself. Officially, the bank's role was limited to financing access to irrigated lands to compensate the peasants forcibly displaced by the Itaparica Dam, which had been completed in 1988.[14]

For the leaders of the Pólo Sindical do Sub-médio São Francisco (Union Coalition of the São Francisco Region)—a coalition of all the peasant unions of the entire region flooded by the dam—the bank was a quasi-ally, or even an ally, since it was supposed to finance the project they had demanded. As a result, the peasants had a strong sense of ownership of the project. From the point of view of their leadership, the project was more the bank's than the Brazilian government's.

In late 1996, almost ten years after the dam was completed, more than two thousand families had still not received land. After fruitless negotiations between the Pólo and the World Bank and the Brazilian government power company in charge of the Itaparica hydroelectric dam, the Pólo's leadership debated intensely what to do to put the issue on the political agenda. The pending final disbursements of the loan set a deadline for the possible use of the Inspection Panel, and Pólo Sindical met with Rede Brasil and Oxfam to evaluate the possibility of filing a claim. The strategy was to mobilize nationally by winning in the international sphere, thus reviving the struggles to solve the now-chronic problems. A national coalition was formed to draft the claim and the international contacts were made to evaluate the proposed strategy. As the claim was sent to Washington signed by dozens of adversely affected peasants, thousands of signatures continued to be collected in the region.

Coordinated with a national campaign, the panel claim put the issue back on the political agenda; indeed, there were speeches in both houses of the Brazilian Congress, major media coverage, meetings between the government and the World Bank in Brazil, and a petition with thousands of signatures calling on the president to change the position of Brazil's representative to the bank. The panel recommended that the board authorize an investigation, and the government responded by proposing an action plan that would commit $290 million in Brazilian government resources to Itaparica, after years of neglecting the resettlement problem. The board split largely along North–South lines, defeating by a slim margin the panel's recommendation to investigate in favor of the government's proposed response.[15]

The action plan turned out to be a tool to weaken the peasant organization, since the government offered monetary compensation to the displaced peasants instead of the irrigated land for which they had been waiting for nearly a decade. For the union leaders, this compensation strategy, which had been used years before by the Brazilian government's power agency for the people displaced by the Sobradinho dam—built on the same river and in the same region as Itaparica—was the government's way of avoiding responsibility for the future of the displaced families. Resettlement with irrigation would allow the peasants to continue to be peasants, strengthening the base of the union, while cash payments meant, according to the leaders, division of the base, moving to the cities, and poor use of resources. The government managed to use the cash compensation to bolster alternative political brokers. Overall, the national mobilization succeeded in generating a policy response, but one that dealt a major defeat to the peasant organization.

CÉDULA DA TERRA: THE PANEL PROCESS AS AN INSTRUMENT IN THE CAMPAIGN OF THE NATIONAL FORUM FOR AGRARIAN REFORM

The project called "Cédula da Terra"[16] in Portuguese, and the "Land Reform and Poverty Alleviation Project" in English, was designed in 1996 by the Brazilian government and World Bank technical staff as a pilot "market-based land reform." The project was launched in 1997 in several states of northeast Brazil.

The Land Reform and Poverty Alleviation Pilot Project worked with and accepted the general notion of land reform, albeit distorting it, which provoked opposition from Brazil's broad-based small farmer and landless movements. Their organizations had a strong sense of ownership of the land reform issues and a stake in both the project itself and its broader policy implications, in a national context where "disappropriation" of unproductive land (with compensation) had long been the principal legal instrument for land reform. The World Bank's explicit direct involvement in the project also got the attention of the landless movements. In 1997, their criticisms of the project were included in the policy advocacy agenda of the Grito da Terra–Brasil (Cry of the Earth–Brazil), a long-standing campaign that mobilizes much of the national peasant movement each year. Traditionally, after marching on Brasília, the organizations negotiate a series of demands with the government. They argued that the World Bank should not use scarce credit for buying land to redistribute when existing laws should be used for land reform. Instead, loans should support infrastructure and land-use management for land reform settlements.

The World Bank, through its Brazil office, which was not part of the Grito da Terra agenda, came to play a prominent role in the negotiations, as did the minister of agrarian reform. The minister stated that he was willing to review the project with the World Bank.[17] In late 1997, getting directly into the debate involving the Brazilian government and the World Bank, the CSOs sought a public hearing in the Senate Committee on Economic Affairs, prior to its approval of a new World Bank loan to expand the project.[18] Criticisms of the project by the MST, CONTAG, and other CSOs became more explicit and a matter of public debate in Congress. The Senate authorized the loan for the land reform project, yet doubts persisted. In the process, the project provoked an uneasy political coalition between the MST, a radical social movement, and CONTAG, a more moderate confederation of peasant unions.

When the Brazilian government created the *Banco da Terra,* or Land Fund, in 1998, expanding the Land Reform and Poverty Alleviation Project to the whole country, the social movements, unions, and NGOs working in support of land reform began to come together more intensely around the issue. The Forum for Agrarian Reform—which included the MST, CONTAG, and other organizations—collaborated more intensely with Rede Brasil, and began considering the possible use of the Inspection Panel. This discussion was informed by the Itaparica claim (which had been filed by Pólo Sindical, a grassroots movement with political stature in the eyes of CONTAG, and also, to a lesser extent, in the eyes of the MST) and by the problems with the design of the Pilot Program. The expansion of a pilot program prior to its in-depth evaluation was identified as violating the World Bank's supervision policies. In addition, the onerous loan conditions for land purchasers were seen as having violated the bank's antipoverty policies because research suggested that the future beneficiaries would be unable to pay their loans, end up in bankruptcy, and lose their land. In addition, the lack of effective participation by the national organizations of the future beneficiaries was seen as conflicting with the World Bank's policies on participation.

The discussion about the Inspection Panel focused on the national CSOs' distrust of using a World Bank instrument, since it would lend legitimacy to the bank. Other critics questioned the political effectiveness of embarking on an Inspection Panel claim, with so many variables and so many unknown actors from the World Bank apparatus involved. The Itaparica experience, despite all its problems, was the basis for the unanimous decision by the Forum for Agrarian Reform to make a claim to the panel. By late 1998, in spite of their political differences, MST and CONTAG leaders came together and played a key role in the forum's initiative. The forum and Rede Brasil were designated to coordinate the claim process. At the same time, in the national arena, the forum promoted hearings in both houses of Congress in an effort to defeat a proposed bill for supplemental federal resources for the Land Fund, which ended up being approved.[19]

The panel claim itself, despite having some political rhetoric, was based on a solid technical analysis detailing violations of World Bank policies, including public access to information, supervision, antipoverty, and participation policies. One of CONTAG's central concerns was that the land purchasers were not informed of the high interest rates they would have to pay, which would allegedly lead them further into poverty. The MST's critique highlighted the government's strategy of replacing Brazil's tradition of land reform by compensated expropriation with land purchases through the market. This was the most important point. In spite of these different perspectives, the common ground was firm enough to sustain the unity of the different groups.

From that point on, the forum's national and international campaign included demonstrations in front of the World Bank offices in Brasília, contacts with state-level authorities, church offices, and the mobilization of international organizations to pressure the World Bank to support the inspection of the pilot project and to block funding for the proposed Land Fund (*Banco da Terra*). The forum's advocacy campaign also included a trip to World Bank headquarters in Washington, D.C., in March 1999 to meet with its executive directors. The Global Campaign for Land Reform also drafted and released an open letter supporting the claim to the governments and legislators of several countries.[20]

As in the process involving Itaparica, but more broadly, an international campaign was organized based on the demands and national agenda of the struggles waged by the forum in an effort to involve groups that were not already involved in land reform issues. Yet at the same time, also as a result of the Itaparica process, the World Bank ended up changing the rules governing the panel's operations, taking away the possibility of undertaking a preliminary analysis, even before making a recommendation to the board. To the surprise of all those involved, even though the claim had been presented when the previous rules were in force, it was analyzed under the new rules, in keeping with the new procedures. The claimants saw these changes in the rules as weakening their case.

The panel responded to the forum's claim, came to Brazil, participated in meetings, and went to areas where the project was being implemented. Even though the areas were chosen by mutual agreement, there was manipulation by the World Bank. Bank technical staff and Brazilian government officials accompanied the panel's visit and participated in the field interviews, which undermined the reliability of the findings.

In May 1999, the panel submitted a report to the board recommending that the investigation not go forward, naively using the data compiled in their project site visits in Brazil, accepting as true the clearly false responses of the bank and the government. Hence, the panel's report to the board looked more like simple praise for the project. The result was considered by the executive director for Brazil and by the Brazilian government as an acknowledgment of the project's "excellence."[21] The panel report was translated into Portuguese and disseminated nationwide by the Ministry of Land Policy. The panel report became part of national and local politics and the disputes between the government and the social movements.

From that moment, the pro-agrarian reform alliance organized around the forum began to come apart, with the World Bank and the government seeking an accommodation with CONTAG by offering changes in the project to win its support and to isolate the MST and other organizations outside the forum. World Bank technical staff knew that the claimants' arguments in part actually pointed to real problems that had to be corrected, such as the onerous terms of the loans to land buyers—a position not originally shared by the government of Brazil. For these technical and political reasons, the new project was modified, including less harsh loan conditions as well as the exclusion of land purchases from areas subject to traditional legal "disappropriation." These changes addressed some of MST's demands, and the main demands of CONTAG, which, in turn, had an opportunity to distinguish itself politically from the MST (and from the Pastoral Land Commission, or CPT). These substantive policy differences were reinforced by their long-standing rivalry for leadership of Brazil's peasant movement. Because the MST and CONTAG are the leading actors in the land reform movement, the other member organizations in the Forum for Land Reform remained on the sidelines.

Itaparica: Desperation and the One Claim That Was at Least Considered by the Panel—An Outmoded Project?

On April 23, 1999, the Pólo Sindical, with the support of Rede Brasil (though without its previous international support), sent a letter to the president of the World Bank, the executive directors, and the Inspection Panel, outlining the history of what had happened since the 1997 board vote.[22] The panel had not been authorized to monitor the design and implementation of the action plan, and in April 1999 the government had still not met its commitments. The government paid monetary compensation to about 25 percent of the resettled families (some 1,500 families),[23] who were already resettled and who "sold" their lots to the government. The government and the bank accepted this, violating both their agreements with the peasant movement and the bank's Operational Directive on Involuntary Resettlement. At the same time, the government encouraged the creation of new peasant associations in the region, with the goal of undermining the Pólo Sindical. In this context, the Pólo Sindical once again sought to activate the Inspection Panel.

The U.S. and European NGOs that had played a key role in the first claim did not get involved the second time because the case was considered officially closed since the World Bank had completed its disbursements. Even the panel staff, with which the Brazilian CSOs always maintained a good relationship, opted to not even answer the Pólo's demand or others sent later when there was still no response to the panel claim. The national organizations—including Rede Brasil—that had organized a considerable international network in support of the claim did not invest sufficiently in the second Itaparica request.

Cédula da Terra: The Second Try

After the response of the panel and the World Bank, the CSOs called for a new public hearing in the Senate, which was held on June 23, 1999. Once again, the CSOs displayed unity and the hearing was quite well attended; those present included the president of the National Institute for Colonization and Agrarian Reform (INCRA) and representatives from the main member organizations of the forum and Rede Brasil. The World Bank turned down an invitation to attend, arguing that it was not authorized to get involved in political meetings.[24] In other words, an official meeting of the Brazilian government in the Senate was classified by the bank as a "political" meeting in the sense of involvement in domestic politics. That hearing was useful for educating the senators on the new project that required Senate approval.

Information was presented at the hearing that flatly contradicted the panel report, using official data from studies commissioned by the government but not presented to the panel team. The document, which was not submitted to the panel but sent to the Senate, stressed that there were problems related to the purchase of lands from areas that could be expropriated by Brazil's traditional land reform policy, that there were still no changes in the interest rates being charged, and that a large number of the beneficiaries did not know the content of the contract they had signed.[25] The meeting was tense. One of the outcomes was that the senators sought a meeting with the president of Brazil, which was held July 8, 1999. When the Brazilian government's conservative nationalist position on the panel was raised with the president, he drew on the national sovereignty argument to say that the representative of Brazil will always oppose imperialist interventions by the World Bank, a discourse that he knew would have some resonance with the grassroots movements.

The forum presented a new inspection claim on August 27, 1999. This second claim reaffirmed the first one, but with increased support from the new technical evidence provided by the official Brazilian government study confirming the original criticisms. At the same time, the forum embarked on a new area of struggle, as it filed more complaints with the federal and state Public Ministries (one of the accountability innovations in Brazil's 1988 constitution).

In November 1999, Rede Brasil and the forum held a seminar on Cédula da Terra in Brasília, with organizations from both coalitions, academics, and three former presidents and directors of INCRA, in which a more solid foundation was laid for the criticisms and new lines of consensus were created. Opposition to Cédula increased, leading to the resignation of an important adviser to the Ministry of Agrarian Reform.

In January 2000, the forum received the panel's response in which it reported that once again it had not called for an investigation, this time not because of the merits of the claim, but because the forum had refused to engage in dialogue with representatives of the World Bank. In effect, because of the first claim, the World Bank sought a rapprochement with the forum with a view to furthering the dialogue, which it was already doing with CONTAG. Yet the wounds opened by the bank itself in its response to the first claim, where its refusal to recognize the forum, the MST, or even CONTAG as legitimate representatives of the beneficiaries, led the forum to establish certain conditions for an authentic and effective dialogue that would not be reduced to co-opting leaders for the project. In other words, the technical issues that had been raised more than once, but now with more consolidated data, had not been considered by the panel, which made for a strictly political reading of the claim, leading to a resolution that was also strictly political.

The World Bank continued to have contact with CONTAG and reworked the *Banco da Terra* project (the Land Fund), which was being forwarded to the board for approval in an effort to take into account some of the criticisms made by the forum. These included the guarantee that the Cédula project would not fund the purchase of any lands that might be subject to legal expropriation and that the interest rates to be paid by the beneficiaries would be lowered. CONTAG agreed to the changes, believing that the bank had agreed to finance the land fund and not the land reform (though this was not yet confirmed), since the changes were not guaranteed by legislation. In other words, CONTAG relied on a series of informal commitments signed by the bank and the government, and continued to depend on the performance of those commitments in maintaining its support for the "new" project. While the divisions between MST and CONTAG became more conflictive, CONTAG won a huge political space within the World Bank, which may result in more effective participation by its member organizations in a series of World Bank–financed rural development projects.

CONCLUSION

Using the Inspection Panel requires knowledge about the World Bank and its policies, as well as how its decision making regarding specific projects affects specific constituencies. It may seem obvious, but prior knowledge of the World Bank as an institution and of its role in specific projects that affect particular people is a key precondition for CSO campaigns. Few organizations "know" the bank well enough to be able to prepare a claim that relates a project to its internal rules (complex operational directives, among others). Indeed, that technical knowledge is not even widely disseminated within the government.

In the case of Brazil, the Planafloro claim had the technical backing not only of international NGOs that had already amassed such knowledge, but also of a national NGO that maintained an office and a highly qualified technical expert on the subject in Rondônia. By the time of the Itaparica claim, that technical contribution was provided by Rede Brasil, which facilitated CSOs' access to this necessary prior knowledge. In effect, for the claims sent in, and for many others that were not sent in but that were actively considered by several Brazilian CSOs, people turned to—and continue to turn to—Rede Brasil for information. Rede Brasil filled a strategic gap by providing political and technical knowledge of these multilateral institutions, which until now had been so distant and mysterious.

Working with people negatively affected by a project to establish the bank's role and responsibility for negative impacts is not exclusively a technical or theoretical exercise. For it is the bank's active participation in the negotiations or field missions far more than the documentary evidence that makes it known, as an institution, to those who work with the grass-roots organizations that may present claims to the panel. Because of this, in all the cases analyzed, the active participation of bank technical staff alongside the CSOs involved—whether the "affected" or "beneficiary" population—was decisive. In other words, the effective involvement of the CSOs and the population directly affected by the project in the panel process was also due to face-to-face contact with the bank's technical personnel, whether full-time staff or consultants. A sense of "ownership" was a precondition for Brazilian campaigns that tried to use the panel process to change projects.

As of the late 1980s, alongside the many Brazilian CSOs with a strictly anti–World Bank or "Bank-bashing" vision, other CSOs were established that used alliances with sectors within the World Bank (and the Inter-American Development Bank) to block or change socially or environmentally disastrous projects or to propose compensatory projects. The emergence of this set of actors is related to what may be one of the most important explanations of the use of the Inspection Panel in Brazil. The three projects that provoked the five claims filed are all *compensatory* projects—all three were designed ostensibly as official efforts to address pressing social and environmental problems. For example, Planafloro was a response to a previous World Bank–financed project and was considered a sustainable development project. The Itaparica project involved bank financing to ensure that resettlement with access to irrigated land—a key demand of the dam-affected persons—was effectively carried out. Cédula da Terra was a project that sought to address the demand of the rural social movements for land reform. In other words, these are projects that, despite their problems, sought to address social demands. The claimants felt it was their "right" to make demands of the bank regarding these projects, not because they were worse than others, but because claimants had a greater sense of ownership over them.

Other problematic projects that were under way in Brazil at the same time, and in which CSOs were adversely affected, did not trigger the use of the panel, perhaps because they had no sense of ownership. Civil-society ownership creates the potential for a claim sent to a remote and unknown alternative authority—the Inspection Panel—to become a grassroots campaign taken up locally by the communities affected. In addition, the bank's sense of ownership leads its staff to consider their responsibilities more directly, because it also makes it easier for the other actors to consider a given project a bank project and not just a government project with World Bank financing. Furthermore, a government's *lack* of ownership, as is the case of the Rondônia state government in relation to Planafloro, may lead the government to be more inclined to negotiate changes, as it views the project as a bank project, not its own.

Filing a Claim with the Inspection Panel Needs a Campaign, or to Be Part of a Campaign

The five claims filed in Brazil showed that garnering greater visibility for the claims through national and international campaigns can get the project and its problems onto, or back onto, the political agenda. The only claim that was not even officially considered (the second one from Itaparica) was also the only one in which the claimants came forth in merely "technical" fashion (without national and international mobilization).

The success of the Brazilian claims insofar as they put the projects on the national agenda—particularly in the cases of Itaparica and Cédula da Terra—leading the Congress to become directly involved, also appears to have provoked a greater response on the part of the Brazilian government within the World Bank Board, where it has attacked the panel, which certainly contributed to the board's decision to review the panel.

Debates on Transparency and Accountability Policies Need to Address the World Bank's Governance System

The fact that the government invoked the sovereignty argument in opposition to the panel, and did not invoke it when, for example, the nonsovereign clauses were signed in the agreement with the International Monetary Fund, is an important issue. The more important challenge to national sovereignty, however, is the absence of democracy in the system for governing the World Bank, in which the countries of the North, and particularly the United States, enjoy hegemony. In spite of this dramatic power imbalance in the multilateral governance process, however, in the rare case of a roll-call vote of the bank's board on whether to authorize a claim in the case of Itaparica, the leading countries of the North were defeated.

Here perhaps an analysis is needed that places more emphasis on the effective political involvement of the countries of the North in relation to those processes. Along the same lines, the Northern NGOs have faced greater difficulties taking action when they have had to reconcile the agendas and arguments of the South with those of the North, for in many cases the panel claim is a means of pressuring national governments almost in the same fashion that they are pressured by the multilaterals' famous "conditionalities."

Using the Inspection Panel Requires Reconciling Local, National, and Transnational Political Logics

The Inspection Panel is not a simple instrument, nor is it used in just one way or with a single rationale. Since it involves different levels of advocacy and political coalition-building—subnational, national, and transnational—the meanings attributed to the panel largely depend on the context of a given institution's work.

To speak of global citizenship today necessarily means speaking of one of the few real instruments available for global advocacy that need not go through national channels. The panel is just such an instrument, and in this context, depending on the panel is not only important—it is necessary.

Furthermore, if the panel is to prove effective in terms of the lives of the people directly affected by World Bank policies or projects, the logic of the subnational and local levels should be accorded priority in political advocacy strategy. The political decisions regarding the use of the Inspection Panel should be limited primarily to the local and national organizations directly involved. These organizations should be the ones to determine whether to pursue international dimensions in their strategies, to avoid possible conflicts with more effective national political processes. The panel—or any external reform conditionalities—cannot take the place of national political processes for societal monitoring of bank projects.

NOTES

1. CSOs are understood to constitute a very broad and diverse group of civil-society organizations, formal and informal, including NGOs, institutionalized social movements, and trade unions.

2. Brazil's Network on Multilateral Financial Institutions (Rede Brasil) published a collection that assesses the Brazilian experiences with the panel process (see Flavia Barros, ed., *Banco Mundial, participação, transparência e responsabilização* [Brasília: Rede Brasil, 2001] and www.rbrasil.org.br). Rede Brasil is a broad coalition of national and regional NGOs and mass membership organizations.

3. See Jonathan Fox, "O Painel de Inspeção do Banco Mundial: lições dos cinco primeiros anos," in Barros, *Banco Mundial,* 56 (Portuguese translation of "The World Bank Inspection Panel: Lessons from the First Five Years," *Global Governance* 6, no. 3 [July–September 2000]: 279–318).

4. See discussion by Dana Clark in chapter 1 of this volume.

5. See Aurélio Vianna Jr., "Civil Society Participation in World Bank and Inter-American Development Bank Programs: The Case of Brazil," *Global Governance* 6, no. 4 (October–December 2000): 433–56 (also published as "La participación de la

sociedad civil en los programas del Banco Mundial y del Banco Interamericano de Desarrollo: El caso de Brasil," in *Luces y sombras de una nueva relación: El Banco Interamericano de Desarrollo, el Banco Mundial y la Sociedad Civil,* ed. Diana Tussie [Buenos Aires: FLACSO/Temas, 2000]).

6. The basic information was drawn from Brent Millikan, "O Painel de Inspeção do Banco Mundial e o pedido de investigação sobre o Planafloro," in Barros, *Banco Mundial,* and also benefited from the comments of anthropologist Stephen Schwartzmann of the EDF, who was actively involved in the process. See also Maria Guadalupe Moog Rodrigues's detailed analysis in chapter 3 of this volume, and Margaret Keck, "The Limits of Leverage," in *The Struggle for Accountability: The World Bank, NGOs and Grassroots Movements,* ed. Jonathan Fox and L. David Brown (Cambridge: MIT Press, 1998), 181–218.

7. See Bruce Rich, *Mortgaging the Earth* (Boston: Beacon, 1994).

8. Margaret Keck and Kathryn Sikkink, *Activists Beyond Borders* (Ithaca: Cornell University Press, 1998).

9. The international NGOs that worked directly in the state of Rondônia included Oxfam–U.K., EDF, the Amazon Program of Friends of the Earth International (FOEI), and the World Wide Fund for Nature (WWF).

10. Millikan, "O Painel de Inspeção do Banco Mundial," in Barros, *Banco Mundial.*

11. See chapter 3 by Maria Guadalupe Moog Rodrigues in this volume.

12. The creation of this new position in the bank's country mission was not limited to Brazil; it was part of a bankwide response to years of campaigning by mainly Southern development NGOs. The bank hired a Brazilian-American development professional with extensive contacts in Brazilian civil society. For an overview of his perspective, see John Garrison, *From Confrontation to Collaboration: Civil Society–Government–World Bank Relations in Brazil* (Washington, D.C.: World Bank, 2000).

13. See Aurélio Vianna Jr., ed., *As Estratégias dos Bancos Multilaterais para o Brasil* (Brasília: Rede Brasil, 1998); see also www.rbrasil.org.br/publicacoes/livros/ [accessed May 26, 2003].

14. Despite those statements, the bank made a sectoral loan to the Brazilian power sector that was used to build the Itaparica Dam. See details in Aurélio Vianna Jr.,"O Painel de Inspeção do Banco Mundial para Itaparica," in Barros, *Banco Mundial.*

15. See Fox, "O Painel de Inspeção."

16. See Luciano Wolff and Sérgio Sauer, "O Painel de Inspeção e o caso do Cédula da Terra," in Barros, *Banco Mundial.*

17. See Wolff and Sauer, "O Painel de Inspeção e o caso do Cédula da Terra," 177.

18. Loans to the Brazilian government must be authorized by the federal Senate.

19. Author interviews with leaders of Rede Brasil and the Brasilian Land Reform Forum, Brasília, 2001.

20. Wolff and Sauer, "O Painel de Inspeção e o caso do Cédula da Terra,"180; see also www.foodfirst.org/action/cgar/ [accessed May 26, 2003].

21. Ministério do Desenvolvimento Agrário, *Banco da Terra* (preface by Minister Raul Jungmann) (Brasília [DF]: Ministério do Desenvolvimento Agrário, 1999).

22. Eraldo José de Souza, general coordinator, Pólo Sindical, to James Wolfensohn, the board of executive directors, and members of the Inspection Panel, April 23, 1999.

23. The total number of families who had to be resettled varies from six thousand to seven thousand, depending on the source. For an assessment of the problems with project implementation by the World Bank's evaluation department, see the chapter titled "Good Intentions, Costly Mistakes in Brazil," in *Involuntary Resettlement: Comparative Perspectives,* vol. 2, ed. Robert Picciotto, Warren Van Wicklin, and Edward Rice (Somerset: Transaction, 2001).

24. Letter from World Bank country director, Gobind Nankani, to the president of the Senate Commission on Economic Affairs, Senator Ney Suassuna, and to the president of the Senate Commission on Social Affairs, Senator Osmar Dias, transcribed in the official proceedings, "Ata da 15a Reunião da Comissão de Assuntos Sociais e 22a da Comissão de Assuntos Econômicos do Senado Federal, 51a legislatura. 23 de junho de 1999." The text reads: "I am honored by your invitation, but I must report that it is impossible for me to attend this public hearing because the World Bank's Statute prevents participation of its staff in official activities that are not part of the technical cycle of projects or that could have a political nature" [*que possam ter cunho político*].

25. "Relatório de Avaliação Preliminar do Programa Cédula da Terra (PCT)," Brasilia, June 1999, unpublished document presenting findings of a study coordinated by the Núcleo de Estudios Agrários e Desenvolvimento.

8

Singrauli: An Unfulfilled Struggle for Justice

Dana Clark

This water and electricity are not important. It wasn't there before and we
didn't need it. Before, we had food, and access to water. We were given
false promises that anyone who owned land or had a house would be given
a job, but they didn't stick to this promise. Look at me, and my condition.
If I had land, I would be healthy. The food that we buy from the market is
pesticide-laden, and causes sickness, so we have to spend more money on
health. Somehow I'm just able to manage one meal a day. The World Bank
people used to come and click snapshots; they assured us we would be
provided with alternative jobs. When we had our own fields, everything
around the house was green, and the heart was happy. Now everyone is
dying of hunger.[1]

—Ram Prasant, living in Bijpur resettlement colony, Singrauli, India

In the Singrauli region of central India, there once was a village called Mitihini, where hard-working people practiced subsistence agriculture on fertile,
spring-fed lands. They were largely independent of the market, growing
enough to meet their needs, and occasionally selling surplus to buy commodities like kerosene, oil, and salt.[2] However, the government of India and
the World Bank had other uses for Mitihini's land. Vast areas in and around
the village would become ash dikes, holding ponds for the expanding tide of
waste from the neighboring coal-fired power plants. The homes would be
bulldozed, and the people relocated to a resettlement colony.

Singrauli is located about a thousand kilometers southeast of Delhi, strad-
dling the states of Madhya Pradesh and Uttar Pradesh. The area was once

densely forested and rich in biodiversity, including tigers. But the defining characteristic of the region are the vast deposits of coal that lie beneath the surface. Although the colonial British government began some extraction activities in the area, Singrauli's real transformation began when a hydroelectric dam was built on the Rihand River in 1960, displacing approximately two hundred thousand people.

The Rihand Dam was one of the first large dams inaugurated in India, and the impacts were devastating. Despite local attempts to organize opposition, most people were given only one day's notice that the reservoir would be flooded. People living in more remote areas, who had no advance notice, were evacuated in boats, forced to abandon their homes, possessions, crops, and farm animals. They received almost no compensation from the government for their losses.[3]

What few people realized at the time was that the Rihand Dam and reservoir represented the first of many significant waves of displacement, as well as the first phase of an industrialization process that has since transformed the area's physical, economic, cultural, and social landscape. The World Bank has described the transformation of Singrauli as follows:

> Until the early 1960s Singrauli was a little known, isolated and economically backward rural area. . . . Today, Singrauli is one of India's largest and most important centers for coal mining and power generation consisting of massive open-cast coal mines, several super thermal power plants and a large number of energy-dependent heavy industries. The Region as a whole is still predominantly agricultural but urbanization is proceeding rapidly around the industrial activity and along the reservoir. The reservoir is a major source of water for industrial consumption.[4]

THE WORLD BANK'S ROLE IN SINGRAULI

The World Bank provided the government of India with the seed money to transform Singrauli into a coal-producing, coal-burning pocket of economic activity and environmental squalor. In 1977, the World Bank loaned $150 million to the National Thermal Power Corporation (NTPC) to help finance the construction of the Singrauli Super Thermal Power Plant, the first coal-fired power plant in the region, and financed an expansion of the same plant in 1980. The bank also helped finance one of the first open-pit coal mines in the area, Dudhichua, in 1985. The bank helped connect the power plants to the northern grid with a loan to NTPC for the Rihand Power Transmission project in 1985.[5]

Challenging Displacement, Challenging the World Bank

Singrauli has suffered from a spiral of development-induced displacement, as prime agricultural land has been appropriated for the dam and reservoir, coal mines, power plants, waste disposal areas, railroad lines linking the mines and power plants, roads and markets, homes and recreational grounds for NTPC workers, and eucalyptus "forest offset" plantations. The *Indian Express* reported that as of 1987, between two and three hundred thousand people had been displaced in Singrauli, some of them "three to five times in 25 years. The land, once covered with prime tropical forests on the fertile Gangetic Plain is totally destroyed, a dust trap for those who live on it."[6] The people displaced by these various projects have been forced into resettlement colonies or have moved away in search of increasingly scarce arable land.

For more than forty years, local people and their national (and later, international) supporters have complained about the environmental and social justice issues at stake, described in the claim as follows:

> The master plan of the Singrauli region is targeted to produce "cheap" electricity from the estimated 10,000 MT [megatonnes] of coal reserves—up to 20,000 MW [megawatts] is the estimated power potential of Singrauli. The cost of this development model is being borne by the local people whose lives have been disrupted and destroyed. The legacy of the World Bank's involvement in Singrauli includes greater impoverishment, the wholesale disruption of communities, abuse of basic human rights and an increasingly bleak future for the local people.[7]

In 1984, the Delhi-based NGO Lokayan helped launch the Srijan Lokhit Samiti, an NGO based in Singrauli, to focus on the displacement problems in the region. In February 1987, Lokayan and the Environmental Defense Fund (now known as Environmental Defense) organized a site visit to Singrauli. Their trip report, which highlighted problems with displacement, triggered the NTPC and the World Bank to follow up with their own field investigations. As a result, project authorities made significant promises, including the concession to local demands that people losing land should be provided with comparable replacement lands, and that there would be at least one job per family. The NTPC and the bank also committed to undertake additional environmental and social impact studies.

One of these additional studies, an environmental assessment commissioned by the World Bank and NTPC in 1991, found that 90 percent of the local people had been displaced at least once, and 34 percent had been forced to move multiple times.[8] The same study found that resettlement "appears to have failed in practically all cases," and noted in particular "the inadequacy of facilities and equipment necessary for water supply, sewage treatment, schools and education, and medical care."[9]

The result of this failed resettlement is that formerly self-sufficient farmers have been converted to beggars. The elderly and landless have been particularly hard-hit, and women have traditionally not been compensated for their lost livelihoods or given proportional employment by NTPC.[10]

The 1993 Loan: Expanding Production, Shallow Promises of Environmental and Social Mitigation

In 1993, the bank loaned NPTC $400 million for the expansion of the Rihand and Vindhyachal coal-fired power plants,[11] thereby surpassing the $4 billion mark in loans and credits, and making NTPC the single largest borrower in the history of the bank at that time.[12] In addition to the power plant and ash dike expansion, the 1993 loan included an environmental action plan that was supposed to improve environmental management and monitoring, introduce a program of remedial environmental measures, address outstanding resettlement and rehabilitation ("R&R") issues, and upgrade NTPC's R&R capacity.[13]

As part of this capacity upgrade, NTPC adopted a new resettlement and rehabilitation policy that applied to all of its operations in India. In setting this policy, which was to deal with past and current resettlement issues, the NTPC, "under advice from the Bank," adopted differential treatment and entitlements for what it called "Stage I" and "Stage II" oustees.[14] Under this framework, Stage I referred to remedial exercises to mitigate the failures in R&R from earlier displacement, and Stage II applied to people who would be displaced by work financed under the new loan.[15]

Despite the commitments made in the loan agreement, the R&R situation has continued to be grim. This chapter will explore the failed implementation of these anticipated remedial measures, and the insufficient commitment or capacity on the part of NTPC or the bank to ensure that the project met the environmental and social objectives of the loan. The chapter also describes a claim to the Inspection Panel and its outcome, including the adoption of a unique problem-solving approach that had mixed results.

The "Energy Capital of India"

While Singrauli's power production supports India's industrial sector and helps meet national demands for power, the local and regional economy has suffered from "decades of uncoordinated and poorly managed heavy industrial developments, creating serious environmental problems and a large population of displaced people . . . some of whom have moved more than once as initial relocation sites have been taken over for further industrial development, township schemes, or waste disposal."[16]

According to the bank, the social and environmental problems in Singrauli result from "the imposition of a formal industrial sector on an essentially traditional society with an economy based on subsistence agriculture and forest products. The development problems have been exacerbated by absence of effective governance in the Region. As industry has expanded, so central and state governments have been unable to adequately address the Region's underlying environmental and development problems."[17]

For people stuck in resettlement colonies, the absence of effective governance means that neither NTPC nor the local government is willing to take responsibility for ensuring that water flows in the hand pumps, that sewer and sanitation systems function properly, or that people in the resettlement colonies have access to adequate schools, health care, burial grounds, or potable water.[18] Now known as the "energy capital of India," Singrauli's development path, stimulated by World Bank financing, has been inherently unsustainable and is not meeting the needs of the people who live there.[19]

The Social Fabric Is Torn Asunder

Displacement in Singrauli has meant that agriculturalists were forced to abandon their way of life and means of livelihood, which have not been replaced. Displaced agricultural workers have become just "one among the faceless crowd hovering in vain around factories, construction sites, and plants in search of work."[20] Women, in particular, face discrimination in the payment of compensation for lost livelihood, discrimination in being hired by the project authorities, and harassment if they do receive jobs in the plants.[21] "Women were rarely offered jobs or monetary compensation despite the crucial role they have traditionally played in farming and supporting their families."[22]

The surrounding area has not been able to absorb the repeated waves of dispossessed farmers, nor can it produce enough food to feed the population in the region. This is partly due to lack of proper land-use planning and the continual conversion of farmland to industrial use, but it is also a result of the pollutant load in the system. There has been a massive loss of soil fertility. As explained by Atri Lal, a farmer formerly from Adhaura:

> The crops are not the same anymore. Since the [Rihand power] plant has come, the yield of maize has drastically gone down. *Urad* [a lentil] turns white when fly ash settles on the field. Then, when the pod comes, there is no seed in it. The beans no longer have the same yield. Pumpkins are no longer there in the same quantity. Cucumbers have totally disappeared. The taste of food is not the same.

There is a fly ash pond adjoining our village, and when the wind blows it carries the fly ash, which falls on the vegetation.[23]

Food security studies required under the 1993 loan have never been undertaken.

Singrauli has been compared to "the lower reaches of Dante's Inferno."[24]
Giant smokestacks dominate the horizon, encircling the Rihand reservoir,
continuously emitting plumes of smoke.[25] The power plants provide a continuous landmark; travelers can gauge their location by the number of smokestacks—four for the Singrauli Super Thermal Power Plant, three for Vindhyachal Super Thermal Power Plant, and one for the Rihand Power Plant, all
managed by NTPC and funded at one stage or another by the World Bank.[26]
Three other power plants are also located nearby, though they are not managed by NTPC or funded by the bank.[27] At night, the power plants are gar-
ishly present, glowing with lights, burning coal.

Attracted by the power plants like moths to a flame, the region also hosts
hundreds of industrial plants—chemical factories, aluminum companies, cement factories. Emissions from these plants, combined with dust from the
coal mines and fly ash from the power plants, result in highly polluted air.
There has been a concomitant rise in tuberculosis and other pulmonary ill-
nesses. The 1991 environmental assessment concluded that dust pollution
was severe (in some areas 50 percent of the people were affected by lung infections) and mercury was present in the food chain (with the stacks of thermal power projects being an important source).[28]

All local surface and groundwater has been compromised; the 1991 environmental study found that "none of the waters extracted from the ground
meet the standards for drinking water."[29] Water drawn from a well in the resettlement colonies sparkles with fly ash.[30] The reservoir, upon which local
people depend for fish, agriculture, and water for their stock, also quenches
the thirst of the industries. Used as a dumping ground for mines, factories,
and power plants, it is contaminated with heavy metals and mercury.

The physical landscape has also been irrevocably altered. The western
horizon is defined by massive heaps of overburden removed from the mines,
piled high to create an artificial ridgeline. On the other side of those false
mountains the Earth has been laid bare, and nine open-pit coal mines are in
operation twenty-four hours a day. Ninety-eight percent of the coal is consumed by the nearby power plants, which also operate around the clock.

The ash by-product of coal combustion has been a plague for local communities, because in addition to contaminating their bodies, crops, animals, and
water supplies, the ash is now the leading cause of displacement. The three
NTPC power plants together produce 5.2 million tons of ash per year, 97 percent of which is mixed with water to form slurry and then dumped in ash

dikes.[31] Massive ponds of grey sludge have consumed vast quantities of fertile agricultural lands, choking out life and invoking both despair and resistance.

Residents of Mitihini Resist Unjust Resettlement

The residents of Mitihini, who had been witness to and surrounded by a wave of NTPC-induced displacement that had shattered the lives of their neighbors, were themselves threatened with displacement by the 1993 loan, which included expansion of the Rihand ash dike. In 1993, they formed a new organization called Grameen Kalyan Sangharsh Samit (GKSS, or the Rural Upliftment Struggle Committee). GKSS coordinated with local and national organizations and peoples' movements already active in Singrauli, including Srijan Lokhit Samiti, Lokayan, and the Public Interest Research Group (PIRG).

International support for the struggle for justice in Singrauli was catalyzed when Lokhit Samiti and PIRG organized another national and international site visit to Singrauli in 1994, joined by Lokayan, Narmada Bachao Andolan, Prayas, Environmental Defense Fund, AidWatch, Greenpeace, Urgewald, a professor from Japan, and the Berne Declaration (BD).[32] Later, the Delhi Forum and the National Alliance of Peoples' Movements also allied themselves with the Singrauli struggle.

In 1995, Madhu Kohli, an activist who had been monitoring the situation for PIRG, moved to Singrauli to live and work directly with the affected communities. Ms. Kohli served as a liaison between the local communities and national and international supporters, keeping others apprised of the situation in Singrauli through faxes, phone calls, and e-mails. Working with GKSS, Ms. Kohli also engaged NTPC management and the bank to demand that they pay attention to the environmental issues, the inadequate resettlement package, and the human rights abuses.

In November 1996, when NTPC was pressuring resisting villagers to give up their lands, a fact-finding team from the BD, based in Switzerland, and the Center for International Environmental Law (CIEL), based in Washington, D.C., visited Mitihini and the surrounding area. During their visit, BD and CIEL staff met with local people resisting resettlement and those who had already been displaced, with NTPC management, and with the World Bank office in Delhi. While in the project area, the NGOs discussed the requirements of the World Bank's policies with local people and provided them with information about the Inspection Panel.

The decision to file an Inspection Panel claim was not taken lightly. The villagers of Mitihini first attempted to negotiate with NTPC, raise their concerns with the World Bank, and seek relief from domestic courts and domestic human rights bodies. Their attempts did not lead to change, however. Local people grew increasingly frustrated by NTPC's refusal to consult with them or respond effectively to their concerns. Meanwhile, the NTPC increased its pressure on residents near the Rihand and Vindhyachal power plants to vacate their land, which had been acquired years before. To gain possession of the lands, NTPC was offering the equivalent of a small plot of land in a resettlement colony and a one-time cash payment. The money offered by the NTPC was far below replacement cost for lost assets such as land, housing, fruit trees, crops, and freshwater springs.[33]

The people had identified their priorities for compensation to both the World Bank and the NPTC: sustainable livelihoods or alternative lands. The resisting families said that they would not abandon possession of their lands until they were provided with a resettlement plan and a rehabilitation package that would compensate them for their losses and allow them to recover their standards of living so that they could live with dignity and self-reliance in the future.[34] As their neighbors were dispersed and construction machinery roared around their lands, eighteen families of Mitihini stayed put. "We saw the condition of the oustees—no rehabilitation, and no facilities," said Bhagwandas, standing amongst the ruins of his bulldozed village years later. "Seeing their troubles we said we could not believe what NTPC was saying, and we decided not to leave."[35]

When the people insisted on fair compensation, and when they demanded that their rights under World Bank policies be respected, they were met with harassment, intimidation, and human rights violations.[36] They were blacklisted from jobs with NTPC and were basically besieged by construction equipment. Bulldozers would stray from the work site to target and attempt to destroy the standing crops and wells of villagers who were refusing to shift, a form of economic coercion to pressure resisting families into accepting the compensation package. Villagers would place their bodies in front of the bulldozers, to try to protect each other's lands. Sometimes the bulldozers were forced to turn back, but other times the people were beaten and arrested.

In one incident, Ram Narain Kumari, a young man who was a vocal leader of the families demanding fair treatment, was run over by a dump truck on orders from the NPTC, as he squatted in the truck's path to try to prevent it from destroying his neighbor's property.[37] According to witnesses and Ram Narain himself, the truck driver had stopped work when an NTPC official arrived and threatened the driver's job if he didn't do the work. The driver started his engine and drove over Ram Narain, who was knocked unconscious. His body fell between the wheels of the truck, and his friends and family pulled him free. The NTPC official and the contractor fled the scene and failed even to send an ambulance. Ram Narain later became one of the claimants to the Inspection Panel.

Filing the Claim

Facing increasing abuse and threats of eviction, the remaining families of Mitihini decided in April 1997 that they had no other recourse than to request an investigation by the Inspection Panel. Madhu Kohli filed a claim on her own behalf and as the authorized representative of thirty-three other affected people, whose names were kept confidential out of fear of reprisals.[38] The claimants articulated their rights and interests as follows:

> First and foremost the people of Singrauli have a right to be treated as human beings. They have a right to a livelihood that enables them to live with dignity and self-reliance. They have a right to timely information about the project, and the manner in which it would affect their lives. They have a right to participate in the planning of projects that will so dramatically affect them. They have a right to a life without fear of being deprived again and again for the sake of abstract "public interest" which is not defined in a democratic way. They have a right to make [a] choice about their future, a right to be consulted about their future. They have [a] right to benefit from the project. They have [a] right to voice their opinions and negotiate for fair compensation without being assaulted, insulted, intimidated and driven from their lands. Their interest lies in being treated as a community and not as "disparate" individuals—a community sharing common resources, relationships of mutual support, a culture and a way of life and common interests and concerns. They have a right to information about World Bank directives and procedures. None of the above rights and interests were ever acknowledged much less respected under the present project.[39]

The claim alleged violations of the following bank policies: Environmental Assessment, Involuntary Resettlement, Indigenous Peoples, Project Supervision, and Economic Evaluation of Investment Alternatives. The claim focused in particular on the bank's failure to ensure that displaced persons would receive effective rehabilitation and have their livelihoods restored.

> While the most critical issue has been that of livelihood this has remained fundamentally unaddressed in Singrauli. . . . People were not given a genuine option of maintaining their agricultural lifestyle. The compensation was given in the form of money to a community which had little experience of handling monetary transactions. Even this money was inadequate to reestablish their former living standards or to purchase replacement land and rebuild lost assets. The WB [World Bank] policy on involuntary resettlement recognizes the insufficiency of

cash compensation particularly in situations such as Singrauli. The policy stresses the importance of land based compensation schemes, even in areas with a high population density. The pattern of resettlement in Singrauli runs completely counter to the WB policy on resettlement.[40]

The claim also documented violations of the environmental action plan, including failure to (1) analyze the impacts of ash leachate on groundwater, (2) study the fate and transport of mercury, (3) monitor the contamination of food crops, and (4) conduct a baseline survey of community health. The claim noted that the "unmitigated environmental effects have adversely affected the health of the people of Singrauli."[41]

The Response: Increased Repression

Filing the claim triggered a retaliatory backlash from NTPC, which moved into the project area with police force and heavy machinery.[42] In the area around the Vindhyachal power plant, people were beaten and physically restrained while their homes were bulldozed in the presence of and at the behest of NTPC. International NGOs alerted World Bank officials in Washington to the human rights violations, noting with alarm that through these tactics, NTPC was seeking to irreversibly alter the status quo, thereby preempting "the ability of the Panel to investigate and the ability of the Bank to design effective remedies."[43] The NGOs urged the bank to put a halt to the forcible evictions and to restrain NTPC from acts of violence.

Robert Drysdale from the bank's South Asia region responded by saying that in the face of conflicting reports from the local people and NTPC about what was happening in the project area, the bank's hands were tied.[44] When the bank did finally send a supervision mission to the field weeks later, their report documented the use of violence against several project-affected people, the police presence, and threats to residents to vacate or have their homes bulldozed.[45] Nonetheless, bank management refused to publicly condemn the human rights violations or compel NTPC to desist from disruptive activities until after the panel could conduct its investigation.[46]

On November 21, 1997, Madhu Kohli was beaten by a bulldozer operator when she tried to prevent him from destroying the crops of a family that had not agreed to shift. The assault took place in the presence of four officials from the NTPC, who failed to intervene.[47] When NGOs and, in response, the World Bank's Washington-based vice president for South Asia called for an investigation into the assault on the claimants' representative, the bank's India country director, Edwin Lim, refused to send a mission to the field, saying that such an investigation would be "inconvenient" for the Delhi staff.[48]

Human Rights Watch, on the other hand, did send a team to monitor the situation in Singrauli. In a memorandum sent to President Wolfensohn and the board of executive directors, they reported, "Many of the displaced we interviewed described a cycle that would begin with physical abuse and harassment, and lead to arbitrary arrest and detention, ill-treatment and threats in custody, arbitrary application of the law, and intimidation to discourage further protest."[49]

Bank Management Admits Policy Violations, Failed Rehabilitation

In its June 1997 response to the claim, bank management acknowledged that it had not fully complied with bank policies and that the bank had failed to effectively supervise the project and had failed to undertake "appropriate remedial actions" to "overcome project implementation problems."[50] The response also acknowledged that NTPC was in violation of loan covenants relating to implementation of the environmental and resettlement action plans and that the project was operating in violation of Indian law regarding thermal pollution.[51]

Management committed itself to "the principle that it is the results on the ground which ultimately count."[52] In an apparent effort to address the shortcomings in question, management proposed two "Action Programs" that it pledged would "bring the Bank into full compliance with ODs 4.01; 4.30; and 13.05."[53] One of these action plans covered all resettlement projects in India and the other was specific to Singrauli. Neither plan was discussed with the claimants or other affected people.

Panel Visit to the Field and Recommendation for Investigation

To determine the eligibility of the claim and verify allegations of harm, the Inspection Panel sent a team to Delhi and Singrauli from July 6 to13, 1997. During this visit, the panel met with the requesters, representatives of the World Bank, and the Indian government. At the local level, there was some frustration with the panel's visit:

> The July 1997 visit of the panel was conducted in great haste and was rather disorganized. The affected people did not get sufficient opportunity to present their case. A sudden change in the itinerary of the panel's visit created chaos and an atmosphere of uncertainty. Lack of prior information about the panel's schedule of meetings prevented many people from reaching the panel. Even the claimants were given hardly any time for a reasonable interaction.[54]

Nonetheless, the panel confirmed that the claimants had established their eligibility to file a claim and also found prima facie evidence of harm resulting from the violations of bank policies:

> harm has occurred because many PAPs [project-affected people] have not been, and may not expect to be restored to at least their previous standard of living . . . most of the displaced population does not appear to be receiving benefits from the project (for example, electricity), despite this being the express objective of the Bank's resettlement policy (OD 4.30, para. 3). As for those who have not yet shifted, given the experience and dashed expectations they see of so many who have already shifted, their reluctance to move can be well understood.[55]

The panel also found that:

> Basic infrastructure in the resettlement colonies appears to have been provided but not maintained. . . . drains are filled with garbage and mud, water pumps are not working, etc. Residents complained of a lack of electricity and water. . . . There was no evidence of medical supplies, and a temporary doctor was appointed just two months ago.[56]

Furthermore, the panel found that "Management's Response and Action Programs fail to address current problems on the ground."[57] On July 24, 1997, the panel recommended that the "Executive Directors authorize—as a matter of urgency—an investigation into the involuntary resettlement and related aspects of the project."[58] On the question of indigenous peoples, however, the panel accepted management's assurances that there were no indigenous or tribal people affected by the project without careful independent analysis, and did not recommend an investigation of those allegations.[59]

THE TUMULTUOUS SEPTEMBER 1997 BOARD MEETINGS

During the second week of September 1997, the board met to determine how to respond to panel recommendations calling for investigations into two troubled projects: Singrauli and Itaparica in Brazil. At the same time, the panel was preparing the report of its limited investigation into the Yacyretá claim in Paraguay and Argentina.[60] India and Brazil rallied support from other borrowing-country executive directors to resist the Inspection Panel's recommendations.

At the board meeting on September 9, 1997, the board rejected the recommendation for an investigation into the Itaparica resettlement project by a narrow margin, and instead accepted Brazil's "action plan."[61] Trouble was also brewing for the Singrauli claim that week, as the government of India quietly made it known to the board that it would not allow the panel to enter India to conduct an investigation.[62] In addition, just before the meeting, bank management distributed a document to the board that it had not shared with the panel—a proposal for a revised action plan in Singrauli—designed to preempt the need for a panel investigation. Management's strategy was to convince the board to reject the panel's recommendation for an investigation into the project and to instead authorize management to rectify the problems without independent oversight.

With strong resistance from both the borrower and management, the board allowed only a limited investigation to be "conducted at the Bank's Headquarters in Washington to further determine the extent to which the Bank adhered to its own policies and procedures under the project."[63] Thus, the board rejected the panel's recommendations for full investigations in both the Singrauli and Itaparica projects, deferring instead to the borrowing governments and management, which did not want the panel to investigate. This was arguably the lowest point in the history of the Inspection Panel, as the panel's independence was undermined and the claimants were deprived of an opportunity to have an investigation into claims that the panel had found to be meritorious.

The high degree of tension around the Singrauli, Itaparica, and Yacyretá cases, and the clear North–South split on the board of executive directors, served as a wake-up call to the board, which recognized that it was not allowing the panel to operate as originally intended. Accordingly, as more fully discussed in chapter 1, the board created a six-member working group to review its experience with the panel, a group that included board members representing India and Brazil.

Inspection Panel Desk Review and Final Report: "Victims Rather than Beneficiaries"

With a limited mandate from the board, the Inspection Panel conducted a Washington-based investigation of the policy violations in Singrauli. The panel also drew from information gathered during its preliminary field visit and received supplemental information from the claimants and NGOs. On December 22, 1997, the Inspection Panel delivered its report on its desk investigation to the board. One of the most significant new findings of its Washington-based investigation was that "violations of policies and procedures can be attributed to pressure to accelerate the process of loan approval and to not granting the same relevance to Resettlement and Rehabilitation and Environmental matters as to other project components."[64] The panel found that "Senior Regional Management pressured staff to accelerate processing of the loan in order to meet fiscal year 1993 lending targets."[65] The project had been approved just two days before the close of that fiscal year.

The panel reported that "[t]he resulting implementation problems can be attributed largely to the failure of the Bank to follow the process of R&R preparation as required in OD 4.30."[66] It found that the NTPC R&R plan, tacked onto the project just two weeks prior to board approval of the 1993 loan, had not been prepared in consultation with local people, and that the borrower lacked ownership of its provisions. The panel noted that "the Bank's processing of the loan violated the Bank policy and furthermore set the stage for the Bank continuing to violate policies during implementation."[67]

The panel's desk report linked the bank's policy violations to the harm suffered by the claimants, saying that local people had become "victims rather than beneficiaries of the project."[68] The panel further found that bank supervision had "effectively failed" and that rather than properly supervising the project, the bank had passively relied on information provided by NTPC, with "little meaningful direct consultation with [project-affected persons]."[69] "Bank staff relied heavily on NTPC staff—who might obviously have conflicts of interest—for information it required for supervision when NTPC itself admits that this was a new area in which it had no expertise."[70]

The Independent Monitoring Panel

One part of management's response to the claim was the development of an Independent Monitoring Panel (IMP), a three-member body of well-respected Indian nationals whose members were appointed following a period of consultation with local, national, and international civil-society organizations that had been active in Singrauli. Although the IMP was created in response to the claim filed to the Inspection Panel, it had no relationship to the panel. Instead, the IMP reported to bank management and NTPC; this would prove to be a major drawback.

The task of the IMP was to "systematically & regularly review and advise on implementation of R&R program for the NTPC power generation project funded by the World Bank," which covered both "Stage I" (the people displaced earlier) and "Stage II" (the people being displaced by expansion of the ash dikes).[71] The IMP was to be "fully independent, with the right to investigate any element of the R&R action plans." The R&R program adopted as part of the 1993 World Bank loan was designed to deal with resettlement failures in Singrauli for all stages of displacement, including those affected by stages of the projects that were not financed by the bank. Pursuant to the 1993 loan, "NTPC agreed to take remedial measures as part of the project."[72]

The IMP established effective communication with local people about their grievances, which helped to defuse tension and identify problems and potential solutions. It ultimately made recommendations to the NPTC and the World Bank for remedial compensation provisions. NTPC accepted many of the IMP's recommendations and rejected others, with the end result being an "IMP package," whereby NTPC offered improved compensation to approximately 1,250 Stage II families affected by the expansion of the Vindhyachal and Rihand ash dikes. One resident of Vindhyachal observed that

Because of the IMP we got some relief, definitely. And some peace. There was some respite from the harassment because of the presence of the IMP. They came to the village and had a dialogue. But there were two outstanding issues, relating to the landless and the situations of expanded families with expanded properties. IMP's recommendations about compensation for the landless people were not adopted by NTPC. Also, IMP in general wanted to include major sons and daughters in the package, but the NTPC did not accept this.[73]

The IMP package was an improvement on the status quo before the claim, but it did not appear to meet the bank's policy requirements of full replacement value for lost assets. Most fundamentally, the communities' demands about restoration of livelihood were not met. In addition, the IMP compensation package was generally not made available to women (except widows) who lost their livelihoods—it was chiefly available only to men. As a result, household livelihoods were effectively halved, and women were further marginalized.[74]

Most fundamentally, the NTPC refused to accept any recommendations from the IMP regarding Stage I people. As a result, women living in the Navjivan Vihar resettlement colony sent a letter to the head of the World Bank Mission demanding attention to the problems with Stage I and the fact that the NPTC was ignoring the IMP's findings:

People displaced by the same project should be given the same set of rehabilitation facilities. The Independent Monitoring Panel (IMP) clearly stated in its report that the plight of Stage 1 oustees is worse and that their problems cannot be ignored. The package recommended for Stage 2 oustees should therefore be extended to Stage 1 oustees as well.

Another problem with the NTPC's response to the IMP process was the coercive manner in which some people were forced to accept its terms and the treatment that was meted out after the package was administered. In October 1999, for example, Churchuria village was surrounded by approximately five hundred policemen and women, and bulldozers were parked in front of peoples' homes. Villagers were required to report to the local police, where they were interrogated, threatened, and in some cases beaten, all in the presence of NTPC officials.[75] Under these circumstances, they signed documents indicating their "acceptance" of the IMP package. They were then loaded into trucks and their homes were destroyed. In both Mitihini and Churchuria, a common complaint was that once people had accepted the IMP package, they were fired from jobs they had at NPTC and/or denied any future employment with NTPC.

The IMP process undoubtedly helped to relieve some of the social tension in the project area, provided a forum for local grievances to be aired, and resulted in some improved compensation. The resettlement and rehabilitation efforts in Singrauli are still unsatisfactory, however. Now that the people have shifted off their lands, they have very little leverage to assert additional demands. For these reasons, many local observers see both the Inspection Panel and the IMP as having been tools that served NTPC's objectives, which was to remove the Stage II villagers from the project area and complete construction of the ash dikes. The bank remained passive, allowing NTPC to flout the IMP findings. Facts subsequent to the disbursement of the loan lend support to the local view of the IMP as a tool for getting people off their land. As noted by residents of Navjivan Vihar resettlement colony:

> World Bank policy on rehabilitation clearly states that unless the oustees regain their earlier standard of living, the rehabilitation efforts must continue. However, NTPC after evicting oustees from the ash dike villages, has almost shut down rehabilitation programs. According to World Bank policies, these would continue to be effective until a particular loan is fully repaid. In reality, the rehabilitation programs have been wound up soon after the release of the last installment of the World Bank loan to NPTC.[76]

Despite these difficulties, the claim to the Inspection Panel filed by the eighteen families of Mitihini resulted in the adoption of a compensation package for 1,250 Stage II families that granted significantly more compensation than they would have otherwise received. As stated by one of the claimants:

> If we did not go to the Inspection Panel, then our treatment would have been the same as happened to the Stage I families. By going to the Inspection Panel, at least we got something. Although it is not enough to replace all that we have lost, it is better than it would have been. If the Panel had not been there, NTPC would have just thrown us off.[77]

Ram Lakhan Yadav, a former resident of Churchuria village, was not a claimant but he and his family benefited from the revised compensation package offered to Stage II people. "I bought one acre, which I could not have afforded if the IMP had not come," he said. "We wouldn't have been able to feed ourselves, much less be able to buy land."[78]

Update on Mitihini

In 1999, the people of Mitihini were forced to abandon their homes and move to a resettlement colony. Ram Narayan and his family and neighbors pooled their money from the IMP package to buy a few acres of agricultural land about 20 kilometers from their homes, which was unirrigated, rocky, and had a disputed claim to title. When the author visited in 2001, they were having difficulty adjusting to the new location, explaining that they had to take a bus from the resettlement colony out to the agricultural land, which was expensive for them and meant time away from their families. When the author visited again in September 2002, food security had improved somewhat because they had been successful, with much hard work, in making the new land productive and had cleared up the title dispute. Karnamati Kumari reflected on her situation in September 2002 three years after displacement and five-and-a-half years after filing the Inspection Panel claim. When asked whether things were finally improving, she responded with the following:

> There we had so much freedom. Here it is like we have been caged—we don't know where to grow food, we don't even know where to defecate. The new thing we've been given is electricity and it costs money. What good is this electricity? They've taken our land, and over and above they are charging us for this electricity.[79]

CONCLUSION

The Singrauli case involved human rights abuses combined with well-documented environmental and social devastation, and yet the bank failed to take responsibility for effectively remedying the situation on the ground. The project has suffered from a lack of commitment by either the bank or borrower to the terms of the bank's social and environmental framework. The NTPC basically refused, with impunity, to meet or adopt World Bank standards. Bank management, in turn, failed to ensure that either bank staff or the borrowing government complied with project requirements, and neglected to undertake critically important work relating to basic issues of food security, public health, environmental impacts, and development-induced displacement.

The Singrauli case also illustrates the significance of the North–South split at the board and the extent to which that division constrains the board's ability to use the Inspection Panel to improve accountability at the bank. As noted above, following the turmoil over the Singrauli and Itaparica claims, the board recognized that it was not allowing the panel to operate in the manner in which it was intended, and launched the second review of the Inspection

Panel. Sustained advocacy by NGOs and local communities—including representatives from Singrauli, Itaparica, and many other claims to the Inspection Panel—resulted in an agreement among board members that was designed to bring the panel process back on track and in accordance with the original board resolution.

The 1993 NTPC loan closed on March 31, 1999, but the World Bank's policies and procedures continue to apply to projects until the loan has been repaid. Accordingly, the bank has a continuing obligation to monitor resettlement and environmental issues in Singrauli and to ensure that the project is brought into compliance with bank policies. As of 2002, the bank had failed to live up to these obligations, and the board had also failed to evaluate the IMP process, or the rest of management's action plans, to determine the extent to which those plans had resolved the problems and addressed the policy violations.

Despite some improvement in compensation as a result of the claim, the fundamental objectives of the resettlement policy have been completely violated in Singrauli. People have been impoverished and have not had their livelihoods restored, nor have they been adequately compensated for their losses. Although the claimants to the Inspection Panel feel that they are better off than they would have been in the absence of the claim, they have not regained their previous standard of living, and they mourn their lost way of life.

> What we have lost, we have not regained here. We lost more and received less. There is no comparison between life before and now. We never worried before about food running short. Earlier, all the grain and fruit was available in plenty, and we could sell extra on the market. Now, we have to buy everything, and we cannot buy enough for our family because it is too expensive. Water was in plenty, now it is scarcity. Our land had a spring, and all of the land was irrigated. We didn't get any compensation for the loss of the spring.[80]

The eighteen families that were the claimants to the Inspection Panel, together with about twelve hundred of their Stage II neighbors, received a slightly better compensation package than they would have received had they not filed the claim. However, the people who have been designated as Stage I feel even further betrayed by the process, because even though the IMP held hearings with them and they were covered by the IMP's mandate, they were nonetheless arbitrarily excluded by NTPC from benefits under the IMP package. The World Bank has ignored their long-standing grievances relating to lost livelihood and inadequate compensation. As the years pass, Stage I families remain mired in poverty and Stage II people have fallen behind the living standard they once knew.

The story of the people of Singrauli is a microcosm of a larger struggle for justice, dignity, and survival, in India as around the world, against a form of development that allows the sacrifice and impoverishment of local communities in favor of industrial expansion. This case provides a graphic illustration of the human and ecological costs that are associated with the World Bank's failure to learn from past mistakes as well as its failure to live up to its mandate of poverty alleviation.

NOTES

1. Ram Prasant, interview by author, Bijpur resettlement colony, September 7, 2002.

2. Dashmatia, interview by author, Dodhar resettlement colony, February 7, 2001; also Rukmatia, interview by author, Dodhar resettlement colony, February 7, 2001.

3. Smitu Kothari, telephone interview by author, April 26, 2002. Mr. Kothari is the director of Lokayan and was actively involved in Singrauli for a number of years. See also SETU-Lokayan, *Vikes Ki Kimat* (Delhi: SETU-Lokayan 1986), the first major report in Hindi on the historical and cultural context as well as the range of issues highlighted by the Singrauli situation.

4. World Bank, "Management Response to the Inspection Panel, NTPC Power Generation Project," June 1997, appendix 4, paragraphs 1–2 (hereinafter "Management Response").

5. In addition, the World Bank has provided financing to Coal India and its subsidiaries, Northern Coal Fields Limited (which operates in Singrauli) and Central Coal Fields Limited (which operates in Bihar and Jharkhand states).

6. *Indian Express,* "Singrauli Fall-Out in US Congress, April 21, 1987, drawing from Smitu Kothari, "Submission on World Bank's Investment in Involuntary Displacement in Singrauli and Narmada," April 1987.

7. Madhu Kohli, "Request for Inspection, NTPC Power Generation Project Cr. 3632 25," April 1997, paragraph 6 (hereinafter "Request for Inspection").

8. NTPC, "Environmental Study of Singrauli Area" (performed by Electricité de France [EdF] International), July 1991, 52 (hereinafter EdF study).

9. EdF study, 109. The study concluded that "The resettlement policy for displaced families, including those both compensated and uncompensated, has been a failure" (p. 48).

10. Interviews by author, Singrauli, February 2001 and September 2002. See also Human Rights Watch memorandum: "Displaced women we met also drew attention to discrimination in the compensation system" (Sidney Jones and Mike Jendrzejczyk, Human Rights Watch, Memorandum to James Wolfensohn, President and Executive Director, the World Bank, "World Bank Projects in the Singrauli Region of India," April 16, 1998, 10 [hereinafter "Human Rights Watch Memorandum"]). Note that the World Bank's policy on involuntary resettlement requires that project authorities provide special attention to the rights of the landless, the semilandless, the elderly, and women (World Bank, Operational Directive 4.30 [1990], paragraph 16).

11. The 1993 loan of $400 million was intended to be the first of three additional loans to NTPC, for a total of $1.2 billion. The 1993 loan was eventually used for the Vindhyachal and Kayamkulam projects (in southern India), not for Rihand as originally envisioned. The two planned follow-on loans were later dropped.

12. "Management Response," appendix 1. As of April 30, 1997, IBRD and IDA had provided the National Thermal Power Corporation with $4,182,700,000.00 in loans and credits ("Management Response").

13. World Bank, "Staff Appraisal Report, India NTPC Power Generation Project," June 4, 1993.

14. World Bank, "Implementation Completion Report," June 2000, appendix D, n. 6 (hereinafter "Implementation Completion Report").

15. "Implementation Completion Report," 13. Although people considered to be Stage II were supposed to be compensated on the basis of "project-affected persons/PAPs" (rather than "project-affected families/PAFs" for Stage I), as discussed later in the chapter, the NTPC has refused to apply the PAP standard and has only allowed compensation for one member of each displaced family, even for Stage II displacement.

16. World Bank, "Management Action Program," paragraph 23.

17. "Management Response," appendix 4, paragraph 13.

18. During a visit to Chilkadand resettlement colony, local residents explained that a school in in the colony with capacity for three hundred children takes five hundred children, while thousands of other children are turned away for lack of space (personal communications with author, Chilkadand resettlement colony, February 9, 2001).

19. "Management Response," paragraph 24.

20. Madhu Kohli, "Singrauli: Saga of Displacement and Dispossession," 1994, 9.

21. For example, Basanti, interviewed by the author at Bijpur Resettlement Colony on September 8, 2002, stated that NTPC had told her "there is no work for women." See also letter signed by twelve women oustees of VSTPP Resettlement Colony Navjvan Vihar, given to The Head World Bank Mission, New Delhi, February 13, 2001 (translated copy on file with author; hereinafter "Demands of Women Oustees). See also note 74.

22. "Human Rights Watch Memorandum."

23. Atri Lal, interviewed by author, Singrauli, February 7, 2001.

24. Bruce Rich, Madhu Kohli, and Smitu Kothari (PIRG), "The Price of Power," 1995.

25. The six plants combined currently generate 8,241 megawatts, although there are plans to expand to 20,000 megawatts (EdF study, 24).

26. England and Russia helped NTPC to finance the initial stages of the Rihand and Vindhyachal power plants and the World Bank financed the expansion of those power plants. The bank provided initial financing for, and expansion of, the Singrauli power plant.

27. Bilateral assistance from Germany, France, and Japan contributed to the development of the Anpara, Renu Sagar, and Obra power plants.

28. Problems include "mercury, cadmium, sulphates, particulates contamination" and "contamination of sediments and of the food chain by mercury and pesticides"

(EdF study, 107). Also according to the EdF study, "A definite contamination of groundwater has been observed near Singrauli and Renusagar ash ponds" (p. 134).

29. EdF study, 107. The bank has acknowledged "industrial pollution in the form of high levels of contamination of ground and surface water and air pollution" ("Management Response," appendix 4, paragraph 15[c]).

30. Witnessed by the author during a field visit, February 4–10, 2001.

31. World Bank, "Management Response to the Inspection Panel: Update of the Action Program," September 1997, paragraph 18.

32. "Site Visit of Indian and International NGOs to Singrauli Region: Report Findings and Recommendations," 1994.

33. People's Union for Civil Liberties, "Dalit Villagers of Mitihini-Khairi Face Displacement for a Second Time," 1996, 7.

34. A World Bank back-to-office mission report concluded that participation and consultation "are very much an NTPC controlled process. This controlled process consists of meetings organized by NPTC in its premises where, in addition to NTPC officials, government officials . . . are present. These meetings are documented and videographed but are not representative of the affected community" (as quoted in letter from Madhu Kohli to David Marsden, World Bank, May 30, 1996, 2).

35. Bhagwandas, interview by author, in the ruins of Mitihini, February 6, 2001, explaining the decision to resist resettlement and file a claim to the Inspection Panel.

36. Human Rights Watch determined that villagers "had been beaten and arbitrarily detained for peaceful protests. . . . The underlying cause of the human rights violations has been a failure to resolve villagers' complaints about levels of compensation, conditions of resettlement, and environmental damage" (Human Rights Watch, "World Bank Should Monitor Abuses in India," press release and memorandum to World Bank president and executive directors, April 21, 1998).

37. Incidents reported to the author in a visit to the project area in November–December 1996. Many of these incidents were documented in contemporaneous correspondence with the World Bank (see, e.g., Peter Bosshard [Berne Declaration], "The Singrauli Experience: A Report of an International NGO Fact-Finding Tour to the World Bank Projects of Singrauli/India," *xxx* 1997; HRW memo; British Broadcasting Corporation, *The Price of Power* [1997] [hereinafter BBC video]).

38. "Request for Inspection."

39. "Request for Inspection," paragraph 24.

40. "Request for Inspection." Although the claimants asked the panel to keep their names confidential, over time their identities were determined by the project authorities and are no longer secret.

41. "Request for Inspection," paragraphs 57–58.

42. "Three weeks after the filing, the N.T.P.C. brought police into four villages to evict people from their homes, a transparent bid to roust the complaining villagers and destroy their homes before an investigation could take place" (*The Nation,* "Late Can Mean Never," July 21, 1997, 7; see also BBC video).

43. CIEL letter to President Wolfensohn, July 11, 1997.

44. Robert Drysdale, telephone conversations with the author, May 1997.

45. World Bank, memorandum from Sam Thangaraj and Mohd. Hasan to David Marsden, June 14, 1997.

46. It is interesting to note that although the bank failed to stop the borrower from altering the status quo through forced evictions, the Inspection Panel also did not make any recommendations for a cessation of the harmful activities. The former General Counsel of the World Bank has observed that "The Panel, in recommending inspection, may indicate whether in its view suspension of preparatory work would be needed for the purposes of its inspection (e.g., if the continuation of such work would have the potential of making the alleged harm irreversible)" (Ibrahim F. I. Shihata, *The World Bank Inspection Panel* [New York: Oxford University Press/World Bank, 1994], 78).

47. See, for example, e-mail from Delhi Forum to Dana Clark, November 24, 1997, documenting the events that culminated in the assault on Madhu Kohli (copy on file with author).

48. In a letter dated November 25, 1997, to Dana Clark of CIEL, Mieko Nishimizu, vice president for the South Asia region, responded to news of the attack on Madhu Kohli by saying "I have instructed our Director in India [Edwin Lim] to advise me on this situation by obtaining a first hand report, on an urgent basis and in whatever manner he deems necessary." In a meeting one week later, Ms. Clark asked Mr. Lim what steps he had taken to obtain this urgent, firsthand report. Mr. Lim responded that he had not gone to the field, had not discussed the incident with Madhu Kohli, and had not interviewed the NTPC staff involved (Dana Clark, notes of meeting with World Bank staff, December 1, 1997).

49. "Human Rights Watch Memorandum," 5.

50. "Management Response," 3.

51. "Management Response," 3, n. 8.

52. The World Bank, Memorandum to Richard Bissell, chairman, the Inspection Panel from Guatam Kaji, Acting President, June 3, 1997, paragraph 4.

53. "Management Response," 1.

54. Madhu Kohli, interview by author, June 2000.

55. Inspection Panel, "Report and Recommendation: India: NTPC Power Generation Project," July 24, 1997, paragraph 48 (hereinafter "Panel Report").

56. "Panel Report," paragraph 43.

57. "Panel Report," paragraph 72.

58. "Panel Report," paragraph 74.

59. See "Panel Report," paragraph 19, where the panel notes that management cited socioeconomic surveys that showed no indigenous peoples were affected by the expansion of the ash dikes in Stage II. The report then notes: "The Inspector raised the question in the field and in discussion with GOI representatives. They confirmed the information provided in the Management Response. Since the inspector received no contradictory information during his field visit, the Panel will therefore not further address this allegation."

60. For more information about Yacyretá, see chapter 4 by Kay Treakle and Elías Díaz Peña.

61. The board split 52.9 percent against an inspection in Itaparica, and 47.09 percent in favor (see Jonathan A. Fox, "The World Bank Inspection Panel: Lessons from

the First Five Years," *Global Governance* 6, no. 3 [July–September 2000]: 305). For further discussion of Itaparica, see chapter 7 by Aurélio Vianna Jr.

62. Prior consent by the borrowing government is required for full panel investigations in the territory of any borrowing country, although it is not required during the panel's preliminary assessment of eligibility. See World Bank, Resolution no. 93-10, Resolution no. IDA 93-6, September 1993, paragraph 21, "Inspection in the territory of such country shall be carried out with its prior consent" (compare with paragraph 19). The bank acknowledged that "There were strong complaints from the Indian Government against what they saw as an investigation into internal affairs, and they argued that the Inspection Panel's mandate was only to investigate the Bank's own conduct, not the conduct of the Indian Government or its agencies. Since the complaint against the Bank was based on the argument that NPTC did not adequately implement the provisions of project resettlement plans, and that the Bank failed to take adequate action to improve matters, it would be difficult to conduct a full investigation without also pointing out the shortcomings of the Borrower" ("Implementation Completion Report," appendix D, n. 21).

63. World Bank, "World Bank Board Agrees to Inspection Panel Investigation," press release, September 12, 1997.

64. Inspection Panel, "Report on Desk Investigation," December 22, 1997, paragraph 16 (hereinafter "Desk Investigation").

65. "Desk Investigation," paragraph 84.

66. "Desk Investigation," paragraph 19 (emphasis added).

67. "Desk Investigation," paragraph 89.

68. "Desk Investigation."

69. "Desk Investigation," paragraph 21, 22.

70. "Desk Investigation," paragraph 121.

71. NTPC, "NTPC Independent Monitoring Panel" (undated).

72. "Management Response," 2. Note that management conveniently remained silent on its role in providing initial financing for the Singrauli Super Thermal Power Plant (Stage I) in 1977, and its, expansion in 1982, which resulted in the forcible displacement of tens of thousands of people.

73. Ram Lakhan Yadav, formerly of Churchuria village, now living in Chargoda, interview by author, February 10, 2001.

74. Dana L. Clark, "An Overview of Revisions to the World Bank Resettlement Policy" (paper presented at a workshop on Engendering Resettlement and Rehabilitation Policies and Programmes in India, New Delhi, September 12, 2002; copy on file with author).

75. Dirja Ram Rajak, formerly of Churchuria, now homeless, interviewed by author, February 9, 2001. Dirja Ram Rajak rejected the IMP package, one of only six people to do so. The account of police presence and beatings at the time Churchuria villagers "accepted" and signed up for the IMP package was confirmed by Ram Lakhan Yadav, formerly of Churchuria, interview by author, Chargoda, February 10, 2001.

76. "Demands of Women Oustees," paragraphs 6–7.

77. Rukmatia, formerly of Mitihini village, now Dodhar resettlement colony, interview by author February 7, 2001. Her neighbor, Bhagwandas, also stated that "After

going to the Inspection Panel, things are better than earlier, but not as much as our demands" (interview by author, February 6, 2001).

78. Ram Lakhan Yadav, interview by author, Chargoda, India, February 10, 2001.

79. Karnamati Kumari, interview by author, Dodhar resettlement colony, September 9, 2002.

80. Rukmatia, interview by author, February 7, 2001.

9

Social Protection Conditionality in World Bank Structural Adjustment Loans: The Case of Argentina's Garden Program (Pro-Huerta)

Víctor Abramovich[1]

In 2001, over one-third of the World Bank's lending was for structural adjustment. In the 1990s, this type of lending encouraged governments to pursue policies that would make their economies more competitive in the world market. These policies weakened the welfare state, labor laws, and social security systems, thus increasing inequality and the vulnerability of the poor. To mitigate the impact of these policies, the World Bank began including social conditionality clauses in structural adjustment loan agreements.[2] These conditions sought to assure that certain budgets would not be cut, especially for those programs targeted to the poorest of the poor. The first claim that challenged government failure to comply with a social conditionality clause was presented to the World Bank Inspection Panel in 1999.

In 1998, after the Brazilian economic crisis, Argentina received a structural adjustment loan from the World Bank for $2.5 billion, designed to encourage changes in economic policy to forestall a currency devaluation. The loan was intended to help the country reduce its vulnerability as it confronted abrupt changes in international financial markets; at the same time the loan was intended to reinforce the country's capacity for sustained economic growth with social equity. This loan included "Social Budget Conditions" to ensure a minimum $680 million budget to support a package of ongoing social safety net programs listed in the agreement.

Convinced that it was the only way to stabilize the national currency, the Argentine government greatly reduced public spending in 1999. In deciding where to make the budget cuts, however, the government took certain precautions to

Translated by Angela Hollowell-Fuentes and Charles Roberts

avoid weakening the governing party's prospects in legislative elections that year. The government allocated the overall amount of the social spending budget specified in the loan agreement, which assured the disbursement of the almost $1.5 billion remaining in the loan. But the government redirected the "social budget" funds to favor those programs traditionally used as instruments of political clientelism. This diversion led the other social programs in the package to suffer deep budget cuts, completely eliminating many of them.

The Garden Program (Programa de Promoción de la Auto-Producción de Alimentos, or Pro-Huerta), which was listed among the guaranteed social programs, was one of those programs threatened with extinction. The program encourages self-sufficient food production based on seed distribution and technical assistance for private and community gardens. Administered by a government agricultural technology agency, the program reached some 2.7 million of the poorest of the poor in 1998, with an annual budget of $11.2 million. Only $4 million was allocated to the program's 1999 budget, which meant that it would disappear altogether by mid 1999.

The same networks of community organizations created for the efficient distribution of seed and technical assistance allowed participants in grassroots programs to organize a resistance campaign. Program staff helped community participants to organize and channel their demands. Some political sectors and mass media echoed the participants' concerns, which were largely ignored by government authorities.

In June 1999, a group of program participants, with the help of the Center for Legal and Social Studies (CELS), a human rights organization, reported to the World Bank's Subregional Office that the budget cut constituted a breach of the social conditionality clause in the loan agreement. Though the government had met its commitment in terms of overall spending on social programs, the group alleged that the government's contractual obligations included a commitment to provide the funds needed for the continuity of all the programs specified in the loan agreement. The program participants argued that this was the only interpretation of the loan conditions compatible with the official goal of the special structural adjustment loan, which was to limit budget cuts that would negatively affect programs that met the most pressing needs of the poorest of the poor.

In July 1999, faced with the inaction of the bank managers in Buenos Aires, Garden Program participants presented a formal claim to the Inspection Panel, charging the local bank officials with failing to comply with the bank's policy directives relating to poverty reduction, project supervision, and public access to information. In their claim, program participants asked the panel to recommend that the bank withhold the undisbursed tranches as a precautionary measure until compliance with the social budget condition could be verified.

Upon learning that a formal claim had been presented to the Inspection Panel, World Bank and government officials suddenly displayed a social conscience. While the bank officials in Argentina were possibly attempting to prevent the panel from taking the case, government officials wanted to avoid any threat to the imminent disbursement of new loan funds, which would have cast more shadows on Argentina's already bleak economic landscape. In any event, shortly after the claim was presented to the panel, the government allocated an additional $4.5 million to the Garden Program budget.

Panel members released a report in December 1999 after visiting Argentina. Although they concluded that the issue was resolved since new funds were granted, thereby enabling the program to continue, they also took positions on several issues raised by the claim. In particular, the panel affirmed its mandate to consider claims involving structural adjustment loans. In addition, the panel rejected the attempt by the bank's regional office to require that the claimants be identified. The panel also accepted the status of the beneficiaries of the guaranteed programs as affected persons and recognized their standing to bring a case before the Inspection Panel.

This chapter presents the background of the case, including the terms of the structural adjustment loan and the Garden Program. Second, it analyzes how the claim was organized and the challenges confronting low-income sectors in their relationship with the World Bank. Next, the chapter analyzes some of the main technical issues debated in the case: the interpretation of the social conditionality clause, the impact of government noncompliance on the rest of the loan agreement, the standing of the beneficiaries to go before the Inspection Panel as persons harmed by the budget cut, the role of the panel in protecting the claimants' confidentiality, and the panel's jurisdiction to hear the case. Finally, the chapter attempts to reach some conclusions about the possibilities of using the Inspection Panel to demand the protection of social interests. More important, the chapter aims to reach conclusions about the value of conditionality clauses in structural adjustment loans as a part of the bank's policies aimed at mitigating the effects of extreme poverty.

SOCIAL CONDITIONALITY IN THE SPECIAL STRUCTURAL ADJUSTMENT LOAN FOR ARGENTINA

In 1998, the international financial system was in turmoil. Imbalances in international financial markets temporarily shut off access to most foreign loans, provoking severe economic instability in Argentina. With the closing of markets and the disruption of capital flows, Argentina was unable to finance its deficit or refinance its external debt. In this context, the Argentine government appealed to the World Bank for "extraordinary assistance" to "make payments on the debt and avoid the contraction of international financial reserves, which would produce a severe recession and increases in unemployment . . . [resulting] in the curtailment of government services and critical social programs."[3] Since its inception in November 1998, the Special Structural Adjustment Loan (SSAL), in conjunction with the Special Repurchase Facility Support Loan (SRFL, the contingent loan), aimed to mitigate "the deleterious effects of the current international fiscal instability on the economy and protecting vulnerable groups."[4]

On November 11, 1998, the $2.525 billion loan agreement was signed, structured in three tranches: the first was to be released in November 1998 for $1.025 billion, the second in March 1999, and the final tranche would be released after June 1999. The loan agreement included a package of reforms with four main objectives, with the principal goal being to "safeguard current social protection programs, which in a time of financial stress might be vulnerable, and to advance reforms in health and education."[5] The SSAL set the requirements, based on bank criteria, which would need to be met by national authorities prior to withdrawing any funds. These requirements included maintaining a set of social programs with a total budget of $680 million.[6]

In choosing which social programs would be included in that set, consideration was given to the fact that the budget allocations for food programs accounted for only 3.6 percent of social spending and that such programs could offset the negative impact of the adjustment financed by the same loan agreement. Accordingly, the programs aimed at bolstering the nutrition of children and the elderly, as well as the program of food production for family consumption called the Garden Program, were included. In this way the bank sought to comply with its own operational directives, including the obligation to safeguard against any immediate harm caused by the transition costs of the adjustment programs, paying particular attention to food security.[7]

THE GARDEN PROGRAM FOR FOOD AND NUTRITION AND THE GUARANTEED SOCIAL PROGRAMS

The federal government created the Garden Program in 1990. The National Institute of Agricultural Technology (Instituto Nacional de Tecnología Agropecuaria, or INTA) was entrusted with designing a food security program to support small-scale production of foodstuffs for family consumption. The program goal was to provide the neediest social sectors with access to a balanced diet of diverse, high-quality, fresh foods. The program was also expected to help families better manage their food expenses, to promote community participation in food production, to generate appropriate technologies for agricultural production for family consumption, and to encourage small-scale alternatives for food production. The program distributed seed for private and community gardens, advised families on techniques for the gardens, and offered nutritional advice on incorporating the foods produced into the regular diet. In addition to provincial cities, the program targeted the impoverished zones on the outskirts of large cities.

The Garden Program is operated by a small staff of less than 600 people, since it is carried out by more than 15,000 promoters, who are recruited from among the beneficiaries themselves. Problems and needs, as well as the possibility of cultivating unused land to meet food needs, are discussed in open conversations among neighbors. INTA's technical staff train the promoters, who are drawn from the program participants themselves. The promoters organize and supervise the gardeners. Training meetings are held in the community at schools, rural cooperatives, and neighborhood clubs.

The areas where the program has been implemented are in a deep social crisis, characterized by high unemployment and poverty, with practically no public assistance. In this context, local social networks have been revived as the last viable recourse for addressing such extreme poverty. Unlike other public assistance programs, in the Garden Program the attitude required of participants is far from passive; rather, they must participate in training workshops for planting, harvesting, and using the crops, as well as throughout the entire cycle, coordinating the distribution of seed and tools to other neighbors.[8]

Interviews with the program participants revealed that they clearly made a strong connection between the garden harvest and community effort. Indeed, they said, "what we get is what we pay for with our sweat and tears," and added, "we are not asking that they give us handouts."[9] Hence, participants clearly distinguish their relationship with the Garden Program from other sorts of welfare programs. The provision of seed and training, adapting nutritional habits to the foods produced, balancing the diet, and observing which foods are most suitable for each season, all differ greatly from handing out a box lunch or providing access to a school cafeteria. The participants in the outlying areas of Buenos Aires emphasize that they are primarily "provincial" people (people who had to migrate to the cities), who "had stopped working the land" and are now rediscovering the activities of their childhood.[10] Thus, in addition to the contribution of the technical staff, recovering the participants' lost knowledge is itself a valuable contribution. In the opinion of the program staff, this active participation by beneficiaries is the program's comparative advantage.

Many of the participants in the Garden Program are women: they are the ones who feel the pressure to put food on the table (*parar la olla*)—to put an end to the desperation of having nothing to feed their children. These women work the gardens, and, with their children, were the driving force behind the claim (four of the five people who signed the original claim are women). The logic of participation and the community networks created for program outreach enabled the beneficiaries to resist the effort to dismantle the Garden Program.

THE GARDEN PROGRAM BUDGET CUT

The Garden Program was launched with the expectation that its coverage would grow over time. Indeed, despite having 2,744,000 participants in 1998, the Garden Program's coverage fell far short of potential demand, since its potential number of participants was the entire national population with unmet basic needs, estimated to number some 6,247,000. By virtue of INTA's technical work, and the organization and discipline it assured in the volunteer labor provided by the institutions, organizations, and individuals in solidarity with the program's objectives and functions, the number of participants skyrocketed. To reach more people, the program's budget had to increase, reaching $11,200,000 for the 1998 fiscal year. With the 1999 budget cuts, however, the Social Development Ministry received 4 million pesos specifically earmarked for the Garden Program, equivalent to 32 percent of the total that was originally budgeted by the secretariat. This made it impossible to hide the fact that the government had decided to use certain social programs as adjustment variables in reducing the budget deficit.

The budget cut also hurt other important social programs, such as the ASOMA program (Apoyo Solidario a los Mayores, or Solidarity Assistance to the Elderly) and PRANI (Programa Alimentario Nutricional Infantil, or Food and Nutrition Program for Children), which, like the Garden Program, were guaranteed in the loan agreement. The government was careful, however, to maintain the overall sum of $680 million allocated to social programs in the agreement's budget condition list. The government was also acutely aware that legislative elections were approaching, and used the cut funds to increase the budget for social programs that involved creating temporary jobs, which were run by the provincial and local political authorities in the context of the election campaigns.

Reviewing the budget ultimately approved, the Secretariat for Social Development was faced with the dilemma of either drastically reducing the number of Garden Program beneficiaries or maintaining the current number, which would exhaust all the funds before the end of the year. Under the first scenario, the government would have had to cut off 1.7 million of the poorest of the poor (58.52 percent of the participants in 1998). It was difficult, however, to define or conceive of a "reasonable" criterion for cutting off such a large proportion of the target population, that is, people in extreme need. So the INTA decided to proceed with the program for all participants, even though this would bring the Garden Program to a standstill by midyear. Among the activities threatened by this decision, perhaps the most important was purchasing of seed. The disruption in the program's time line for distribution led to its suspension in March (seriously setting back the activities set for fall/winter 1999), and threatened to shut down the program for good after June. The Garden Program suffered another setback when a related loan being negotiated with the Inter-American Development Bank was blocked.

ORGANIZING THE CLAIM: COLLABORATION BETWEEN TECHNICAL STAFF, PROGRAM PARTICIPANTS, AND CELS

In response, the technical staff sought to defend the participants and their access to Garden Program services, and to defend their own jobs. Their efforts received the unconditional support of the program's beneficiaries and promoters, bolstered by the very logic of community organization on which the program was based. INTA staff ensured that federal authorities received written protests from the participants and their allies. Approximately 1,200 letters were presented to the federal government from organizations, provincial legislatures, and individual supporters.

Facing an unresponsive government, INTA staff members decided to seek legal support from CELS. Some of them knew of CELS because of its activities under the military dictatorship. In the democratic era, CELS had become known for its participation in the prosecution of military officers implicated in human rights violations, as well as for its more recent involvement in police brutality cases. CELS had also developed a legal program for protecting economic, social, and cultural rights.

At first, INTA staff and the CELS attorneys discussed the possibility of taking action before the local courts, or possibly pursuing an *amparo,* or constitutional injunction, which would block budget cuts on the grounds that they infringed the right to adequate nutrition. After considerable discussion and analysis of the alternatives, the CELS legal team predicted that judicial action in the domestic courts would be unlikely to succeed.

Several scenarios were explored, including the possibility of using the very logic of the program as a source of state obligations. In this approach, since the program prepared families to live off of community gardens, by abruptly blocking the beneficiaries' access to the seed the state had failed to address the nutritional needs that it had itself established. The state could not contradict its own actions by creating a dietary program dependent on public assistance and later suddenly cut that assistance without any compensatory measure, thereby aggravating the poverty it had once sought to address.

The team also examined the possibility of challenging the budgetary law as unconstitutional, since it called for cutbacks at odds with the loan agreement. In the Argentine Constitution, treaties have higher rank than statutes, such that if the agreement between the Argentine state and the bank were a treaty, the contradictory budget law could be ruled null and void. The possibility of successfully pursuing any of these approaches was minimal, however: the Argentine judiciary had an extremely conservative track record when it came to questioning administrative or congressional decisions regarding the design or implementation of public policy.

Also significant when analyzing the possibility of suing the Argentine government in the domestic courts was the highly vulnerable position of the participants. They faced great risks in formally suing the government because they depended on public assistance for their subsistence. Since it would be impossible for participants to keep their identities confidential while filing a lawsuit, various forms of collective lawsuits were explored, including the possibility of CELS filing the suit on the participants' behalf.

It was the technical staff who noted that the Garden Program had sought financing from the Inter-American Development Bank. They knew that the program was somehow related to the government's commitments to the World Bank, although they were not sure whether it was funded directly by the bank. With this scant information, the CELS team began its research. Through the Secretariat for Social Development, CELS learned that the program was mentioned in the SSAL agreement. CELS then asked the World Bank office in Argentina for the text of the loan agreement. The request for information was informal and there was no mention of specific motives. Initial contacts were made between students of the University of Buenos Aires (UBA) interning at the Human Rights Legal Clinic at CELS, who worked actively on the preliminary investigation, and lower-level staff at the bank mission. During this phase of the case there were no difficulties gaining access to the information requested from the bank. Bank staff were completely open to supplying all the documents on the SSAL, and even helped the students understand the more difficult and unclear aspects of the texts. In contrast, asking the Secretariat of Social Development and the Ministry of Economy for information on their agreements with the bank turned out to be a fruitless undertaking.

Prior to the requests, the UBA students, along with the CELS lawyers, had already begun to understand and analyze the World Bank's Inspection Panel. Once it was discovered that the Garden Program was among the programs protected by the social budget condition of the loan agreement, they analyzed the possibility of using the Inspection Panel to ensure bank compliance. The CELS lawyers, along with the students, then held a series of meetings with INTA staff and program participants. In these meetings they discussed the risks and advantages of such an approach, including the possible risks that such an action could pose to the participants. They discussed the possibility of the authorities taking reprisals against the staff, and particularly against the participants, whose sustenance largely depends on access to the public assistance controlled by these authorities. In an effort to avoid or minimize reprisals, it was decided that the technical staff would not be claimants and the identity of the program participants signing the claim would be protected under the panel's confidentiality guarantee.

While the CELS lawyers prepared the claim with the assistance of the clinic students, the technical staff and promoters organized a series of meetings using the program's networks to get the word out. They distributed a petition in support of the claim, explaining the scope of the action being taken and the guarantee of confidentiality. While the initial group of participants who signed the claim sufficed to meet the standing requirement (i.e., that claimants must be persons actually affected by a bank-supported project), organizers also recognized that getting as many participants as possible to join the claim would strengthen it. Outreach and word-of-mouth efforts succeeded, such that while only 5 participants signed initially, 418 signed after the claim was filed.

PRINCIPAL ARGUMENTS OF THE CLAIM PRESENTED TO THE WORLD BANK'S BUENOS AIRES OFFICE

On June 11, 1999, CELS presented its concerns to the World Bank's Subregional Office in Buenos Aires, requesting urgent measures in response to what was alleged to be the Argentine state's violation of the social budget condition in the SSAL agreement. After describing the operation of the program, CELS provided its interpretation of the scope of the "social budget condition," acknowledging that while the Argentine government had notified the bank that the total social budget met the commitment, the government did not inform the bank of the drastic cuts in some of the programs to be protected.

The argument was simple. The purpose of the social conditionality clause in the structural adjustment loan is precisely to protect social programs targeted to the poorest of the poor from drastic budget cuts. Beyond the total amount of spending set in the conditionality clause, each program specified for protection has an essential value in the context of the agreement since each is tailored to the characteristics of the sectors affected and to the types of services to be protected. Even when the government guarantees a fixed sum for social programs, it must also guarantee the continued existence of those programs, such that the targeted social sectors are not deprived of the services deemed necessary when the protected social programs were initially selected. In this sense, the government's failure to fund the services guaranteed by the programs would be sufficient grounds for blocking later disbursements.[11] This does not prevent the government from making changes in the budgetary allocations, but it does rule out cuts that might endanger a listed program, unless it is shown that the benefits for the social sectors originally guaranteed by such a program are otherwise safeguarded.

The argument was that the government had violated the loan's social conditionality clause by drastically cutting the Garden Program's budget to the point of condemning it to extinction by mid 1999. CELS further argued that the reduction of funds made the organization of the program impossible since its services, such as distribution of seed, were essential for every participant, and since it was impossible to establish a reasonable criterion for excluding some social sectors from the food support program. They also cited the United Nations Economic and Social Council and the Food and Agriculture Organization's official conclusions on the role of the international financial institutions in social impacts structural adjustment.[12]

In summary, the claim presented to the bank's Buenos Aires office requested postponing disbursement of the third tranche until the Argentine government earmarked sufficient funds to the Garden Program to keep it in operation. The social conditionality guarantees of the SSAL, it argued, should be interpreted as the express resolve of the bank to preserve essential social services to the greatest extent possible. By protecting such social programs, the bank sought to mitigate the effects of the declining living standards of the vulnerable groups caused by economic difficulties and by implementation of the structural adjustment programs promoted by the bank.

The claim was presented on June 9, 1999. On June 23 CELS received a fax from the World Bank's Argentina country director, Myrna Alexander, which stated: "the situation this year may be having a negative impact on the financing of various government programs, including the Garden Program," and that "the loan agreement does not specify the amount of funds to be earmarked to each particular program; rather, it approves the general financing of all the programs." The bank's reply was diplomatic in tone and recognized the potential impact of adjustment on the program, but also suggested that it would be impossible to adopt any measures to avoid such an impact. The bank's reference to the total amount in the social budget condition suggested that it interpreted the government's contractual obligations in a manner clearly at odds with the claim.

In response, on June 24 the claimants sent a fax to the local bank office re-iterating their position on the serious threat to the program. Moreover, aware of the approaching disbursement, they asked that the local bank office notify them of the specific measures to be adopted. In an interview in the daily newspaper *La Nación* the claimants warned that if they did not receive a re-sponse from the local bank office, they would present the claim to the In-spection Panel in Washington, D.C. The bank did not reply; CELS reiterated their concerns on July 15. When there was still no reply, the claimants pre-sented their formal request for inspection to the Inspection Panel on July 28, 1999, claiming that bank management was violating its own directives in its supervision of the loan agreement and that such negligence was leading to the imminent shutdown of the Garden Program , which would result in direct ma-terial damage to the program participants.[13]

PRINCIPAL ARGUMENTS IN THE CLAIM PRESENTED TO THE WORLD BANK INSPECTION PANEL

The claimants argued that the loan conditioned disbursements on the bank be-ing satisfied with government implementation of the actions set forth in the loan agreement.[14] The agreement included the sustained operation of the des-ignated social programs.[15] This was a decisive point, given that the bank could argue that the breach of social conditionality was not the type of breach that could condition the disbursement of the structural adjustment loan tranches—as its Buenos Aires office claimed. From the bank's perspective, failure to comply with just one condition was not enough to suspend the dis-bursement; rather, it argued that the agreement as a whole should be evalu-ated in considering a suspension. From the claimants' perspective, the nature of structural adjustment loans was such that the social conditionalities were essential to the economics of the agreement, so that any breach of the condi-tionality would constitute a breach of the agreement as a whole, requiring the suspension of disbursements.[16]

To make such an argument, the claim sought to put these conditionalities in context, appealing to the bank's public positions. Thus, it argued that social conditionalities had to be understood in the context of what World Bank Presi-dent Wolfensohn has called "balanced development," the idea that sustainable development demands a "balanced economic and social program," including social protections for the poor.[17] The bank's policy on poverty reduction (Op-erational Directive [OD] 4.15) recognized that the transition costs of structural adjustment can adversely affect the poor. "Bank-supported adjustment pro-grams, therefore, include measures to protect the most vulnerable from declines in consumption and social services—with particular attention paid to food and nutritional security—in the context of an agreed public expenditure program."[18] This policy further specified that "special efforts should be made to safeguard, and increase where appropriate, budgetary allocations for basic health, nutrition, and education, including programs that benefit the most vulnerable groups among the poor."[19]

Thus, the failure of the Buenos Aires office to block the disbursement violated the bank's directives on project supervision. Claimants noted that the bank's conduct violated provisions of the loan agreement and several of its own operational policies: Poverty Reduction (OD 4.15), Project Supervision (OD 13.05), Project Monitoring and Evaluation (OP/BP 10.70), Supervision of Disbursements (OP/BP 13.40), and Operational Information Disclosure (OP/BP 17.50).

Although it is not within the scope of this chapter to explain each argument associated with these bank standards, the main argument is worthy of discussion, for it proved to be the most revealing of bank management's failure to supervise effectively each of the listed social programs. Because the budget cuts for social programs stemmed directly from the December 1998 budget law, had there been diligent supervision, the Buenos Aires office would have been able to detect the threat to the Garden Program prior to March 1999. This meant that management had failed in its duty to identify the problems that could arise during the loan's implementation,[20] given that one of its main objectives was precisely to protect the most vulnerable social sectors.

The claim also noted that the local bank office could have done more to monitor and evaluate the loan, including contacts with the program beneficiaries to closely monitor attainment of the social goals.[21] In the case of the Garden Program, its organizational structure could have facilitated contact with the regional promoters and with the participants at the various meeting centers nationwide. Even so, at no time did management make contact with them or find out what was happening—not even after receiving the claim. Finally, the claim alleged that the bank office's response (which literally stated that the budget cut "might" affect the financing of the Garden Program) constituted evidence of the absence of adequate supervision.

KEY ACTORS' REACTIONS AFTER PRESENTATION OF THE CLAIM

CELS did not formally notify bank management that it had presented the claim to the Inspection Panel; in early August, management found out informally. At a seminar on mechanisms for civil-society participation in the World Bank that was organized by the Buenos Aires–based subregional office, a lawyer from CELS described the case of the Garden Program in a panel discussion and concluded by informing the conference members of the claim presented in Washington. A bank official who was moderating the discussion interrupted him and, in front of the conference participants, reproached him for having failed to notify the Buenos Aires office. After that incident, this particular official contacted Country Director Myrna Alexander, and soon after assured the CELS lawyer that she would address the issue immediately. A few days later, the same official told CELS by telephone that the country director had a meeting with the chief of the cabinet ministers, Jorge Rodríguez, where the government had committed to supplying additional funds to the program. Indeed, on August 27, 1999, the government announced a resolution, signed by Rodríguez, which allotted an additional $3 million to the Garden Program from funds reallocated from customs auctions. Another $1.5 million was added to the program by the Secretariat for Social Development as part of a reorganization of its funds. Less than a month after submitting the claim to the Inspection Panel, the program was allotted an additional $4.5 million.

It is clear that the response of the bank staff in Buenos Aires came after the request for inspection was filed in Washington and was not a result of the claimants' original report submitted to them in June. Bank Country Director Alexander, as a defense in response to the request for inspection, reported to the Inspection Panel that her supervisory effort to increase funding, having begun on July 6, 1999, had inspired the government's commitment to increase funding for the program. While it is not possible to prove that this version of the facts is false, one can conjecture that had there been major supervisory efforts in July, as the director claims, they would have been reported to the claimants to forestall them from taking the case to the panel. It seems that the only measure taken by Director Alexander that CELS was told about was her August meeting with the presidential chief of staff, which occurred after the bank office had found out that the panel would get involved; the resolution to increase funding for the program also came in August.

It is also clear that the success of the claimants' action was linked directly to Argentina's financial vulnerability at that time. This does not mean that just any sort of step taken by the bank to ensure compliance with the social conditionalities would have been equally successful, or that the government lacked any room for maneuver to contest the bank's recommendations. When the claim was presented to the panel, the bank had disbursements pending for two tranches of the SSAL totaling approximately $1.5 billion. In the middle of the fiscal adjustment under way, and with the backdrop of an unstable national economy, any rumor of delays in the arrival of fresh funds to the public coffers would have made the markets tremble. In this context, the additional funds for the Garden Program were a tiny cost compared to the risk of suspension or postponement of the disbursement.

Presenting the claim to the panel not only unleashed the pressure of the local bank office on the government, but also highlighted the position of those government sectors, specifically officials of the INTA and the Secretariat for Social Development, that were pushing for an increase in the program's funding. The Secretariat for Social Development, which was in direct contact with the beneficiaries, had been receiving hundreds of letters and complaints about the status of the program. The bank's intervention thus helped to bolster the position of the social development secretary vis-à-vis the fiscal conservatism of the economic policymakers.

In stating its defense to the panel on September 13, 1999, management reported that an additional $3 million had been allotted to the Garden Program fund, thanks to its own supervisory efforts. Paradoxically, it failed to report that another $1.5 million had been allocated, revealing persistent weaknesses in its supervision capacity. The office recognized that during the first semester, $3.8 million of the $4 million assigned to the Garden Program in the budget had been spent, which, as the claim charged, threatened the continued operation of the program.

Bank management also tried to prevent the panel from hearing the case by challenging its "eligibility." In short, management argued that the participants in the guaranteed social programs lacked standing to make a complaint, since they could not be considered victims of specific bank policies as such, nor could the budget cut be considered to have had a material adverse effect on their interests. Following this argument, management also objected to their identity being kept confidential, since this made it impossible to verify whether the claimants were actually beneficiaries of the program in question, or whether they were receiving equivalent services from other programs. In addition, management maintained that no supervisory errors had been made and that the disbursement should not be suspended based merely on the budget cuts since such an exceptional measure required analyzing the entire agreement. Bank management also challenged the Inspection Panel's jurisdiction over a case of alleged violations of the SSAL conditions.[22]

The Inspection Panel made an on-site visit to Argentina in November 1999, including panel chair Jim MacNeill, panel member Maartje van Putten, and the panel's executive secretary, Eduardo Abbott. Panel members interviewed program participants, visited some of the community gardens in the outlying areas of Buenos Aires, and met with the authorities of the Buenos Aires office and CELS. It was during this visit that the panel learned that the program had received an additional $1.5 million from the Secretariat for Social Development, which had never been reported by the local bank office. This was significant, since they had reported that the $3 million assigned by the chief of staff was enough to solve the problem.

THE INSPECTION PANEL REPORT

The Inspection Panel's report, released in December 1999, found that the claim met the eligibility requirements for opening a case.[23] The panel expressly recognized its jurisdiction to examine a case that alleges government failure to comply with bank directives related to the supervision of social conditionality in structural adjustment loans. The panel also concluded that the beneficiaries had standing as affected persons. What is unique about this case is that the claimants are not directly affected by a bank action or by an action of a government that was designed or sponsored by the bank. Rather, the harm derives from government actions that violated the conditions agreed upon with the bank, such that the responsibility of the bank's Buenos Aires office is based on its failure to monitor or supervise the action of the borrower government. If one were to apply the analysis of the international responsibility of states in the human rights system to the bank, one would say that this case involves indirect, rather than direct responsibility. The bank holds indirect responsibility because while negative effects are not the result of the bank's direct action, they are the consequence of its failure to prevent the actions of another actor (in this case the government) from causing the harm. This is analogous to when a state violates a human rights treaty by failing to take the measures needed to prevent a non-state actor from somehow impeding, limiting, or affecting the exercise of a basic human right.

The panel stated in its report that the eligibility rules were met since the claimants were indeed participants of the Garden Program and "would sustain harm if the program were to be terminated and they were without any other forms of nutrition assistance."[24] Thus, the panel accepted the claimants' standing in light of the fact that a serious violation of the bank's policies and operational procedures could have a material adverse effect on them, such as being deprived of the food obtained through the program, without receiving an alternative benefit.

It is important to note that the panel also accepted the request to keep the claimants' identities confidential. Management had objected, reasoning that it

would impede an examination of the claimants' eligibility. The panel concluded that although it would not guarantee anonymity, it would guarantee
confidentiality by keeping the claimants' identities under seal and possibly
extending this protection to certain correspondence. "To imply that the Panel
should divulge their names to Management to enable it to comment on eligibility," the panel argued, " reveals a surprising and worrying level of understanding about this part of the Panel's process." And it added, "The Panel . . .
determines whether a request is eligible—subject, of course, to the approval
of the Board."[25]

The panel also concluded that management's work in supervising and monitoring compliance with the loan conditionality seemed to have been limited
to a review of the federal budget allocation to the totality of social programs
listed in the loan agreement. In the case of the Garden Project, the panel
stated, "no attempt was made to contact the executing agency or program
beneficiaries to ascertain whether the proposed budgetary allocations were
sufficient to sustain the program throughout the fiscal year." In fact, the panel
affirmed, "both Management and GOA [the Government of Argentina] officials acknowledged the fact that the Bank 'urged the Argentine authorities to
revisit the [Garden Program's] budget' only after CELS brought this matter to
their attention on behalf of the Requesters."[26] Moreover, the panel repri-
manded management for not being aware that an additional $1.5 million was
allocated to the program from the Secretariat for Social Development. This
allocation, according to the panel, was essential for the uninterrupted operation of the program, since the acquisition of seeds before the start of the new
planting season was urgent. Management had authorized disbursement of the
second tranche of the SSAL while the case was still under review, unaware of
this essential contribution to the program's budget, and underscoring the serious shortcomings in supervision.

The panel concluded that when it issued its report, the Garden Program
had adequate financing to assure its operation during that year (1999). Moreover, the panel was informed that the program would be maintained
throughout the period covered by the SSAL. The panel stated, "the potential
harm rightly feared by the Requesters when they submitted the Request for
Inspection—which was based on the information available to them at that
time—seems to have been avoided both by their own actions in submitting
the Request, and by the subsequent favorable reaction of both the Argentine
authorities and Bank Management."[27] Because the issue was resolved, the
panel did not recommend an investigation into the case, adding that "a more
open dialogue between management and CELS as representatives of the then
potential Requesters (within the boundaries of the Bank's stated policies,

which favor disclosure) could have perhaps avoided the need for a Request for Inspection."[28]

CONCLUSION

This case has opened possibilities for using the Inspection Panel as an international mechanism for protecting social interests covered by social programs—under certain circumstances. Affirmation of the panel's jurisdiction and its position on the standing of the beneficiaries of social programs no doubt strengthens clauses that condition SSALs on the implementation of certain benefits aimed at alleviating extreme poverty.

The case demonstrates, moreover, how the panel and the request to withhold disbursements can bring considerable crosscutting pressure to bear on the borrower governments, in the opposite direction of the kind of pressures they usually receive from the multilateral banks. The Inspection Panel's involvement provoked various reactions in the bank's Buenos Aires office and in the different spheres of government. It was the dynamic of all these actors with different interests, together with the mobilization of the program participants, that culminated in the approval of the additional funds.

However, the success of this case and the possibility of presenting claims in Washington should not lead us to lose sight of the limitations that CELS staff has faced and continues to face as they work to uphold the social rights of those who suffer poverty vis-à-vis the states. It is quite paradoxical that the beneficiaries of the social program guaranteed in the loan agreement had to make their claim to the bank expressly keeping their identities confidential to avoid reprisals from the government providing the benefits they were trying to defend. Moreover, there was no possibility of effectively denouncing the bank's inaction in local courts.

For more than a decade, Argentina, like many other countries that receive financial support from the bank, has pushed structural adjustment reforms that dismantled mechanisms to protect social rights, rolled back labor rights, and privatized or weakened social security systems. Along with the dismantling of these universal social protections, new targeted social programs sought to guarantee basic benefits to the indigent population—the poorest of the poor. In short, the social policies blessed by the bank have tended to erode social *rights,* previously recognized as individual rights, while fostering the institution of welfare sorts of *benefits*—subject to the discretion of government officials. As a result, the possible avenues for program beneficiaries to defend the benefits they receive are minimal: to receive government assistance, one must "qualify" as indigent, yet those who defend these benefits run the risk of losing everything. This sort of social policy invariably tends to further stigmatize and marginalize vast sectors of the population, ultimately weakening the ability of society, and of each citizen, to hold the state accountable and to call on it to provide some appropriate form of protection. In this context, international supervisory mechanisms such as the Inspection Panel and social loan conditionalities are of enormous value, but are far from sufficient to compensate for the legal and social vulnerability caused by structural adjustment.

NOTES

1. The author would like to thank Juana Kweitel, Julieta Rossi, and Martín Serrano, from the Program on Economic, Social and Cultural Rights at CELS, for their collaboration. Thanks are also due to Martín Abregú, the former executive director of CELS, who cosponsored the claim presented to the Inspection Panel.

2. These social conditionality clauses make disbursement of the loan's second and third tranches conditional on the government's earmarking set funds to maintain certain antipoverty programs. In the loan agreement and bank documents, they are called "Social Budget Condition."

3. This is as it appears in the loan agreement signed with the bank (see II. "FACTS"; II.2. "Special Structural Adjustment Loans," annex 5; annex B).

4. See II. "Facts"; II.2. "Special Structural Adjustment Loan," annex 5; annex B.

5. See II. "Facts"; II.2. "Special Structural Adjustment Loan," annex 5; annex B.

6. The conditionality clauses mentioned explicitly prohibit any withdrawal of funds from the accounts opened for that purpose without first showing, based on reasonable evidence in the view of the bank, that the actions provided for in schedules 3 and 4, respectively, of the agreement have been carried out. Those actions include the national government's commitment to keep the budgetary outlays of the social programs listed in the annex to schedule 3 of the SSAL to no less than U.S.$680 million for 1999 (see II. "Facts"; II.2. "Special Structural Adjustment Loan," annex 6; annex B).

7. See World Bank, OD (Operational Directive) 4.15, "Poverty Reduction," December 1991, paragraph 25.

8. The gardens are generally cultivated for subsistence. However, program participants who have high yields have a margin to market what they do not consume, and on occasion they barter with neighbors for other types of food and goods.

9. Interview by author, Buenos Aires, 2000.

10. Interview by author, Buenos Aires, 2000.

11. This is the meaning that should be attributed to what the bank said in paragraph 17 of annex 5 to the report (annex B), according to which the SSAL consists of a package of reforms "in four main areas . . . and most importantly (d) the reform package also has measures to safeguard the current social protection programs, which in a time of financial stress could be compromised, and to advance reforms in health and education."

12. See United Nations Economic and Social Council, E/CN.4/1999/45, E/CN.4/1999/50, and E/CN.4/1999/51.

13. The claimants moved quickly to present the claim since they knew that the disbursement of the remaining tranche was coming soon. At that time, they were under the impression that there was only one more tranche to be disbursed, the third tranche, but as it turned out, there were two more tranches pending disbursement. Based on the panel's rules, the claim had to be submitted before the last disbursement. According to article 14 (c) of Resolution BMRD 93-10/ADI 93-06 of September 22, 1993, which defines the scope of the panel's functions, the panel cannot hold a hearing for "requests filed after the Closing Date of the loan financing the project with respect to which the request is filed or after the loan financing the project has been substantially disbursed."

14. The conditions for disbursing the second and third tranches were established in the agreement itself. There were twenty-two separate conditions to authorize the disbursement of the second tranche, and twenty-six for the third. These conditions had to do with a wide range of objectives, actions, and policies aimed at introducing fiscal, financial, and regulatory reforms, and also reform in the human development sector.

15. This was stated literally: as it was shown in the claim presented to the World Bank Subregional Office, the text of the loan agreement in the clauses 2.02 (d) (ii) (C) and 2.02 (e) (ii) (C) conditions the withdrawal of funds from the loan account unless the "Bank shall be satisfied, after an exchange of views as described in Section 3.01 of this Agreement based on evidence satisfactory to the Bank . . . (C) *that the actions described in Schedule 3 to this Agreement* have been taken in form and substance satisfactory to the Bank" (emphasis and parentheses added; see annex 6, annex B). Schedules 3 and 4 describe the actions to be followed by the borrowing government (Argentina) to fully comply with the conditions of the SSAL. In these sections, the "Actions of the Human Development Sector" are explained (see schedules 3 and 4 of annex 6, annex B), which include a statement that the Argentine government's 1999 budget for the social programs listed in the annex to schedule 3 (also in 4) must be maintained at an aggregate minimum of $680,000,000 (see schedules 3 and 4 of annex 6, annex B). The annex to schedule 3 provides a list of the social programs that the bank has prioritized in the fight against poverty. Among others, the Garden Program (Pro-Huerta) is listed in the subtitle referring to nutrition programs; this establishes the Garden Program as a requisite sine qua non for the effective disbursement of each tranche of the SSAL and/or the REPO (see schedule 3 of annex 6, annex B).

16. The argument was not rhetorical, but rather sought to interpret the reach of OD 13.05 in conjunction with the OP/BP (Operational Policy/Bank Procedure) 13.40, which determine the suspension and/or cancellation of the corresponding portion of the loan in cases where the borrower does not meet the conditions for disbursement (see World Bank, OD 13.05 (1989), "Project Supervision," paragraph 2.

17. James D. Wolfensohn, "The Other Crisis" (presentation before the governing board, Washington, D.C., October 6, 1998).

18. OD 4.15, paragraph 25. For the full text, see www.worldbank.org.

19. OD 4.15 paragraph 24.

20. OD 13.05, paragraph (1) (b).

21. OP/BP 10.70, paragraphs 14 and 16.

22. These arguments derive expressly or implicitly from the considerations section of the Inspection Panel's final report. Four days before presenting its defense, management authorized the release of the second disbursement. The office justified the disbursement arguing that by then the additional funds had already been guaranteed to the program.

23. The concept of eligibility refers to the admissibility of the claim based on meeting the indispensable requirements (exhaustion of prior remedies, timely submission, existence of harm to the claimants, etc.).

24. According to Ibrahim F. I. Shihata "an affected party" is "a party whose rights or interests have been or are likely to be directly or adversely affected in a material way as a result of a serious violation by the Bank of its operational policies and procedures with respect to the preparation, appraisal, or implementation of projects" (see Ibrahim F. I. Shihata, *The World Bank Inspection Panel: In Practice* [New York: Oxford University Press, 2000], chapter 2, section III, 56).

25. Inspection Panel, "Request for Inspection—Argentina: Special Structural Adjustment Loan (Ln 4405-AR) Panel Report and Recommendation," December 22, 1999, 6.

26. Inspection Panel, "Request for Inspection—Argentina," 7.

27. Inspection Panel, "Request for Inspection—Argentina," 7.

28. Inspection Panel, "Request for Inspection—Argentina," 7.

10

The China Western Poverty Reduction Project

Dana Clark and Kay Treakle

On April 27, 1999, the London-based Tibet Information Network (TIN) broke the news that the World Bank was developing the China Western Poverty Reduction Project, which would have moved approximately fifty-eight thousand farmers westward onto the Tibetan plateau to become settlers in an area that has historically been inhabited by Tibetan and Mongol no-madic peoples.[1] The TIN report set off alarms within the Tibetan community, which considers China's long-standing population transfer program to be one of the single greatest threats to continued Tibetan cultural identity. The story also quickly circulated to the bank-watching community, which has cam-paigned against previous disastrous World Bank–sponsored population-transfer projects, including the trans-Amazon highway in Brazil and the In-donesian government's transmigration program.[2]

The dramatic, fifteen-month campaign to stop the project, which was launched by Tibet supporters and bank activists, captured the attention of en-vironmental and human rights organizations, academics, members of Con-gress and Parliaments, and the press. Public interest in the campaign was sus-tained by a plethora of controversial issues, including threats to Tibetan and Mongol nomadic cultures, violations of the bank's environmental and social policies, the detention and abuse of independent investigators, and severe ten-sions within the World Bank.

A claim filed to the Inspection Panel provided a critical link in the strategy to stop the project. After the Inspection Panel issued its highly critical report, the board of directors of the World Bank met to decide on the project's fate. On July 7, 2000, the majority of the board rejected the resettlement project.

211

The cancellation of the project served as a vindication of the role of the Inspection Panel, and the role of civil society, in holding the bank accountable to its social and environmental policies.

This chapter will explore the issues at stake in the China Western Poverty Reduction Project: the social and environmental policy violations, the institutional weaknesses that allowed the project to be pushed forward despite its flaws, the global campaign that mobilized to challenge the project, the role of the World Bank Inspection Panel, and the decisions made by the board of executive directors. It will also examine the internal ripple effects, including the ways in which the controversial project catalyzed potentially significant changes in the bank's approach to compliance with the environmental and social policy framework.

BACKGROUND ON THE CHINA
WESTERN POVERTY REDUCTION PROJECT

The China Western Poverty Reduction Project (CWPRP, or China/Tibet project) claimed to promote poverty alleviation in three western provinces of China: Gansu, Inner Mongolia, and Qinghai.[3] The Qinghai component of the project attracted the most public scrutiny and concern, because it would have involved, among other things, World Bank support for China's plan to resettle approximately fifty-eight thousand poor farmers onto the Tibetan plateau, displacing at least four thousand local people, including Mongol and Tibetan nomadic peoples. The incoming migrants, called "voluntary" resettlers by the bank, were predominantly Han Chinese or Chinese Muslim (Hui and Sala), with smaller numbers of Tibetans and Mongols. The Inner Mongolia and Gansu components focused on intensification of agriculture and did not involve resettlement.

The CWPRP would fundamentally alter the resettlement area's social, ecological, and economic relationships. The environmental assessment report noted that the local environment would be completely transformed: "the project will break down the desert, semi-desert and grassland ecological system, which is primitive and low efficient. Oasis agricultural system, which is efficient and steady, will be established."[4]

Proponents of the project at the World Bank proclaimed that they would convert the hummocky and windswept Tibetan plateau "from a desert into an oasis" and that all that was needed to do so was water,[5] which would be supplied by damming seasonal water flows and building canal networks to divert the water to the agricultural settlements. According to the plan, the "oasis" would depend on chemical inputs of pesticides and fertilizers.

The diversion of scarce water resources to agricultural irrigation threatened wetlands, migratory birds, and wildlife. The project also threatened to deprive traditional inhabitants of scarce resources needed for survival. The incoming settlers would occupy prime pastureland, bisecting the seasonal migration routes of nomads and their herds of yaks.[6] An internal World Bank memo recognized that the "lifestyles of the hosts patterned on pastoral rhythms will be irreversibly changed by settled agriculturalists who will now constitute nearly 90% of the population." The memo further noted that China's resettlement plan "offers few remedial measures other than propaganda, education, policing and homogenization ('national unity')."[7]

The new settlement would create an agriculture and infrastructure base for further exploitation of the natural resources in the Tsaidam Basin, one of the Tibetan plateau's most resource-rich areas. The environmental assessment report explicitly noted that

> The project region and its surrounding areas are rich in metal and non-metal mineral resources, which are worthy of exploitation. The Qinghai-Tibet highway also runs through the south side of the project region, providing a very convenient transportation. The main metal resources are copper, iron, gold, lead and zinc. Of the nonmetal resources there are coal, natural gas, oil. . . . There are more than 10 coal deposits with at least 13–18 million tons of coal.[8]

However, there was no analysis by the bank or the Chinese government of the environmental or social impacts of the resource extraction that would be stimulated by the project. When confronted with the fact that one of China's development objectives in the western provinces is to "establish the infrastructure that is needed to fully exploit the valuable and extensive mineral resources in the region," the World Bank simply "denie[d] that it shared these long-term aims."[9]

Understanding the Terrain

To fully understand the controversy around the project, one must consider the complicated political landscape of the project area. The "move-in area" (where the fifty-eight thousand new settlers would be placed) has been inhabited by Mongol and Tibetan nomadic peoples for thousands of years. On Chinese maps, the move-in county (Dulan in Chinese) is shown to be part of Qinghai Province, a geographical designation that was established by the Chinese government in 1929. However, the Tibetan government-in-exile (TGIE) and many Western scholars of Tibet view the project as part of a traditional Tibetan area known as Amdo Province to most Tibetans. According to this perspective, Amdo, Kham, and U'Tsang provinces together constitute the geographically contiguous Tibetan areas that share a common culture, religion, written language, and heritage. The Chinese government designated all Tibetan areas as autonomous counties, prefectures, or regions; the move-in area is within the Haixi Mongol and Tibetan autonomous prefecture. The Tibetan Autonomous Region, which is often referred to as "Tibet," roughly corresponds to the traditional U'Tsang Province.

World Bank staff indicated that they had accepted the Chinese demarcation of Tibet. One staff person argued, for example, that "in fact we are not involved in settling anyone in Tibet. . . . The farmers are not moving into Tibet but rather within an area of the Chinese province of Qinghai, which borders Tibet."[10] And because the place from which the settlers were shifting (the move-out area) and the place where they were going (the move-in area) are both located within Qinghai Province, World Bank staff downplayed the significance of the population transfer, responding to the public outcry by describing the project as "all within one province." In fact, geographically, environmentally, historically, and ethnically, the areas are completely different. The move-out area is part of the Chinese valley plain, whereas the move-in area is high steppe or plateau; thus, throughout history each has been part of a different civilization and ecosystem.[11]

Since 1950, the Chinese government has pursued an aggressive campaign to shift Chinese settlers into ethnic minority areas. The government has promoted the settlement of urban areas in Tibetan zones and has offered incentives to Chinese citizens to move to Tibet. In Eastern Qinghai, Chinese settlers have colonized former pastoral lands. The government has built numerous prison labor camps in eastern Tibet, and released Chinese prisoners, who often lack the means to return home, have also served to alter the demographics of the region.

Voices of Objection

Local and international observers were concerned that the World Bank's involvement in the CWPRP would constitute an international seal of approval of China's population transfer program as a legitimate form of development, potentially leading to other similar projects by the multilateral development banks. China's population transfer policy is seen by local Tibetans and Mongols, as well as by the TGIE and other exiled Tibetans and Mongols as posing a significant threat to continued Tibetan and Mongol cultural identity.[12] However, the Chinese government does not tolerate criticism of its program of encouraging Chinese settlement of ethnic minority areas. Indeed, Tibetans in Qinghai have been imprisoned for expressing objections to the government's population transfer program.[13]

Because of this intolerance of domestic dissent, Tibetans living in the project area sent appeals to the Dalai Lama, their temporal and spiritual leader, who has been living in exile in Dharamsala, India, since 1959. Local people also wrote to international Tibet-support organizations, asking supporters to raise concerns with the World Bank and the world's governments on their behalf. One letter read:

> Recently we have heard of a plan to settle tens of thousands of Chinese Muslim and Han Chinese in our nomadic region of Tulan Dzong [Dulan County]. This is very dangerous for us, an evidence of the Chinese policy of ethnic cleansing of the Tibetan people. We have heard the World Bank may be financing this project. . . . In the event the resettlement project is carried out with World Bank financing, then the World Bank will have participated in passing a death sentence to us here. Please forward this appeal to the World Bank on our behalf.[14]

Kalon T. C. Tethong, the minister of information and international relations for the TGIE, wrote to bank Vice President Jean-Michel Severino to register his concerns:

> [F]or the last four decades the Chinese authorities have been engaged in finding a Final Solution to China's Tibet problem. They have found this in a policy of ethnic swamping, drowning the Tibetans in a sea of Chinese. . . . If this is going to be the end result of the World Bank's project in Tibet then it will not only be a tragedy for the Tibetan people but will also rebound on the World Bank which will come to be perceived as an instrument of the disappearance of a distinct people and an important cultural heritage of the world.[15]

A representative of the Inner Mongolian Peoples' Party, a small exile organization based in the United States, also objected:

> The project will encourage the Chinese government to further consolidate the occupation of lands traditionally belonging to the Mongols and Tibetans, whose culture and language is completely different from the Han Chinese. Funding this project will send a message to the Chinese government that the World Bank condones the population resettlement policies of the Chinese Government, a policy that allows them to annihilate minority cultures with impunity. You must understand that the Chinese government's resettlement policies are not really an economic tool, they're a political tool by which the Chinese government subdues the nascent opposition felt by the minority people towards the violation of their human rights by the Chinese government. . . . The devastating effect it has had on the Mongols of Inner Mongolia in eliminating our language and culture, the effects on our environment through desertification are now perhaps close to irreversible, and this project will add further force to the devastation of our people.[16]

The project was seen as a threat to the way of life of indigenous peoples living in the project area, with potentially serious environmental and social impacts. Tibetans living in the project area expressed concern about the danger of resource conflict and ethnic tension associated with the project:

> This is Communist Chinese policy to create conflicts between the Tibetans and the Muslims. There have been many conflicts and many killings over pasture land. In view of this, the settlement is designed to create a dangerous situation in the region. Many of us will die in the conflicts and even if we survive where do we go? As it is we do not have sufficient pastureland to support our animals, how is the land going to support tens of thousands [of] new Muslim Sala settlers?[17]

In another letter, local Tibetans who described themselves as "living on the threshold of extermination and survival" appealed to the Dalai Lama for assistance after learning about the World Bank project on a May 7 Voice of America broadcast. They wrote: "Please tell the World Bank to think about the adverse effects their project will bring on our villages. Please save our people from the threat of extinction."[18]

A Campaign Is Launched

When news of the project broke in late April 1999, the CWPRP was already on the calendar to go to the board of directors for approval in early June. This left only a short window of time within which to mount a challenge to the project. Tibet supporters began to request information from the World Bank, and for advice and advocacy assistance they turned to the Center for International Environmental Law (CIEL) and the Bank Information Center (BIC), nonprofit organizations that promote accountability at the international financial institutions and provide support to local communities affected by bank-financed projects.

In an early strategy meeting, CIEL explained the Inspection Panel process to several Tibet-support organizations. The coalition decided to use the panel only as a last resort, hoping to achieve cancellation of the project without having to file a claim. However, the NGOs immediately began laying the groundwork for a claim, by analyzing the project in the context of bank policies and sharing and documenting their concerns with bank officials through written analyses, meetings, e-mails, and phone calls. The coalition brought together experienced World Bank campaigners from around the world with a well-connected network of Tibet-support organizations.[19] These groups shared information, strategies, and resources, and brought a diverse set of skills and political contacts to the campaign.

During the time leading up to the board meeting to decide on the loan, coalition representatives held a series of meetings at all levels of the World

Bank, explaining their concerns and sharing their analysis of policy violations with project staff, external affairs staff, executive directors' offices, and senior management, including the president of the bank. As documents slowly became public—late and in violation of the bank's information disclosure policies[20]—they were analyzed against the policy framework. Significant policy violations were identified and documented in correspondence and meetings with bank officials.[21]

Conference calls and e-mail communication allowed for rapid information sharing and strategizing between watchdog groups on different continents. In addition to the bank, these groups engaged members of Congress and Parliament, treasury departments and finance ministries, and ministries of foreign affairs. The campaign reached out to the public through action alerts, media advocacy, protests, leafletting, Internet organizing, and simultaneous Tibetan Freedom concerts on four continents. The coalition was able to mobilize a strong and engaged response from tens of thousands of people around the world, who wrote, faxed, and called the World Bank and their government representatives to register their concerns. The fax machines of several executive directors' offices (and reportedly President Wolfensohn's as well) broke down under the strain.[22] Organizers called for the project to be scrapped, emphasizing the violations of the World Bank's social and environmental policies, and the human rights implications of giving an international seal of approval to China's population transfer program.

THE WORLD BANK TURNS A BLIND EYE

All of the policy violations described below were exacerbated by the bank's failure to release information about the project as required by its information disclosure and environmental assessment policies. Bank staff had fast-tracked the project, in part because they wanted it approved before China "graduated" from receiving cheap IDA loans. The project was thus slated for approval before the close of the fiscal year at the end of June and was on the board's calendar before the public even learned about the project. The restricted time frame put intense pressure on all players as the project raced toward approval before the end of June, the close of the bank's fiscal year.

The Environmental Assessment Policy

According to the bank's environmental assessment policy, projects involving involuntary resettlement, dams, irrigation, land clearance and leveling, reclamation, and new land development—all of which were present in the

CWPRP—should be considered "Category A," requiring a full Environmental Assessment (EA) and mitigation plan.[23] Despite this rather clear policy guidance, bank staff chose to classify the China/Tibet project as "Category B," requiring less careful analysis and scrutiny. Not surprisingly, the EA failed to accurately assess the environmental and social risks associated with the project, or include adequate mitigation measures.

In March 1998, a World Bank staff person traveled to the project area to review the draft environmental assessment in light of World Bank and Chinese government guidelines. He concluded that because the project involved "large-scale population transfer including minority nationalities, acquisition and compensation of land belonging to minority people and large-scale changes in natural resource use, it should have been classified as Category A."[24] This recommendation was ignored or rejected by bank management and the project remained classified as Category B.[25] The decision to classify the project as a B rather than an A project was based largely on its perceived consistency with "accepted practice" in China.[26] This theme would recur throughout the controversy over the project: the bank accepted a lower standard of compliance for projects in China.

After the controversy broke, President Wolfensohn sent the deputy vice president of the East Asia and Pacific Region, Julian Schweitzer, to Qinghai to evaluate the situation. Schweitzer's back-to-office memorandum to Wolfensohn contended that "the project was correctly categorized as a 'B' and upgrading it now carries serious risks. We are concerned that NGOs would regard this as carte blanche to insist on more A categories, thus needlessly raising the costs of project preparation."[27]

The Indigenous Peoples' Policy

The World Bank's policy on indigenous peoples requires that bank staff take special action to ensure that the rights and interests of ethnic minorities are respected in bank-financed projects. The policy explicitly states, "the strategy for addressing the issues pertaining to indigenous peoples must be based upon the *informed participation* of the indigenous peoples themselves."[28] In addition, projects impacting ethnic minorities must have an Indigenous Peoples' Development Plan and must be designed to protect and promote the cultural integrity of indigenous and ethnic minority populations. The policy further requires that bank staff evaluate each borrower's policy and laws affecting ethnic minorities, as reflected in the country's constitution and legislation.[29]

In stark contrast with the objectives of the indigenous peoples' policy, the planners of the CWPRP did not consider, protect, or promote the development priorities of the local Mongol and Tibetan ethnic minorities. The project lacked an Indigenous Peoples' Development Plan, it lacked informed participation, and it was not designed to respect or defend the cultural integrity and viability of the ethnic minorities in the area.

In the bank's view, the displaced ethnic minorities were "beneficiaries" of the project. Rather than receiving culturally appropriate benefits, however, households in the move-in area would be offered "the opportunity to join the program," "providing them with the same level of benefits as the settlers."[30] Thus, bank staff gave nomadic pastoralists the option of joining the settled agricultural lifestyle of their new, mostly Chinese, neighbors—or leaving the project area. This raised concerns about Bank complicity, intentional or otherwise, in a long-term policy by the Chinese authorities of forcing or pressuring nomadic communities to give up pastoralism.

The Involuntary Resettlement Policy

According to the project documentation, the incoming wave of settlers would have displaced at least four thousand local people. The CWPRP, however, did not develop or provide a separate resettlement plan for those people, in violation of the bank's involuntary resettlement policy.[31] In fact, the project documentation incorrectly characterized *all* of the resettlement impacts as "voluntary," including the impacts on the people already living in the move-in area, who faced physical and cultural displacement.[32] Only after the public controversy had erupted and the project came under heavy scrutiny did the bank prepare and place in the public information center a seven-page "involuntary resettlement plan" for the CWPRP. The plan was six months late; it should have been prepared prior to appraisal of the loan. Moreover, the document was devoid of substantive content—it merely recited the requirements of the bank policy without providing any detail about how those requirements would be accomplished.[33]

When questioned about the inadequacy of the involuntary resettlement plan in a meeting with President Wolfensohn and NGOs, Julian Schweitzer replied that there was no problem because "only 63 herder families" would be adversely affected by the project, and they had personally assured him that they wanted the project. This, despite the fact, as the NGOs pointed out, that the project documentation indicated that thousands of people would be displaced and that bank policy required an involuntary resettlement plan for those people.[34]

Flawed Social Assessments

The bank claimed to have conducted a detailed social assessment.[35] According to the World Bank, "social assessment work was used to build comprehensive mechanisms to facilitate stakeholders' . . . participation in project decision-making as well as implementation."[36] Analysts of the project, however, felt that the social assessment was problematic in many ways.

For one thing, the situation in the project area must be factored into an assessment of the consultation. Bank staff acknowledged that all of the interviews of local affected people had been conducted in the presence of Chinese officials,[37] that the social assessment methodologies in China "often compromise respondent confidentiality," and that records of the consultation, including the names of those interviewed, were available to Chinese officials.[38] These methodological weaknesses are compounded by the fact that Chinese citizens face the risk of serious punishment if they criticize certain government or party policies.

Although the bank's project appraisal document proclaimed that "the herders welcomed the project," the social assessment data actually showed that only 29 percent of those interviewed said that migrants were "welcome," 62 percent "did not object," and 9 percent "did not welcome" the settlers.[39] That 71 percent of the people were not enthusiastic should have alerted the project team to a problem. Bank management downplayed (and distorted) this information, but those with experience in the region found it to be quite significant. "No serious study of opinion among Tibetans would assess support for government policy, where sensitive or national security issues are involved, without assuming that a significant percentage of stated approval is coerced or strategic, and that any dissent will almost always be expressed indirectly if at all."[40]

Despite these constraints, local people did express their concern about several issues that were at stake in the project. Thus, 100 percent of the local people interviewed by Chinese researchers for the World Bank said that they feared that the new settlers would "destroy the ecological environment."[41] Furthermore, 21 percent expressed concern that the influx of immigrants and the increase in population would cause more social unrest.[42]

The Bank's Response to Public Concern

As noted above, one of the initial problems facing the coalition was the bank's failure to provide substantive information about the project. The bank was actually placed in a very uncomfortable position once the public began to demand information about the project, because over time it became clear that there was little to disclose—the bank had simply failed to require the Chinese government to prepare the detailed project documents required by its policies.

Adding to the dearth of information was the refusal by both the bank and China to release any project documents that were deemed to belong to the

Chinese government. This excuse led to the withholding of even the Voluntary Settlement Implementation Plan (VSIP)—the very document that purportedly provided the poverty alleviation rationale for the project, which was never released to the public or the board.

Rather than providing project documentation, the bank team initially put its energy into rhetoric and spin. For example, in response to the growing public controversy, the East Asia and Pacific (EAP) region produced and circulated to executive directors and the media a "Summary Paper" about the Qinghai component of the project. That document claimed that the "immediate" move-in area "has no Tibetans at all," as though seeking to discredit the thousands of faxes and phone calls that executive directors were receiving from concerned constituents,[43] and divert attention from the indisputable fact that ethnic minorities were adversely affected by the project.

THE CRISIS DEEPENS

The China/Tibet project was one of the most controversial projects in the history of the World Bank, and it generated an enormous internal crisis. President James Wolfensohn was pulled between the competing interests of the bank's largest borrower, China, which insisted that the loan proceed, and the largest donor, the United States, which believed that the project violated the bank's social and environmental policies.

In response to these countervailing pressures, and conscious of the way the project was threatening the bank's reputation, President Wolfensohn sought assurances from the EAP region and from the central Environment Department that the project was in compliance with the bank's policies. In an internal memo sent to Wolfensohn on June 10, senior management insisted that there were "no technical reasons why this project should not go ahead."[44] The wisdom behind this advice was questionable, because the technical issues provided exactly the exit strategy that Wolfensohn could have legitimately used to withdraw from the politically charged project. Nevertheless, bank staff continued to argue, to Wolfensohn and the board, that the project was in compliance with bank policies and should be approved.

Board members were apparently frustrated with management's insistence on moving forward despite their concerns about the project. In an unprecedented move, eleven out of twenty-four board members sent a letter to President Wolfensohn expressing their concerns about the project and requesting that he refrain from submitting the Qinghai component of the project to the board because it failed to meet World Bank standards.[45]

At the same time, activists from around the world were flooding the bank with letters, faxes, e-mail messages, and telephone calls. NGOs argued that by rushing such a controversial project through to the board for approval without carefully considering its weaknesses and potentially devastating impacts, bank management was abdicating its responsibility to ensure that projects sent to the board for approval are in compliance with the bank's policies.

A week before the board meeting, sixty members of the U.S. Congress wrote to President Wolfensohn, citing numerous concerns about the project and urging the bank to withdraw support for the CWPRP.[46] At the same time, parliamentarians from Europe were also contacting Wolfensohn and weighing in with their finance ministries and executive directors. Concerns were raised about substantive policy violations as well as the risk to the World Bank's reputation of being associated with China's controversial population policies in Tibetan areas.

But despite the groundswell of public concern and the intensifying controversy within the bank, the project remained on a fast track for board approval. On June 17, 1999, in a tense meeting with members of the NGO coalition, Vice President Severino declared that the project would be sent to the board for approval within a matter of days. He said that the bank had successfully financed several projects in China similar to this one, and that it met the bank's "usual standards" for projects in China. Severino concluded the meeting by saying that his staff could not take "moral and political" concerns into consideration. The NGO delegation responded that its concerns were entirely within the scope of the bank's policies and that if the bank staff had complied with the policies they would have recognized the risks to the Tibetan and Mongol cultures.[47]

THE CLAIM TO THE INSPECTION PANEL

As management finalized the project for board approval, the International Campaign for Tibet (ICT)[48] worked to finalize a claim to the Inspection Panel. With technical support from BIC and CIEL, ICT filed the claim on June 18, 1999, asking the Inspection Panel to investigate the alleged policy violations in the China/Tibet project.[49] The claim alleged that the bank had violated, among others, its policies on Indigenous Peoples, Involuntary Resettlement, Environmental Assessment, Information Disclosure, Natural Habitats, and Agricultural Pest Management. The claim was filed six weeks after the effort to stop the project was launched, and one week before the board meeting to decide the fate of the project.

As documented in other chapters of this book, many of the claims brought to the Inspection Panel have involved transnational coalitions in support of local claimants who were directly affected by the project in question. The China/Tibet case was unique in that it was filed by an international organization on behalf of anonymous, locally affected people.

Since NGOs cannot operate in China without government sanction, and internal statements against the project could be considered "splittist," NGOs within China could not realistically provide a channel for critical concerns raised by local people.[50] Lacking organizations to represent their interests locally or nationally, Tibetans looked to the TGIE as well as international Tibet support groups, such as ICT, for international support.

In filing the claim, ICT argued that, pursuant to the resolution creating the panel, it was serving in a representative capacity for local Tibetans who would be directly and adversely affected by the violations of bank policies.[51] The resolution provides for nonlocal representation (provided there is written authorization, submitted to the panel) of affected people in those "exceptional cases" where "appropriate representation is not locally available."[52] While local people living in the project area provided written authorization to ICT, which ICT provided confidentially to the Inspection Panel, they did not directly participate in Inspection Panel process. The China/Tibet case marked the first time that such a claim was filed by an international organization, and it illustrates the importance of "exceptional cases" provision in allowing some degree of access to the panel for those who are living without access to basic human rights.

China's Position

As the controversy heated up, China vocally expressed its disapproval of the public scrutiny of issues that it considered its "internal affairs." For instance, China criticized the United States for opposing the loan, saying, "We demand the US side change its opposition to the World Bank loan and stop using the Tibetan issue to interfere in China's internal affairs."[53] Then-Secretary of the Treasury Lawrence Summers issued a statement clarifying that U.S. opposition to the project was based on concern with noncompliance with bank policies: "The United States will be voting to oppose the project because of concerns in environmental areas and concerns in the resettlement areas."[54] The media picked up on the U.S.–China tension and described the standoff over the project in those terms—as a clash between the bank's most powerful donor and its most powerful borrower, with the president of the World Bank caught in the middle.

Although denouncing opposition to the project as being "based on politics," the Chinese government engaged in some hardball politics of its own in the time leading up to the board vote. Among other things, China threatened to withdraw from membership in the World Bank if the project was not approved.[55] This put enormous pressure on President Wolfensohn, who, according to insiders, felt that he would have to resign if he were responsible for losing the bank's largest client.[56] In addition, the Chinese government apparently called on donor-country ambassadors in Beijing, and in a diplomatic demarche, linked continued donor-country access to foreign investment in China with their support for the CWPRP.[57]

The June 24, 1999, Board Meeting

Board members, faced with one of the most difficult and contested decisions in the history of the bank—and one fraught with complex geopolitical ramifications—turned to their capitals for guidance. As editorials ran in major newspapers calling for the World Bank to reject the project, decisions about how to proceed were taken at extraordinarily high levels of government in many countries.

The June 24 meeting was highly contentious. At the end of the day, despite the objections of the United States and Germany and the abstention of four other chairs (France, Canada, the Nordic countries, and the Austria/Belgium group), the board decided to conditionally approve the China Western Poverty Reduction Project.[58] The board acknowledged the claim filed with the Inspection Panel, however, and chose to withhold funding for the Qinghai/resettlement component, stipulating that no money could be released and no work could take place on the project until after the claim was investigated and the board had an opportunity to review the panel's findings. The claim, it turns out, had provided the board with breathing room in a situation that had become highly politicized.

In his concluding statement at that board meeting, President Wolfensohn emphasized China's pledge to cooperate with the Inspection Panel investigation.[59] This pledge was described by insiders as having played a decisive role in the negotiations that led to conditional board approval.

Both the bank and China made declarations of openness and transparency that day, with China stating to the board: "we are in favor of transparency. Transparency brings light to facts and scorches all rumors." However, China's statement to the board also warned, "We should work together to create an enabling environment for the Bank's staff to fulfill their development mission free from the interference of special interest groups."[60]

The next day, activists from Students for a Free Tibet protested the board's decision to approve the project by scaling the front of World Bank headquarters in Washington, D.C., and hanging a banner above the entrance at 1818 H Street. The banner proclaimed "World Bank APPROVES China's Genocide in Tibet," while down below a crowd of demonstrators marched in front of the World Bank. Eventually, the two climbers descended to join a delegation that was invited to meet with senior management and project staff, including President Wolfensohn.

In that and subsequent meetings, senior bank management, including President Wolfensohn and Vice President Severino, encouraged NGOs to try to visit the project area and to engage in a dialogue with the Chinese executive director. Bank management admitted that it had violated the information disclosure requirements and pledged to make additional documents available; it also asked that the NGOs provide feedback on that additional information if and when it was made available. The NGOs agreed to continue to have a dialogue about the issues, but only with the clear understanding that cancellation of the project was still an option on the table, and that the campaign against the project would continue.

The Situation Escalates: Broken Promises and a Broken Back

On July 1, a week after the board meeting, Vice President Severino convened a meeting with BIC, CIEL, and ICT with the stated purpose of producing additional documentation and discussing access to the project area. However, during the meeting, management refused to release any actual documents, and only reluctantly released a list of existing project documents. Management pointed out that most of the documents on the list were considered "property of the Chinese government" and hence would not be made publicly available without the government's consent.[61]

During that meeting, bank staff and NGOs also had a frank discussion about access to the project area, including the fact that NGOs and scholars doing research in Tibet typically travel on tourist visas. CIEL and BIC representatives informed the bank project team that they intended to follow up on the proclamations of transparency and access, and that they would seek business-purpose visas from the Chinese government to travel to the project area for monitoring purposes. Vice President Severino said that if the visas were refused, it would be "of major importance for us to know about it."[62]

The NGOs also raised concerns about possible retribution against people living in the project area who, at great personal risk, had expressed their opposition to the project during the social assessments. When asked what the bank would do if there were repercussions for local people, Vice President Severino stated that any such reprisals would constitute a "major point of blockage for us to proceed."[63]

One by one, the promises made by bank management and China's representatives concerning transparency and access to the project area were broken.

Throughout July, the bank continued to refuse to release any further documents (except some nonsignificant agricultural studies).[64] In July and August, the Chinese executive director refused repeated requests for a meeting, and then declined to provide BIC or CIEL with a letter that would enable them to obtain visas to travel to the project area other than as tourists (which would not allow them to carry out monitoring or research legally).[65] In August, the Chinese government tried to support its original declaration that it would allow unfettered access to the area by taking several Beijing-based foreign journalists on a government-supervised visit to the project area. Indira Laskmanan later reported in the *Boston Globe* that the tour was under "strict supervision" with restricted access to local people.[66]

Meanwhile, two independent researchers, Gabriel Lafitte from Australia, and Daja Wangchuk Meston, a U.S. citizen, traveled to the project area to investigate. They went to the move-out and move-in areas to try to learn more about local opinions. Their visit quickly attracted the attention of Chinese security agents, however, and early in the morning of August 15, the police burst into their hotel room in Dulan County and arrested Lafitte, Meston, and their local Tibetan translator, Tsering Dorjee.

The men were separated from one another and taken to what appeared to be an abandoned hotel in Xining, 450 kilometers away. The official Chinese news agency reported that the men "were detained for studying poverty-relief projects in the province" and alleged that "they had conducted illegal covering and photographing in closed areas."[67] Denied access to their embassies for days,[68] Lafitte and Meston later reported that they had been subjected to sleep deprivation, continuous surveillance, threats, and intimidation.[69] When the interrogators demanded to know the names of everyone with whom the researchers had spoken, they feared not only for their own safety, but also for the safety of local people with whom they had met.

On August 19, Meston fell from a third-floor window of the building where he was being interrogated, apparently while trying to escape or call attention to their situation. He landed on the concrete driveway below and suffered life-threatening injuries, including a broken back, internal organ damage, and shattered heels.[70] Meston's ruptured spleen was removed in emergency surgery in a provincial hospital. When he regained consciousness, his hospital room was crowded with the same interrogators from the Foreign Ministry and the Public Security Bureau, together with armed guards, and the questioning continued.[71]

Meanwhile, the U.S. government, the Australian government, the Chinese authorities, the World Bank, and NGOs were engaged in intensive negotiations to secure the release of the three men. The bank, and particularly President Wolfensohn, made significant efforts to obtain their release, including a telephone call to Prime Minister Zhu Rongji.[72] On August 21, Gabriel Lafitte was escorted under custody to Beijing and deported to Australia. On August 25, Meston was medically evacuated out of the country, although only after extensive negotiations through the U.S. Embassy, which included the Chinese government demanding payment for Meston's hospital fees incurred in treatment of the injuries he suffered while in the custody of Chinese security forces. Meston was taken to a hospital in Boston, where he had multiple surgeries. It took months for him to recuperate from his injuries, and although he is now walking again, he is unsteady on his feet and suffers from constant pain. The fate of Tsering Dorjee, a teacher and student, remained unknown until a month later, when reports came that he had been seen again at his university.

THE INSPECTION PANEL INVESTIGATION

On August 24, 1999, after reviewing the claim and management's response, the panel recommended that the board authorize a full investigation into the alleged policy violations in the project.[73] Shortly thereafter, despite the assurances made at the meeting when it was seeking board approval of the project, the Chinese government objected to the investigation, and particularly to the fact that the claim had been filed by the "so-called International Campaign for Tibet."[74]

The board sidestepped China's objection by authorizing the panel to conduct an investigation, on behalf of the board, of all of the policy violations that were alleged in ICT's claim.[75] This was the first time that the board had invoked its own authority to request an investigation. This marked a significant commitment by the board to the panel process, and also reflected the board's intense interest in the case, which in turn resulted from the global pressure that board members were feeling to cancel the project. This was also the first panel investigation to come to the board for approval since the second board review described in chapter 1. The board's decision to accept the panel's recommendation for an investigation of the China/Tibet project marked an important turning point in the panel–board relationship.

After reviewing files and interviewing bank staff in Washington, the Inspection Panel traveled to Beijing and to Qinghai Province to conduct interviews and gather information.[76] They hired experts in environmental and social assessment, and consulted with Tibet scholars and researchers. Ten months later, the panel delivered its report to President Wolfensohn, who then distributed the report to select board members on April 28, 2000. Extraordinary steps were taken to keep the report from being leaked to the public—every page of every distributed copy of the panel's report was watermarked with a large number that was assigned to each recipient, and copies were literally kept under lock and key.[77] Nonetheless, news spread quickly by word of mouth—both inside and outside the bank—that the panel's report was scathing. And despite the security measures, the report was eventually leaked to the press and reproduced on the *Financial Times* website.

The Panel's Report

The panel determined that bank staff had violated the following policies: Environmental Assessment, Involuntary Resettlement, Indigenous Peoples, Natural Habitats, Agricultural Pest Management, and Information Disclosure. The panel report criticized crucial decisions by management that had facilitated the policy violations, such as the decision to maintain a Category B environmental rating. One consequence of that decision was that the bank sought to justify that initial flawed decision by downplaying (rather than carefully considering) the environmental and social impacts that the project would have on the host area and the Tibetan and Mongol people living there.

More fundamentally, the panel found that the bank failed to consider or incorporate the cultural preferences of the ethnic minorities who would be displaced:

> No number of add-on indigenous-culture-boosting activities (bilingual schools, Islamic religious sites, Tibetan pharmacological centers, corridors for nomadic herders) can override the fact that the initial project design is flawed in the failure to recognize, from the outset, the cultural uniqueness of the separate ethnic minorities involved.[78]

Similarly, bank management persisted in characterizing persons facing involuntarily displacement as project "beneficiaries," thereby ignoring both their vulnerabilities and their rights under the bank's involuntary resettlement policy. Furthermore, the panel observed, "[a] network of social, commercial and political interactions clearly exists in Dulan County and in Xiangride Township. Yet no assessment has been made of how these linkages and interactions will be affected, for better or worse, by a Project that will completely change the economy and demography of the County."[79]

The panel report revealed that despite a policy framework that has been in place for more than a decade, there is still a shocking lack of awareness of the policy requirements among bank staff. The panel found that many bank staff members and senior management viewed the social and environmental policies as flexible or discretionary guidelines rather than a binding set of policies.[80] Compliance was also undermined by deficiencies in the management structure between the central environment department and the East Asia and Pacific region.

The Panel Documents a "Climate of Fear"

When the Inspection Panel members visited the project area, they found that local people who were opposed to the project were afraid of expressing those opinions publicly.[81] The Inspection Panel reported that its visit "yielded some disturbing and dramatic examples of what can only be described as a climate of fear." The panel found

> evidence that many people were clearly afraid to talk about the Project; and many of those who were willing to talk about the project were strongly opposed to it. During these interviews, those who opposed the Project clearly felt threatened and asked that their identity be kept secret.[82]

The panel's direct experience thereby belied management's argument that "the will of the move-in host population was adequately expressed."[83] The panel concluded that "[f]ull and informed consultation is impossible if those consulted even perceive that they could be adversely affected for expressing their opposition to, or honest opinions about, a Bank-financed project."[84]

"In China, Things Are Done Differently"

The campaign against the project and the panel investigation encountered, and exposed to public scrutiny, the cozy relationship between bank staff and China, its largest client. It became clear that bank staff tended to excuse the Chinese government from strict policy compliance, and to treat this powerful client deferentially, applying a double standard to bank-financed projects in China. Bank staff repeatedly told the panel during its investigation that "in China, things are done differently."[85]

Management's response to the claim, for example, had argued that "The level and quality of preparation and analysis for this Project were very much in line with Bank practice in applying social and environmental policies to projects in China *in the context of its political and social systems.*"[86] The panel noted that there is no basis in the policy framework to support "the view that precedents in a country, or a country's 'social and political systems,' can in any way determine what is required by the policies."[87] The panel's view is supported by the former general counsel of the World Bank, who has written that "Exceptions that are not authorized in the text of the OD [Operational Directive] or OP [Operational Policy], however, must be kept to a minimum if these documents are to serve their purpose *and if the Bank is to avoid undue differentiation among its borrowers.*"[88]

MANAGEMENT'S RESPONSE: THE PROJECT CAN BE FIXED

Despite all of the failures described above, including the broken promises and human rights violations occurring in the project area, bank management and the Chinese government were not willing to step back from the project. On June 21, 2000, President Wolfensohn delivered the panel's report and management's response to the board. In his cover letter, Wolfensohn recommended that the project should proceed, and argued that management could solve the technical problems identified by the panel's report. Management's plan to fix the project would have included the following:

- conducting a "higher level of environmental analysis," and upgrading the environmental classification from Category B to Category A;
- "upgrading" the social assessments, including initiating a new consultation process;
- providing better documentation;
- improving disclosure of information; and
- creating an environmental and social team of experts to provide the borrower and the bank with "independent professional advice" on the project.[89]

Management basically proposed to retrofit the project, to try to bring it into compliance with the policies after the fact. President Wolfensohn's cover letter complained that because of the public controversy, the bank was being pushed "into a literal and mechanistic application of the OPs and ODs that was never intended when they were written. This is happening at considerable cost both to China and to the Bank."[90] Wolfensohn's concerns about how expensive it would be for China and the Bank to bring the project into compliance were based on management's estimation of the cost of retroactively conducting studies that should have informed the initial decision making about the project. The costs, therefore, represent the costs of noncompliance rather than the costs of compliance. Wolfensohn's letter, however, sent the signal that policy compliance is too expensive, which in turn provided fuel for an internal backlash against the panel and the policy framework (which is discussed more thoroughly in chapter 11 of this volume).

Critics pointed out that this retrofit approach failed to take into consideration the fact that if the policies had been complied with from the beginning, the bank would not have gotten involved with the project. They argued that the expensive add-on studies and experts' reports called for by bank management would not address the underlying problems.[91] In this scenario, fundamental flaws—such as the failure to adequately assess the feasibility of the project, including an assessment of the benefits and costs, or to consider the ability or willingness of the borrower or the bank to mitigate negative impacts—would be glossed over rather than rectified. For instance, the proposed experts would not be authorized to assess the feasibility of the project, but rather would be focused on ensuring its implementation. Management's proposal was geared toward moving forward with the project.

VICTORY!

Management organized a technical briefing for the board on their proposed action plan,[92] and also conducted a video conference for the G7 embassies in Beijing, presumably to ensure that foreign ministry officials would get the message that the project had implications for diplomatic relationships with China.[93] Management's decision to go forward with the project, worked out in negotiations with the Chinese government, meant that the onus of decision making about the fate of the project was placed, once again, on the board of executive directors.

The board meeting to discuss the panel's findings and management's action plans for the China/Tibet project was scheduled for July 6, which just happened to be the Dalai Lama's sixty-fifth birthday. In a further coincidence of timing, the annual Smithsonian Folk Life Festival on the National Mall in Washington was featuring Tibetan culture in exile as one of its programs, and this event drew thousands of Tibetans and others interested in Tibetan culture to Washington, D.C., during the two weeks leading up to the final board meeting. After a meeting with then-President Bill Clinton, the Dalai Lama, who had given a keynote speech at the festival, said that the CWPRP "would be a source of more problems" and should not proceed.[94]

Tibetans participating in the Folk Life festival chose to spend their only day off from their festival responsibilities in a spontaneous vigil in front of the World Bank. Dressed in traditional clothes, they prayed, chanted, and held banners that read "World Bank Are You Listening? Tibetans Say Cancel the Project." They also delivered letters to all of the executive directors, urging them to vote against the project:

> We understand that the Inspection Panel's final report vindicates the concerns of our fellow Tibetans and documents multiple and egregious violations of the Bank's policies that are supposed to prevent harm to people and the environment. We also know that the Inspection Panel documented a "climate of fear." We, as Tibetans, know the consequences of living in this climate of fear and we believe that Bank Management is naïve to suggest that the studies simply need to be redone. We have always believed that this project was not in the best interests of the Tibetan people and any attempt to repair this project will not remedy this fundamental problem.

We hope that you will recognize that the best option for Tibet as well as for the World Bank is to cancel this project.[95]

The chants of protesting Tibetans (including "World Bank, Do the Right Thing, Please") could be heard inside the World Bank, where delegations from CIEL, BIC, Students for a Free Tibet, ICT, Milarepa, and visiting cabinet members of the TGIE conducted discussions with executive directors offices. In the days leading up to the board meeting, many of the executive directors emphasized that they could not consider the political implications of the project—that what was most important to them was the question of lack of compliance with bank policies. There was a great deal of discussion of the policy violations and their implications. Tibetan representatives also explained the devastating human and political costs associated with China's population transfer program.

On July 1, ICT, Students for a Free Tibet, and others sponsored a rally at Lafayette Park and a March for Tibet, during which approximately eight thousand people encircled the World Bank chanting, "World Bank Out of Tibet," and then marched up Connecticut Avenue to the Chinese Embassy. On Monday, July 3, activists began a continuous, colorful, twenty-four-hour-a-day occupation of a small park in front of the World Bank, complete with giant puppets, prayer flags, Tibetan flags, leaflets, and megaphones.

Outside of Washington, the media, NGOs, and parliamentarians from around the world also stepped up the pressure on the bank. The European Parliament passed a resolution to "ask the World Bank to suspend the decision on the CWPRP and to monitor all the potential effects of this project on the ethnic, cultural and social balance of Tibet."[96] A *New York Times* editorial urged board members "to reject this poorly designed project" and the *Los Angeles Times* called on the board to "scrap it."[97]

When the board of executive directors convened to discuss the Inspection Panel's report and management's response and recommendation to proceed with the project, the meeting was reported to be tense and chaotic. Board members were dealing with a difficult situation in which the Inspection Panel report had found egregious violations of the bank's social and environmental framework, and yet bank management and China were arguing that the board should allow the project to proceed after conducting additional social and environmental studies. Executive directors from both the North and South raised questions about management's credibility and capacity to conduct further analysis of the project in light of management's incorrect assurances to the board in June 1999 that the project was in compliance with bank policies.

The United States and Japan (the two most powerful donor countries) were firmly opposed to the project moving forward, on the grounds that it was not technically feasible, and they did not believe that management's proposal to fix the project would cure the fundamental violations of the safeguard policies. Their executive directors were also concerned about accountability and felt that allowing the project to move forward despite the very apparent flaws would send an inappropriate signal to bank staff about policy compliance.[98]

The Europeans, meanwhile, were prepared to take more of a compromise position. They were willing to support the new environmental and social impact studies proposed by management, but they insisted on further board review of the findings of those studies before giving their final approval for the project to move forward. Finally, while some borrowing country executive directors took the unusual step of praising the Inspection Panel for its investigative work, the borrowers as a block were prepared to support China and bank management and vote in favor of the project.

In her statement at the board meeting, United States Executive Director Jan Piercy noted the perverse situation that

> A project that was clearly non-compliant with basic Bank policies was brought to the Board despite enormous effort by Board members to persuade Bank Management to step back and reassess. Bank staff has no consistent understanding of basic policies that have been in place for years.[99]

Piercy also identified the question of accountability, saying "It is time for this organization to see the issue for what it is—delivering on its own commitments to credible internal controls and faithful execution of agreed policies and procedures."[100] In his statement to the board, Chinese Executive Director Zhu Xian said, "We are greatly concerned . . . that compliance policies have been interpreted by some to an extreme, and used for political purposes."[101] And so the two opposing executive directors laid out a road map for the debate that would follow.

As day turned into night, it became clear that the majority of board members felt uncomfortable giving management and China authorization to proceed with the project. The discussion reached an impasse, and the board adjourned. In late-night negotiations between the U.S. Treasury Department and various finance ministries, the Europeans, Canada, Australia, and other donor countries decided to join the United States and Japan in opposition to management's action plan. On the morning of July 7, 2000, the board reconvened and rejected management's proposal to undertake additional studies and then move forward with the project without further board involvement. China then withdrew the project, proclaiming that it would proceed without the bank's financing.[102]

The Immediate Aftermath

As protesters gathered outside the bank erupted in celebration, news of the cancellation was broadcast inside Tibet by Radio Free Asia and Voice of America. When asked later about the outcome, John Ackerly, president of ICT, which had represented the claimants in the request for inspection, noted the broad implications of the victory: "The World Bank project would have imposed a development model that was antithetical to the aspirations of the Tibetan people. The cancellation of this project will hopefully cause future investors to look more carefully at projects planned for Tibetan areas."[103] Thubten Samdup, an exiled Tibetan who is president of the Canada Tibet Committee, issued a press release in which he extolled the role of civil society in giving voice to local Tibetans:

> China's defeat at the World Bank today is a monumental victory for the Tibetan people. Governments that for years have turned a blind eye towards Chinese actions in Tibet have shown, in the clearest way, that their tolerance has a limit. The voiceless citizens of Dulan have been heard thanks to a wonderful coming together of non-governmental organizations, students and activists who have valiantly held their ground in order to represent the unrepresented.[104]

The unprecedented outcome stunned the World Bank, which continued to insist that it would have been better if the project had been approved. While admitting that the bank had done "an inadequate job on the project," President Wolfensohn also continued to insist that "at the end of the day it would have been better if we were involved in the project than if we were not at all."[105]

Better If the World Bank Were Involved?

The frequently used argument that it was better for the World Bank to be involved in controversial projects was an important strategic issue that had already been considered and rejected by the Tibetan support groups at the earliest stages of the campaign. The coalition fully recognized that there was a significant risk that China would continue with the project even if the World Bank withdrew, given that the Chinese government has been steadily promoting population transfer of Chinese settlers into eastern Tibetan areas for the last fifty years.

However, Tibetans and their supporters felt that any potential benefit of having the bank involved was outweighed by the risk that the World Bank would legitimize population transfer onto traditional Tibetan lands as an acceptable form of development. Furthermore, the coalition was skeptical of the extent to which the bank's involvement in the project would have improved performance.[106] The poor quality of the scant project documentation, combined with the panel's findings about the bank's failure to ensure that the project actually complied with the bank's environmental and social policy requirements, indicates that the bank's involvement did not sufficiently raise project quality to meet World Bank standards, at least in terms of the impacts on ethnic minorities and the environment.[107]

CONCLUSION

The outcome in the China/Tibet case demonstrates that sustained advocacy coupled with serious policy analysis can have an impact on decision making. There are many aspects of the campaign that are not easily replicable, however, such as the intense media interest in issues involving Tibet and the international advocacy network of Tibetan exiles and supporters of the Tibetan cause. It took fifteen months of campaigning and analysis by a coalition of organizations, combined with intense pressure by tens of thousands of people, to ensure that the system worked. While the cancellation of this project was a significant victory, it was hard-won. The hope is that the precedents set by this case will lay an easier path for future claimants. The risk is that the backlash will make things more difficult for all who care about truly sustainable development.

The precedents set by this case are numerous. Perhaps the most visible are related to the process and substance of the decision—the board took the highly unusual step of rejecting a project promoted by bank management, thereby depriving China of international support for its population transfer program. In addition, the board of executive directors acted with newfound authority to uphold the policy framework and take ownership of the Inspection Panel process. For the first time since the Arun claim in 1994, the board authorized the panel to conduct a full investigation.[108] The China/Tibet case also marked the first time that the board adopted a claim filed by an NGO, and requested the panel to investigate on the board's behalf. The case demonstrated the panel's value in assisting the board in making an informed decision about whether to proceed with a controversial project.

The case also had longer-term impacts, which are discussed below. These included structural changes at the World Bank; internal concern about the "costs of compliance;" impacts on the bank's relationship with civil society; and the bank's relationship with China.

Structural Change and Mixed Attitudes at the World Bank

One thing is clear: nobody at the bank wants to endure "another China/Tibet." In the aftermath of the claim, institutional changes were implemented to increase the staffing and budget devoted to policy compliance, including expanding the

"Quality Assurance and Compliance Unit" (QACU) within the Environmentally and Socially Sustainable Development Department (ESSD). Ian Johnson, vice president for ESSD, has stated that the controversy over the CWPRP "was of a magnitude different than anything that had come before. And word gets out, that we are taking this very seriously. No doubt CWPRP was the Waterloo of the World Bank."[109] He also emphasized the heightened priority assigned to the environmental and social "safeguard" policies at the bank as a result of the controversy around the CWPRP: "We hadn't taken these issues as seriously as we should have done. We had no money here to oversee anything regarding safeguards before CWPRP broke. . . . All of us were guilty, including myself. It was the wakeup call we needed."[110]

The ESSD has also staffed a Safeguards Help Desk to help bank staff "ensure adequate attention to safeguard policies in project design and implementation."[111] In addition, the question of uneven application of safeguard policies among different countries and regions, which was criticized by the Inspection Panel, is ostensibly being addressed. Furthermore, the bank's new environment strategy, approved by the board in July 2001, stresses a heightened commitment to policy compliance and includes provisions for increased training and resources for bank staff and management.[112]

Nevertheless, while Ian Johnson has explained that the bank is now placing greater emphasis on the need to perform "due diligence" in meeting the requirements of the environmental and social policies in the design of projects, he acknowledged that the bank has been less effective in accomplishing the policies' objectives and that more work needs to be done in terms of deepening bank and borrower ownership of the policy requirements.[113]

Challenge to Civil-Society Influence on the Bank

The high-profile campaign and the dramatic cancellation of the project added to a backlash against World Bank engagement with civil society, despite the fact that the NGOs involved in the campaign had been engaged in constant dialogue with bank staff and management and had openly shared their concerns and analysis with the bank. Many borrowing countries, including the Chinese government, have challenged the bank's relationship with civil society and NGOs, and their voices have resonated with senior management. For instance, at a meeting with NGOs in Washington, D.C., in April 2002, President Wolfensohn noted, "I have recently met with twenty-two African heads of state and most of them have complained that the bank has gone too far in working with civil society and allowing unrepresentative NGOs to influence government decision making."[114]

Many borrowing-country board members argue that elected governments are the only legitimate representatives of local peoples' interests, and since civil-society groups lack such representational authority, they should therefore be disallowed a voice in development decision making. This argument lacks credibility, however, in the context of development projects where national governments have made calculated decisions that local communities or ecosystems should be sacrificed, thereby subordinating the interests of local communities to the "greater good" of the nation.[115] Local concerns are often ignored by the country's representatives at the bank, a situation that was particularly stark in the context of the China/Tibet project.

The tension between civil society and certain borrowing-country executive directors and bank staff has been particularly acute in the context of accountability and the Inspection Panel. Many borrowing-country governments have long been uncomfortable with the Inspection Panel precisely because it gives voice to local people who challenge development plans negotiated between national governments and the bank. They also resent the support that local communities receive from international NGOs. In the China/Tibet case, project proponents resented the influence of the groups campaigning against the project; one such person insisted that the CWPRP had been well prepared and that it was derailed only because of an overly rigid Inspection Panel and by "politically motivated" "outside agencies."[116]

The Chinese government has venomously denounced the actions of what it refers to as "the Dalai clique." A leaked internal Chinese government document reveals the official resentment of the success of civil society in challenging this project, among others:

> In the last few years, the Dalai clique has openly focussed its splittist campaign on weakening China's economic power and interfering in our nation's economic relations with other countries. Since last year, the Dalai groups, with support from anti-China western forces, have undertaken campaigns to cut off the World Bank loan to our population transfer program in the Tulan county of Quinghai province, to disrupt PetroChina's entry into the American stock market, to prevent our entry into WTO, to obstruct the granting of US permanent trade relations status to China, and to get people in different countries to boycott our goods. Under the pretext of environment and development issues, they submitted petitions, openly targeting our economic interests.[117]

Scaled Back, the Project Goes Ahead

From the time that the campaign was launched, there was an open question of what would happen if the project were cancelled. Would the project go forward without the involvement of the World Bank as vowed by the Chinese government? One and a half years after the World Bank project was cancelled, there was evidence that a resettlement program had begun. The Associated Press reported the following in January 2002:

> China is moving 17,000 mostly Chinese and Muslim settlers to a traditionally Tibetan region in its remote west, reviving a plan abandoned after protests by critics of China's Tibetan polices. . . . Zou Hanbin, a spokesman for the Dulan county government . . . said $80 million is earmarked for the project. He said preparatory work began in September but didn't know when the first settlers would move in.[118]

According to John Ackerly of ICT:

> We have heard that the Dulan resettlement project is going forward in a scaled down, and quite different way. Apparently they are now planning on moving 17,000 people, less than a third of the original plan. This would still be a very significant population resettlement, but not nearly as large as the one the World Bank would have supported. The biggest design change, however, appears to be a plan to resettle the 17,000 onto land that is currently a 200,000 hectare "reform through labor" camp. Migrants will be housed in existing buildings, although it is not clear whether this could include former cell blocks. By moving migrants into a former labor camp, it could mean that fewer Tibetans and Mongols will be displaced.[119]

Thus, the predictions of the Tibetan exile community that China would continue to pursue population transfer in Dulan County with or without the bank's support have been confirmed. However, the number of people moving is much smaller, and the design change means that the project impacts on ethnic minorities and the environment may be significantly less. Furthermore, the project lacks the imprimatur of approval of the world's governments.

T. C. Tethong, the former foreign minister for the TGIE, indicated that interviews with Tibetans arriving in Dharamsala, India, after leaving Amdo have shown that "the Tibetans and Mongols in Dulan and Xining appreciated our effort to put a stop to the World Bank loan to the Chinese government to carry out the western poverty development project."[120] Others, who have encountered Tibetans who left Amdo and went to India following the cancellation of the project, reported that local people expressed pride and a sense of empowerment from having the project stopped.[121] Only time will tell what the longer-term impacts of this victory will be for the Tibetan people.

NOTES

1. The project would have transferred fifty-eight thousand settlers into the Haixi Mongolian and Tibetan Autonomous Prefecture. See Tibet Information Network

(TIN), "World Bank Funds Controversial Population Transfer Scheme," TIN news update, April 27, 1999. For more information about TIN, see www.tibetinfo.net.

2. For a description of the Polonoreste trans-Amazon project, see chapters 3 and 7 of this volume. In March 2001, *National Geographic* concluded that Indonesia's transmigration projects and related voluntary migration have been linked to "recent eruptions of violence" on Irian Jaya (now West Papua), Sumatra, Kalimantan, and the Molucas: "The World Bank has concluded that its half billion dollars in transmigration loans produced 'irreversible impacts' on indigenous peoples—including seizure of land and destruction of traditional subsistence patterns by short-sighted development schemes" (Tracy Dahlby, "Indonesia—Living Dangerously," *National Geographic,* March 2001, 80, 87).

3. The project involved a loan of $100 million from IDA and $60 million from IBRD. For the perspective of bank management and staff for why the project was "a potentially good anti-poverty project," see Pieter Bottelier, "Was World Bank Support for the Qinghai Anti-Poverty Project in China Ill Considered?" *Harvard Asia Quarterly* 5, no. 1 (Winter 2001): 47–55.

4. Qinghai Institute of Environmental Science, "Environmental Impact Assessment for the Agricultural Development and Poverty Reduction Project in Xiangride-Balong," Qinghai, October 1998, annex 4.

5. Julian Schweitzer, deputy vice president, East Asia and Pacific Region, the World Bank, statements made during meeting between NGO representatives, including the authors, and World Bank staff and management, to discuss the CWPRP, Washington, D.C., June 17, 1999.

6. Gabriel Lafitte, "World Bank Seen through Tibetan Eyes," *US Tibet Committee News Archives* (June 1999), available online at www.ustibet.org/facts/lafitte.html [accessed March 13, 2003].

7. World Bank, "China—Western Poverty Alleviation Project—Note on Social Issues," internal memorandum (undated) (copy on file with the authors).

8. World Bank, "CHINA: Western Poverty Reduction Project, Environmental Information Package" (undated), 33 (hereinafter cited as "Environmental Information Package"). See also Paul Lewis, "U.S. May Try to Stop Loan Seen as Bad for Tibetans," *New York Times,* May 30, 1999.

9. TIN, "World Bank Funds Controversial Population Transfer Scheme."

10. Lucy Oh, World Bank, e-mail to John Hocevar, Students for a Free Tibet, May 4, 1999 (copy on file with the authors).

11. Robbie Barnett, research scholar, East Asian Institute, Columbia University, e-mail correspondence with the authors, May 22, 2002.

12. See, for example, "Guidelines for International Projects and Sustainable Development in Tibet," promulgated by the TGIE, which requests that agencies wishing to pursue development projects in Tibet take steps to ensure that their participation does not "facilitate the migration and settlement of non-Tibetans into Tibet," www.tibet.net, May 1999 [accessed May 25, 2003].

13. "Request for Inspection, China Western Poverty Reduction Project," submitted by the International Campaign for Tibet, June 18, 1999, section 3.3.2 (hereinafter cited as "Request for Inspection").

14. Undated letter from Tibetans in Tulan Dzong, written to "fellow Tibetans living in independent countries" (copy on file with the authors).

15. Minister Kalon T. C. Tethong, Department of Information and International Relations, Central Tibetan Administration, to Jean-Michel Severino, vice president, the World Bank, June 16, 1999.

16. Oyonbilig, Inner Mongolian Peoples' Party, to James D. Wolfensohn, president, the World Bank, June 17, 1999 (copy on file with the authors).

17. "Tibetan Citizens of Tulan," letter to American Friends of Tibet (undated) (copy on file with the authors).

18. Letter from Tibetans in Tulan County to His Holiness the Dalai Lama, May 14, 1999 (copy on file with the authors).

19. For instance, in the United Kingdom, the Free Tibet Campaign worked closely with the Bretton Woods Reform Project; in Canada the Canada Tibet Committee joined with Probe International; in Italy the Reform the World Bank Campaign teamed with Italian Greens.

20. World Bank policies require the public release of information well before a project is scheduled to go to the board for approval. The environmental impact assessment, for example, should have been publicly available in January 1999 (prior to project appraisal), but it was not released until June 1999, after the controversy broke and just two weeks prior to board consideration of the project.

21. See, for instance, CIEL, "Preliminary Analysis of World Bank Policy Violations in the China Western Poverty Reduction Project," June 15, 1999, available online at www.ciel.org/ifi/tibet3.html [accessed March 13, 2003].

22. "Tibetan Tinderbox," *The Economist,* June 19, 1999, 70; also, personal communications between the authors and bank staff.

23. World Bank, Operational Directive (OD) 4.01, October 1991, paragraph 17, annex A.

24. Inspection Panel, "Investigation Report," Washington, D.C., April 28, 2000, paragraph 160; World Bank, "China—Western Poverty Alleviation Project—Note on Social Issues" (undated), 7.

25. Inspection Panel, "Investigation Report," paragraph 313.

26. Inspection Panel, "Investigation Report," paragraphs 176–79.

27. World Bank, internal memorandum, forwarded to President Wolfensohn from Jean-Michel Severino, June 10, 1999, designated "Emergency" (on file with the authors).

28. World Bank, OD 4.20, "Indigenous Peoples" (1991), paragraph 8 (emphasis in original).

29. OD 4.20, paragraph 15(a).

30. World Bank, "Management Response to the Request for Inspection," July 19, 1999, 7, available online at wbln0018.worldbank.org/IPN/ipnweb.nsf/(attachmentweb)/Report_and_Recommendation/$FILE/Report_and Recommendation.pdf [accessed March 13, 2003] (hereinafter cited as "Management Response").

31. World Bank, OD 4.30, "Involuntary Resettlement" (1990), paragraph 4.

32. World Bank, "Project Appraisal Document," June 1, 1999, 6.

33. Qinghai Provincial PMO, "China Western Poverty Reduction Project: Involuntary Resettlement Plan," May 1999.

34. Meeting at the World Bank, June 18, 1999, between James D. Wolfensohn, Julian Schweitzer, and John Clark of the World Bank; Bhuchung Tsering and John Ackerly of International Campaign for Tibet; and Dana Clark of the Center for International Environmental Law.

35. World Bank, "Management Response," 17.

36. World Bank, "Summary Paper," June 2, 1999, 7–8, available online at www.worldbank.org/html/extdr/offrep/eap/projects/china/wprp/chindex.htm [accessed March 13, 2003].

37. World Bank, "Summary Paper," 7; this information was also confirmed by bank staff in meetings with NGOs.

38. World Bank, "Project Appraisal Document," 102.

39. World Bank, "Project Appraisal Document," 109.

40. Robbie Barnett, research scholar, East Asian Institute, Columbia University; personal communication with authors, June 1999, and e-mail correspondence with the authors May 22, 2002.

41. World Bank, "Environmental Information Package," 3 and 65.

42. World Bank, "Environmental Information Package," 66.

43. World Bank, "Summary Paper," 6. See also Agence-France Presse, "World Bank Plays Down 'Tibet Issue' in Mass Relocation Project," June 17, 2001.

44. Jean-Michel Severino, memorandum to Wolfensohn, June 10, 1999.

45. See, for example, Paul Blustein, "World Bank to Vote on Controversial Project," *Washington Post,* June 22, 1999.

46. Letter from Congress of the United States, House of Representatives, to Mr. James D. Wolfensohn, president, the World Bank, June 17, 1999, signed by sixty members of Congress; coordinated by Reps. Benjamin Gilman, Nancy Pelosi, Frank Wolf, and Barney Frank (on file with the authors).

47. Statements made at meeting between World Bank staff and NGOs, including the authors (representing CIEL and BIC), as well as Tibet-support organizations, three exiled Tibetans from the project area, and a lawyer from Mongolia, June 17, 1999.

48. The International Campaign for Tibet (ICT) is an organization based in Washington, D.C., with eighty thousand members, that is dedicated to promoting human rights and democratic freedoms for the people of Tibet. See www.savetibet.org.

49. ICT, "Request for Inspection," annex B1.

50. U.S. Department of State, "China Country Report on Human Rights Practices for 1998," 28, attached to "Request for Inspection" as annex B5: "There are no independent domestic NGO's that publicly monitor or comment on human rights conditions."

51. Inspection Panel, "Operating Procedures" (1994), paragraphs 5, 11, 39. In support of its standing as a nonlocal representative, ICT submitted confidential letters from people living in the project area, affidavits from experts on Chinese criminal law, copies of the U.S. State Department's human rights report for China, and a statement from the Lawyers Committee for Human Rights (LCHR).

52. World Bank, Resolution no. 93-10, IDA Resolution no. 93-6, *The World Bank Inspection Panel,* September 22, 1993, paragraph 12.

53. World Bank, *Development News,* June 24, 1999, quoting from Reuters reports.

54. Lawrence Summers, quoted in David E. Sanger, "World Bank and Treasury Nominee at Odds over Loan to China," *New York Times,* June 23, 1999, A3.

55. See, for example, "Tibetan Tinderbox" and David E. Sanger, "A Stick for China, a Carrot for Tibet's Lobby," *New York Times,* July 11, 1999, 18.

56. Some analysts, including, apparently, President Wolfensohn, saw China's withdrawal from either the bank or this project as being a lost opportunity for "Western" control over Beijing. The *New York Times* described Wolfensohn as saying that China "didn't need the Bank's money—but with it, the West would have a voice in what China does in the region" (Sanger, "A Stick for China, a Carrot for Tibet's Lobby," 18).

57. Conversations between the authors and internal World Bank sources, including executive directors, June 1999.

58. James D. Wolfensohn, World Bank, telephone call to Dana Clark, CIEL, June 24, 1999, describing the outcome of the board meeting.

59. James D. Wolfensohn, concluding statement to the board, June 24, 1999 (on file with the authors).

60. World Bank, memorandum on Western Poverty Reduction Project from Xian Zhu to executive directors, June 24, 1999 (on file with the authors).

61. Authors' notes of meeting, July 1, 1999, at the World Bank.

62. Authors' notes of meeting, July 1, 1999.

63. Authors' notes of meeting, July 1, 1999.

64. Julian Schweitzer, acting regional vice president, to Kay Treakle, BIC, July 21, 1999; Kay Treakle, BIC, to Jean-Michel Severino, July 16, 1999.

65. Dana Clark, CIEL, to Jean-Michel Severino, vice president of the World Bank (summarizing attempts to gain access to information and visas to visit to the project area), September 8, 1999.

66. Indira Laskmanan, "China's Long March," *Boston Globe,* August 22, 1999, A1.

67. "China Spokesman Says Detained American Severely Injured after Attempting Escape" *Xinhua News Agency,* August 20, 1999.

68. Human Rights Watch, "World Bank Should Intervene in Detentions in China," press release, August 19, 1999.

69. Personal conversations between the authors and Gabriel Lafitte and Daja Wangchuk Meston.

70. U.S. State Department, DRL press guidance, "China: Activists Detained in Quinghai," August 19, 1999.

71. Telephone interview with Daja Wangchuk Meston, by Dana Clark, August 30, 2001.

72. Telephone call from Peter Stephens, World Bank External Affairs, to Dana Clark, CIEL, August 19, 1999, relaying the news that James D. Wolfensohn had telephoned Prime Minister Zhu Rongji, and that the Chinese government had promised to release the men.

73. Inspection Panel, "Report and Recommendation on Request for Inspection, Re: Request for Inspection: China Western Poverty Reduction Project," August 18, 1999, available online at wbln0018.worldbank.org/ipn/ipnweb.nsf [accessed May 25, 2003].

74. Office memorandum from Xian Zhu to James D. Wolfensohn, August 13, 1999.

75. World Bank, "Proposed Decision on Request for Inspection—China: Western Poverty Reduction Project" (credit no. 3255-CHA and loan no. 4501-CHA). China did not object to this board request.

76. Inspection Panel, "Inspection Panel Returns from China," press release, October 28, 1999.

77. Inside sources told the authors that these steps to prevent leaking were triggered by the U.S. government, which did not want the report to be leaked at a time when the U.S. administration was trying to persuade Congress to grant China Permanent Normal Trade Relations (PNTR), a first step toward admitting China to the World Trade Organization, which was a high priority for both governments.

78. Inspection Panel, "Panel Investigation Report, Executive Summary," paragraph 11.

79. Inspection Panel, "Investigation Report, Executive Summary," paragraph 18.

80. Inspection Panel, "Investigation Report, Executive Summary," paragraph 9.

81. Inspection Panel, "Investigation Report, Executive Summary," paragraphs 119–20.

82. Inspection Panel, "Investigation Report, Executive Summary," paragraph 120.

83. World Bank, "Management Response," 1.

84. Inspection Panel, "Investigation Report, Executive Summary," paragraph 29.

85. Inspection Panel, "Investigation Report, Executive Summary," paragraph 14.

86. World Bank, "Management Response," 5 (emphasis added).

87. Inspection Panel, "Investigation Report," paragraph 43.

88. Ibrahim F. I. Shihata, *The World Bank Inspection Panel: In Practice* (New York: Oxford University Press, 1994), 43 (emphasis added).

89. James D. Wolfensohn, president, "Management Report and Recommendation in Response to the Inspection Panel Investigation Report," June 21, 2000, INSP/R2000-4/2 (hereinafter cited as "Management Report and Recommendation"). Project proponents argued that this action plan, and specifically the provision for independent experts, constituted "a historic breakthrough" that was "unprecedented in China. Everyone who cares about China's political liberalisation should celebrate" (Robert Wade, "A Move for the Good in China," *Financial Times,* July 3, 2000).

90. Wolfensohn, "Management Report and Recommendation."

91. See, for example, "China Project Shakes Bank," *Bretton Woods Update,* August 2000, 3.

92. World Bank, "China: Western Poverty Reduction Project, Questions and Answers," July 5, 2000.

93. Conversations between the authors and bank staff and executive directors.

94. Harry Dunphy, Associated Press, "World Bank Fails on Tibet Loan," *Washington Post,* July 7, 2000.

95. Tibetan participants in the Year 2000 Smithsonian Institute Folklife Festival, letter to each executive director, June 29, 2000.

96. European Parliament Resolution on the Western China Poverty Reduction Project and the Future of Tibet, July 6, 2000, Doc.: B5-0608/2000.

97. "A Misguided World Bank Project," *New York Times,* July 5, 2000; "Bank Should Retract China Loan," *Los Angeles Times,* June 27, 2000.

98. Jan Piercy, "Qinghai Component of Western China Poverty Reduction Project: Inspection Panel Report and Management Response," statement of U.S. executive director to the World Bank, July 6, 2000 (on file with the authors) (hereinafter U.S. statement).

99. Piercy, U.S. statement.

100. Sathnam Sanghera and Stephen Fidler, "World Bank Chief under Fire after Chinese Project," *Financial Times,* July 14, 2000, 5.

101. "Chinese Government Statement on the Inspection Panel Investigation Report for the China: Western Poverty Reduction Project (Qinghai Component)," lnweb18.worldbank.org/eap/eap.nsf/Attachments/chinastatement.pdf/$File/chinastatement.pdf, July 6, 2000 [accessed March 13, 2003].

102. World Bank, "China to Implement Qinghai Component of the China Western Poverty Reduction Project with Its Own Resources," press release, July 7, 2000.

103. John Ackerly, president, ICT, telephone interview by Dana Clark, December 3, 2001.

104. Canada Tibet Committee, "Statement Regarding World Bank Decision on Tibet," www.tibet.ca/wbstatement.htm, July 7, 2000 [accessed May 25, 2003].

105. Sanghera and Fidler, "World Bank Chief under Fire."

106. E-mail communication from John Ackerly, president, ICT, to Dana Clark, September 6, 2001 (on file with authors).

107. The situation in China/Tibet is reminiscent of the situation in the Biobío case described in chapter 6. In that case, the report of an independent review of the project found that "From an environmental and social perspective IFC added little, if any, value to the Pangue project" (Pangue Audit Team, *Pangue Hydroelectric Project [Chile]: An Independent Review of the International Finance Corporation's Compliance with Applicable World Bank Group Environmental and Social Requirements,* April 1997, executive summary, 4).

108. It was also the first time that there did not need to be an intense campaign around the question of authorizing a panel investigation, because that had been negotiated at the time of the first board meeting on the project.

109. Ian Johnson, interview by authors, May 2, 2002.

110. Johnson, interview by authors, May 2, 2002.

111. James D. Wolfensohn, "Memorandum to the Executive Directors re: Operational Policy on Involuntary Resettlement," draft OP/BP 4.12, September 28, 2001.

112. World Bank, "Making Sustainable Commitments: An Environmental Strategy for the World Bank," July 2001, available online at www.worldbank.org [accessed May 25, 2003].

113. Ian Johnson, interview by authors, May 2, 2002.

114. Meeting between President Wolfensohn and NGOs, including BIC and CIEL, April 19, 2001 (notes on file with the authors).

115. See Arundhati Roy, *The Greater Common Good* (Bombay: India Book Distributor, 1999), available online at narmada.org/gcg/gcg.html [accessed May 25, 2003].

116. Bottelier, "Was Support for the Qinghai Anti-Poverty Project in China Ill Considered?"

117. Statement by Zhao Qizheng, "Tibet-Related External Propaganda and Tibetology Work in the New Era" (in Chinese), June 12, 2000. Zhao is minister in charge of the Information Office of the State Council, People's Republic of China.

118. "China Going Ahead with Resettlement," Associated Press, January 22, 2002.

119. E-mail from John Ackerly to Dana Clark and Kay Treakle, "Update on Dulan Resettlement," January 8, 2002.

120. E-mail correspondence from T. C. Tethong to Dana Clark, April 15, 2002.

121. Personal communications with Dana Clark, Dharmsala, India, February 2001.

11

Lessons Learned

Kay Treakle, Jonathan Fox, and Dana Clark

The Inspection Panel has inserted a key political concept into the World Bank's governance model—that the institution must be accountable to the people directly affected by its lending. The Inspection Panel has given increased legitimacy to the claims of local people affected by the World Bank, and it serves as a forum through which their voices have been amplified within the institution. The panel represents the bank's formal acknowledgment of civil-society actors as stakeholders with rights and interests that are affected by the bank's decisions and operations. Thus, an important test of its effectiveness is whether the claims filed have had any impact on the projects they address. The panel has also been a catalyst for broader change at the World Bank. In particular, it has heightened the debate about the bank's commitment to, and effectiveness in, promoting environmentally sustainable development, through the lens of its environmental and social safeguard policies. Another test of the panel's effectiveness, then, is its impact on the institution.

The case studies presented in this book have explored both realms: how the process has affected projects on the ground and whether the panel's case history has changed the way the bank does business. Both of these inquiries help to determine whether the Inspection Panel has led to increased accountability at the World Bank. This chapter draws on lessons from the specific cases profiled in this volume, as well as the entire set of claims, to draw out broad trends that help to determine the panel's impacts.

Claims and the Trends They Reveal

Between 1994 and 2002, twenty-eight claims were submitted to the Inspection Panel. This section reviews broad trends across the claims: what types of projects trigger complaints of environmental and social harm? What Bank policies have been violated? Who brought the claims, and were they assisted by national and/or international NGOs? And how did the powerful react?

What Types of Projects Tend to Trigger Claims?

The bulk of claims filed with the panel—sixteen of twenty-eight—have come from people affected by large infrastructure projects, including six dams (in Nepal, Chile, Argentina/Paraguay, Brazil, Lesotho, and Uganda) and four energy and extractive industry projects (in India, Ecuador, and Chad–Cameroon). In addition, five claims were brought in rural development projects (in Itaparica, Land Reform, and China/Tibet) and three addressed issues related to structural or sectoral adjustment programs (in Bangladesh, Argentina, and Papua New Guinea). Two claims were related to failures in ostensibly positive environmental and social projects (in Brazil and Kenya) and one addressed the negative social side effects of the creation of a protected area (India). Table 11.1 summarizes the types of projects in which claims have been filed.

What Policy Violations Did Claimants Allege?

To be eligible, claimants must assert that they have suffered or are threatened with material harm as a result of violations of bank policies and procedures. The types of projects that cause or threaten the most obvious harm are those that involve high environmental and social risks, such as energy and extractive industry projects, and especially those that involve involuntary resettlement. In many cases, these projects also threaten the lands and livelihoods of indigenous peoples or other vulnerable populations. Such projects also tend to be highly visible and unite project critics, both those directly affected and environmental and human rights advocacy groups.

The bank's environmental and social safeguard policy framework is designed to prevent or mitigate harm to the environment and vulnerable people in bank-financed projects. Not surprisingly, they are the policies most often cited as having been violated (see table 11.2).

Table 11.1. Project Types: Sectors in Which Claims Have Been Filed with the Panel

Inspection Panel Claims Filed	Rural Development	Infrastructure/ Energy/ Extractive Industries	Sustainable Development/ Environment/ Protected Areas	Structural/ Sectoral Adjustment
1. Arun III Hydro, Nepal. October 1994		X		
2. Expropriation, Ethiopia, April 1995				
3. Emergency Power VI, Tanzania, May 1995		X		
4. Rondônia Natural Resources Management Project (Planafloro), Brazil, June 1995			X	
5. Biobío (Pangue) Dam, IFC, Chile, November 1995		X		
6. Jamuna Bridge, Bangladesh, August 1996		X		
7. Yacyretá Hydropower, Paraguay–Argentina, September 1996		X		
8. Jute Sector, Bangladesh, November 1996				X
9. Itaparica Resettlement, Brazil, March 1997	X			
10. Singrauli/NTPC 1 India. May 1997		X		
11. Ecodevelopment, India, April 1998			X	
12. Lesotho Highlands Water, South Africa, May 1998		X		
13. Lagos Drainage and Sanitation, Nigeria, June 1998		X		
14. Land Reform, Brazil, December 1998	X			
15. Lesotho Highlands Diamond, Lesotho, April 1999		X		
16. Itaparica Resettlement, Brazil (second claim), April, 1999	X			
17. China Western Poverty Reduction, June 1999	X			
18. Pro-Huerta, Structural Adjustment, Argentina, July 1999				X
19. Land Reform, Brazil (second claim) September 1999	X			
20. Lake Victoria Environment, Kenya, September 1999			X	
21. Prodeminca, Ecuador, December 1999		X		
22. Singrauli/NTPC 2 India, December 1999		X		
23. Chad–Cameroon Pipeline, Chad, March 2001		X		

(continued)

Table 11.1. Project Types: Sectors in Which Claims Have Been Filed with the Panel (*continued*)

Inspection Panel Claims Filed	Rural Development	Infrastructure/ Energy/ Extractive Industries	Sustainable Development/ Environment/ Protected Areas	Structural/ Sectoral Adjustment
24. Coal Sector Project, India, June 2001		X		
25. Bujagali Hydropower, Uganda, July 2001		X		
26. Structural Adjustment, Papua New Guinea, December, 2001				X
27. Yacyretá Hydropower, Paraguay–Argentina (second claim), May 2002		X		
28. Chad–Cameroon Pipeline, Cameroon, September 2002		X		
Total:	5	16	3	3

Sources: World Bank, *Inspection Panel Annual Report 2002* (Washington, D.C.: World Bank, 2002) and chapters 2 through 10, this volume.
Note: IFC = International Finance Corporation; NTPC = National Thermal Power Corporation.

Table 11.2.   Allegations of Policy Violations in Inspection Panel Claims

Bank Policy	Number of Claims in Which Violations Alleged
Environmental Assessment	15
Project Supervision	14
Involuntary Resettlement	14
Indigenous Peoples	12
Information Disclosure	11
Poverty Reduction	9
Economic Evaluation of Investment Operations	7
Natural Habitats (Wildlands)	6
Forestry	4
Cultural Property	4
Pest Management	2

Source: World Bank, *Inspection Panel Annual Report 2002* (Washington, D.C.: World Bank, 2002). (The *Annual Report* is based on a smaller number of claims than those shown in table 11.2. Here, we are including the second claims for Itaparica, Yacyretá, and the Chad–Cameroon Pipeline.)

However, other policies have also been cited in panel claims. The Supervision Policy has been critically important in many claims, because it clarifies that the bank has a responsibility to ensure that government and project authorities meet the safeguard policy requirements and loan conditions during project implementation. The policy prevents the bank from simply shifting blame for implementation failures, such as inadequate mitigation or compensation measures, to the borrower. Other policy violations that have been cited include Economic Evaluation of Investment Options and Poverty Reduction.

Which Civil-Society Actors Led the Claims?

Some critics of the panel have charged that claims to the Inspection Panel are catalyzed by Northern NGOs, but as table 11.3 shows, exclusively Southern actors have led most claims. In other cases there has been significant support from Northern NGOs, acting in coalition with local and or national partners.

Seventeen claims were generated exclusively by Southern civil-society actors in collaboration with affected people, or Southern private-sector actors; ten were generated through South–North coalitions involving local, national, and international groups; and one was initiated by an international NGO on behalf of local people who lacked the freedom of expression necessary to file a claim on their own.[1]

Table 11.3. Which Civil-Society Actors Led the Claims?*

Inspection Panel Claims Filed	Exclusively Southern-led	South–North Coalition	Exclusively Northern-led
1. Arun III Hydro, Nepal		X	
2. Expropriation, Ethiopia	X		
3. Emergency Power VI, Tanzania	X		
4. Rondônia Natural Resources Management Project (Planafloro), Brazil		X	
5. Biobío (Pangue) Dam, IFC, Chile		X	
6. Jamuna Bridge, Bangladesh	X		
7. Yacyretá Hydropower, Paraguay–Argentina		X	
8. Jute Sector, Bangladesh	X		
9. Itaparica Resettlement, Brazil	X		
10. Singrauli/ NTPC 1 India		X	
11. Ecodevelopment, India	X		
12. Lesotho Highlands Water, Lesotho	X		
13. Lagos Drainage and Sanitation, Nigeria	X		
14. Land Reform, Brazil	X		
15. Lesotho Highlands Diamond	X		
16. Itaparica Resettlement, Brazil (second claim)	X		
17. China Western Poverty Reduction			X
18. Pro-Huerta, Structural Adjustment, Argentina	X		
19. Land Reform, Brazil (second claim)	X		
20. Lake Victoria Environment, Kenya	X		
21. Prodeminca, Ecuador		X	
22. Singrauli/ NTPC 2 India	X		
23. Chad–Cameroon Pipeline, Chad	X		
24. Coal Sector Project, India		X	
25. Bujagali Hydropower, Uganda		X	
26. Structural Adjustment, Papua New Guinea		X	
27. Yacyretá Hydropower, Paraguay–Argentina (second claim)	X		
28. Chad–Cameroon Pipeline, Cameroon		X	
Totals	17	10	1

Sources: Case studies documented in this volume as well as personal communications with claimants, Inspection Panel members, and NGOs that were involved in particular cases.

Note: IFC = International Finance Corporation; NTPC = National Thermal Power Corporation.

* Of the five claims that appear to be brought twice, three are claims that were generated by some of the same claimants (Itaparica, Land Reform, and Yacyretá) and are considered "second claims," while two are claims that were generated by separate claimants on the same project (Singrauli and Chad–Cameroon Pipeline). We refer to Singrauli claims as Singrauli/NTPC 1 and Singrauli/NTPC 2. In the case of the Chad–Cameroon Pipeline, one claim was brought in Chad and the other in Cameroon.

The majority of the South–North coalitions that supported Inspection Panel claims evolved out of international campaigns that had already formed around particular "problem projects" or high-risk lending (Arun, Planafloro, Biobío, Yacyretá, Singrauli, China/Tibet, Cameroon, Bujagali, and Papua New Guinea).[2] In the claims processes that emerged, and in particular in the early claims where campaigns were needed to get board approval for investigations or quasi-investigations, transnational coalitions have been critical. Northern groups such as Bank Information Center, Center for International Environmental Law, Environmental Defense, Friends of the Earth–U.S., and International Rivers Network have played a particularly important role in these coalitions due to their proximity to information and their bank watchdog functions. Indeed, they have helped to inform Southern NGOs and affected people of the potential to use the Inspection Panel as a tactic in their campaign, and have often tracked the claim inside the institution to ensure that claimants were kept informed of the panel process. Together, transnational coalitions have generated international political pressure on decision makers and catalyzed press coverage.

South–North coalitions were especially critical in the context of the Board Second Review of the Panel. As described in chapter 1, Washington-based NGOs sounded the alarm about threats to the panel's independence and mobilized responses from donor governments and NGOs, but the key to reversing the attack on the panel was the testimony of claimants delivered directly to the board.

As noted by Víctor Abramovich, an Argentine human rights lawyer who helped file the Pro-Huerta claim remarked, a key distinction between the roles of Southern and Northern civil-society actors is that "Southern civil society actors bring the cases and Northern civil society actors protect the procedures and the Panel itself."[3]

As information about the panel and its potential became more available,[4] and as the process became more navigable, more claims were generated by local and national actors without the direct support of international experts or the need for high-profile international campaigns (for example, Jamuna, Ecodevelopment, Lesotho Highlands Water, Pro-Huerta, Land Reform, Lake Victoria, Prodeminca). There is still a need for coalitions, though not necessarily transnational ones. Due to the technical nature of the claims process, NGO support to help claimants develop a claim that will withstand the technical requirements continues to be a factor to facilitate the accessibility of the panel to directly affected people.

How Did the Powerful React?

The World Bank

Bringing claims to the Inspection Panel almost inevitably triggers strong reactions from both bank management and the board. As the case studies have shown, the tendency has been for management to respond defensively—denying that they violated any policies, challenging claimants' eligibility, and in some cases, challenging the panel's findings. Before the second review (described in chapter 1), the board accepted the panel's recommendation to investigate only once—in the first claim on the Arun Dam. After that first claim, the board either rejected the panel's recommendation to investigate or limited the panel's terms of reference. Table 11.4 shows how management, the panel, and the board reacted to the claims.

In the vast majority of cases, management responded by denying they had violated any policies and/or contesting the claimants' allegations of harm. In only four cases did management acknowledge some failure to comply with bank policies. This should be contrasted with the fourteen cases in which the panel found evidence that at least some of the claimants' allegations of policy violations were valid.[6]

Management and the bank's legal department also routinely challenged the eligibility of claims.[7] And before the second review, in several claims the board accepted borrower and management-generated "action plans" to preempt investigations (Rondônia, Yacyretá, Itaparica, and Ecodevelopment).

In the Yacyretá case, management took extraordinary steps to subvert the panel findings and avoid accountability by misrepresenting to the Paraguayan public the findings of the panel investigation (which had identified a number of policy violations) in a letter published in Paraguayan newspapers claiming that the panel had found the project to be "satisfactory" to the bank.[8]

Management's aggressive responses and the influence it had on the board undermined the panel's independence and led to a chronic animosity between the panel and management. This tension also played out at the board level. Ibrahim Shihata, then the bank's general counsel, observed that

> An attitude against investigation whenever it could be avoided thus evolved among borrowing countries and created a divisive climate every time the Board had to discuss a Panel recommendation to investigate a complaint. Even when [an] investigation was authorized, the term investigation/ inspection had to be avoided in one case (Yacyretá) and the process had to be limited to inspection at the Bank's headquarters in another (NTPC).[9]

The often-antagonistic relationships between the panel and bank officials, particularly in claims filed before the second review, reflects a predictable resistance to challenges to the status quo. The bank's long-standing culture of impunity has allowed staff, management, and the board to avoid having to answer for the sometimes-disastrous results of their decisions. When the panel started making findings of policy noncompliance, and substantiated the claimants' allegations of harm, the reaction from bank managers and borrowing-

Table 11.4. Management, Panel, and Board Responses to Claims

Inspection Panel Claims Filed	Bank Management Response	Panel Recommendation	Board Approves Investigation
1. Arun III Hydro, Nepal	Deny violations	Yes	Yes
2. Expropriation, Ethiopia	N/A	Not registered[a]	
3. Emergency Power VI, Tanzania	Deny violations	Found ineligible[b]	No
4. Rondônia Natural Resources Management Project (Planafloro), Brazil	Acknowledges some failure to comply	Yes	Asked panel to review progress on project implementation
5. Biobío Dam, IFC, Chile	N/A	Not registered[c]	
6. Jamuna Bridge, Bangladesh	Deny violations	No	Restricted
7. Yacyretá Hydropower, Paraguay–Argentina	Deny violations	Yes	Investigation limited to "review and assessment" of action plan
8. Jute Sector Adjustment, Bangladesh	Deny violations	No	No
9. Itaparica Resettlement and Irrigation, Brazil	Deny violations	Yes	Government action plan
10. Singrauli/ NTPC 1 India	Acknowledges some failure to comply	Yes	Restricted Investigation limited to Washington desk review
11. Ecodevelopment, India	Acknowledges some failures to comply	Yes	No Board agrees to review progress in six months
12. Lesotho Highlands Water, South Africa	Deny violations	Found ineligible[d]	
13. Lagos Drainage and Sanitation, Nigeria	Deny Violations	No	
14. Land Reform, Brazil	Deny Violations	Found ineligible[e]	

(continued)

Table 11.4. Management, Panel, and Board Responses to Claims (continued)

Inspection Panel Claims Filed	Bank Management Response	Panel Recommendation	Board Approves Investigation
After the Second Review Inspection Panel Claims[5]			
15. Lesotho Highlands Diamond	Deny violations	Found ineligible[f]	
16. Itaparica, Brazil (second claim)	N/A	Not registered[g]	
17. China Western Poverty Reduction	Acknowledges some failure to comply	Yes	Yes
18. Pro-Huerta, Structural Adjustment, Argentina	Deny violations	No	
19. Land Reform, Brazil (second claim)	Deny violations	Found ineligible[h]	
20. Lake Victoria Environment, Kenya	Deny violations	Yes	Yes
21. Prodeminca, Ecuador	Deny violations	Yes	Yes
22. Singrauli/NTPC 2 India	N/A	Not registered[i]	
23. Chad–Cameroon Pipeline, Chad	Deny violations	Yes	Yes
24. Coal Sector Project, India	Deny violations	Yes	Yes
25. Bujagali Hydropower, Uganda	Deny violations	Yes	Yes
26. Structural Adjustment, Papua New Guinea	Deny violations	No	
27. Yacyretá Hydropower, Paraguay–Argentina (second claim)	Deny violations	Yes	Yes
28. Chad–Cameroon Pipeline, Cameroon	Deny violations	Yes	Yes

Sources: World Bank, *Inspection Panel Annual Report 2002* (Washington, D.C.: World Bank, 2002); case studies for chapters 2 through 10, this volume; and the claims, management responses, and panel reports available at www.worldbank.org/ipn/ipnweb.nsf.

Note: IFC = International Finance Corporation; NTPC = National Thermal Power Corporation.

a Ethiopia was not registered by the panel because it found no linkage to acts or omissions by the bank (see www. inspectionpanel.org/summary of all Requests.doc [accessed February 18, 2003].

b In Tanzania, the panel found that claimants lacked standing, so the claim was found to be ineligible.

c The Biobío claim was inadmissible because the panel does not have jurisdiction over IFC projects.

d In the Lesotho Highlands Water case, the panel found no evidence linking complaints of harm to World Bank actions or omissions.

e In the first Land Reform claim, the panel found no evidence of harm, and thus it was determined to be ineligible.

f In the Lesotho Highlands Diamond claim, the panel found no link between complaints of harm and World Bank actions or omissions.

g The Lesotho Highlands Diamond case was not registered by the panel, which did not respond to the claimants, who had sent a letter on April 23, 1999, to the president of the bank, the executive directors, and the panel (see Vianna, chapter 7, this volume). The Inspection Panel maintains that it never received a formal complaint; moreover, the claim was filed after the loan was closed.

h The panel found that the claim was ineligible because it determined that the claimants had not previously raised concerns with bank management.

i The claim was filed after the loan was closed.

country governments was to deny wrongdoing, obstruct the truth, and attempt to discredit the panel's work, while the board, often split along North–South lines, failed to empower the panel to do its job.

Subsequent procedural changes, coupled with growing board acceptance of the panel's role in the bank, have allowed the panel to operate more in keeping with the original intent—to provide the board with an independent perspective on the concerns raised by citizens experiencing negative side effects of bank lending. In every case since the second review, board members have approved panel recommendations for investigations.

Responses to Claims in Country

Bringing claims to the Inspection Panel is a daunting process for most claimants. For some, inviting international scrutiny of problems in projects can be dangerous. Leaders have sometimes been targeted for retribution, or in extreme cases, human rights violations. As described in chapter 8, in the Singrauli project, local people were subject to intimidation from the National Thermal Power Corporation (NTPC), the implementing agency. Madhu Kohli, the representative of the claimants, became a target of project authorities, whose frustration with her leadership role culminated with her being beaten by project contractors in the presence of four officials from the NTPC.[10]

More recently, Ngarledjy Yorongar, a Chadian member of Parliament, was an opposition candidate running for president when he filed a claim on behalf of many of his constituents, who live in the oil-drilling area of the Chad–Cameroon pipeline. At the time of the national elections, Yorongar and five other opposition candidates were imprisoned. Yorongar was beaten and tortured and was released only upon the intervention of World Bank President James Wolfensohn, who placed a telephone call to Chad's President Idriss Deby.[11]

The Panel's Impacts on Projects

A key test of the panel's impact is whether the claimants have been satisfied by the outcome. Through the Inspection Panel process, claimants have sought to receive adequate compensation for being forcibly displaced; to demand implementation of environmental protection and mitigation measures; to have their livelihoods restored; to receive support for social programs; to prevent threatened harm by stopping or delaying potentially destructive projects; and to hold the bank accountable for its role in causing their problems.

The panel does not have the power to issue an injunction, stop a project, or award financial compensation for harm suffered. Rather, the most that the panel can do is produce a public report with the impartial findings of its investigation. It is up to the board, after reviewing the panel's report of its investigation, to announce whether remedial measures will be undertaken. Thus claimants use the process because they anticipate that the bank will take steps to effectively address the problems articulated in their complaint. So what difference did the claim process make? What were the tangible impacts of the claim for those directly affected by the project? To what degree were claimant's goals met? Table 11.5 compares the claimants' objectives to outcomes, and also summarizes the broader impacts of the panel on the institution.

Despite the objectives and expectations of many of the claimants that the panel process will help solve problems, unfortunately there is no guarantee that a claim will lead to improvements at the project level. Ten of the twenty-eight claims filed had (in some cases limited) positive project-level impacts. These include Arun, Planafloro, Jamuna, Yacyretá, Jute Sector, Itaparica, Singrauli 1, Land Reform (first claim), China/Tibet, and Structural Adjustment Argentina. (It should be noted that nine claims were found to be ineligible or were not registered by the panel.)

The panel process has also had some direct, though limited, policy-level impacts. As table 11.5 shows, the Biobío, China/Tibet, and Structural Adjustment Argentina claims resulted in positive institutional changes. Four claims—Planafloro, Yacyretá, Itaparica, and Singrauli 1—aggravated board tensions with the panel (which actually began with Arun), catalyzing the second review. As we note in chapter 1, that review resulted in changes in the panel procedures, some of which were positive (e.g., the agreement by the board to accept panel recommendations for investigation), and some negative (e.g., the definition of the standard of harm, which raised the eligibility bar for claimants). Overall, a total of eleven of the twenty eight claims resulted in some direct impact on the project or the institution more broadly. The following section explores some of the constraints to the panel process that have limited its impact at the project level, and expands on the cumulative impact of the panel on the institution.

Constraints to the Panel Process

The unevenness of satisfactory outcomes on the ground points to a fundamental flaw in the panel's architecture: it is designed to present findings to the board of directors, not to prescribe or oversee the development and implementation of solutions to problems raised by the claimants. Moreover, while the panel's investigations (or reviews) have often confirmed that the harm was caused by bank policy violations, the solutions (action plans) have been proposed by management, which is also responsible for their implementation. This means that

Table 11.5. Impact of the Panel Claims[12]

Inspection Panel Claims Filed	Claimants' Objectives	Outcome at Project Level	Broader Bank Institutional Response/Impact
1. Arun III Hydro, Nepal	Secure adequate compensation; overhaul the energy sector; postpone the project	Loan cancelled, dam stopped, claimants satisfied	Institutional resistance to panel process began
2. Expropriation, Ethiopia	Obtain compensation for expropriated assets	None: claim found ineligible	
3. Emergency Power VI, Tanzania	Challenge decision related to procurement	None: claim found ineligible	
4. Rondônia Natural Resources Management Project (Planafloro), Brazil	Meet sustainable development goals	Partial project reform, including compensation, creation of protected areas, and civil-society legitimacy (power-sharing); may have triggered state government backlash against environmental commitments	Triggered backlash against the "harm" standard, which was changed by board of directors during second review
5. Biobío (Pangue) Dam, Chile	Cancel project	No discernable outcomes on the ground; partial compensation for a group of those affected	Creation of CAO and adoption of social and environmental policies at IFC and MIGA

(continued)

Table 11.5. Impact of the Panel Claims[12] (continued)

Inspection Panel Claims Filed	Claimants' Objectives	Outcome at Project Level	Broader Bank Institutional Response/Impact
6. Jamuna Bridge, Bangladesh	Include char people in project planning and compensation	Partial compensation, with high transaction costs for affected people; creation of new, precedent-setting project-level policy for "erosion and flood-affected" people	Claim fueled borrower backlash against the panel, leading to second review
7. Yacyretá Hydropower, Paraguay–Argentina	Secure expanded compensation and environmental mitigation; stop increase in reservoir level; stop privatization	Management cover-up of panel findings; reservoir level height has not increased, avoiding displacement of thousands of people; privatization stopped. Still unresolved issues with resettlement, compensation, and mitigation.	
8. Jute Sector, Bangladesh	Keep jute mills open by bringing loan into compliance with loan agreement to restructure the jute sector	Bank conceded that jute sector reform program, which had been "on hold," was a failure and cancelled loan	

9. Itaparica Resettlement, Brazil	Find solutions to chronic problems of lack of land and livelihoods related to displacement	Board accepted Brazilian government action plan; panel process avoided; cash compensation instead of land for a minority of those affected; divided social organizations; problems remain unresolved	Claim fueled borrower backlash against the panel, leading to second review
10. Singrauli/NTPC 1 India	Secure fair resettlement and rehabilitation and environmental mitigation	Board accepted management action plan, including innovative Independent Monitoring Panel; improved compensation package for 1,200 families out of hundreds of thousands of affected people	Claim fueled borrower backlash against the panel, leading to second review
11. Ecodevelopment, India	Stop evictions of indigenous people from protected area	No evidence of problems being solved; claimants dissatisfied by bank response	

(continued)

Table 11.5. Impact of the Panel Claims[12] (continued)

Inspection Panel Claims Filed	Claimants' Objectives	Outcome at Project Level	Broader Bank Institutional Response/Impact
12. Lesotho Highlands Water, South Africa	Challenge economic rationale of the project; improve access to water in South Africa townships	No impact, claimants dissatisfied with panel process	
13. Lagos Drainage and Sanitation, Nigeria	Secure fair resettlement, rehabilitation, and compensation	Panel satisfied by management steps to compensate additional people; claimants dissatisfied by panel process and inadequate compensation	
14. Land Reform, Brazil	Stop market-based land reform; continue government expropriation of unproductive land	Interest rates for loans for land reduced; some modifications in project design; bank reworked National Land Fund, guaranteed not to fund purchase of lands subject to legal; civil-society organizations divided over response; expropriation	
15. Lesotho Highlands Diamond, Lesotho	Unknown	None: claim found ineligible	

16. Itaparica Resettlement, Brazil (second claim)	Request implementation of the unfinished action plan	None: claim not recognized by the panel	
17. China Western Poverty Reduction Project	Block the resettlement component of the project	Board rejected management action plan: China withdrew project; bank financing of resettlement component cancelled; government project scaled back; claimants satisfied	Management expanded internal safeguard compliance efforts
18. Pro Huerta Structural Adjustment, Argentina	Protect funding for food security program for urban poor	Funding restored; claimants satisfied	Affirmed panel's jurisdiction over claims regarding structural adjustment loans
19. Land Reform, Brazil (second claim)	Call attention to deficiencies of response to first claim	None: claim found ineligible by the panel	
20. Lake Victoria Environment, Kenya	Challenge the project design; improve public participation in project design and benefits	Project completed; panel findings about consultation violations moot	Board chastised management for distorting factual data and for challenging panel's findings

(continued)

Table 11.5. Impact of the Panel Claims[12] (continued)

Inspection Panel Claims Filed	Claimants' Objectives	Outcome at Project Level	Broader Bank Institutional Response/Impact
21. Prodeminca, Ecuador	Sought to prevent release of mapping data about mineral resources in protected areas to forestall exploitation		
22. Singrauli/ NTPC 2 India	Unknown	None: loan closed before claim was filed	
23. Chad–Cameroon Pipeline, Chad	Delay the project	Claimant arrested and tortured because of his opposition to the project; Wolfensohn intervened to secure release of claimant; project continues	
24. Coal Sector, India	Challenge project design and implementation; extend benefits and rehabilitation to excluded affected people; target remaining funds for restoration of livelihoods and environmental mitigation	Pending	

Project	Objective	Status	Notes
25. Bujagali Hydropower, Uganda	Reevaluate project justifications, including economic and environmental impacts	Project delayed due to corruption scandals; claimants satisfied (for now)	Project was also submitted to the Compliance Advisor/Ombudsman at IFC
26. Structural Adjustment, Papua New Guinea	Improve governance in forest sector and protection of claimants' forests	Bank disbursed loan; made commitment to address governance problems through new project; claimants not satisfied; governance problems persist	
27. Yacyretá Hydropower, Paraguay–Argentina (second claim)	Improve environmental and social compensation and mitigation	Pending	Investigation pending
28. Chad–Cameroon Pipeline, Cameroon	Improve resettlement, compensation and environmental mitigation	Pending	Investigation pending

Note: NTPC = National Thermal Power Corporation; CAO = Compliance Advisor/Ombudsman; IFC = International Finance Corporation; MIGA = Multilateral Investment Guarantee Agency.

the same bank officials—whose actions or omissions may have caused the claimants' problems—are tasked with resolving the very problems that they have caused. This is particularly ironic given that, as table 11.4 shows, staff and management-generated have frequently denied that problems existed.

The board, which is tasked with announcing what, if any, remedial measures the bank will implement, has explicitly prohibited the panel from having an oversight role in management-generated action plans. Oversight of those plans is left to the board, but the board has abdicated its responsibility; it neither follows up itself, nor requires independent reviews of the implementation of remedies. Thus, the board, bank management, and project authorities (both governmental and private sector) all too often get away with their failures to resolve claimants' problems. One result of this absence of effective solutions has been the resubmission of claims (e.g., Biobío and Yacyretá) as conditions on the ground have worsened. The lack of effective remedies for claimants is one of the most significant weaknesses of the Inspection Panel process.

Claimants have often had to overcome great odds to bring their grievances to the Inspection Panel. Some obstacles are built into the process and present structural constraints—for example, limiting the scope of the panel's jurisdiction or creating eligibility hurdles for potential claimants to clear. Some are more methodological—that is, the way in which the panel operates while conducting claims. Both sets of obstacles can make bringing a claim and receiving relief a challenge for claimants.

The intent of the bank's board and management was to ensure that only locally affected people would have access to the panel, to avoid having a flood of claims submitted as well as to prevent nonrepresentative Northern NGOs from using the process. While it is supposed to be as simple as two people submitting a letter to the panel, in fact the process requires a fair amount of technical knowledge and work on the part of the claimants. In practice, the requirements have made access to the panel difficult for those very people it was established to serve. Richard Bissell has argued that in establishing the panel:

> The Executive Directors stated that they wanted to enfranchise the weakest and most peripheral people in the global financial system, and yet laid out a legalistic blueprint for obtaining access to the Panel. How many people directly affected by Bank-financed projects would be able to obtain, read and understand Bank policy statements? And then understand how to "request an inspection" of a Bank-financed project?[13]

The lack of information for local people, and the technical nature of the process, means that claimants have often relied upon the assistance of experts (e.g., national and/or international NGOs or lawyers).

Another structural constraint is that the panel can't investigate projects in which the loan has been more than 95 percent disbursed, largely because the bank loses its leverage to influence government implementation once it no longer controls the finances. But many problems with projects don't show up until years after funds are disbursed. While the bank's policies apply to a project until the loan is repaid, the panel is not an option for those people who learn about the panel and choose to file a claim too late in the project cycle to meet the requirements for eligibility. For those affected people, there simply is no official recourse.

As noted previously, one of the most important roles of the Inspection Panel is to give voice and standing to affected people. While the panel does play a significant role in bringing local concerns and complaints to the attention of decision makers at the bank, there are constraints to claimants' involvement in the process. As noted by Richard Bissell in chapter 2, once claimants file a request for inspection, they largely lose control of the panel process. Indeed, their only formal point of engagement after filing a claim is to meet with the panel if it comes to the field. There is no opportunity for claimants to comment on management's response, nor do claimants have access to information before significant decisions are made about their claim. Only after the board decides on the panel's recommendation do the claimants have access to management's response. Moreover, there is no right for claimants to appeal either the panel recommendation or the board's decision about how to respond to their claim.

More fundamentally, there is a stark imbalance in access between the two adversarial parties—the claimants and management—once the panel has developed its final report to the board. At that point, management has the opportunity to react and provide recommendations to the board about how to resolve any identified policy violations. The claimants, in contrast, have no right to comment on what remedial measures would be appropriate to bring the project into compliance or rectify the harm that they have suffered.[14] Thus, the board tends to adopt management-generated action plans, ignoring the experience, knowledge, and preferences of the people who triggered the process in the first place.

Finally, the standard of harm excludes people affected by projects where policies may not appear to have been directly violated, but which have negative impacts nonetheless. As noted earlier, claimants are required to link the harm that they experience to violations of specific bank policies.[15] In the claim brought on the Lesotho Highlands Water Project, claimants alleged that Black townships of Johannesburg, South Africa, were negatively affected by the project. The main complaint was the dramatic increase in water prices for what was Africa's largest-ever dam project. The claimants argued that this project, and the bank's technical advice to the South African government, resulted in a distortion of water management policies and placed a disproportionate cost on poor townships.[16] While expressing sympathy, the panel did not recommend an investigation because it determined that the claimants had not made a link between the conditions they complained of and specific bank policy violations:

> There is no doubt, as the Requesters claim, that for reasons of historical neglect, poor communities suffer widespread inequalities in terms of lack of or limited access to water. Water prices have increased and some are unable to afford water sufficient for basic health and hygiene. . . . Conditions are harsh and unsanitary for millions of people in Alexandra, Soweto, and other poorer townships. . . . The Requesters' concerns about the conditions on the ground are valid but there does not appear to be a connection between these conditions and any observance or not by the Bank of its own policies and procedures. Rather, they appear to be a part of the enormous legacy and odious burden of apartheid.[17]

The limited scope of the panel's mandate—to investigate only when there are clear linkages between harm and policy violations—preempts the kinds of issues that the claimants in South Africa were trying to raise in the Lesotho case.

Feedback from some claimants suggests that the panel process has often provided the first opportunity for affected people to engage in a discussion with bank officials about their concerns, needs, and problems. Indeed, a critical role of the panel is to create an atmosphere where claimants and affected people can feel secure. The panel recognized the importance of maintaining the safety of claimants and designed its Operating Procedures to allow claimants to request that the panel keep their names confidential. The panel's mandate to gather information impartially implies that its engagement with claimants should be independent of government or bank officials.

Yet some claimants have been unsatisfied with field visits by the panel. For example, in the first land reform case, the panel was accompanied by bank officials, and in Singrauli, NTPC officials were present during the field visit. The presence of government or bank officials could stifle the free exchange of information with affected people. Claimants have also noted communication problems regarding the panel's field visits, including short notice of visits (Ecodevelopment) or last-minute schedule changes that limited the participation of local people (Jamuna, Lagos, and Singrauli). In Papua New Guinea, the claimants were confused by the panel's decision not to travel to the area where they lived, and believed that this failure to view firsthand the impacts of governance failures on their lands and forests may have contributed to the panel's determination that the claimants had not adequately demonstrated harm.[18] In Singrauli, claimants felt that the panel did not allow enough time for meetings with affected people. One claimant commented that

> Hope was raised when we came to know that our complaint was being looked into and that someone was coming to visit. But when the Panel came to our village and made a flying visit, we were disappointed. They were there only for about an hour, and there wasn't enough time for us to present what we wanted them to listen to. . . . It looked like a ritual visit. They didn't hear ninety percent of what we had to say.[19]

The panel's visits to the field establish not only the eligibility of the claim, but also the credibility of the process for local people. The methodology that the panel uses in the field is critical to bringing the facts of the cases to light. The panel's field visits can also potentially serve to galvanize claimants and other affected people to articulate their demands and to create momentum for their ongoing organizing efforts and engagement with the bank and their government.

Impact of the Panel on the Institution

The Inspection Panel process has had a profound impact on the World Bank as an institution. There seem to be two distinct directions of change, however. While the bank has moved forward in terms of adopting policies and improving internal structures for compliance, it has also moved backwards in some disturbing ways. In particular, the safeguard policies themselves have come under fire from management and some borrowers who have found numerous ways to undermine the policy framework to avoid the kind of accountability that the panel was intended to foster.

The largest institutional changes may have been at the IFC and MIGA, which adopted environmental and social policies and created the Compliance Advisor and Ombudsman Office (CAO) in 1998 and 1999.[20] Before these changes were made, the IFC and MIGA, which lend to the private sector, were exempt from earlier policy reforms adopted at the public sector arms of the World Bank Group (IBRD and IDA). As described in chapter 6, the international campaign against the Biobío Dam, and the Inspection Panel claim that it generated, included an objective to highlight the need for clear policies and an accountability mechanism in the World Bank's private-sector lending agencies. It is undeniable that the NGO efforts to stop the project succeeded in forcing these two fundamental changes at the IFC and MIGA.

More modest changes in the World Bank (specifically in IBRD and IDA) can also be attributed to the Inspection Panel. Interviews with staff and management suggest that there is the perception in the bank that the panel *has* contributed to better policy compliance on the part of bank staff, in part linked to the internal turmoil and embarrassment that claims can cause. Ian Johnson, vice president for Environmentally and Socially Sustainable Development, noted that

> People are recognizing that the costs of non-compliance are higher than the costs of compliance at the end of the day. An ounce of prevention is worth a pound of cure. It has made quite a big difference. . . . I think there is a genuine desire to do the right thing. If you don't do due diligence, and you get caught, you pay a price.[21]

The panel has also prompted internal restructuring and improvements in transparency. After the China/Tibet controversy raised the reputational costs of noncompliance for the bank, the staff, mandate, and budget of the bank's Quality Assurance and Compliance Unit (QACU)—a team in the Environment Department responsible for oversight of safeguard policy compliance— were significantly expanded. The QACU now oversees coordination of the safeguard policies, trains bank management and borrowers as well as staff, and runs a "Safeguards Help Desk" to assist staff with questions about policies or projects in the portfolio. QACU also advises on high-risk projects that require greater management attention.[22]

New systems have been put in place that are meant to screen bank projects against the policies. The newly instituted Integrated Safeguards Data Sheets now require staff to go on record regarding which, if any, safeguard policies are acknowledged to apply to a specific project under consideration. This means that for the first time since the policies were adopted, information about policy application for each project that the bank is financing is available on the bank's website. [23]

These small steps may contribute to internal compliance by giving bank staff better tools to identify what types of actions should trigger policy application. These changes, however, do not ensure that the policy objectives are actually met. And improved systems have not necessarily led to better accountability. A recent report by the bank's Operations Evaluation Department (OED) found that one internal constraint to the bank's environmental performance has been

> the apparent lack of senior Management commitment to the environment and to IDA environmental policies. This has not only weakened components in country strategies and lending programs, but also led to embarrassing situations in several high-profile projects in which the Inspection Panel and the public have questioned IDA's integrity and the ability to follow its own policies. Senior managers should accept full responsibility for achieving IDA's environmental objectives and hold regional and country managers accountable for their performance in achieving these objectives.[24]

The key question—whether bank management's assertions that there have been actual improvements in policy compliance—remains open. To date there have only been limited studies of compliance improvements, and nothing yet that can definitively affirm whether there has been greater compliance with policies since the panel was created.[25]

Risk Aversion as a Deterrent

One impact of the panel on the bank is that the experiences of panel claims, and the subsequent emphasis on compliance with safeguards, have contributed to certain "allergic reactions" of bank staff to high-risk projects. The threat of a panel claim—or even the potential applicability of safeguard policies—may inhibit bank staff from promoting certain controversial projects. Managing Director Shengman Zhang asserts that "Risk aversion is widespread, among front line managers especially. . . . It comes out in the choice of projects. It looks like staff are avoiding certain types of projects."[26]

Increased risk-averse behavior means that some projects won't make it onto the drawing board because of staff fear of an Inspection Panel claim. Robert Picciotto, former director general for the bank's OED, noted that the panel generates

> a great amount of transaction costs that may be contributing to risk aversion. There is a Vice President here saying no more dams, no more mines, no more forestry. This is very negative. There is an enormous focus on the Inspection Panel and too little focus on the upstream work, or the adaptation of the project instruments to meet social and environmental objectives.[27]

In October 2001, President Wolfensohn requested information regarding risk aversion from increased oversight of the safeguard policies. An OED paper confirmed that bank policies seem to lead to risk aversion, reporting that "There is anecdotal evidence that some managers are discouraging their staff from tackling operations involving safeguard policies."[28] Some observers would view this as a positive, and indeed intended, consequence of the panel and as a logical result of increased accountability. Several interviews with high-level bank officials, however, revealed a view from inside the institution that such risk aversion is bad for business and should be overcome.

From "Policy Conversion" to "Beyond Compliance"

One way to avoid accountability is to change the policy framework. Indeed, as the most frequently cited benchmarks against which the Inspection Panel evaluates claims, the safeguard policies have themselves become a battleground in the struggle for greater accountability. Shortly after the panel was created, the bank embarked on a process to convert its hundreds of pages of bank policies and Operational Directive into a standardized format consisting of three related documents: the Operational Policy (OP) and Bank Practice (BP) documents, which outline mandatory requirements for staff, and the Good Practice (GP) document, which is considered to be merely "guidance" for staff and not actionable through the panel process.[29] Ostensibly the motivation was to make the policies clearer and more operational for bank staff, but, as the senior bank manager initially responsible for the process divulged in an internal memo in 1996, "Our experiences with the Inspection Panel are teaching us that we have to be increasingly careful in setting policy that we are able to implement in practice."[30]

During the ensuing years, the safeguard policies were put through this "conversion" process, and for the most part, NGOs had to fight "hand-to-hand combat" to retain the mandatory language that gave the safeguards their teeth.[31] Bank management's tendency has been to weaken the mandatory language or move important provisions into the Good Practice section of the policy to avoid being accountable to tough standards. Robert Goodland, a former senior environment advisor at the World Bank and one of the original architects of the safeguard policies observed:

In updating its safeguard policies, not one has been modernized and strengthened commensurate with the deteriorating global environment. Remarkably, several policies have stagnated and others have been gutted. The resettlement policy no longer recognizes the indirect impacts of resettlement. In 2002, the Bank rescinded its commendable decade-long ban on financing logging in tropical forests. The World Bank has lost the social and environmental leadership it had between the 1980s and 1990s.[32]

The weakening of bank policies undermines the jurisdiction of the Inspection Panel, the bank's commitment to sustainable development, and has direct negative effects on the rights of local people. Medha Patkar of the Narmada Bachao Andolan, commenting on the conversion process, observed that "with the new water policy, indigenous peoples policy, and resettlement policy, the Panel's position is weakened."[33] Former panel Chair Jim Mac-Neill commented on the crucial role of NGOs in maintaining the standards of the policies:

The safeguard policies are the criteria against which we judge the Bank's performance. If they are rephrased and become vague and without teeth, they won't be used as effectively to judge compliance. The standard will go. If NGOs want to protect the Panel they need to ensure that the policies are not denuded. This is absolutely crucial.[34]

The backsliding on the safeguard policies has recently been overtaken by a new bank initiative to avoid accountability by shifting more responsibility for policy compliance to the borrower. A 2002 strategy paper aims to make the safeguards "more relevant to changing development practices and changing client needs."[35] This paper reflects the bank's growing emphasis on "country ownership" and recommends allowing "more flexibility in how the borrower achieves" development results. The bank argues that such flexibility is needed because "borrowers in the public and private sector generally agree with safeguard principles, but have reservations about the detailed prescriptive requirements that limit their approaches to achieving agreed ends."[36]

While environmental and social impact prevention and mitigation would arguably improve with borrower ownership, a key concern raised by bank critics is that in the process, responsibility for implementation of protection measures will fall to governments (which often lack commitment, capacity, and the political will to accomplish the safeguard policy objectives), while the bank maintains a distant "oversight" function. As Tom Griffiths, an analyst with the U.K.-based Forest Peoples Programme, notes:

> It is highly risky to pass all responsibility for social and environmental issues to borrowers when they still lack the capacity and normative frameworks to address issues effectively. It boils down to the Bank trying to wriggle out of accountability after civil society has tried so hard to pin it down over the last two decades.[37]

Moreover, shifting responsibility for safeguard implementation to borrowers could ultimately undermine the panel's role since its jurisdiction is the bank. While this outcome is not inevitable, it signals that the continuing trend in the institution is to circumscribe the panel rather than use its functions to improve the bank's accountability and development effectiveness.

The Panel's "Net Effect" on Policies

In terms of its impact on the bank, the panel process appears to have had *contradictory* impacts on the social and environmental policy framework. By working to improve future compliance with safeguard policies, bank management focused attention on the internal changes needed to encourage more consistent levels of policy compliance as a direct result of the China/Tibet claim. At the same time, management has continued to pursue its ongoing "conversion" of the safeguard policies into often-weaker standards—a process also motivated in part by the threat of panel claims. Finally, management is now proposing to shift compliance responsibility to borrowers. The "net effect" of these changes in terms of overall social and environmental impact is difficult to predict. Any answer would require extensive independent field-based evaluations of projects launched "before" and "after" these changes.

Impact of the Panel on Accountability Reforms at Other International Financial Institutions

Following the lead of the World Bank, the Inter-American Development Bank (IDB) and the Asian Development Bank (ADB) created inspection mechanisms in 1994 and 1995, respectively. The investigation processes of these regional development banks lack many fundamental guarantees of independence and effectiveness. Neither have a permanent panel, relying instead on ad hoc systems in which they maintain "rosters of experts" from which to choose inspectors in the event that their boards authorize an investigation. The claimants are at a severe disadvantage in these processes, as they lack access to an impartial, independent forum until significant decisions are made by the boards of directors. As of this writing, only a handful of claims have been filed (three at the ADB and four at the IDB).[38]

The experience of the World Bank Inspection Panel has, however, provided valuable lessons in process as well as concepts of accountability. Moreover, growing attention by global civil society to accountability mechanisms at international financial institutions is creating a political imperative for reform. The IDB's Independent Investigation Mechanism has recently been criticized by claimants and NGOs after several claims have revealed the mechanism's appalling lack of transparency and responsiveness.[39] The ADB's Investigation Mechanism was reviewed during 2002 and was reformed in 2003. Both the European Bank for Reconstruction and Development and the Japan Bank for International Cooperation are currently in the process of creating accountability mechanisms, largely in response to civil-society pressure.[40]

Increasing the prospects for accountability at the World Bank has been a slow process of incremental change. Undoubtedly, that change has been brought about by the persistent efforts of civil society and the integrity of the Inspection Panel. The adoption of environmental and social policies, and the creation of the Inspection Panel and CAO to which affected people can appeal, has been the bank's direct response to decades of campaigning by NGOs, grassroots social movements, and affected people demanding that their concerns and interests be addressed and that the bank shoulder some responsibility for solving the problems its lending has caused. As this study has shown, however, project and policy improvements do not always guarantee the substantive project-level outcomes that claimants seek. While the Inspection Panel provides citizens with a tool to raise the profile of their concerns at the highest levels of the bank, civil-society strategies clearly need to include a variety of additional tools and tactics to move the institution toward effective problem solving and greater accountability.

NOTES

1. See Dana Clark and Kay Treakle, chapter 10, this volume.
2. While the claim in Cameroon related to the Chad–Cameroon Pipeline project did evolve from the international campaign to delay construction and ensure adequate compensation and environmental mitigation, the claim in Chad on the same project was brought by a member of Parliament who filed the claim on behalf of his constituents living in the project area.
3. Víctor Abramovich, personal communication with the authors, Washington, D.C., June 23, 2001.
4. CIEL's "Citizens Guide to the World Bank Inspection Panel" was also widely distributed in English, French, Spanish, and Portuguese to environmental and human rights activists around the world, and is geared for use by communities affected by World Bank–financed projects (see Dana L. Clark, *A Citizen's Guide to the World Bank Inspection Panel* [Washington, D.C.: CIEL, 1999]; available online at www.ciel.org). Over the years, several of the claimants have relied on the *Citizen's Guide* for guidance.
5. See Dana Clark, chapter 1, this volume.
6. See BIC, "Select Inspection Panel Claims: Claimant Allegations of Policy Violations and Panel Findings, or Preliminary Findings Based on *Prima Facie* Evidence," www.bicusa.org, August 2001 [accessed February 23, 2003].
7. For example, management responses to Planafloro, Ethiopia, Tanzania, Yacyretá, and Itaparica contained detailed arguments against an investigation, and in Arun, management's presentation to the board, as well as a separate legal opinion, caused board members to question the claim's eligibility. For a discussion of the problems of bank management's interference in Inspection Panel claims, see Lori Udall, *The World Bank Inspection Panel: A Three-Year Review* (Washington, D.C.: BIC, 1997).
8. See Kay Treakle and Elías Díaz Peña, chapter 4, this volume.
9. Ibrahim F. I. Shihata, *The World Bank Inspection Panel: In Practice* (Oxford: Oxford University Press, 2000), 221.
10. See Dana Clark, chapter 8, this volume.
11. Korinna Horta, "Rhetoric and Reality: Human Rights and the World Bank," *Harvard Human Rights Journal* 227, no. 15 (Spring 2002): 236.
12. For more information about claims not covered in this volume, see the following sources: Inspection Panel reports on investigations, available online at www.worldbank.org/ipn/ipnweb.nsf. For information specific to the India Ecodevelopment Project, see Sanghamitra Mahanty, "Conservation and Development Interventions as Networks: The Case of the India Ecodevelopment Project, Karnataka," *World Development* 30, no. 8 (2002): 1369–86.
13. Richard E. Bissell, "Institutional and Procedural Aspects of the Inspection Panel," in *The Inspection Panel of the World Bank: A Different Complaints Procedure,*

ed. Gudmundur Alfredsson and Rolf Ring (The Hague: Kluwer Law International, 2002), 107–25.

14. See letter from Madhu Kohli to Ernst Günther Bröder, the Inspection Panel, September 24, 1997 (copy on file with authors): "An issue of concern in the Panel process so far has been lack of transparency. The requesters were not given access to the Panel's Report until the Board had voted on it. The Bank Management, however, had access to the Report as is very apparent from the update on the Action Programme."

15. Jonathan Fox, "The World Bank Inspection Panel: Lessons from the First Five Years," *Global Governance* 6 (2000): 279–318.

16. See Patrick Bond, "Lesotho's Water, Johannesburg's Thirst: Communities, Consumers and Mega-Dams," in *Unsustainable South Africa: Environment, Development and Social Protest* (Pietermaritzberg: University of Natal Press; London, Merlin Press, 2002).

17. Inspection Panel, "Lesotho/South Africa: Lesotho Highlands Water Project" (Request 1), August 18, 1998.

18. Damien Ase, CELCOR (Center for Environmental Law and Community Rights), to Edward Ayensu, Inspection Panel, May 23, 2002: "The requesters representatives had to travel all the way from their villages in the project area to meet with the Panel due to the fact that the Panel chose not to visit the Kiunga-Aimbak area. They incurred a lot of costs in the process. The Panel's failure to travel to the project area may have undermined the Panel's ability to understand the issues."

19. Ram Narain Kumari, interview by Dana Clark, Dodhar Resettlement Colony, Singrauli, India, September 8, 2002. Note that although thirty-three of the Singrauli claimants requested that the panel keep their names confidential, over time, their identities were determined by the project authorities and are no longer secret.

20. For more recent information about the effectiveness of the IFC's safeguard policies, see International Finance Corporation, Compliance Advisor Ombudsman, "A Review of IFC's Safeguard Policies: Core Business: Achieving Consistent and Excellent Environmental and Social Outcomes," January 2003. The report is available at www.cao-ombudsman.org [accessed May 27, 2003].

21. Ian Johnson, World Bank vice president for Environmentally Sustainable Development; interview by Dana Clark and Kay Treakle, Washington, D.C., May 2, 2002.

22. Steve Lintner, head of the World Bank Quality Assurance and Compliance Unit; interview by Kay Treakle, Washington, D.C., February 1, 2002. It should be pointed out that Lintner did not think that the expansion of QACU was related to the panel or the China/Tibet claim, but rather to a general trend that "the bank started to emphasize quality."

23. To find the Integrated Safeguards Data Sheets, go to www.worldbank.org, and search for the term "Integrated Safeguards Data Sheets."

24. World Bank, "Environmental Sustainability Issues In IDA 10-12," in *OED IDA Review* (Washington, D.C.: World Bank Operations Evaluation Department, 2001).

25. For an overview of the independent and official evidence on bankwide compliance trends through 1997, see Jonathan Fox and L. David Brown, "Assessing the Impact of NGO Advocacy Campaigns on World Bank Projects and Policies," in *The*

Struggle for Accountability: The World Bank, NGOs and Grassroots Movements, ed. Jonathan Fox and L. David Brown (Cambridge: MIT Press, 1998), 485–551.

26. Shengman Zhang, World Bank managing director, interviewed by Kay Treakle, Washington, D.C., June 18, 2002.

27. Robert Picciotto, former director general of the World Bank Operations Evaluation Department, interview by Kay Treakle, Washington, D.C., February 3, 2002.

28. World Bank, Operations Evaluation Department, "Risk Aversion: Safeguards and Post-Conflict Lending," *Lessons and Practices,* October 23, 2001.

29. See BIC, "World Bank Policy Conversion: An Overview," www.bicusa.org/publications/, April 14, 1997 [accessed February 18, 2003].

30. Myrna Alexander, "Conversion of Remaining OD's," World Bank Operations Policy internal memorandum, March 15, 1996 (on file with the authors).

31. Korinna Horta, senior economist, Environmental Defense, personal communication with Kay Treakle, September 2002.

32. Robert Goodland, personal communication with Kay Treakle, February 21, 2003.

33. Medha Patkar, interview by Dana Clark, Badwani, India, September 22, 2002.

34. Jim MacNeill, former chair of the Inspection Panel, interview by Kay Treakle, November 28, 2001.

35. World Bank, "Safeguard Policies: Framework for Improving Development Effectiveness. A Discussion Note" (Environmentally and Socially Sustainable Development and Operations Policy and Country Services), October 7, 2002, paragraph 2.

36. World Bank, "Safeguard Policies: Framework for Improving Development Effectiveness," www.worldbank.org/, October 7, 2002 [accessed February 18, 2003].

37. Tom Griffiths, an analyst with the U.K.-based Forest Peoples Programme, personal communication with Kay Treakle, January 6, 2003. The Forest Peoples Programme has made substantial contributions to the analyses of the safeguard policies during the conversion process. For more information see www.forestpeoples.org; see also letter signed by seventy organizations from thirty-two countries, to Stephen Pickford, World Bank executive director for the United Kingdom, March 2, 2001.

38. For more information on the ADB's Inspection Function, see www.adb.org/inspection, and www.bicusa.org/mdbs/adb/inspectionfunction.htm [accessed February 18, 2003]. For the IDB's Independent Investigation Mechanism, see www.iadb.org/cont/poli/investig/brochure.htm [accessed February 18, 2003].

39. Amy Gray et al. to Enrique Iglesias, February 18, 2003, available online at www.bicusa.org [accessed February 20, 2003].

40. See European Bank for Reconstruction and Development, "Independent Recourse Mechanism at the EBRD," available online at www.ebrd.org ("Inviting Public Comment") [accessed February 20, 2003]. See also "Joint Comments on the EBRD's Proposed Independent Recourse Mechanism," submitted by BIC, CIEL, and Central and Eastern European BankWatch, December 20, 2002, available online at www.bicusa.org [accessed February 20, 2003]. For information on the Japan Bank for International Cooperation proposed guidelines, see www.jbic.go.jp/autocontents/japanese/news/2003/000012/1-3.pdf [accessed February 21, 2003] and www.mekongwatch.org [accessed February 21, 2003].

Concluding Propositions

Jonathan Fox and Kay Treakle

The panel is an experiment in institutional innovation that has become an established presence on the landscape of the World Bank. New claims are investigated through a more streamlined process no longer requiring advocacy campaigns simply to gain the right to an investigation. The panel's investigative process continues to provoke sovereignty concerns from borrowing governments, in spite of the limits of its mandate to focus only on the World Bank's role, but these debates no longer appear to threaten the panel's institutional survival. Though various actors may differ in their assessments of its effectiveness, the legitimacy of the panel's goal of increasing the World Bank's accountability, as well as the legitimacy of an independent investigation process, is no longer in dispute. This chapter concludes with a series of propositions for discussion that emerge from this analysis of the panel process, focusing on the issues of institutional innovation and lessons from its impacts.

The Inspection Panel Creates a Crosscutting Process of Institutional Answerability to Civil Society, Transcending Traditional State-Centered Multilateral Accountability Relationships

Accountability refers to the process of holding actors responsible for their actions. At minimum, accountability involves "answerability" in which actions are held up to standards of behavior or performance. Formally, the World Bank, like other multilateral organizations, is responsible only to its member governments and their representatives that sit on its board of directors. The board created the panel to respond to tensions in its relationship

279

with management, after independent evidence of the bank's politically costly noncompliance with social and environmental policies became too overwhelming to ignore. The panel provides the bank's board with the possibility of third-party verification of concerns expressed by people directly affected by bank operations. The process gives the board discretionary power over whether and how to use this information to redress wrongs or to hold management accountable for policy violations.

Civil-society campaigners promoted an approach to accountability that called for institutional answerability to the people directly affected by bank projects that transcended the bank–nation-state relationship. Two dimensions of the panel process made this *public* answerability possible: the official standing for affected people combined with the commitment to release the panel's findings. The cases analyzed here show that when panel reports publicly verify claims of grassroots critics, they create a new crosscutting accountability relationship, constituting a form of "answerability" of the bank to directly affected communities.[1] When these reports officially recognize institutional failure, they are newsworthy and legitimate the concerns of both external critics and internal bank reformers. This built-in use of "sunshine" to shame the bank has the potential to pressure the board to act when the bank has violated its own standards and can lead to broader policy impacts.

Most Panel Claims Have Been Filed by Directly Affected People and Their Southern Allies, Suggesting That the Process Has Largely Fulfilled Its Goal of Being "Citizen Driven"

The panel process was structured to be used primarily by people who are directly affected by bank-financed projects. This design feature was an attempt to address concerns that Northern NGOs would take advantage of the process to press their agendas on borrowing governments. The requirement of local standing, or local authorization of indirect representation, has had the intended effect. This provision bolstered the legitimacy of the panel process in the face of nationalist backlash from borrowing governments and encouraged Southern organizations to take advantage of the opportunity to make their case directly without governmental or international NGO involvement. This study's review of the sources of leadership in each claim demonstrated that the *majority* of cases so far have been clearly Southern-led (including those brought by private-sector actors) and that most of the rest emerged from coalitions between claimants and their allies from both Southern and Northern NGOs. Only in the exceptional case of the China/ Tibet project did outside representatives lead the claim process. This evidence puts the charge that the "Panel process is a tool of Northern NGOs" to rest, and shows the degree to which diverse Southern civil-society actors have tried to engage with the panel.[2]

Panel Claims Have Led to Clear Project- and Policy-Level Impacts on the World Bank

The impacts of panel claims can be understood in terms of two crosscutting dimensions. The first dimension involves the distinction between influence at the project and policy levels. The second dimension involves the distinction between more tangible and less tangible impacts. Table 5 shows tangible project-level impacts in at least ten cases, clear policy impacts in at least three cases, and because of overlap, eleven cases that had direct institutional impacts.

Direct project impacts refers to identifiable changes in the projects that provoked the claims, such as cancellation of the project (as in Arun and China/Tibet), increased compensation for affected people (as in Singrauli), reversal or reform of project decision-making processes (as in Pro-Huerta and Planafloro), or mitigation of project impacts (as in preventing the increase in the reservoir level at Yacyretá).[3] Other effects are direct but less tangible, such as the nominal recognition of rights of a previously excluded social group or a reported sense of empowerment on the part of those filing claims. The Jamuna Bridge case offers a clear example of the distinction between tangible and intangible direct impacts. The material impacts included extremely small amounts of compensation for a subset of those affected, delivered through a bureaucratic process that—in spite of being NGO-run—was discriminatory toward the very people whose rights were being recognized. The spillover effects of the government's first-ever recognition of the char people's rights to compensation are less tangible, but may well be significant in the future.

The second dimension involves the distinction between impacts on the projects themselves as well as impacts on broader policies. In several important cases—notably the Biobío dam—the most tangible impact of the claim took place far from the affected community. The claim directly provoked the establishment of a new environmental and social policy framework at the International Finance Corporation and the Multilateral Investment Guarantee Agency, as well as the creation of an ombudsman/compliance process to address problem projects. Similarly, the China/Tibet case provoked a major reassessment of the bank's internal approach to policy compliance more generally. Less tangible impacts at the institutional level include the staff's reported "risk aversion" as discussed in chapter 11.

The Inspection Panel Process Deploys Transparency in Two Directions at Once, Exposing Cases of Policy Violations to the Public, While Internally Exposing the Responsible Staff to Their Colleagues

The World Bank has long been criticized for its internal incentive structure, which rewards staff more for moving projects and money through the pipeline than for assuring socially and environmentally sustainable outcomes on the ground. Bank management's mantra of "client focus" in the late 1990s encouraged staffers to choose their battles with borrowing governments carefully. In this context, some staff treated full compliance with the bank's safeguard policies as a costly distraction, especially if compliance risked slowing project preparation or created tension with their official counterparts in borrowing governments. In addition, the bank's internal decentralization in the late 1990s weakened its own limited internal checks and balances by undercutting the autonomy of its social and environmental vetting process.[4]

Most discussion of the power of sunshine to inhibit potential violations of safeguard policies focuses on the threat of external exposure, but "internal exposure" may matter as well. The potential reach of external exposure is inherently limited because of the uneven coverage and capacity of independent civil-society watchdog monitoring around the world. As a result, only some unknown fraction of safeguard policy violations are ever exposed.

At the same time, the bank's own internal monitoring is also limited; until recently the institution lacked a mechanism that allowed management to systematically track individual staff compliance with safeguard policies. In addition, because both staff and managers are regularly rotated among different countries and projects, by the time that problems might unfold on the ground—years after a project was launched—those responsible would often have been transferred elsewhere. As a result, from the individual staff or manager's point of view, the costs of compliance with safeguard policies could be higher than the career risks of noncompliance. In response to the China/Tibet panel claim, however, for the first time management created a bank-wide internal oversight mechanism, the Integrated Safeguards Data Sheets, which could potentially detect those individual staff members who fail to comply. The impact of this reform remains to be seen. Bank management also encouraged greater awareness of safeguard policies by encouraging staff training and creating a Safeguards Help Desk. These are necessary but not sufficient conditions for deepening accountability within the institution. The bank still lacks a track record of sanctioning individual staff members for violations of its social and environmental policies.

The threat of exposure used to be limited to denunciations by advocacy groups or occasional criticism in the media. This kind of "sunshine" proved to have very limited shaming power for those staff members and managers who appear to have been responsible for a disproportionate share of disastrous projects. Indeed, the perpetrators could easily hide behind their official anonymity, since external criticism rarely focused on specific individuals in the bank. The panel process created the first institutional mechanism to question the individuals responsible for implementing the bank's social and environmental standards to find out what went wrong and why.

The panel process thus brings a limited kind of exposure to bear on *individual* staff members. Though rarely, if ever, identified by name in the reports, individuals "hauled up on charges" by the panel are widely known within the institution. The widespread discomfort provoked among staff and management by panel investigations suggests that they fear the loss of prestige associated with being exposed in the eyes of their colleagues for policy violations that embarrass the bank. The panel's use of transparency therefore operates on two levels at once: externally, by potentially validating the concerns of affected people, and internally, by potentially holding actual individuals "answerable" to an unprecedented degree. This threat of internal exposure could therefore be interpreted as adding a limited new dimension to the staff's incentive structure.

While Most Panel Claims Have Focused on Infrastructure Projects, Some Have Broadened the Scope of the Process by Addressing Sustainable Development and Structural Adjustment Projects

Infrastructure projects are the "problem projects" that the safeguard policies were designed to prevent or mitigate, so it is not surprising that they dominate the set of claims. However, claimants have shown that they can use the panel process to improve sustainable development projects (Planafloro) and to bolster social protections in structural adjustment loans (Pro-Huerta). By accepting claims brought against structural and sectoral adjustment loans, the panel accepted the standing of, and legitimated the claims by, affected people that macroeconomic policy can have direct, tangible impacts that cause harm. This precedent opens up new possibilities for civil-society actors to hold the bank accountable both to its poverty alleviation mandate and to the negative consequences of its macroeconomic development model.

The Number of Panel Claims So Far Represents Only a Fraction of Potentially Controversial Projects

The bank has approved thousands of loans since the panel was created. The fraction of those projects that provoked panel claims could lead one to conclude that policy violations are few and far between. However, such a conclusion would be based on the assumption that affected people have full access to relevant information about the bank's impacts on their lives, that they have access to freedom of expression and association, and that they determine that filing an Inspection Panel claim would be worth the considerable time and effort involved.

Are the cases that led to panel claims the exception to the rule or the tip of a much larger iceberg? The panel itself addressed this issue in its report on the China/Tibet claim, pointing to systemic weaknesses in the effective application of safeguard policies. Nevertheless, it is difficult to assess the specific patterns of *bankwide* compliance or noncompliance with safeguard policies without access to still-confidential performance data, not to mention extensive independent field testing.[5]

The panel process so far does reveal some of the key obstacles to filing claims, which could explain why there aren't more claims. For example, many people directly affected by bank-funded projects are not aware that the bank is even involved; those on the receiving end see government bulldozers. In addition, many are not aware that the bank has safeguard policies that grant them some minimal rights and set some standards for institutional behavior. Many are not aware of the panel's existence.

Even for those who have access to this information, the decision to file a panel claim is not one taken lightly. Some affected people may be aware of the panel, but are not convinced of its relative autonomy. Some may be wary of pursuing their campaign on the bank's home turf—its own limited policy framework. Others have ideological objections to formally engaging with an institution they see as illegitimate.

For those without these broader objections, other obstacles are quite real. One practical consideration is that the preparation of a full panel claim—and when needed, a broader support campaign—requires substantial investment of human resources, thus raising the question, "Is it worth it?" In some countries, the risks of backlash from borrowing governments are quite high, ranging from the threat of human rights violations, to political attacks for encouraging external intervention. Then there is the further risk that a panel investigation may not validate the claimants' charges. What if the investigation was flawed or the problems claimants were facing were difficult to link directly to bank policy violations? In these cases, the panel's findings could be used by the bank or the government to claim that they were exonerated and to undermine the legitimacy of their critics (as in the case of Brazil's land reform claims, analyzed in chapter 7 of this volume). In other words, from the potential claimants' point of view, the panel's "third-party verification" capacity could be a two-edged sword. Even in cases where the panel finds policy violations, as noted previously, remedial measures are often inadequate.

The Panel Experience Suggests That Getting a "Foot in the Door" Is Quite Different from Gaining a "Seat at the Table"

The international standing gained by panel claimants can be seen in terms of getting a "foot in the door" of the decision-making process. This image of partial opening is especially appropriate because it leaves the outcome open-ended. The question is whether sustained pressure will open the door even further, whether the door will get stuck, or end up being slammed shut. Whatever happens in any one case, the process may let in some light and help those on the outside to see more clearly what the "powers that be" are doing on the inside.

A "foot in the door" is quite distinct from "a seat at the table," which is an image that also suggests official recognition of standing. But being at the table gives citizens the opportunity to participate in negotiations over how decisions are made.[6] The scope of the panel process, in contrast, is limited to the investigation of the application of the bank's already-defined policies and projects. That is, the size and shape of the door is already determined, and the question is whether and how far the door will actually open in the case of any particular claim. This image would be incomplete without highlighting the insiders who react differently to the opening of the crack. Insider reformists pull the door from within, in synergy with those pushing from outside. Others—especially bank managers, who react defensively most of the time—put their shoulder against the door, trying to prevent those outside from coming in.

Meanwhile, some high-level bank policymakers looking at the scuffles in and around the door take the longer view, designing sophisticated strategies that leave the door open a crack, while redesigning the size and shape of the door itself by revising the safeguard policies. This has underscored the importance of sustained monitoring and advocacy of the bank's policy process by public interest groups. So far, organized public interest advocacy campaigns have influenced this process in some cases—often in the form of partial limits on the degree to which policies were watered down. But stakeholders are still far from having gained the right to a "seat at the table" at which the World Bank makes its important decisions.

Accountability at the World Bank: The Long-Term View

Even the limited prospect of accountability represented by the panel has affected the actions and strategies of different actors within the bank. In spite of the panel's lack of powers of enforcement or restitution, powerful forces have reacted defensively to the prospect of institutional accountability—a clear indicator of weakened impunity.

This study has shown that the panel process sometimes permitted people directly affected by bank projects to use reform policies to shift the balance of power in their favor. This process of using a targeted intervention to turn the weight of the institution against itself can be seen as a kind of "institutional judo." The Inspection Panel process shows how grassroots actors can sometimes oblige global authorities to sit up and officially listen. It remains to be seen to what degree this experience will unleash multiplier effects that can further empower citizens in their ongoing struggles over the role of the World Bank in their societies.

NOTES

1. For a definition of a stakeholder approach to accountability, see Hetty Kovach, Caroline Neligan, and Siman Burall, "Power without Accountability?" in *The Global Accountability Report* (London: One World Trust, 2003).

2. This perception nevertheless persists among some policymakers. For example, the recent *Human Development Report* by the UNDP (United Nations Development Program) (New York: Oxford, 2002) speculates that "judicial-style accountability" reforms such as the Inspection Panel "may end up being shaped more by the desire of industrial country NGOs to garner publicity through confrontations and showdowns, not by quiet measures that more modestly improve the lives of people directly affected by projects" (117). The director of the UNDP previously served as head of public relations for the World Bank.

3. The overall pattern of bank and borrowing-government responses to claims—when they do respond—shows that the most common approach is to promise partial compensation or mitigation, but neither full redress nor sanctions. Specifically, management and borrowing governments promise the board to deal with the problems, often through arrangements in which outcomes on the ground are not subject to independent monitoring. As noted earlier, this puts the solutions in the hands of those responsible for the problems in the first place, eludes the panel's mandate, and shifts the political terrain of struggle back to national and local arenas. In these cases, the outcomes of transnational accountability claims that attempt to bring in international actors to change the local or national balance of power, end up being determined by local and national actors.

4. See Andrés Liebenthal, *Promoting Environmental Sustainability in Development: An Evaluation of the World Bank's Performance* (Washington, D.C.: World Bank Operations Evaluation Department, 2002). This official study confirms much of the independent critique in Bruce Rich's "The World Bank under James Wolfensohn," in *Reinventing the World Bank,* ed. Jonathan R. Pincus and Jeffrey A. Winters (Ithaca: Cornell University Press, 2002), 26–53.

5. Fox and Brown, "Assessing Impact," 485–551.

6. The World Commission on Dams, in contrast, is a very significant example of an institutional innovation in which civil-society actors gained a seat at the table at which decision-making criteria are set, although the World Bank did not accept the new standards proposed in the commission's recommendations.

Index

Abbott, Eduardo, 74, 204
Abramovich, Victor, 251
accountability: of aid agencies, xv, xxviin14; Brazilian, 3; definition of, xii, xxiiin2; horizontal, xii, xxiiin3; IFC mechanism of, 135, 140; Inspection Panel and, 41, 54, 183; Inspection Panel and resistance to, 11–14; of international financial institutions, xv, 70, 233, 274–75; public, xii; reforms as window dressing, xxxn31; of WB, 83–86, 162, 233, 271, 273, 279–80, 285–86; Yacyretá Dam and WB's lacking of, 83–86
Ackerly, John, 234, 238
ADB. *See* Asian Development Bank
Adhikary, 39
affected party, 210n24
agriculture: Cédula da Terra and, 157; China, farmers resettlement and, 211; Forum for Agrarian Reform and, 156–59; Garden Program, food production and, 192, 194–96, 202, 205; oasis agriculture, water and, 212–13; Singrauli and lost fertility of, 167, 171–72, 183. *See also* Federation of Agricultural Workers of Rondônia

aid agencies, bilateral, accountability limited in, xv, xxviin14
AidWatch, 173
Alexander, Myrna, 200, 203
Alien Tort Claims Act, xxxn27
Aña Cua, 72
answerability, xii, xxiiin2, 279–80
approval, culture of, 5–6
Araucaria, 117
Arauco Gulf, 117
Argentina, xx, 116; macroeconomic crisis of, 72–73; Social Budget Conditions of, 191–92; Yacyretá Dam and, xx, 70, 75, 90n17. *See also* Garden Program (Pro-Huerta)
Arun Concerned Group, 28
Arun III dam, xix, 12; access road to, 36, 39; background of, 25–28; civil-society claim's led against, *252*; claim, project type and, *249*; claimants disorganized against, 28–29; claimant's frustration of investigation of, 29–31; claim's process, origin of, 28–31; environmental issues of, 29, 30, 35, 39; hydroelectric issues for, 30, 36–37; Inspection Panel claim's impact on, 37–40, 258, *259*;

287

About the Contributors

Víctor Abramovich is a lawyer from the University of Buenos Aires (UBA). He obtained a master's degree in international law (LL.M.) from the American University's Washington College of Law, where he is currently a visiting professor. He has been a visiting professor at the University of Valencia, University of Castilla-La Mancha, and at the Catholic University of Ecuador. He is also a regular adjunct professor of human rights at the University of Buenos Aires School of Law. Abramovich is the executive director of CELS (Center for Legal and Social Studies), a human rights, nongovernmental organization based in Argentina. CELS carries out legal action to protect human rights, including the use of international human rights bodies such as committees of the ICHR and the United Nations.

Richard E. Bissell is the executive director of the Policy and Global Affairs Division of the National Research Council and executive director of the Committee on Science, Engineering, and Public Policy (COSEPUP) at the National Academy of Sciences in Washington, D.C. He was previously the head of the interim secretariat of the World Commission on Dams (Washington, D.C., and Cape Town), a joint initiative of the World Bank and the World Conservation Union (IUCN). Bissell has held a variety of teaching and research positions, including positions at the Johns Hopkins University, Georgetown University, the American University, and the University of Pennsylvania. He has published seven books and numerous articles on issues of international institutional and policy change. He received a B.A. from Stanford University (1968) and his Ph.D. is from Tufts University (1973). During the period 1994 to 1997, Bissell was a founding member and chair of the Inspection Panel at the World Bank. In that role, he was involved in ten different inspections of World Bank projects across three continents.

Dana Clark is an international human rights and environmental lawyer with expertise in international financial institutions, citizen-based accountability mechanisms, and sustainable development. She is the president of the International Accountability Project, a nonprofit organization based in Berkeley, California. She is a former senior attorney at the Center for International Environmental Law (CIEL), where she was the director of the International Financial Institutions Program. She has served as an adjunct professor of law at the American University's Washington College of Law. She has provided advocacy, analytical support, and advice to many of the claimants who have utilized the World Bank Inspection Panel and the Asian Development Bank's inspection function. Clark has also written numerous articles and publications about issues of accountability and international financial institutions, including, most recently, "The World Bank and Human Rights: The Need for Greater Accountability," published in the Spring 2002 edition of the *Harvard Human Rights Journal.* She is the author of *A Citizen's Guide to the World Bank Inspection Panel* (1999). She is a 1992 graduate of the University of Virginia School of Law.

Elías Díaz Peña coordinates the Environmental Sector of SOBREVIVENCIA, Friends of the Earth–Paraguay, an organization that is working to promote sustainable development in national, regional, and international forums such as the National Council on Energy, the UN Commission on Sustainable Development, the Intergovernmental Forum on Forests, Conferences of the Parties for the Convention on Biological Diversity and the Framework Convention on Climate Change, the World Commission on Dams, and others. Representing SOBREVIVENCIA, he participates in various networks and coalitions, including the Network of Environmentalist Organizations of Paraguay, the Bank Network, the Rios Vivos Coalition, Friends of the Earth International (where he coordinates the International Forest Campaign), and IUCN. Diaz Peña coordinates the Campaign to Monitor the Yacyretá Hydroelectric Project and Support of Affected Communities. He also coordinates the Program on Sustainability and Local Autonomy in the Los Altos region of Paraguay. He is an engineer and a hydrologist by training. In 2000, he was awarded, jointly with his colleague Oscar Rivas, the Goldman Environmental Prize for the South and Central American Region. SOBREVIVENCIA has helped local affected people file two claims (in 1996 and 2002), filed jointly in each case to the World Bank Inspection Panel and the Inter-American Development Bank, to challenge implementation failures in the Yacyretá Hydroelectric Project.

Majibul Huq Dulu has been the director of the Jamuna Char Integrated Development Project (JCDP) in Bangladesh since 1989, whose mission is to improve living conditions of the disadvantaged char-dwellers. In August 1996, JCDP filed a claim with the Inspection Panel of the World Bank on behalf of the char-dwellers. After this action. the government of Bangladesh quickly decided on a policy to compensate the people living within the defined impact zone of the bridge for losses due to erosion and flood. The compensation project was not implemented properly, however, and JCDP and the people affected by the project continue to fight for their rights.

Jonathan Fox is professor and chair of the Latin American and Latino Studies Department at the University of California, Santa Cruz. His publications include *Indigenous Mexican Migrants in the US: Building Bridges between Researchers and Community Leaders* (co-edited, forthcoming); *Cross-Border Dialogues: US–Mexico Social Movement Networking* (co-edited, 2002); *The Struggle for Accountability: The World Bank, NGOs and Grassroots Movements* (co-edited, 1998); *Decentralization and Rural Development in Mexico: Community Participation in Oaxaca's Municipal Funds Program* (coauthored, 1996); *Transforming State Society Relations in Mexico: The National Solidarity Strategy* (co-edited, 1994); *The Politics of Food in Mexico: State Power and Social Mobilization* (1992); and *The Challenge of Rural Democratization: Perspectives from Latin America and the Philippines* (edited, 1990). His recent articles have appeared in *Foro Internacional*; *Política y Gobierno*; *Revista Mexicana de Sociología*; *Nonprofit and Voluntary Sector Quarterly*; *Policy Sciences*; *Global Governance*; and *Latin American Research Review*. He currently serves on the boards of directors of the Bank Information Center and Inter-Hemispheric Resource Center and as a research advisor to the Oaxaca Indigenous Binational Transparencia.

David Hunter is the president of Peregrine Environmental Consulting, a senior advisor to CIEL, and the acting executive director of the Bank Information Center (BIC). He also serves as chairman of the Board of Directors for Earth Rights International and for the Project on Government Oversight, and is a member of the Board of Directors of the Environmental Law Alliance Worldwide–U.S. Hunter graduated with a B.A. from the University of Michigan in 1983 and with a J.D. from the Harvard Law School in 1986.

Cristián Opaso is a journalist and environmentalist from Chile. He has worked for almost ten years with Pehuenche communities from the Alto Biobío, which are threatened by the construction of a series of dams. Born and raised in Chile, Opaso lived in the San Francisco Bay Area for thirteen years, where he studied broadcasting and worked as a television and radio journalist. After returning to Chile in 1989, he worked for several publications, and since 1993 has dedicated most of his time to work with the Pehuenche communities, carrying out a campaign at the national and international level through the NGO Grupo de Acción por el Biobío (GABB—Action Group for the Biobío), for which he served as vice president. In 1995, Opaso helped coordinate the research for a claim presented to the Inspection Panel.

Marcos Orellana has been a senior attorney at CIEL since November 2002, where he focuses on trade, finance, and human rights. In that capacity, he has acted on behalf of indigenous communities before the Inter-American Commission on Human Rights and the IFC's Ombudsman. Prior to joining CIEL, Orellana was a Fellow at the Lauterpacht Research Centre for International Law of the University of Cambridge, U.K., and a visiting scholar with the Environmental Law Institute. Orellana previously lectured on international law and environmental law at the Universidad de Talca, Chile, and provided legal support to NGOs in Chile. In 1997–1998, he completed the LL.M. program at American University, during which time he also worked as an intern at the World Bank's Inspection Panel. He has also provided legal counsel to the Chilean Ministry of Foreign Affairs on international environmental issues. Orellana currently lectures on the law of the sea and on international institutions and sustainable development at the American University's Washington College of Law.

Maria Guadalupe Moog Rodrigues is an assistant professor of political science at the College of the Holy Cross in Worcester, Massachusetts. She has a Ph.D. in political science from Boston University. Her areas of interest are environmental politics and Latin American politics. Her book *Global Environmentalism and Local Politics* will be published in 2003. She has recently been awarded a fellowship from the Carnegie Council on Ethics and International Affairs. Her Ph.D. dissertation investigated the challenges faced by transnational advocacy networks of organizations concerned with the environmental protection of the Brazilian Amazon region. The dissertation focused on advocacy networks mobilized around three World Bank development projects—Polonoroeste, Carajas Iron Ore, and Planafloro—and analyzed the impact of filing the Planafloro Inspection Panel claim.

Kay Treakle is currently a program officer in the Environment Program at the Charles Stewart Mott Foundation, focusing on reform of international finance and trade. Treakle comes to Mott after working with BIC since 1992, where she was most recently the executive director. She held a number of positions at BIC, including coordinating BIC's Latin America and Caribbean Program. Before working at BIC, Treakle was the national campaign director for Greenpeace, where she worked in senior management and program coordination positions for fifteen years, covering primarily toxics and nuclear issues. She has published numerous articles and papers on international environmental issues and international financial institutions and has a degree from the Evergreen State College in Olympia, Washington, where she studied ecology.

Aurélio Vianna Jr. has a Ph.D. in social anthropology (National Museum, Rio de Janeiro). He is the top adviser to Rede Brasil; a member of the boards of many Brazilian NGOs; adviser of the Brazilian Association of NGOs; former executive secretary of Rede Brasil; former executive secretary of INESC (Instituto de Estudos Socioeconômicos—Socioeconomics Studies Institute); former advisor of the Brazilian Confederation of Trade Unions (CUT); former advisor of the National Movement of People Affected by Large Dams (MAB); former coordinator of CEDI (Centro Educacional de Desenvolvimento Integrado [Educational Center for Integral Development]) and other Brazilian NGOs; and former professor of social anthropology at the University of Brasília (UnB) and the Federal University of Rio de Janeiro (UFRJ). Vianna has written many articles and several books on peasants and politics in Brazil, international financial institutions in Brazil, and civil-society organizations.